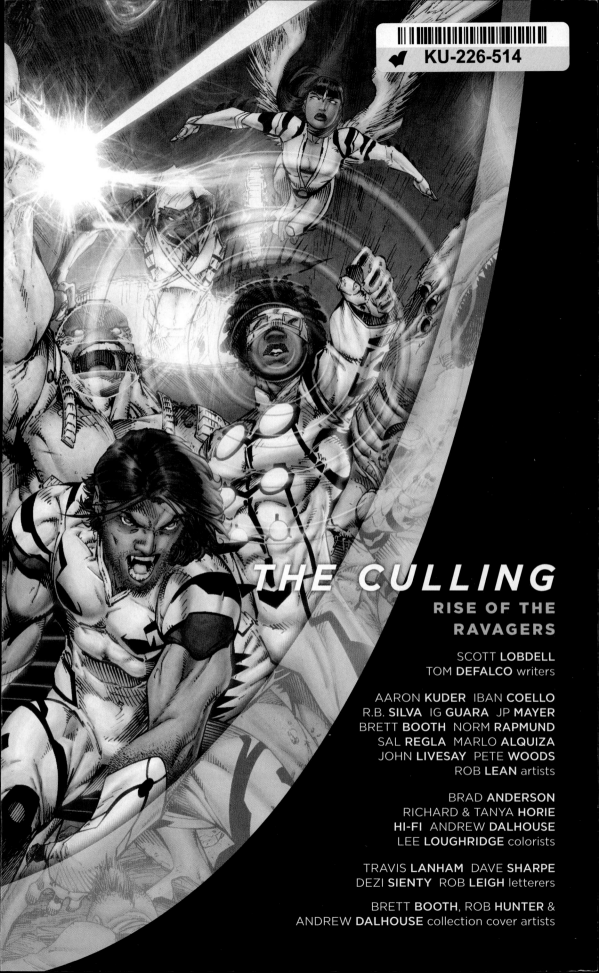

THE CULLING
RISE OF THE RAVAGERS

SCOTT **LOBDELL**
TOM **DEFALCO** writers

AARON **KUDER** IBAN **COELLO**
R.B. **SILVA** IG **GUARA** JP **MAYER**
BRETT **BOOTH** NORM **RAPMUND**
SAL **REGLA** MARLO **ALQUIZA**
JOHN **LIVESAY** PETE **WOODS**
ROB **LEAN** artists

BRAD **ANDERSON**
RICHARD & TANYA **HORIE**
HI-FI ANDREW **DALHOUSE**
LEE **LOUGHRIDGE** colorists

TRAVIS **LANHAM** DAVE **SHARPE**
DEZI **SIENTY** ROB **LEIGH** letterers

BRETT **BOOTH**, ROB **HUNTER** &
ANDREW **DALHOUSE** collection cover artists

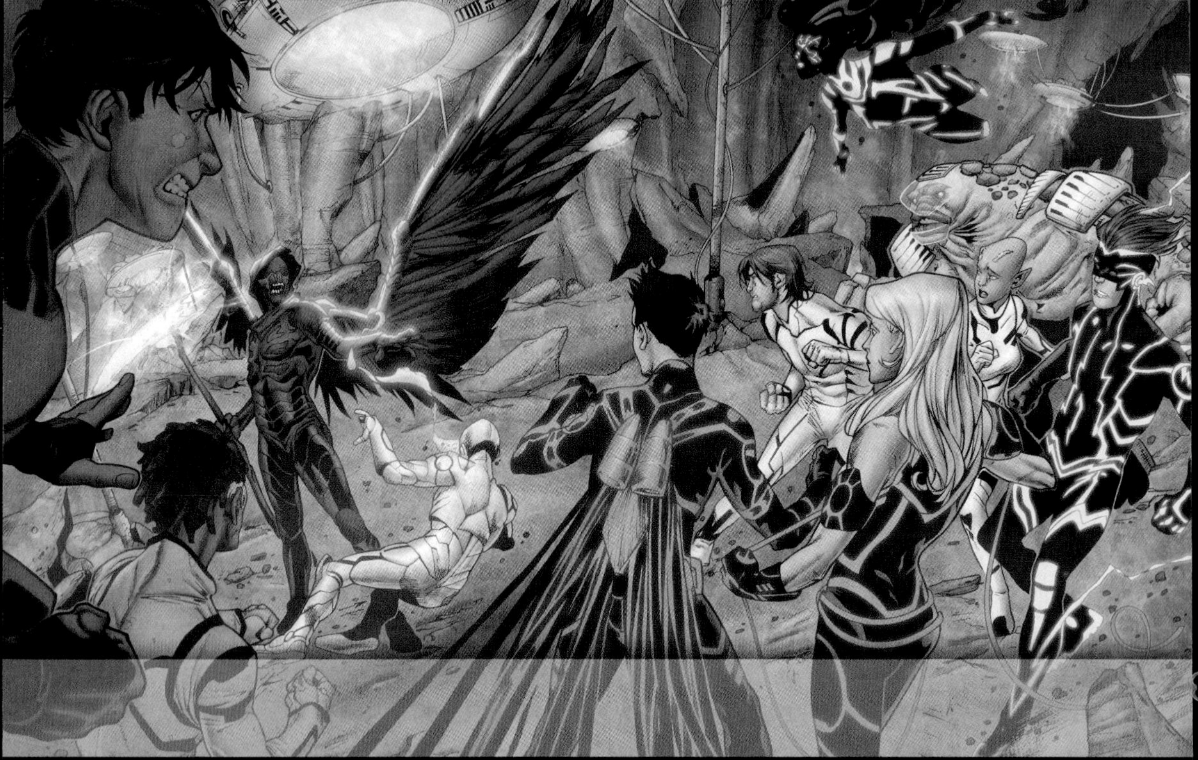

BRIAN CUNNINGHAM CHRIS CONROY BOBBIE CHASE Editors – Original Series
DARREN SHAN KATIE KUBERT Assistant Editors – Original Series
ROWENA YOW Editor ROBBIN BROSTERMAN Design Director – Books ROBBIE BIEDERMAN Publication Design

BOB HARRAS VP – Editor-in-Chief

DIANE NELSON President DAN DIDIO and JIM LEE Co-Publishers GEOFF JOHNS Chief Creative Officer
JOHN ROOD Executive VP – Sales, Marketing and Business Development AMY GENKINS Senior VP – Business and Legal Affairs
NAIRI GARDINER Senior VP – Finance JEFF BOISON VP – Publishing Operations MARK CHIARELLO VP – Art Direction and Design
JOHN CUNNINGHAM VP – Marketing TERRI CUNNINGHAM VP – Talent Relations and Services
ALISON GILL Senior VP – Manufacturing and Operations HANK KANALZ Senior VP – Digital
JAY KOGAN VP – Business and Legal Affairs, Publishing JACK MAHAN VP – Business Affairs, Talent
NICK NAPOLITANO VP – Manufacturing Administration SUE POHJA VP – Book Sales
COURTNEY SIMMONS Senior VP – Publicity BOB WAYNE Senior VP – Sales

THE CULLING: RISE OF THE RAVAGERS

DC Comics, 1700 Broadway, New York, NY 10019
A Warner Bros. Entertainment Company.
Printed by RR Donnelley, Salem, VA, USA. 12/21/12. First Printing.
ISBN: 978-1-4012-3799-8

Library of Congress Cataloging-in-Publication Data

Lobdell, Scott.
The culling : rise of the ravagers / Scott Lobdell, Tom DeFalco, Ig Guara, Brett Booth, R.B. Silva, Aaron Kuder.
p. cm.
"Originally published in single magazine form in Legion Lost 8-9, Superboy 8-9, Teen Titans 8-9, Teen Titans Annual 1."
ISBN 978-1-4012-3799-8
1. Graphic novels. I. DeFalco, Tom. II. Guara, Ig. III. Booth, Brett. IV. Silva, R. B., 1985- V. Kuder, Aaron. VI. Title.
PN6727.L6C85 2012
741.5'973 — dc23
2012032149

SUSTAINABLE FORESTRY INITIATIVE
Certified Chain of Custody
At Least 20% Certified Forest Content
www.sfiprogram.org
SFI-01042
APPLIES TO TEXT STOCK ONLY

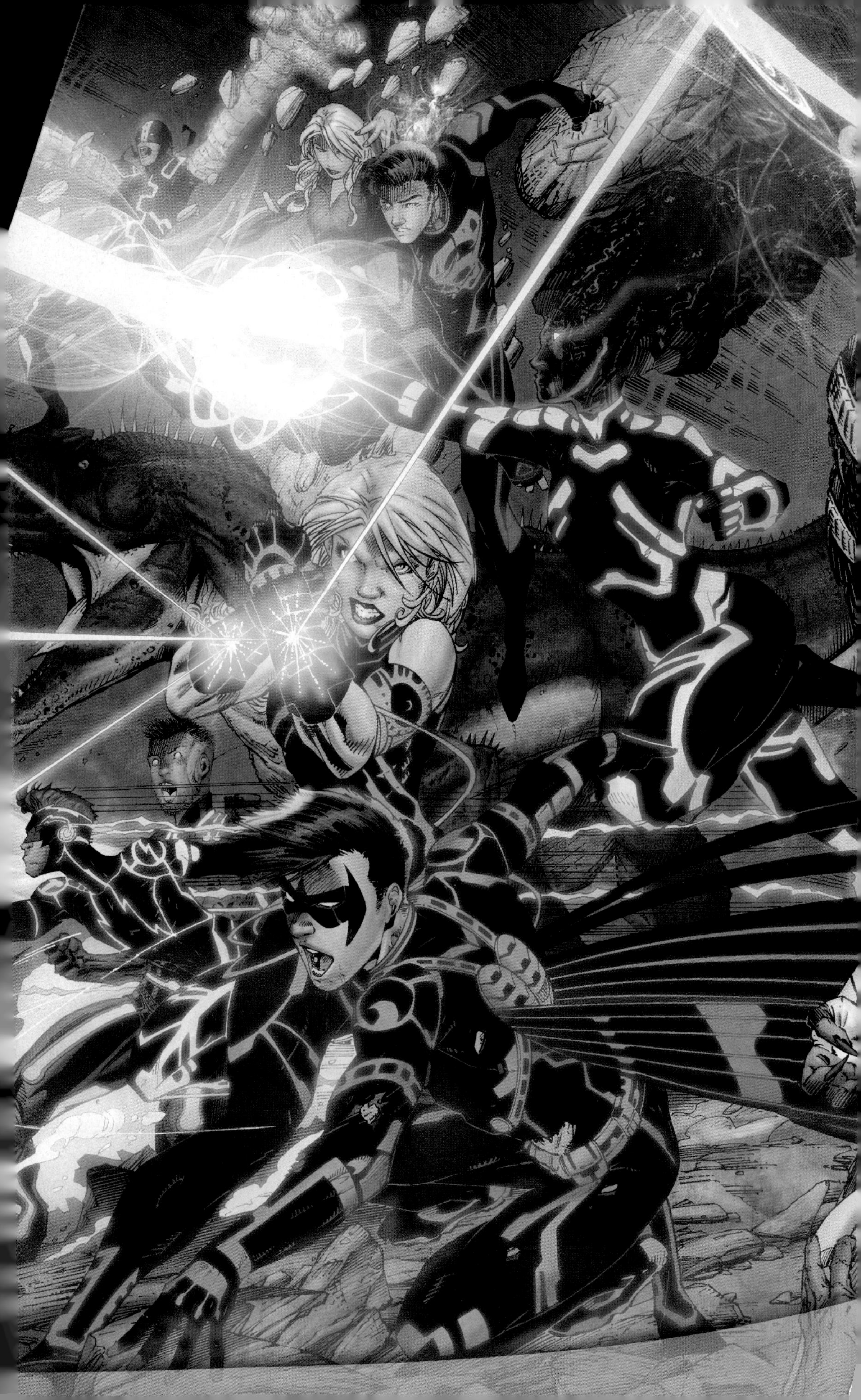

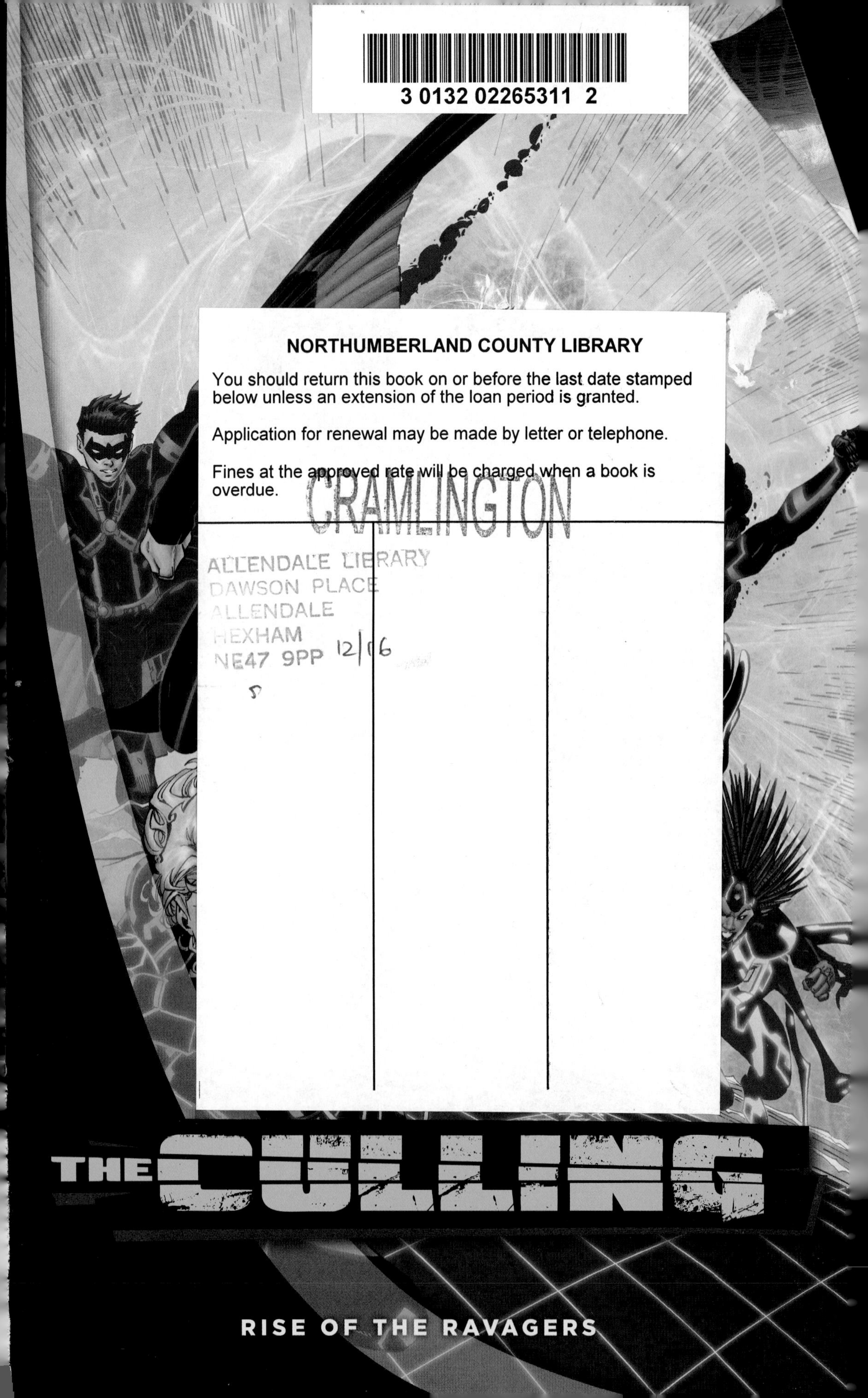
THE CULLING
RISE OF THE RAVAGERS

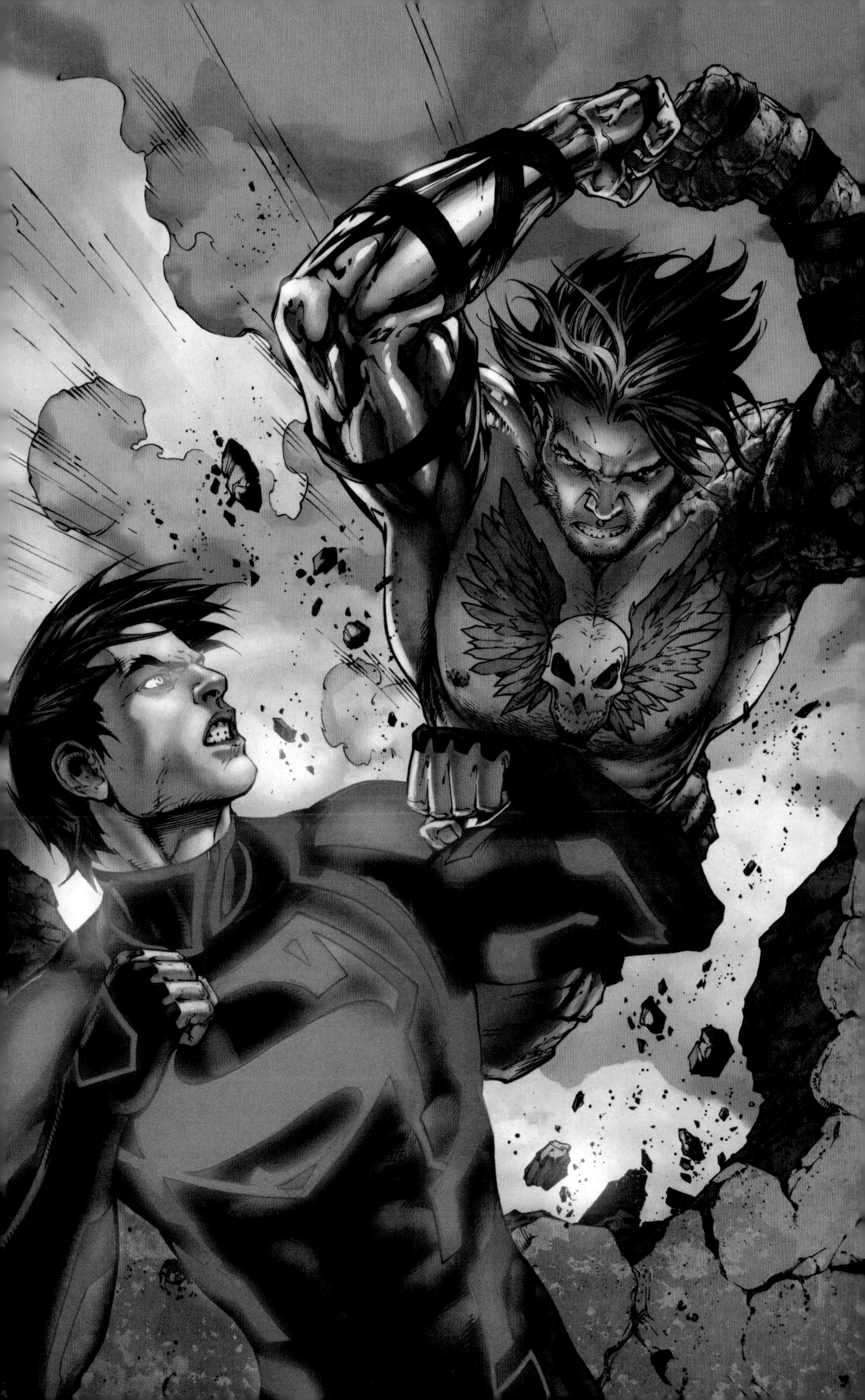

PRELUDE PART ONE: TRAINING DAY
SCOTT LOBDELL & TOM DEFALCO writers IBAN COELLO artist
R.B. SILVA penciller ROB LEAN inker
cover art by SHANE DAVIS, SANDRA HOPE & BARBARA CIARDO

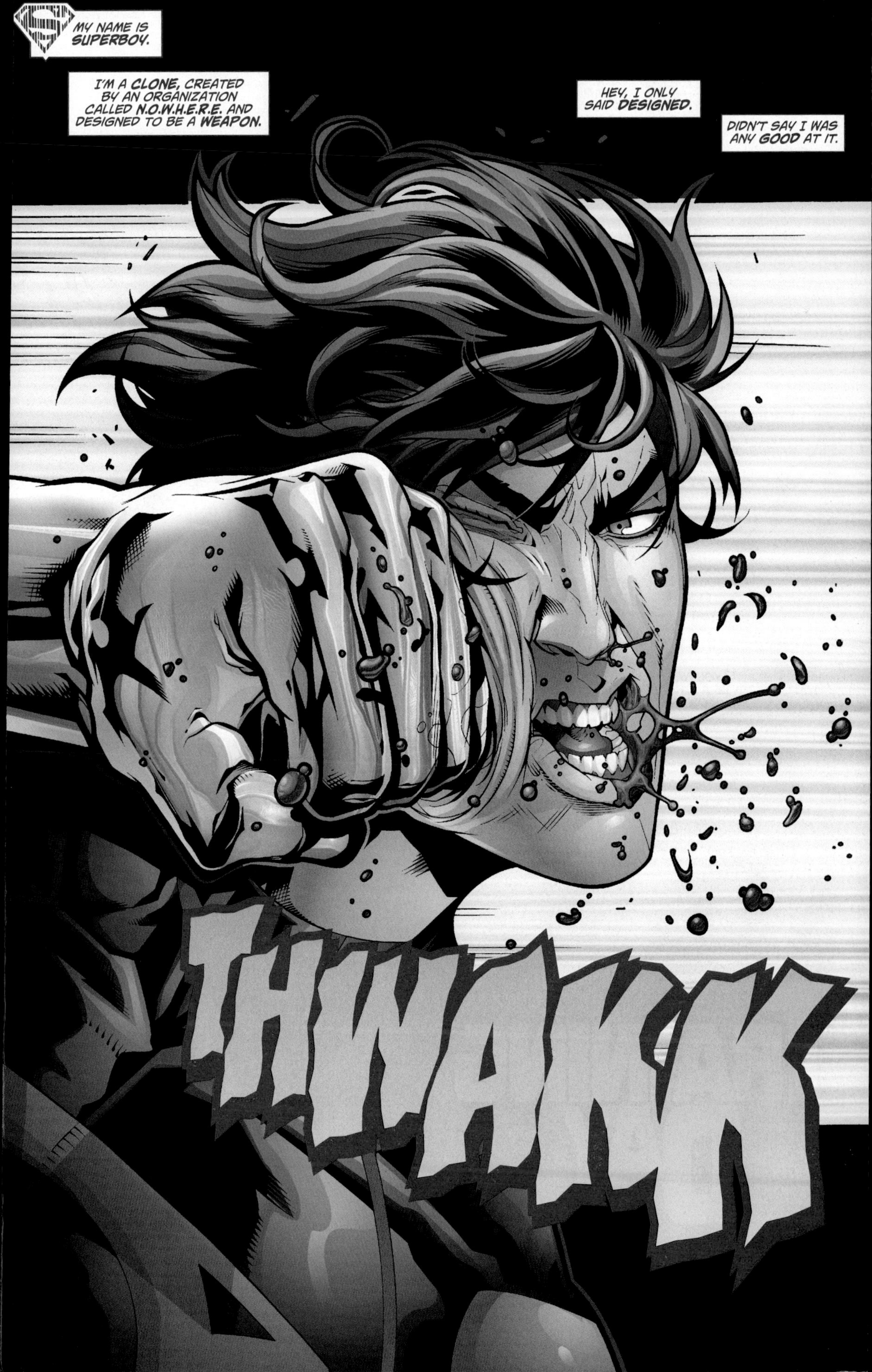
MY NAME IS SUPERBOY.
I'M A CLONE, CREATED BY AN ORGANIZATION CALLED N.O.W.H.E.R.E. AND DESIGNED TO BE A WEAPON.
HEY, I ONLY SAID DESIGNED.
DIDN'T SAY I WAS ANY GOOD AT IT.
THWAKK

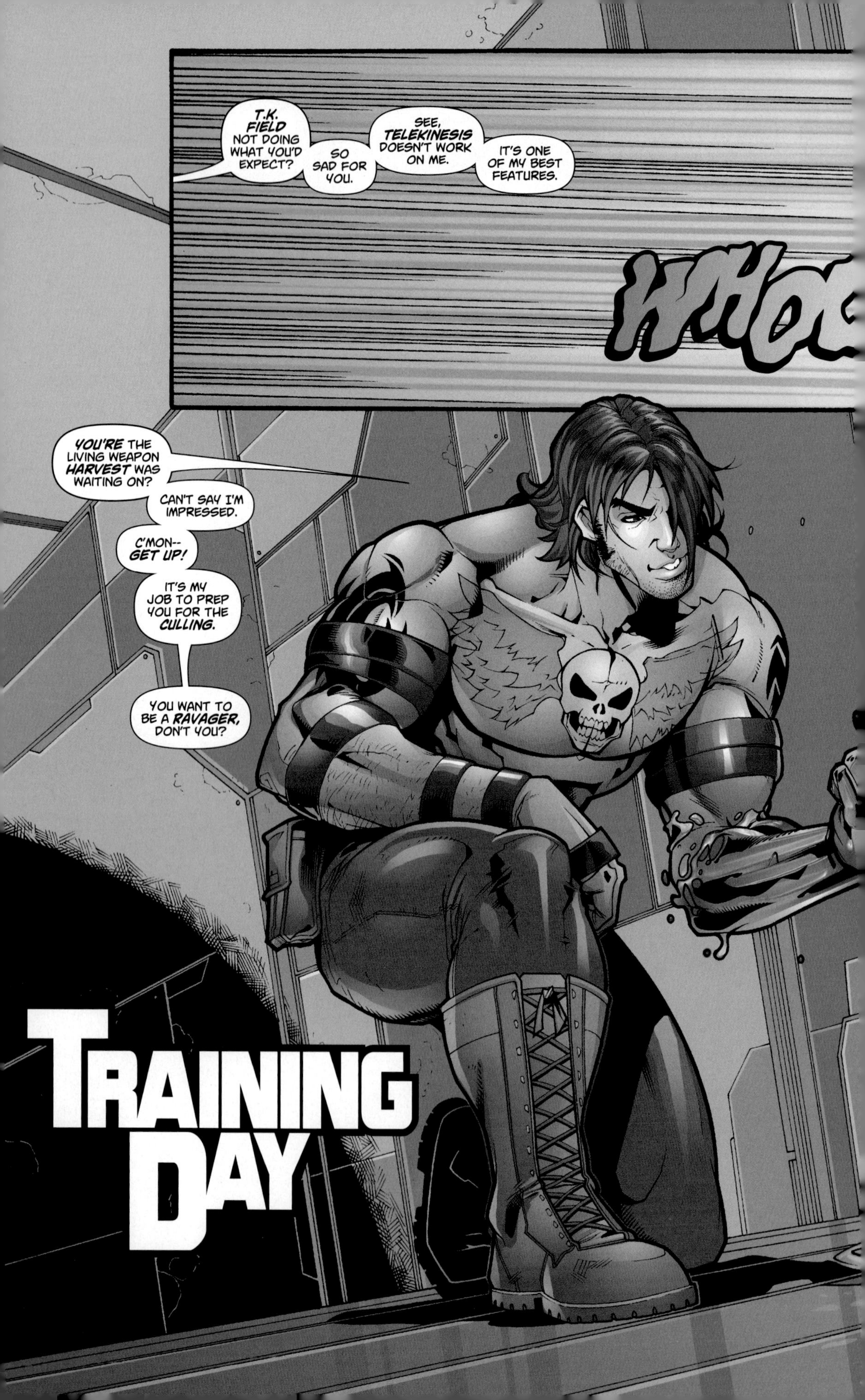
T.K. FIELD NOT DOING WHAT YOU'D EXPECT?
SO SAD FOR YOU.
SEE, TELEKINESIS DOESN'T WORK ON ME.
IT'S ONE OF MY BEST FEATURES.
WHOO
YOU'RE THE LIVING WEAPON HARVEST WAS WAITING ON?
CAN'T SAY I'M IMPRESSED.
C'MON-- GET UP!
IT'S MY JOB TO PREP YOU FOR THE CULLING.
YOU WANT TO BE A RAVAGER, DON'T YOU?
TRAINING DAY

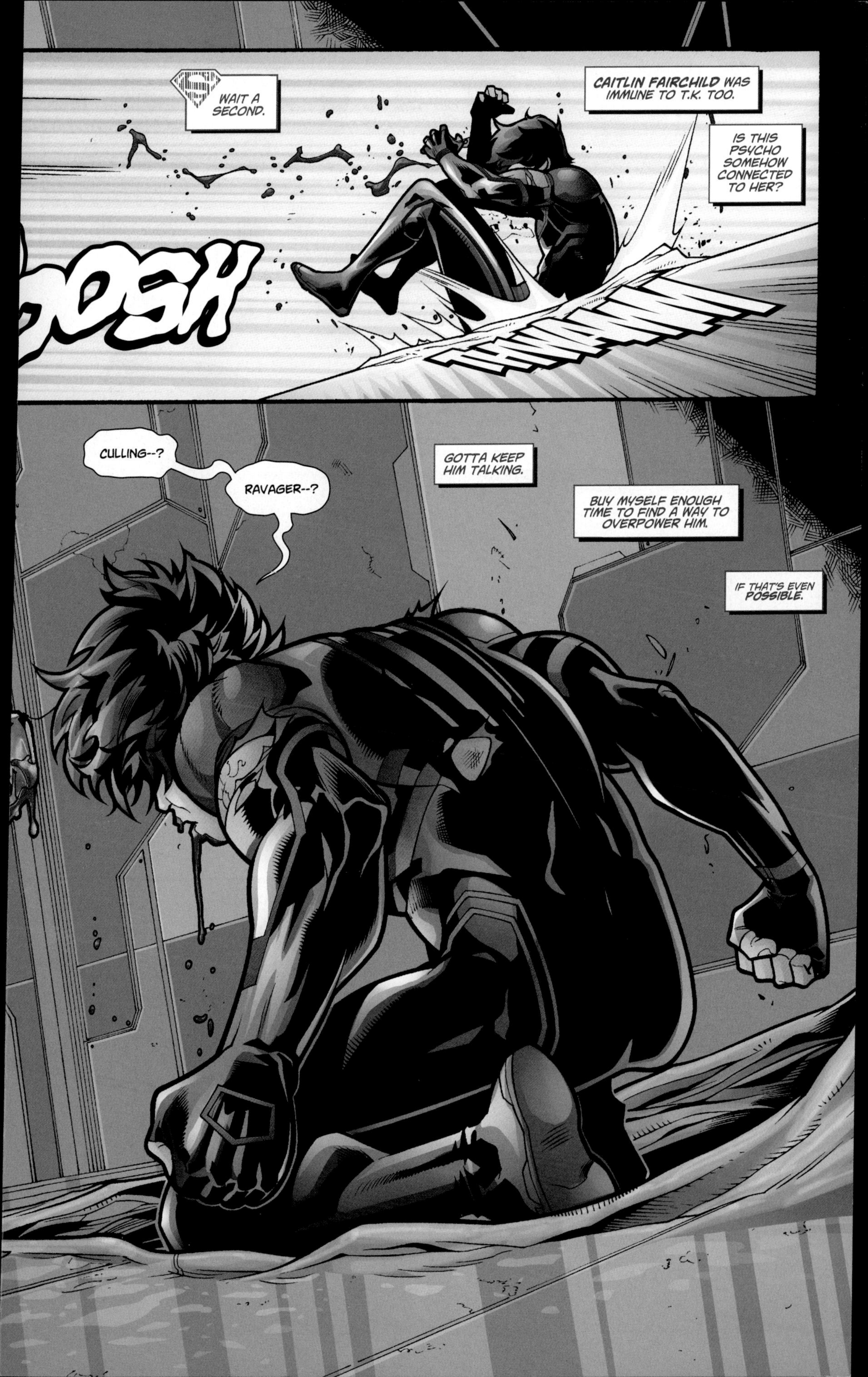
WAIT A SECOND.
CAITLIN FAIRCHILD WAS IMMUNE TO T.K. TOO.
IS THIS PSYCHO SOMEHOW CONNECTED TO HER?
CULLING--?
RAVAGER--?
GOTTA KEEP HIM TALKING.
BUY MYSELF ENOUGH TIME TO FIND A WAY TO OVERPOWER HIM.
IF THAT'S EVEN POSSIBLE.

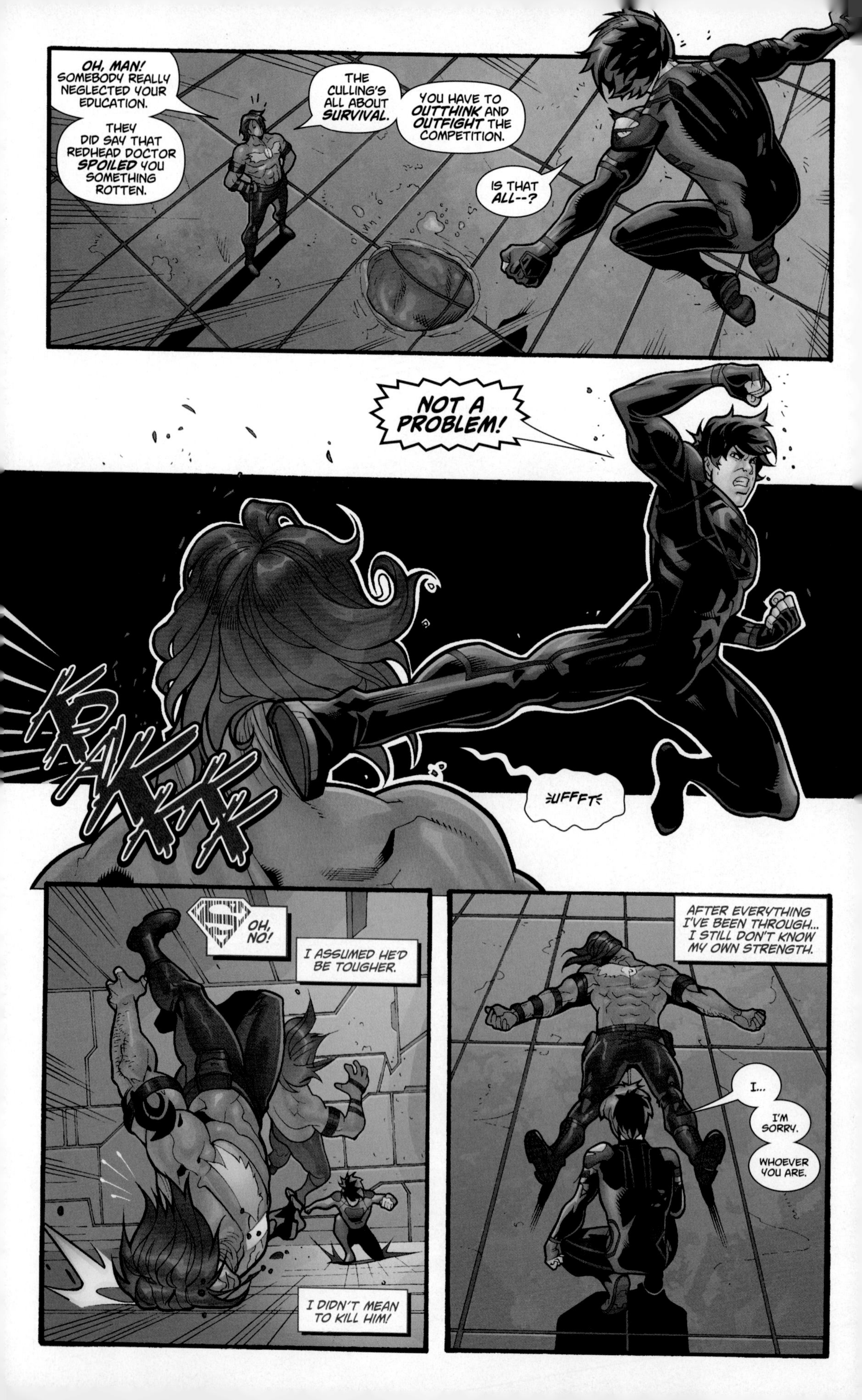
OH, MAN! SOMEBODY REALLY NEGLECTED YOUR EDUCATION.
THEY DID SAY THAT REDHEAD DOCTOR SPOILED YOU SOMETHING ROTTEN.
THE CULLING'S ALL ABOUT SURVIVAL.
YOU HAVE TO OUTTHINK AND OUTFIGHT THE COMPETITION.
IS THAT ALL--?
NOT A PROBLEM!
KRAKKKK
UFFFT
OH, NO!
I ASSUMED HE'D BE TOUGHER.
I DIDN'T MEAN TO KILL HIM!
AFTER EVERYTHING I'VE BEEN THROUGH... I STILL DON'T KNOW MY OWN STRENGTH.
I...
I'M SORRY.
WHOEVER YOU ARE.

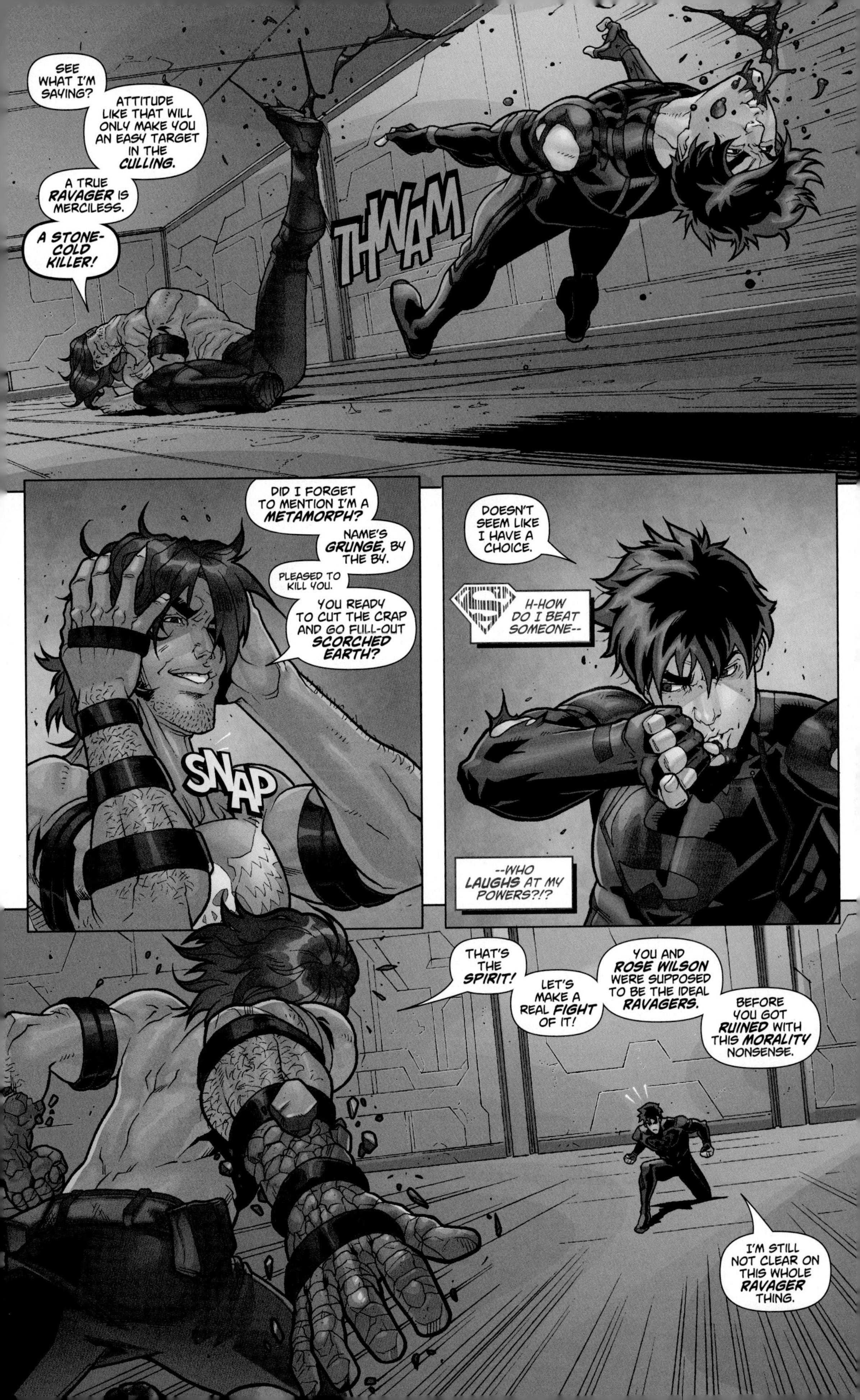
SEE WHAT I'M SAYING?
ATTITUDE LIKE THAT WILL ONLY MAKE YOU AN EASY TARGET IN THE CULLING.
A TRUE RAVAGER IS MERCILESS.
A STONE-COLD KILLER!
THWAM
DID I FORGET TO MENTION I'M A METAMORPH?
NAME'S GRUNGE, BY THE BY.
PLEASED TO KILL YOU.
YOU READY TO CUT THE CRAP AND GO FULL-OUT SCORCHED EARTH?
SNAP
DOESN'T SEEM LIKE I HAVE A CHOICE.
H-HOW DO I BEAT SOMEONE--
--WHO LAUGHS AT MY POWERS?!?
THAT'S THE SPIRIT!
LET'S MAKE A REAL FIGHT OF IT!
YOU AND ROSE WILSON WERE SUPPOSED TO BE THE IDEAL RAVAGERS.
BEFORE YOU GOT RUINED WITH THIS MORALITY NONSENSE.
I'M STILL NOT CLEAR ON THIS WHOLE RAVAGER THING.

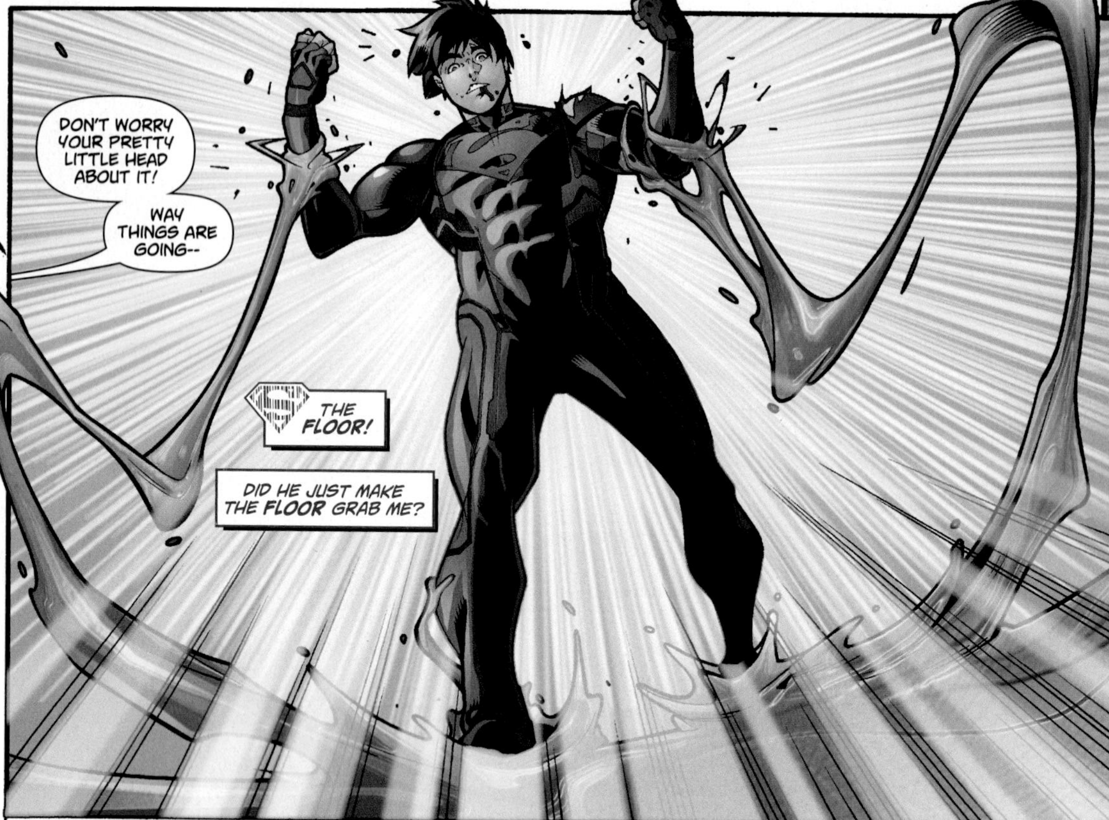
DON'T WORRY YOUR PRETTY LITTLE HEAD ABOUT IT!
WAY THINGS ARE GOING--
THE FLOOR!
DID HE JUST MAKE THE FLOOR GRAB ME?

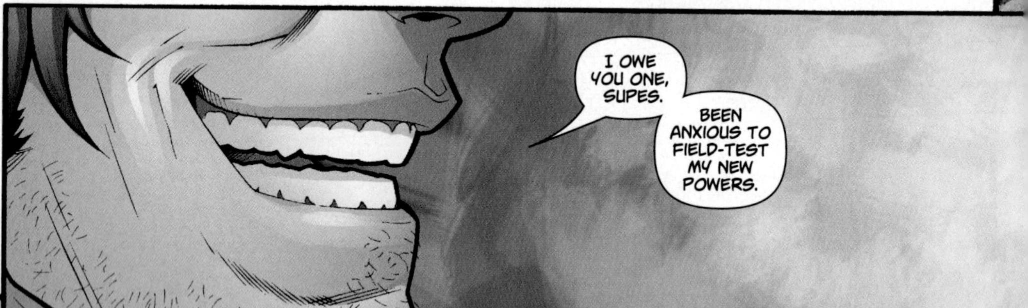
I OWE YOU ONE, SUPES.
BEEN ANXIOUS TO FIELD-TEST MY NEW POWERS.

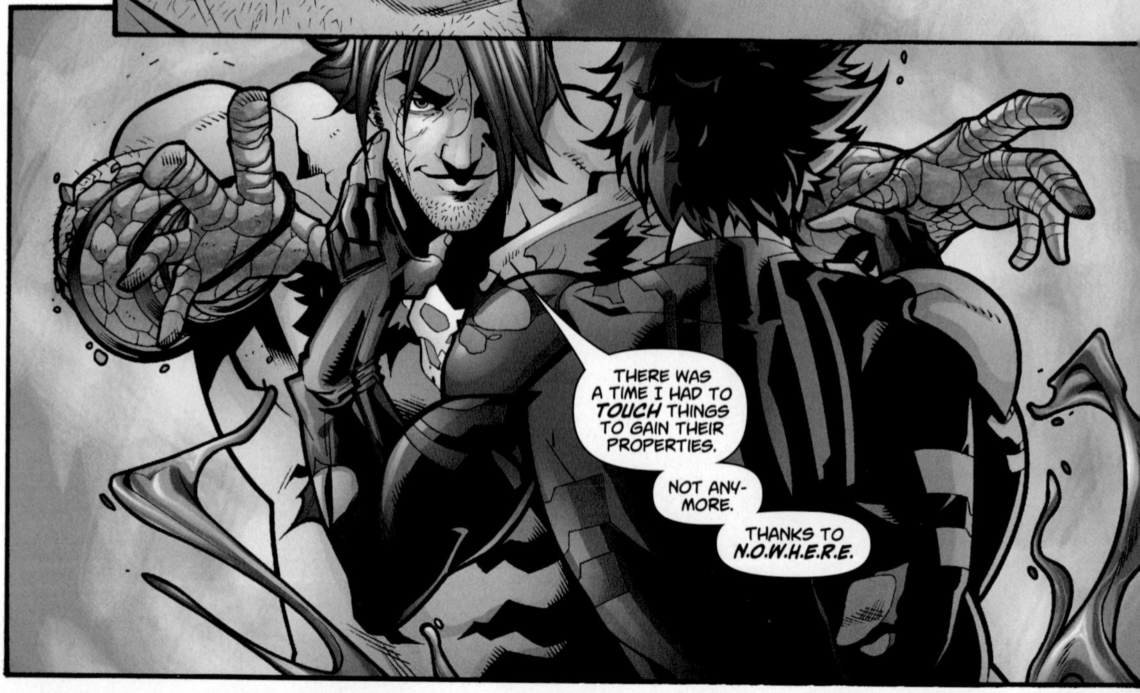
THERE WAS A TIME I HAD TO TOUCH THINGS TO GAIN THEIR PROPERTIES.
NOT ANY-MORE.
THANKS TO N.O.W.H.E.R.E.

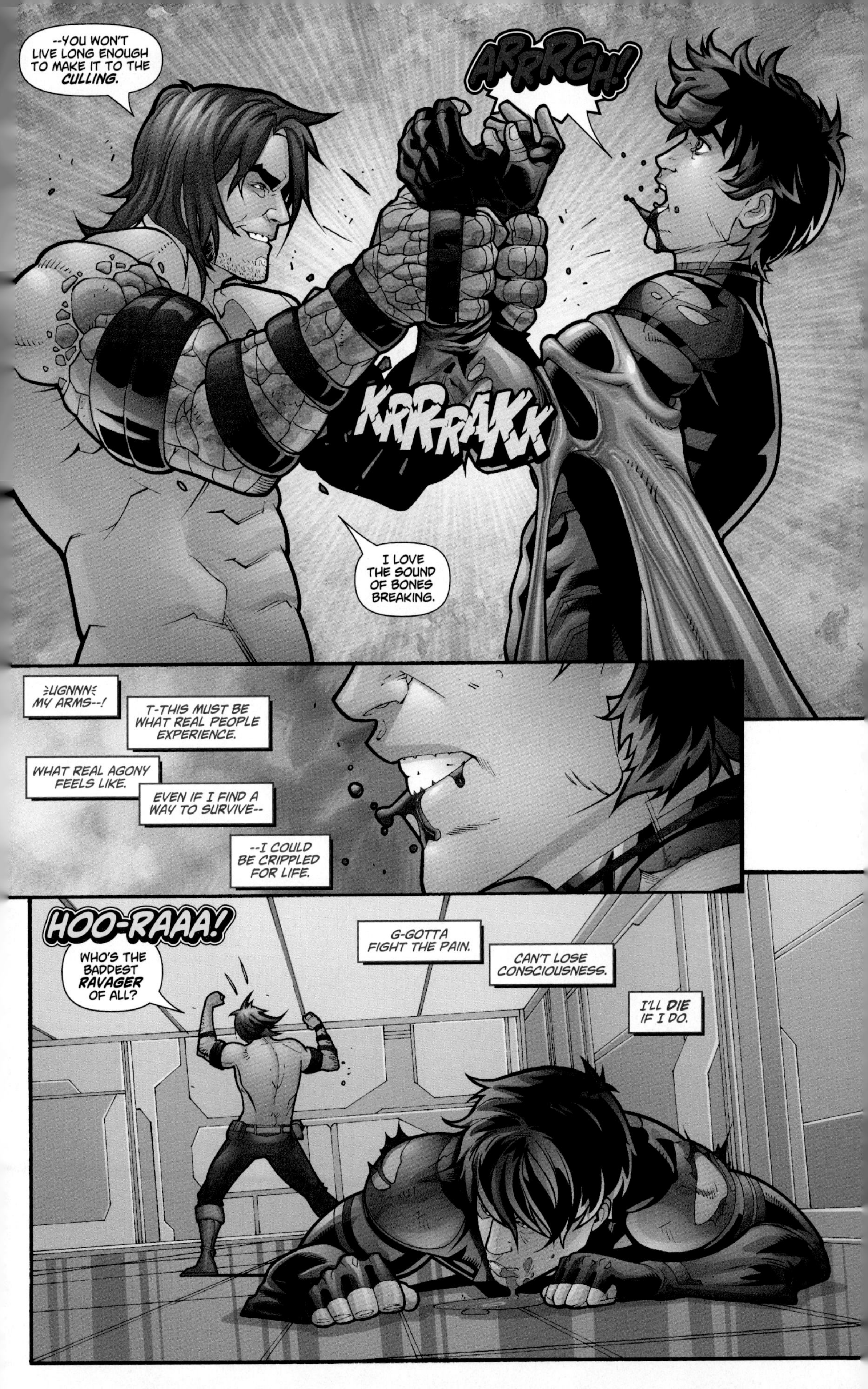
--YOU WON'T LIVE LONG ENOUGH TO MAKE IT TO THE CULLING.
ARRRGH!
KRRRAKK
I LOVE THE SOUND OF BONES BREAKING.
UGNNN MY ARMS--!
T-THIS MUST BE WHAT REAL PEOPLE EXPERIENCE.
WHAT REAL AGONY FEELS LIKE.
EVEN IF I FIND A WAY TO SURVIVE--
--I COULD BE CRIPPLED FOR LIFE.
HOO-RAAA!
WHO'S THE BADDEST RAVAGER OF ALL?
G-GOTTA FIGHT THE PAIN.
CAN'T LOSE CONSCIOUSNESS.
I'LL DIE IF I DO.

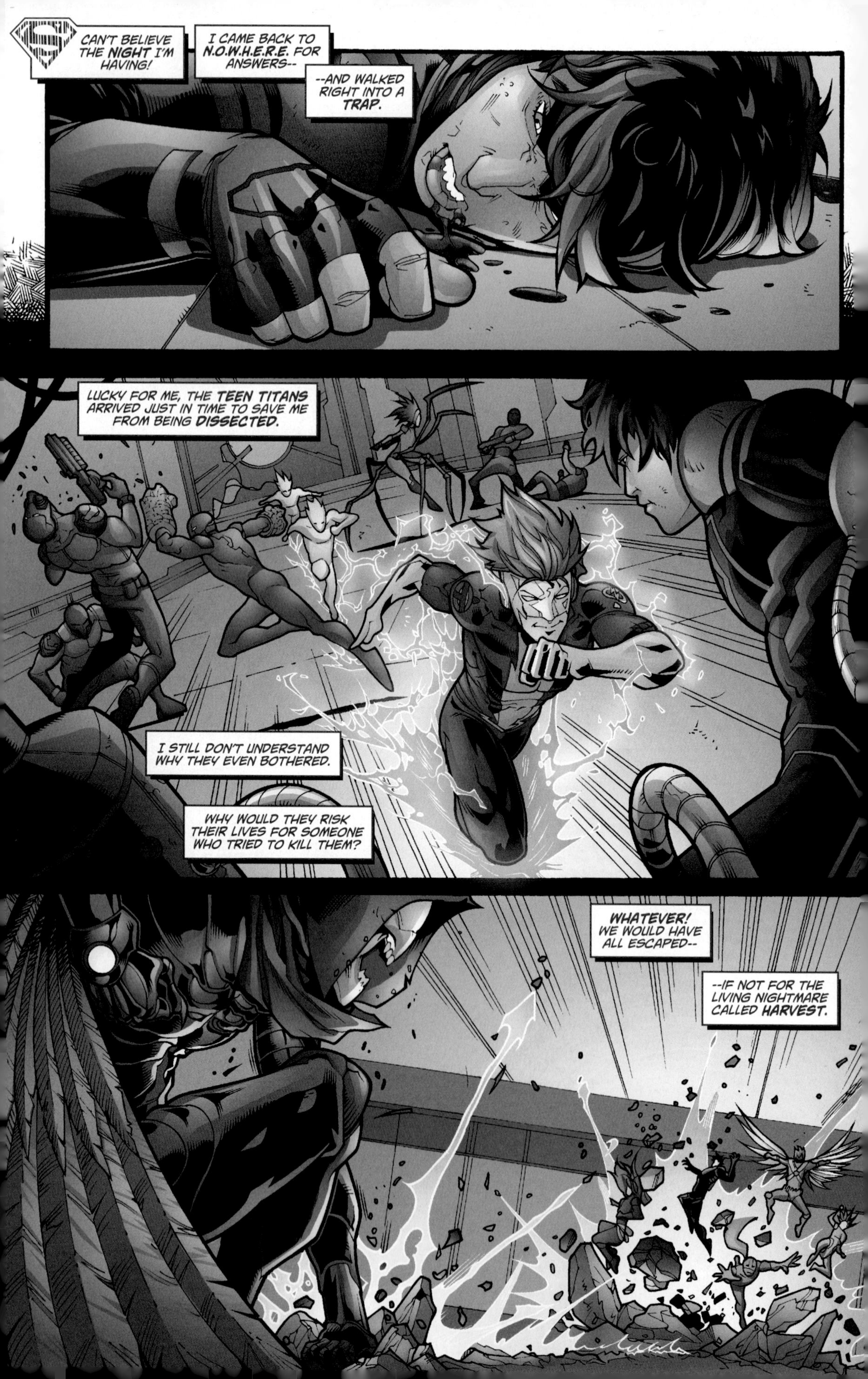
CAN'T BELIEVE THE NIGHT I'M HAVING!
I CAME BACK TO N.O.W.H.E.R.E. FOR ANSWERS--
--AND WALKED RIGHT INTO A TRAP.
LUCKY FOR ME, THE TEEN TITANS ARRIVED JUST IN TIME TO SAVE ME FROM BEING DISSECTED.
I STILL DON'T UNDERSTAND WHY THEY EVEN BOTHERED.
WHY WOULD THEY RISK THEIR LIVES FOR SOMEONE WHO TRIED TO KILL THEM?
WHATEVER! WE WOULD HAVE ALL ESCAPED--
--IF NOT FOR THE LIVING NIGHTMARE CALLED HARVEST.

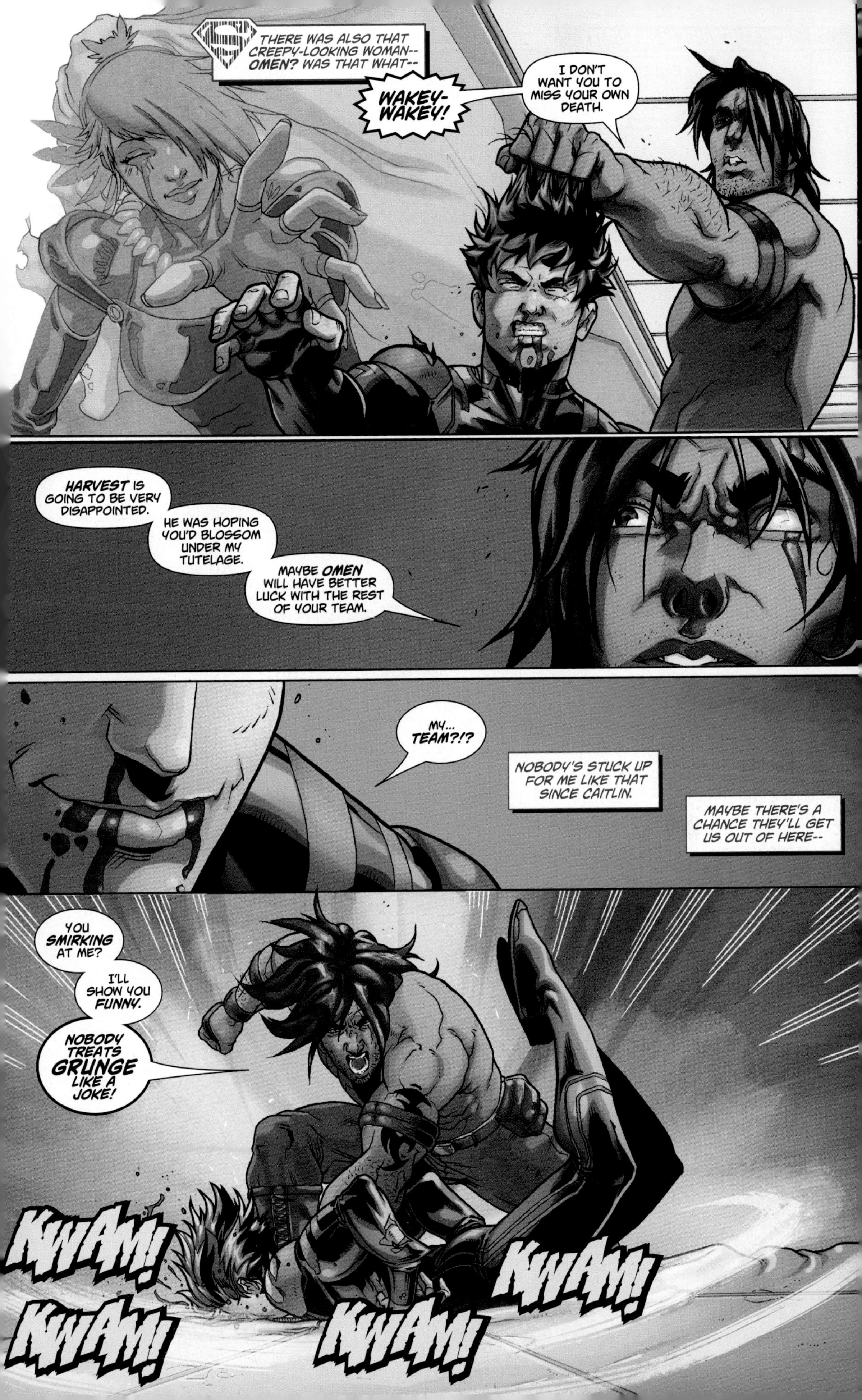
THERE WAS ALSO THAT CREEPY-LOOKING WOMAN-- OMEN? WAS THAT WHAT--
WAKEY-WAKEY!
I DON'T WANT YOU TO MISS YOUR OWN DEATH.
HARVEST IS GOING TO BE VERY DISAPPOINTED.
HE WAS HOPING YOU'D BLOSSOM UNDER MY TUTELAGE.
MAYBE OMEN WILL HAVE BETTER LUCK WITH THE REST OF YOUR TEAM.
MY... TEAM?!?
NOBODY'S STUCK UP FOR ME LIKE THAT SINCE CAITLIN.
MAYBE THERE'S A CHANCE THEY'LL GET US OUT OF HERE--
YOU SMIRKING AT ME?
I'LL SHOW YOU FUNNY.
NOBODY TREATS GRUNGE LIKE A JOKE!
KWAM!
KWAM!
KWAM!
KWAM!

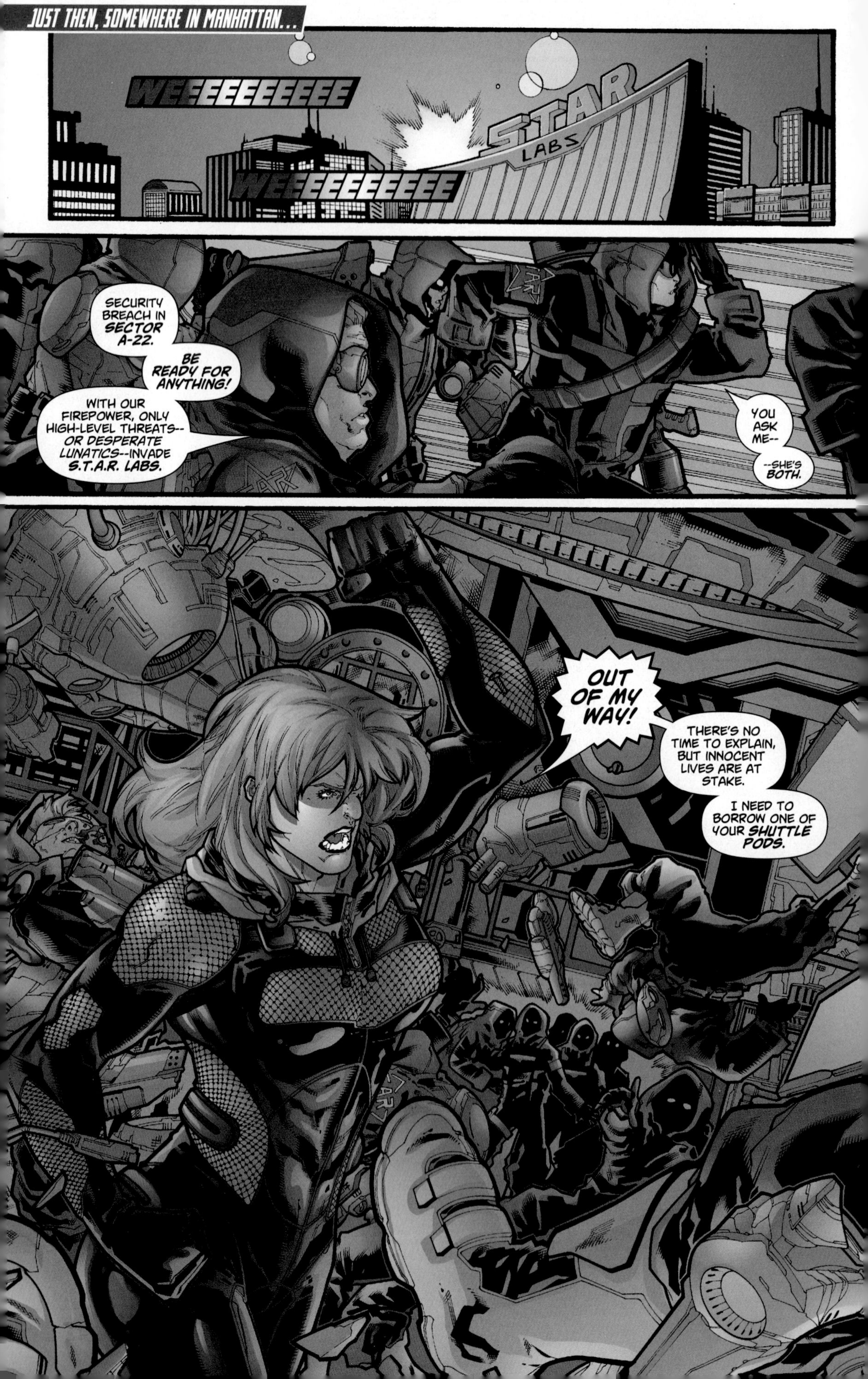
JUST THEN, SOMEWHERE IN MANHATTAN...
WEEEEEEEEEE
S.T.A.R. LABS
WEEEEEEEEEE
SECURITY BREACH IN SECTOR A-22.
BE READY FOR ANYTHING!
WITH OUR FIREPOWER, ONLY HIGH-LEVEL THREATS--OR DESPERATE LUNATICS--INVADE S.T.A.R. LABS.
YOU ASK ME--
--SHE'S BOTH.
OUT OF MY WAY!
THERE'S NO TIME TO EXPLAIN, BUT INNOCENT LIVES ARE AT STAKE.
I NEED TO BORROW ONE OF YOUR SHUTTLE PODS.

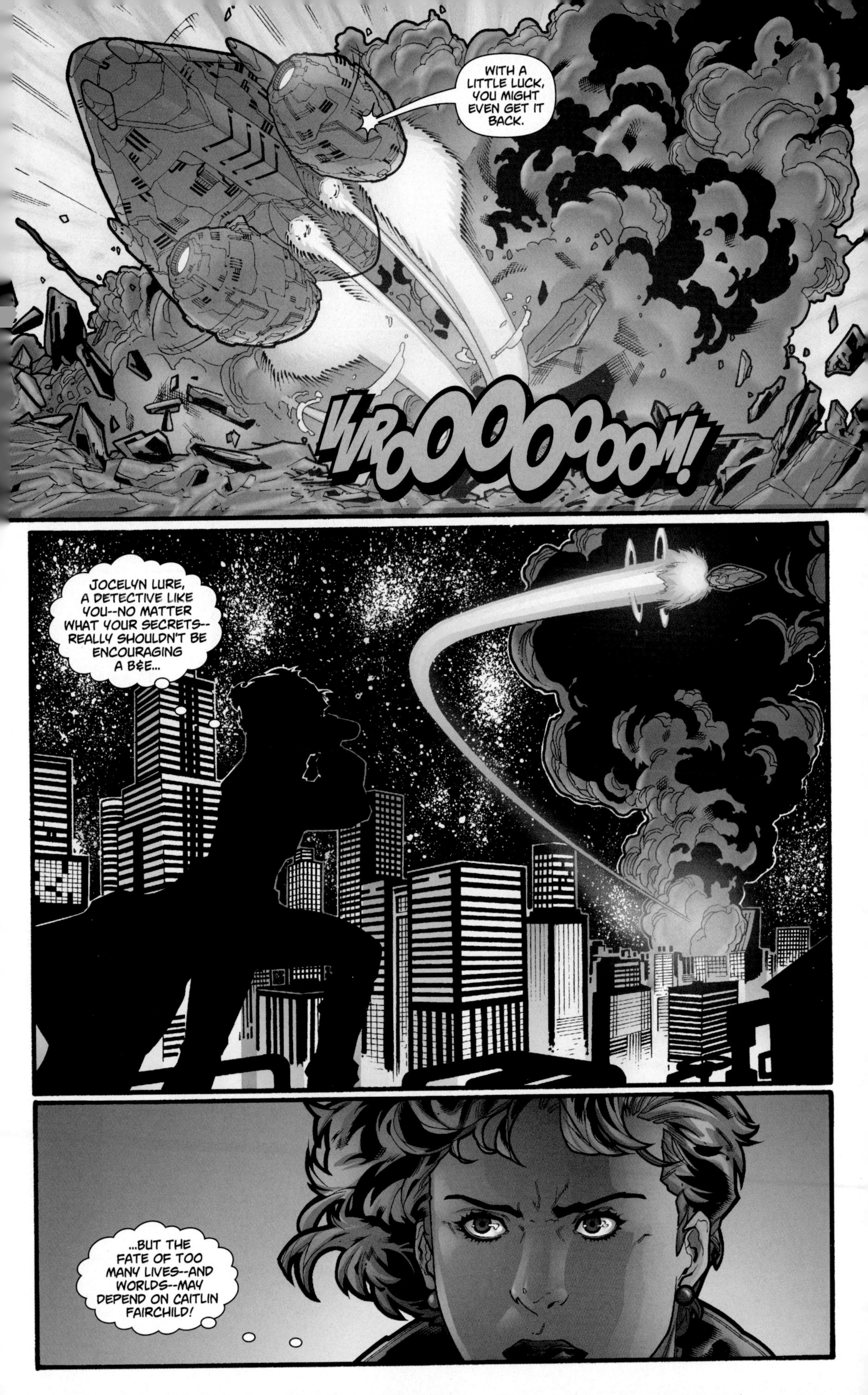
WITH A LITTLE LUCK, YOU MIGHT EVEN GET IT BACK.
VVROOOOOOOOM!
JOCELYN LURE, A DETECTIVE LIKE YOU--NO MATTER WHAT YOUR SECRETS--REALLY SHOULDN'T BE ENCOURAGING A B&E...
...BUT THE FATE OF TOO MANY LIVES--AND WORLDS--MAY DEPEND ON CAITLIN FAIRCHILD!

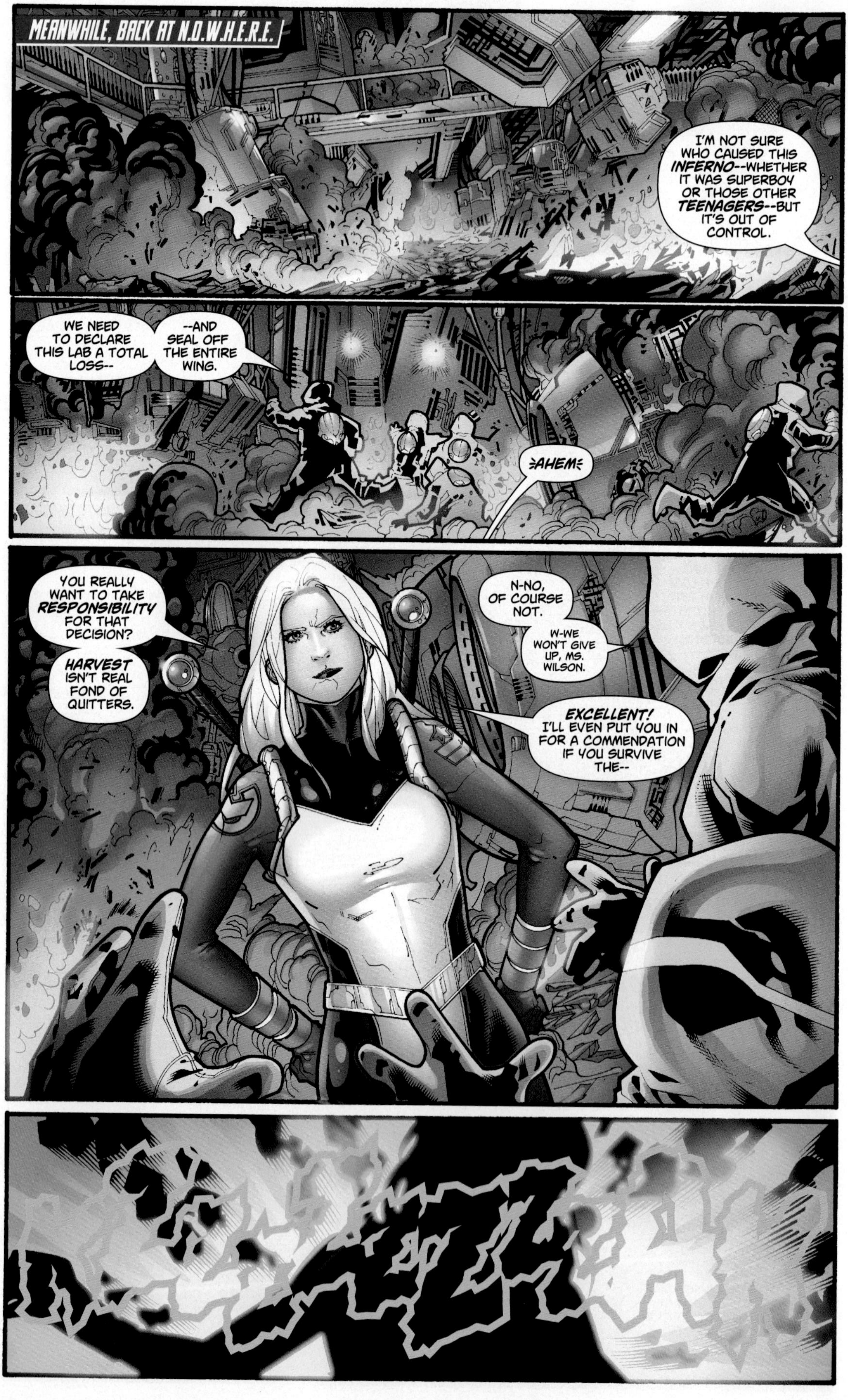
MEANWHILE, BACK AT N.O.W.H.E.R.E.
I'M NOT SURE WHO CAUSED THIS INFERNO--WHETHER IT WAS SUPERBOY OR THOSE OTHER TEENAGERS--BUT IT'S OUT OF CONTROL.
WE NEED TO DECLARE THIS LAB A TOTAL LOSS--
--AND SEAL OFF THE ENTIRE WING.
AHEM
YOU REALLY WANT TO TAKE RESPONSIBILITY FOR THAT DECISION?
HARVEST ISN'T REAL FOND OF QUITTERS.
N-NO, OF COURSE NOT.
W-WE WON'T GIVE UP, MS. WILSON.
EXCELLENT! I'LL EVEN PUT YOU IN FOR A COMMENDATION IF YOU SURVIVE THE--

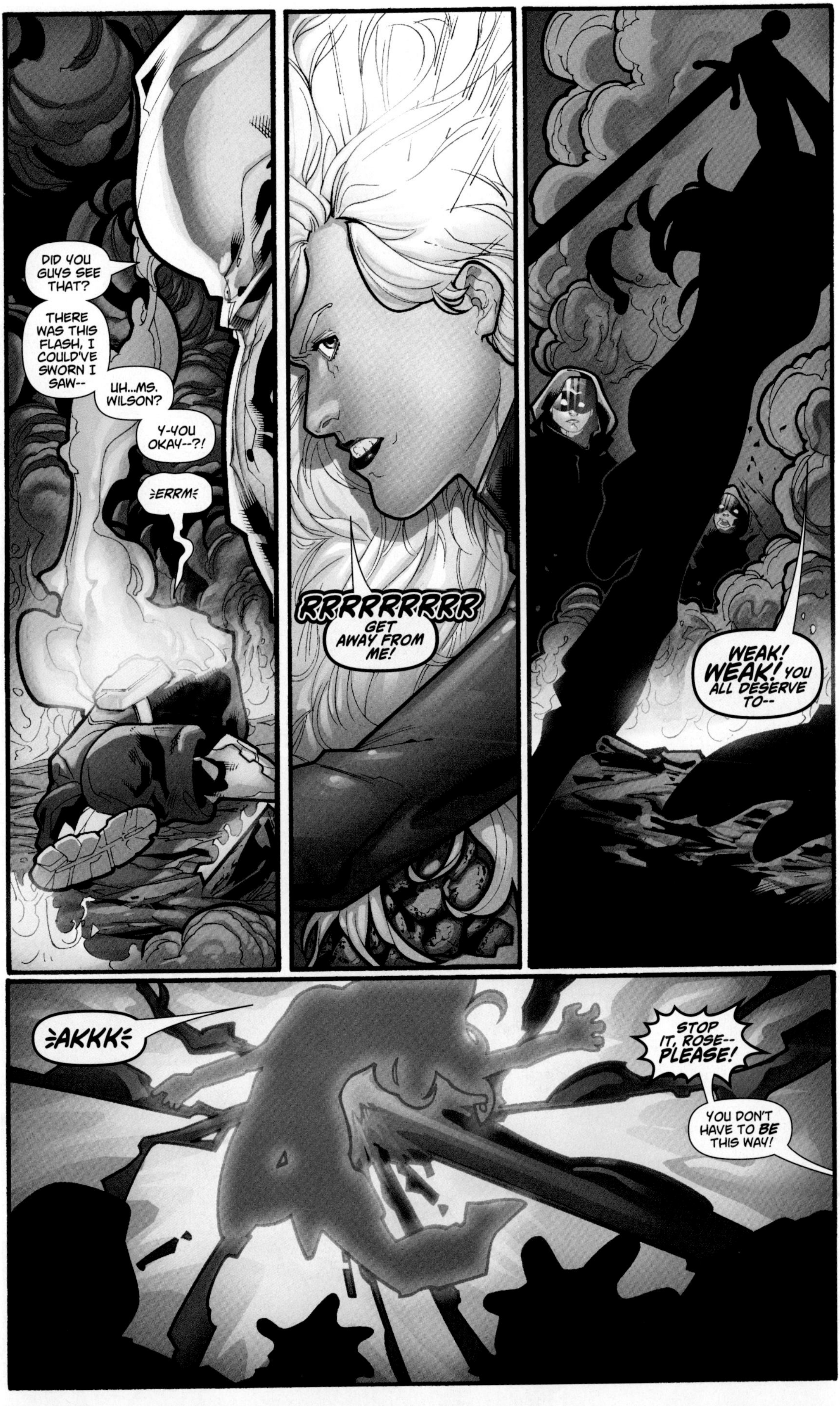
DID YOU GUYS SEE THAT?
THERE WAS THIS FLASH, I COULD'VE SWORN I SAW--
UH...MS. WILSON?
Y-YOU OKAY--?!
ERRM
RRRRRRRRR
GET AWAY FROM ME!
WEAK! WEAK! YOU ALL DESERVE TO--
AKKK
STOP IT, ROSE-- PLEASE!
YOU DON'T HAVE TO BE THIS WAY!

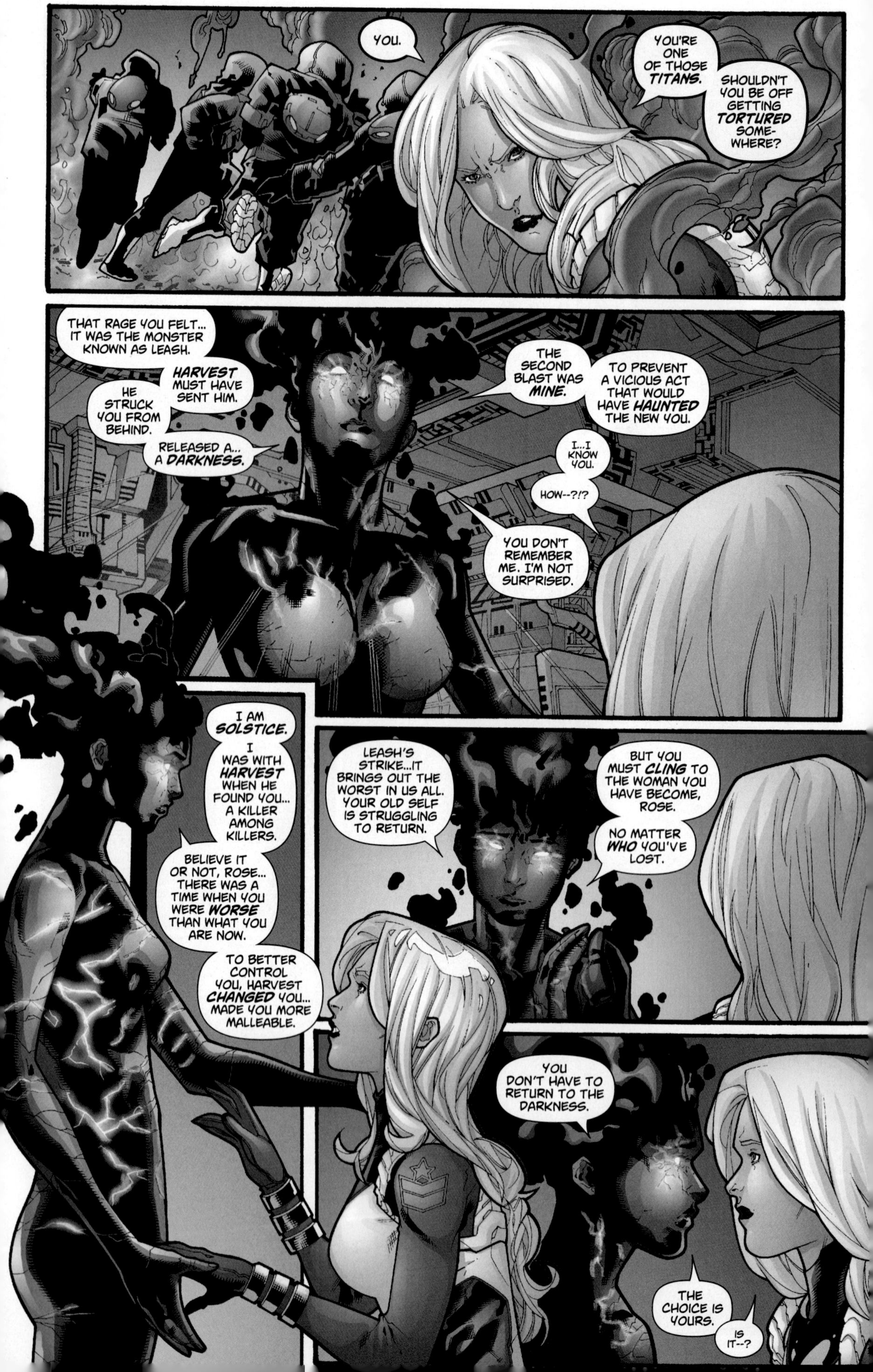

YOU.
YOU'RE ONE OF THOSE TITANS.
SHOULDN'T YOU BE OFF GETTING TORTURED SOME-WHERE?
THAT RAGE YOU FELT... IT WAS THE MONSTER KNOWN AS LEASH.
HARVEST MUST HAVE SENT HIM.
HE STRUCK YOU FROM BEHIND.
RELEASED A... A DARKNESS.
THE SECOND BLAST WAS MINE.
TO PREVENT A VICIOUS ACT THAT WOULD HAVE HAUNTED THE NEW YOU.
I...I KNOW YOU.
HOW--?!?
YOU DON'T REMEMBER ME. I'M NOT SURPRISED.
I AM SOLSTICE.
I WAS WITH HARVEST WHEN HE FOUND YOU... A KILLER AMONG KILLERS.
BELIEVE IT OR NOT, ROSE... THERE WAS A TIME WHEN YOU WERE WORSE THAN WHAT YOU ARE NOW.
TO BETTER CONTROL YOU, HARVEST CHANGED YOU... MADE YOU MORE MALLEABLE.
LEASH'S STRIKE...IT BRINGS OUT THE WORST IN US ALL. YOUR OLD SELF IS STRUGGLING TO RETURN.
BUT YOU MUST CLING TO THE WOMAN YOU HAVE BECOME, ROSE.
NO MATTER WHO YOU'VE LOST.
YOU DON'T HAVE TO RETURN TO THE DARKNESS.
THE CHOICE IS YOURS.
IS IT--?

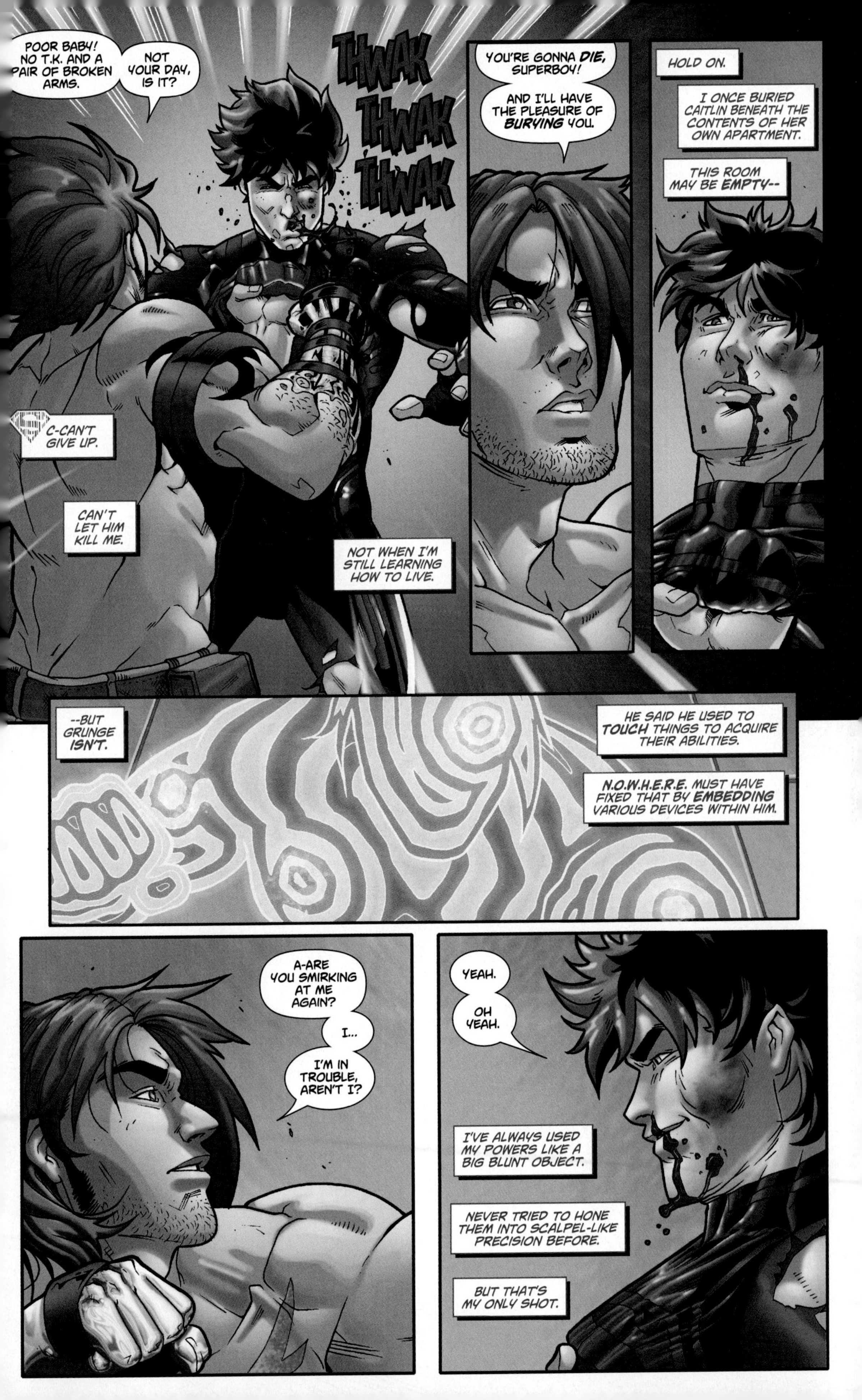

POOR BABY! NO T.K. AND A PAIR OF BROKEN ARMS.
NOT YOUR DAY, IS IT?
THWAK THWAK THWAK
C-CAN'T GIVE UP.
CAN'T LET HIM KILL ME.
NOT WHEN I'M STILL LEARNING HOW TO LIVE.
YOU'RE GONNA DIE, SUPERBOY!
AND I'LL HAVE THE PLEASURE OF BURYING YOU.
HOLD ON.
I ONCE BURIED CAITLIN BENEATH THE CONTENTS OF HER OWN APARTMENT.
THIS ROOM MAY BE EMPTY--
--BUT GRUNGE ISN'T.
HE SAID HE USED TO TOUCH THINGS TO ACQUIRE THEIR ABILITIES.
N.O.W.H.E.R.E. MUST HAVE FIXED THAT BY EMBEDDING VARIOUS DEVICES WITHIN HIM.
A-ARE YOU SMIRKING AT ME AGAIN?
I...
I'M IN TROUBLE, AREN'T I?
YEAH.
OH YEAH.
I'VE ALWAYS USED MY POWERS LIKE A BIG BLUNT OBJECT.
NEVER TRIED TO HONE THEM INTO SCALPEL-LIKE PRECISION BEFORE.
BUT THAT'S MY ONLY SHOT.

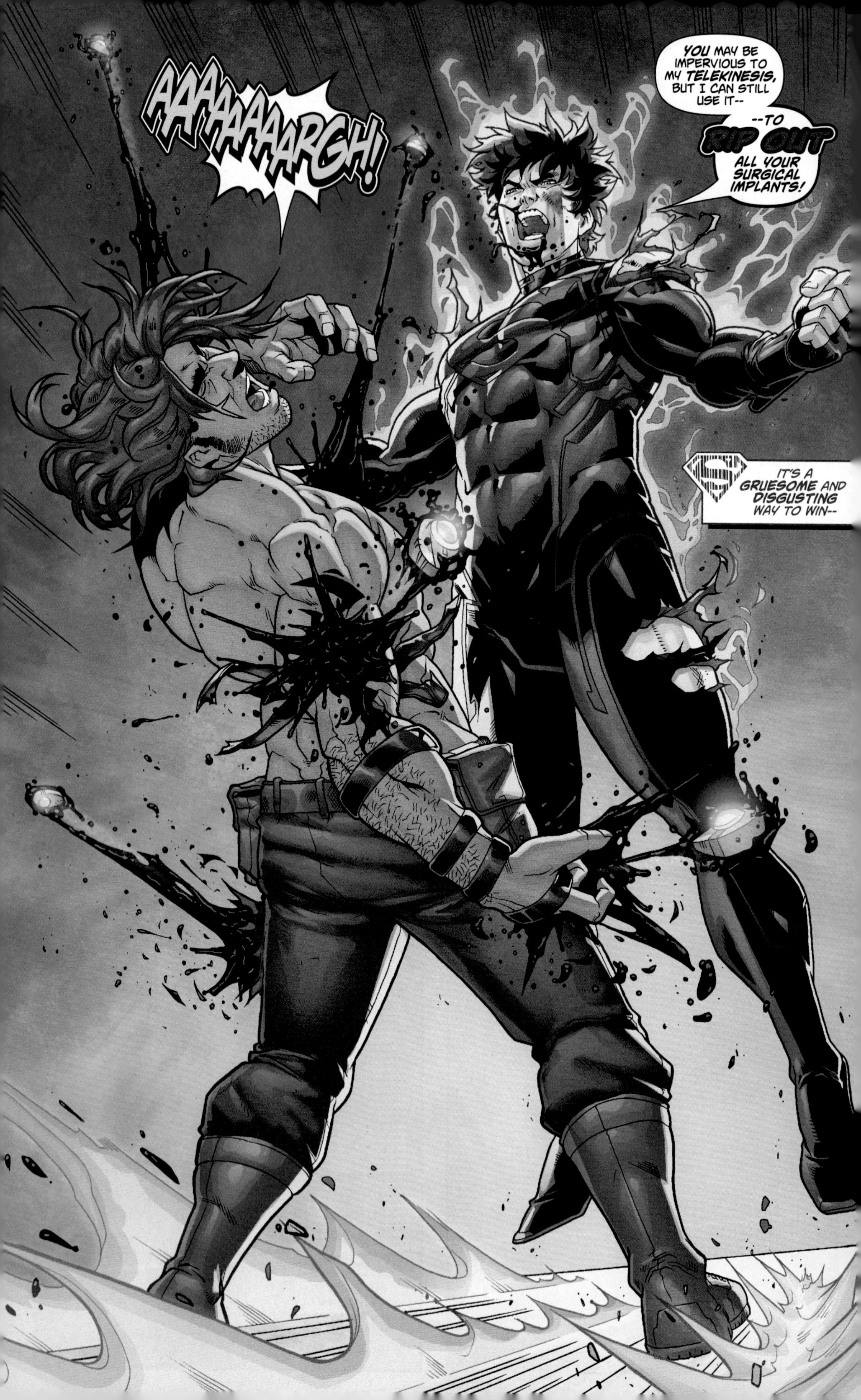
AAAAAAAARGH!
YOU MAY BE IMPERVIOUS TO MY TELEKINESIS, BUT I CAN STILL USE IT--
--TO RIP OUT ALL YOUR SURGICAL IMPLANTS!
IT'S A GRUESOME AND DISGUSTING WAY TO WIN--

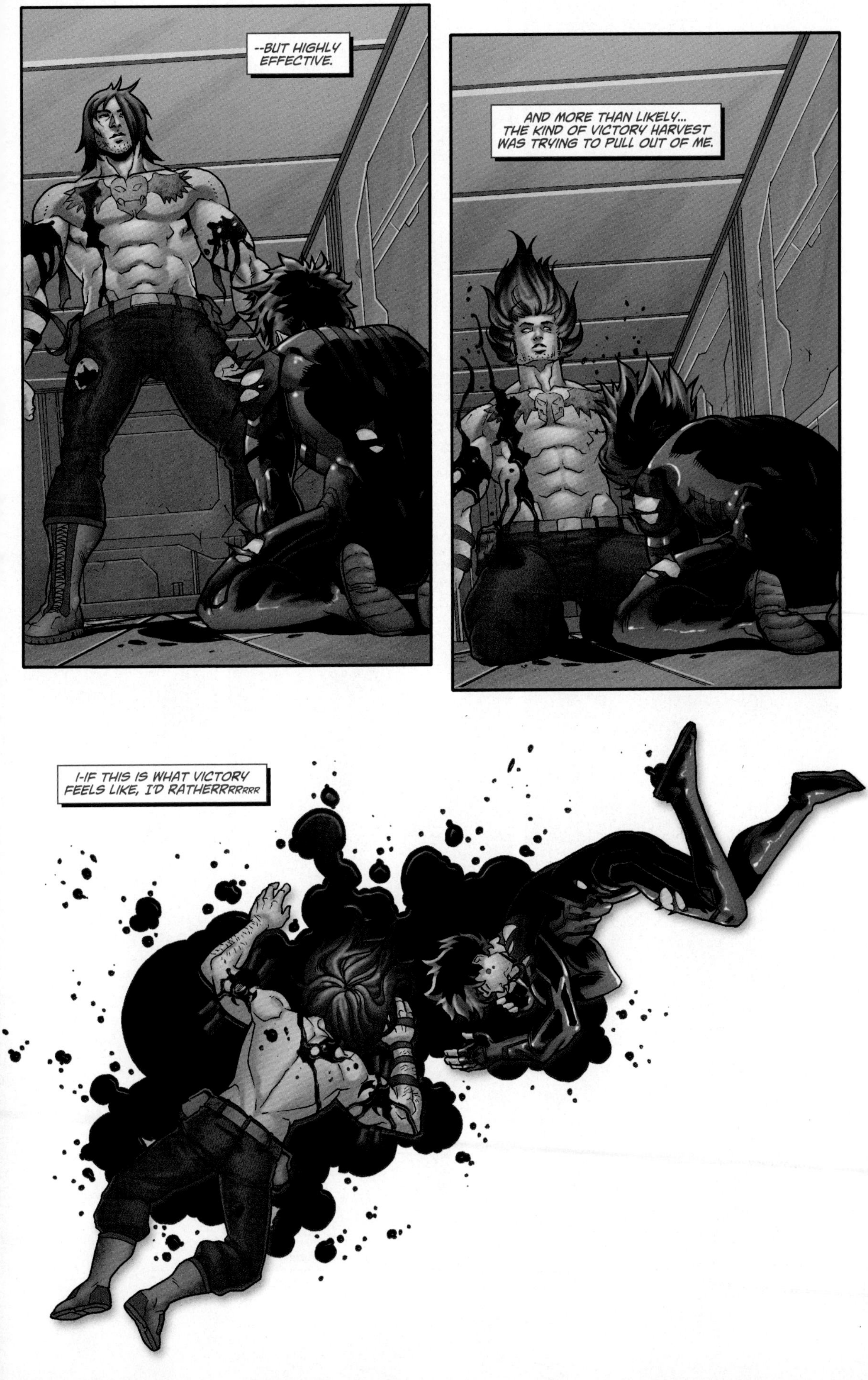
--BUT HIGHLY EFFECTIVE.
AND MORE THAN LIKELY... THE KIND OF VICTORY HARVEST WAS TRYING TO PULL OUT OF ME.
I-IF THIS IS WHAT VICTORY FEELS LIKE, I'D RATHERRrrrrr

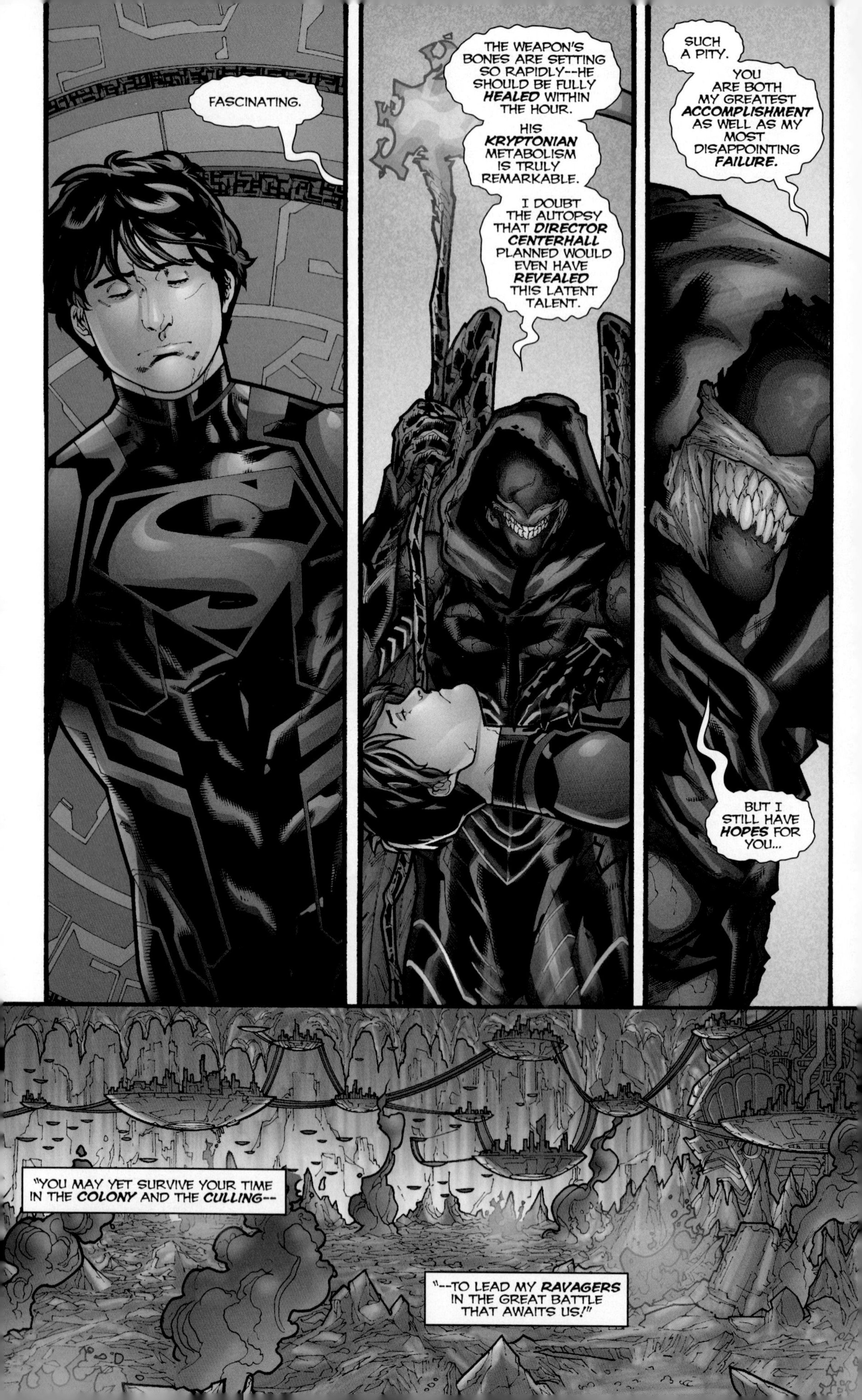
FASCINATING.
THE WEAPON'S BONES ARE SETTING SO RAPIDLY--HE SHOULD BE FULLY HEALED WITHIN THE HOUR.
HIS KRYPTONIAN METABOLISM IS TRULY REMARKABLE.
I DOUBT THE AUTOPSY THAT DIRECTOR CENTERHALL PLANNED WOULD EVEN HAVE REVEALED THIS LATENT TALENT.
SUCH A PITY.
YOU ARE BOTH MY GREATEST ACCOMPLISHMENT AS WELL AS MY MOST DISAPPOINTING FAILURE.
BUT I STILL HAVE HOPES FOR YOU...
"YOU MAY YET SURVIVE YOUR TIME IN THE COLONY AND THE CULLING--
"--TO LEAD MY RAVAGERS IN THE GREAT BATTLE THAT AWAITS US!"

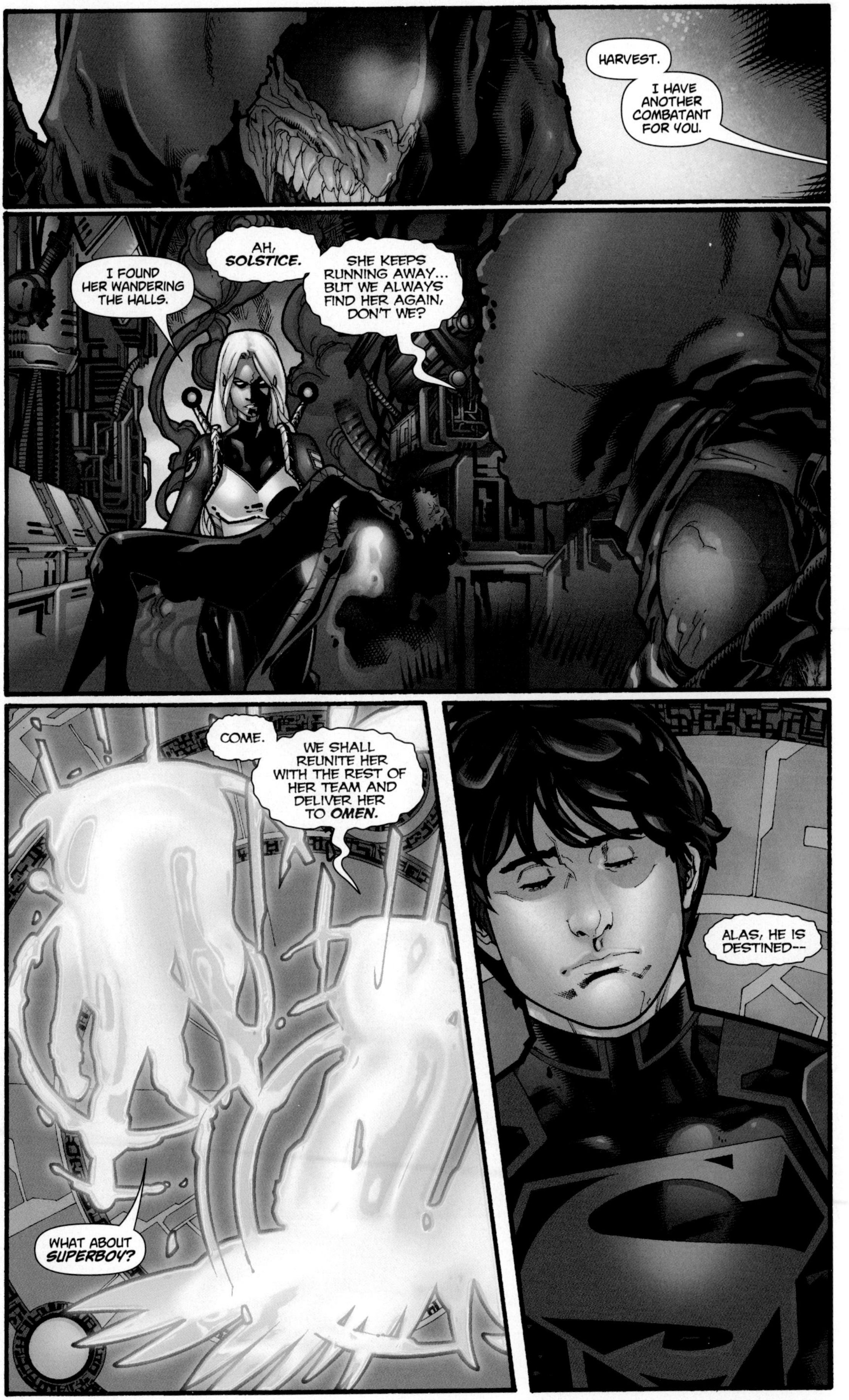
HARVEST.
I HAVE ANOTHER COMBATANT FOR YOU.
I FOUND HER WANDERING THE HALLS.
AH, SOLSTICE.
SHE KEEPS RUNNING AWAY... BUT WE ALWAYS FIND HER AGAIN, DON'T WE?
COME.
WE SHALL REUNITE HER WITH THE REST OF HER TEAM AND DELIVER HER TO OMEN.
WHAT ABOUT SUPERBOY?
ALAS, HE IS DESTINED--

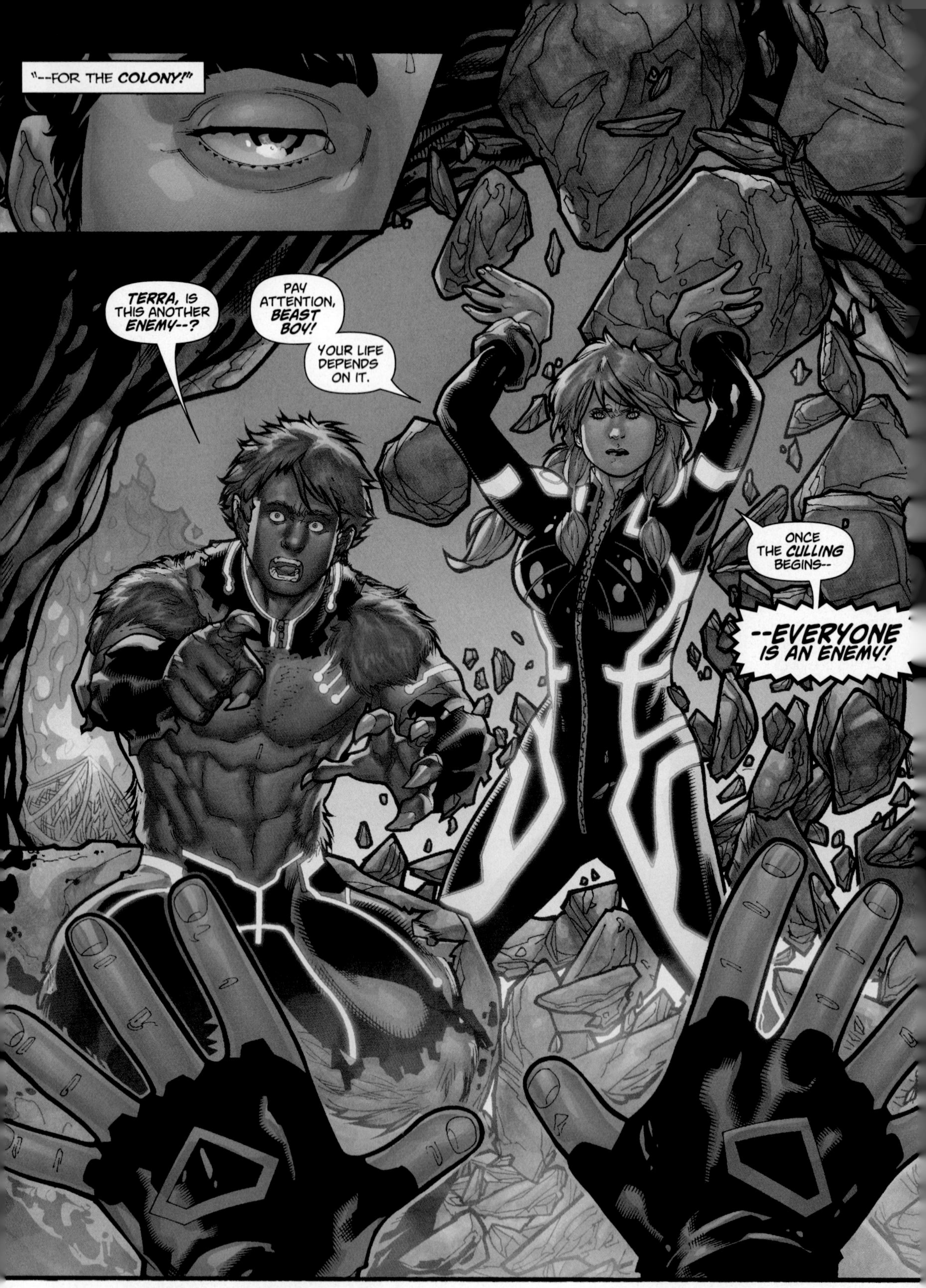
"--FOR THE COLONY!"
TERRA, IS THIS ANOTHER ENEMY--?
PAY ATTENTION, BEAST BOY!
YOUR LIFE DEPENDS ON IT.
ONCE THE CULLING BEGINS--
--EVERYONE IS AN ENEMY!

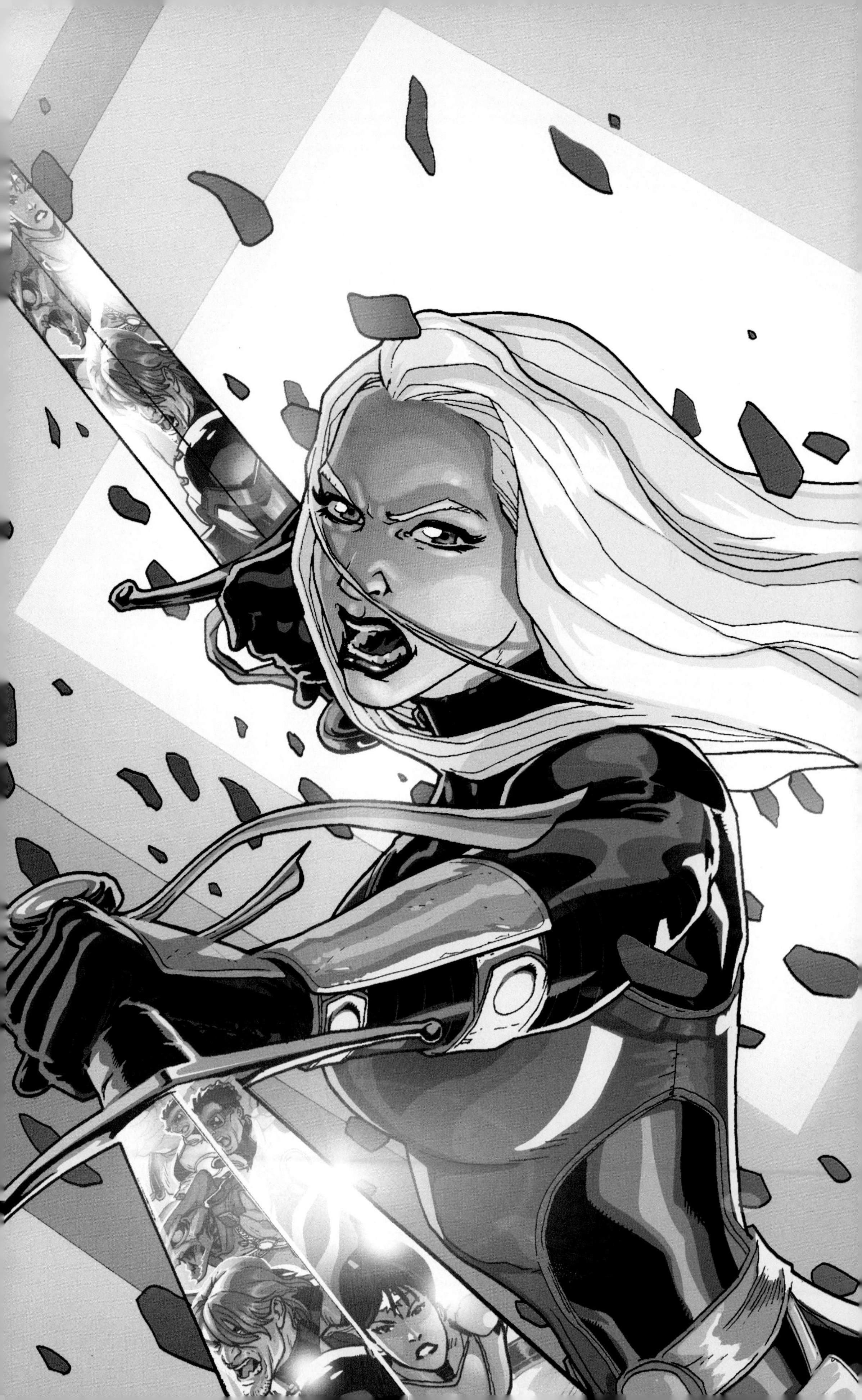

PRELUDE PART TWO: RAVAGED!
TOM DEFALCO writer AARON KUDER artist
cover art by PETE WOODS & BRAD ANDERSON

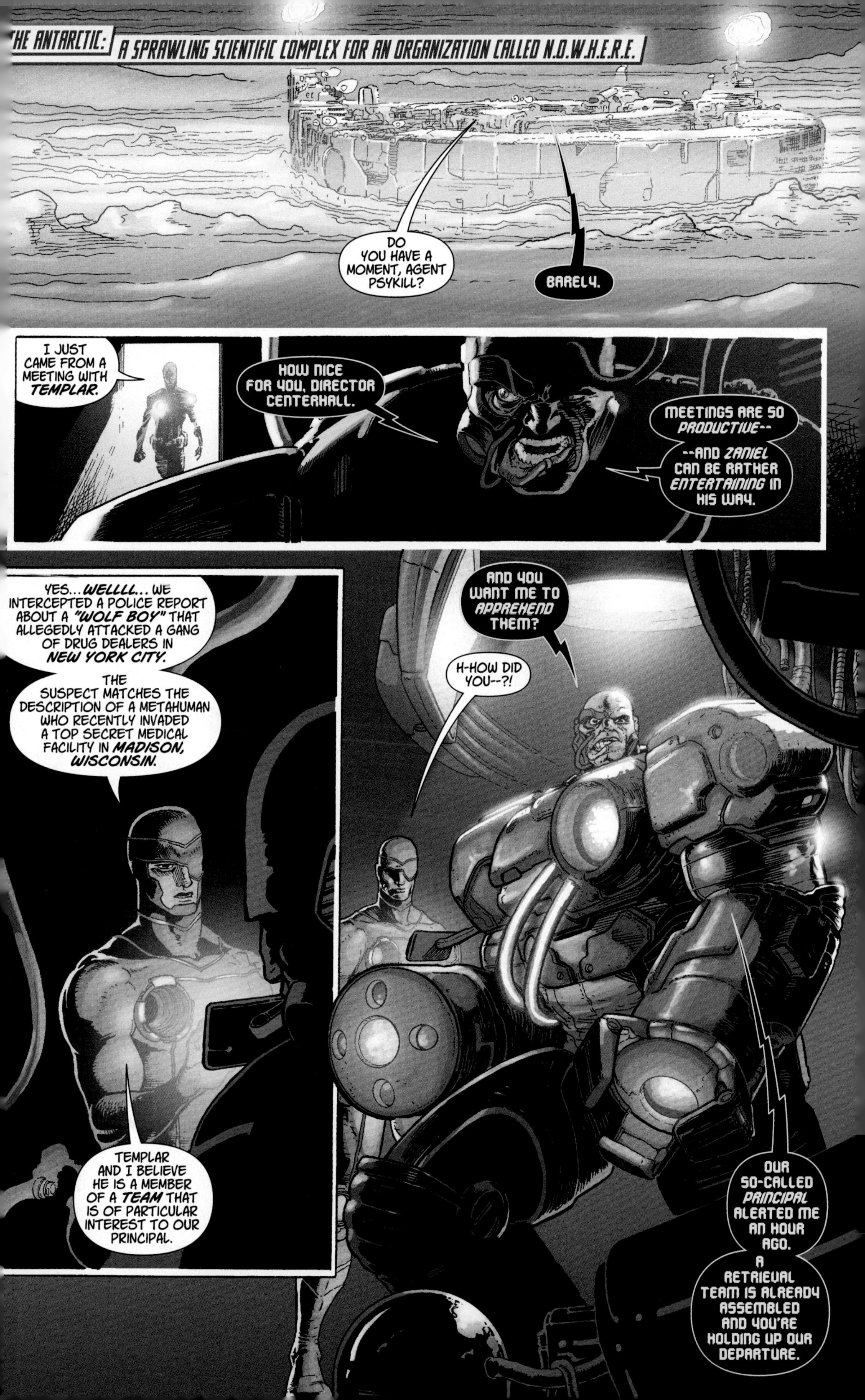
THE ANTARCTIC: A SPRAWLING SCIENTIFIC COMPLEX FOR AN ORGANIZATION CALLED N.O.W.H.E.R.E.
DO YOU HAVE A MOMENT, AGENT PSYKILL?
BARELY.
I JUST CAME FROM A MEETING WITH TEMPLAR.
HOW NICE FOR YOU, DIRECTOR CENTERHALL.
MEETINGS ARE SO PRODUCTIVE--
--AND ZANIEL CAN BE RATHER ENTERTAINING IN HIS WAY.
YES...WELLLL... WE INTERCEPTED A POLICE REPORT ABOUT A "WOLF BOY" THAT ALLEGEDLY ATTACKED A GANG OF DRUG DEALERS IN NEW YORK CITY.
THE SUSPECT MATCHES THE DESCRIPTION OF A METAHUMAN WHO RECENTLY INVADED A TOP SECRET MEDICAL FACILITY IN MADISON, WISCONSIN.
TEMPLAR AND I BELIEVE HE IS A MEMBER OF A TEAM THAT IS OF PARTICULAR INTEREST TO OUR PRINCIPAL.
AND YOU WANT ME TO APPREHEND THEM?
H-HOW DID YOU--?!
OUR SO-CALLED PRINCIPAL ALERTED ME AN HOUR AGO.
A RETRIEVAL TEAM IS ALREADY ASSEMBLED AND YOU'RE HOLDING UP OUR DEPARTURE.

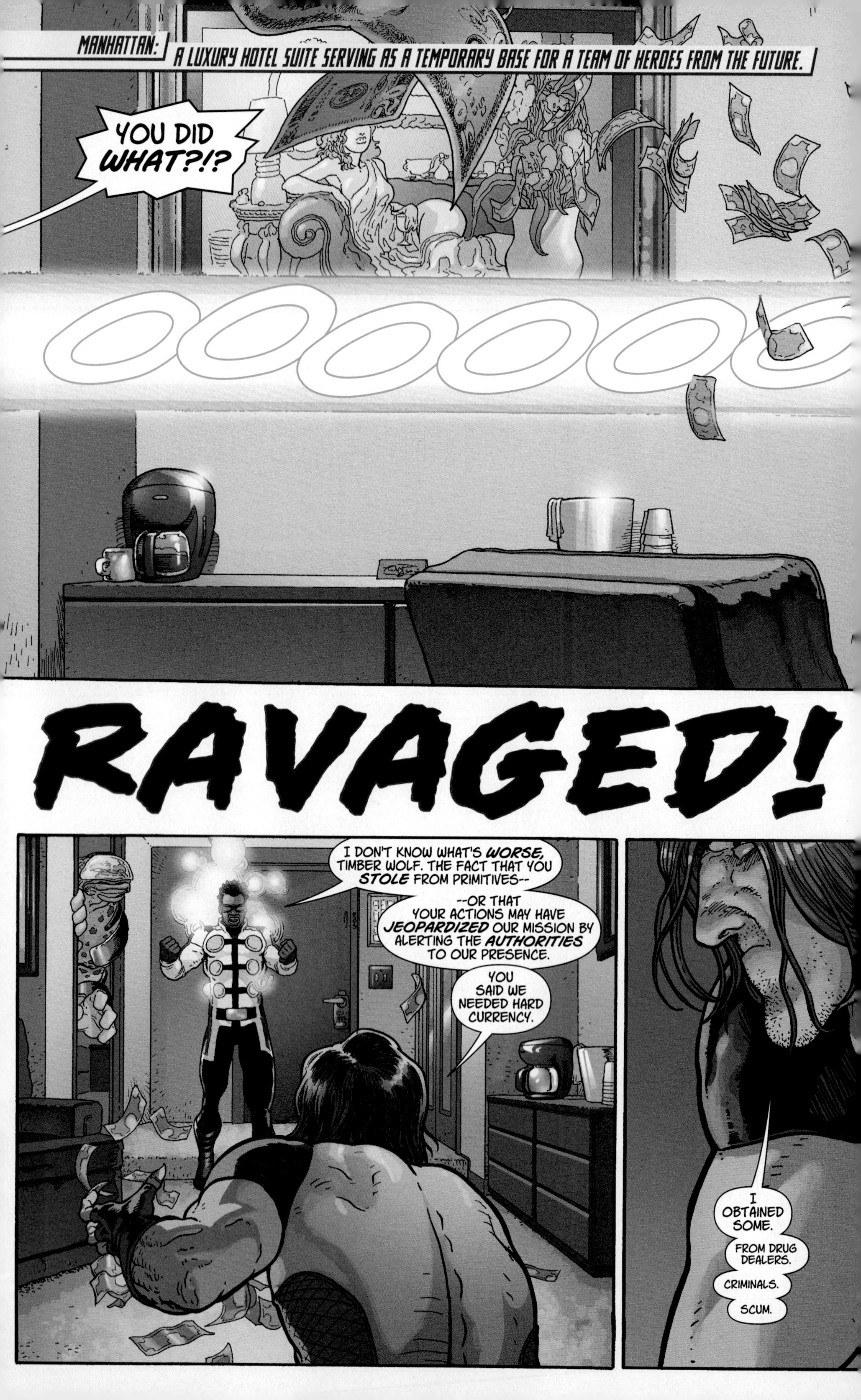

MANHATTAN: A LUXURY HOTEL SUITE SERVING AS A TEMPORARY BASE FOR A TEAM OF HEROES FROM THE FUTURE.
YOU DID WHAT?!?
OOOOOO
RAVAGED!
I DON'T KNOW WHAT'S WORSE, TIMBER WOLF. THE FACT THAT YOU STOLE FROM PRIMITIVES--
--OR THAT YOUR ACTIONS MAY HAVE JEOPARDIZED OUR MISSION BY ALERTING THE AUTHORITIES TO OUR PRESENCE.
YOU SAID WE NEEDED HARD CURRENCY.
I OBTAINED SOME.
FROM DRUG DEALERS.
CRIMINALS.
SCUM.

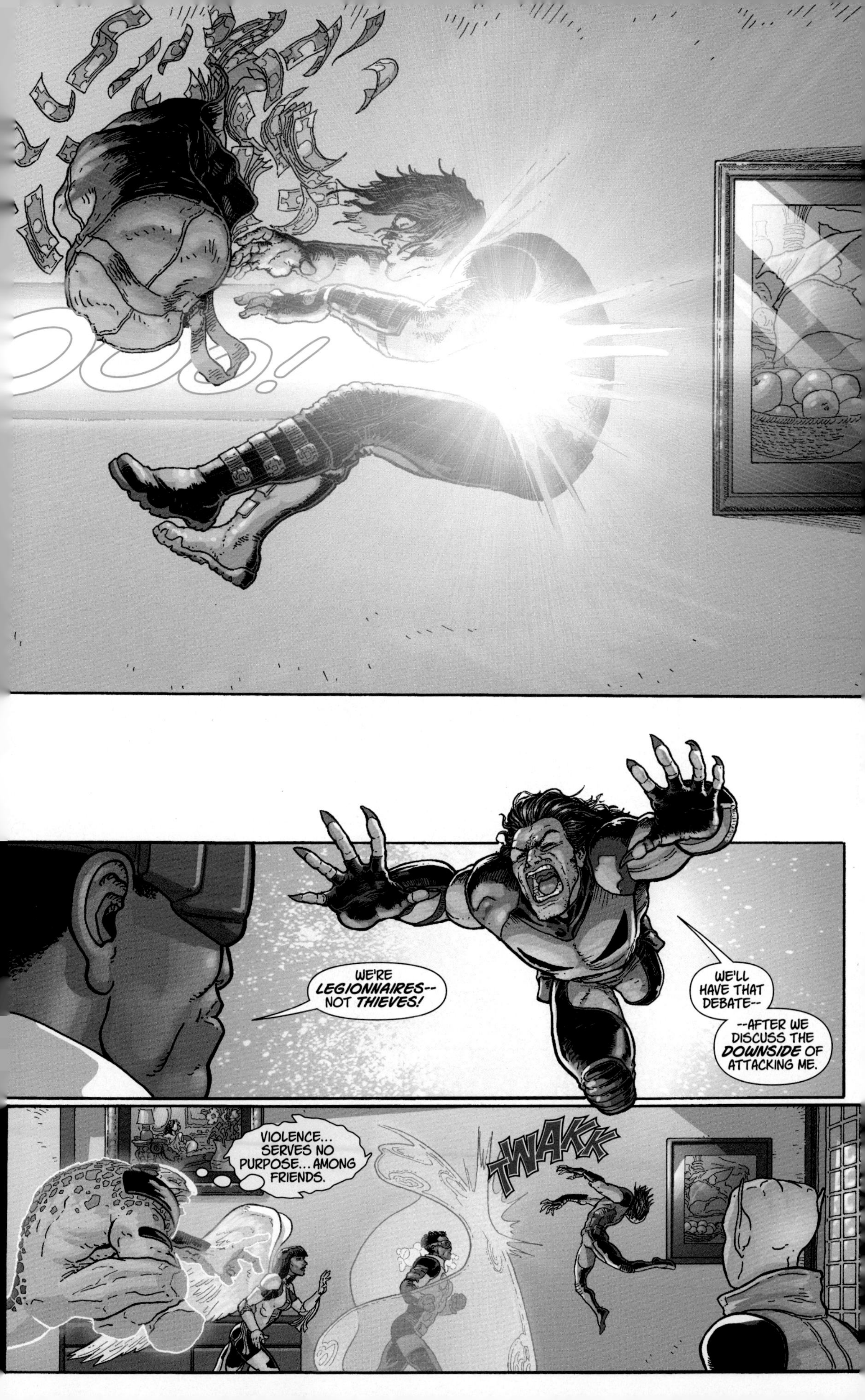
WE'RE LEGIONNAIRES-- NOT THIEVES!
WE'LL HAVE THAT DEBATE--
--AFTER WE DISCUSS THE DOWNSIDE OF ATTACKING ME.
VIOLENCE... SERVES NO PURPOSE... AMONG FRIENDS.
TWAKK

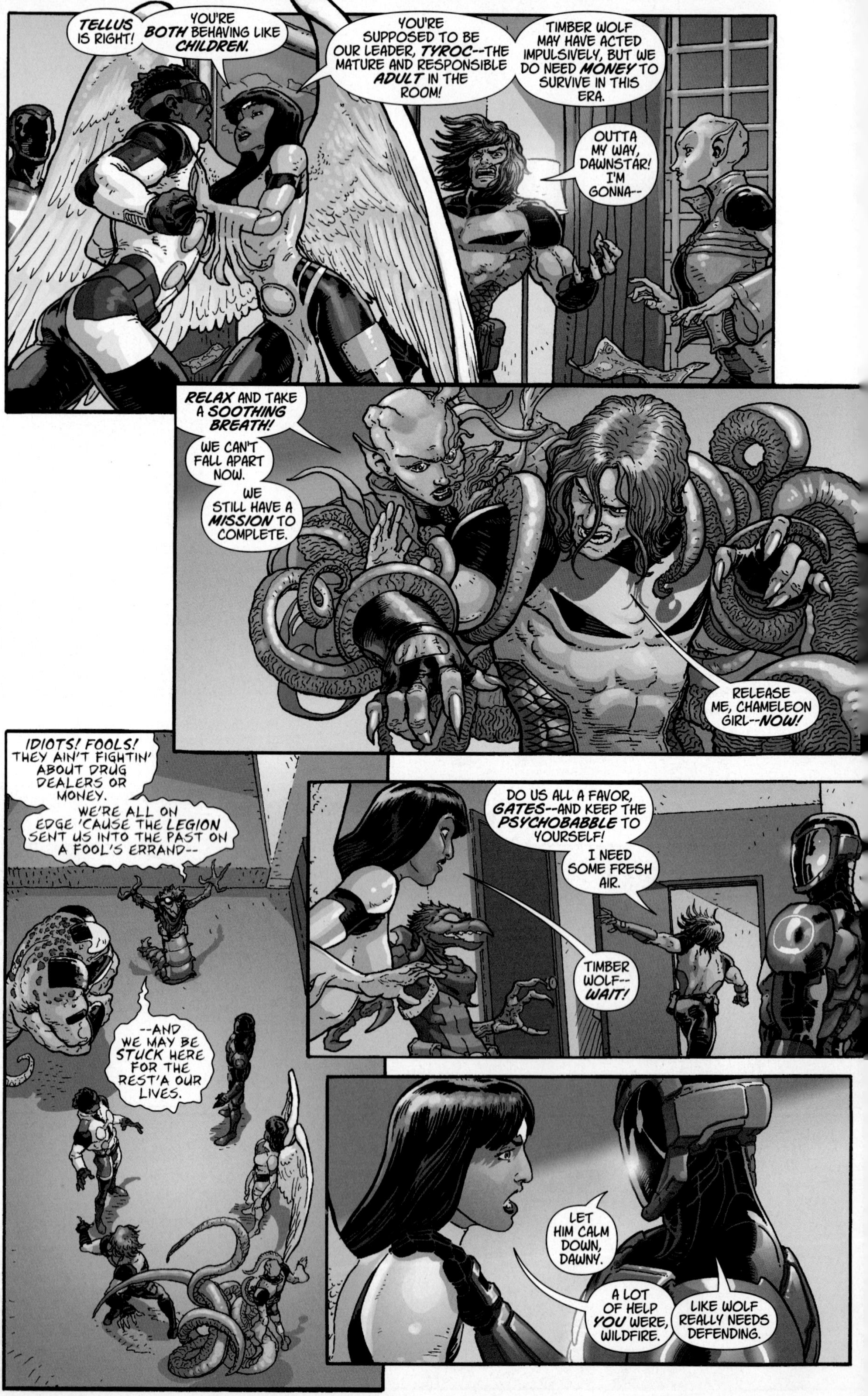
TELLUS IS RIGHT!
YOU'RE BOTH BEHAVING LIKE CHILDREN.
YOU'RE SUPPOSED TO BE OUR LEADER, TYROC--THE MATURE AND RESPONSIBLE ADULT IN THE ROOM!
TIMBER WOLF MAY HAVE ACTED IMPULSIVELY, BUT WE DO NEED MONEY TO SURVIVE IN THIS ERA.
OUTTA MY WAY, DAWNSTAR! I'M GONNA--
RELAX AND TAKE A SOOTHING BREATH!
WE CAN'T FALL APART NOW.
WE STILL HAVE A MISSION TO COMPLETE.
RELEASE ME, CHAMELEON GIRL--NOW!
IDIOTS! FOOLS! THEY AIN'T FIGHTIN' ABOUT DRUG DEALERS OR MONEY.
WE'RE ALL ON EDGE 'CAUSE THE LEGION SENT US INTO THE PAST ON A FOOL'S ERRAND--
--AND WE MAY BE STUCK HERE FOR THE REST'A OUR LIVES.
DO US ALL A FAVOR, GATES--AND KEEP THE PSYCHOBABBLE TO YOURSELF!
I NEED SOME FRESH AIR.
TIMBER WOLF-- WAIT!
LET HIM CALM DOWN, DAWNY.
A LOT OF HELP YOU WERE, WILDFIRE.
LIKE WOLF REALLY NEEDS DEFENDING.

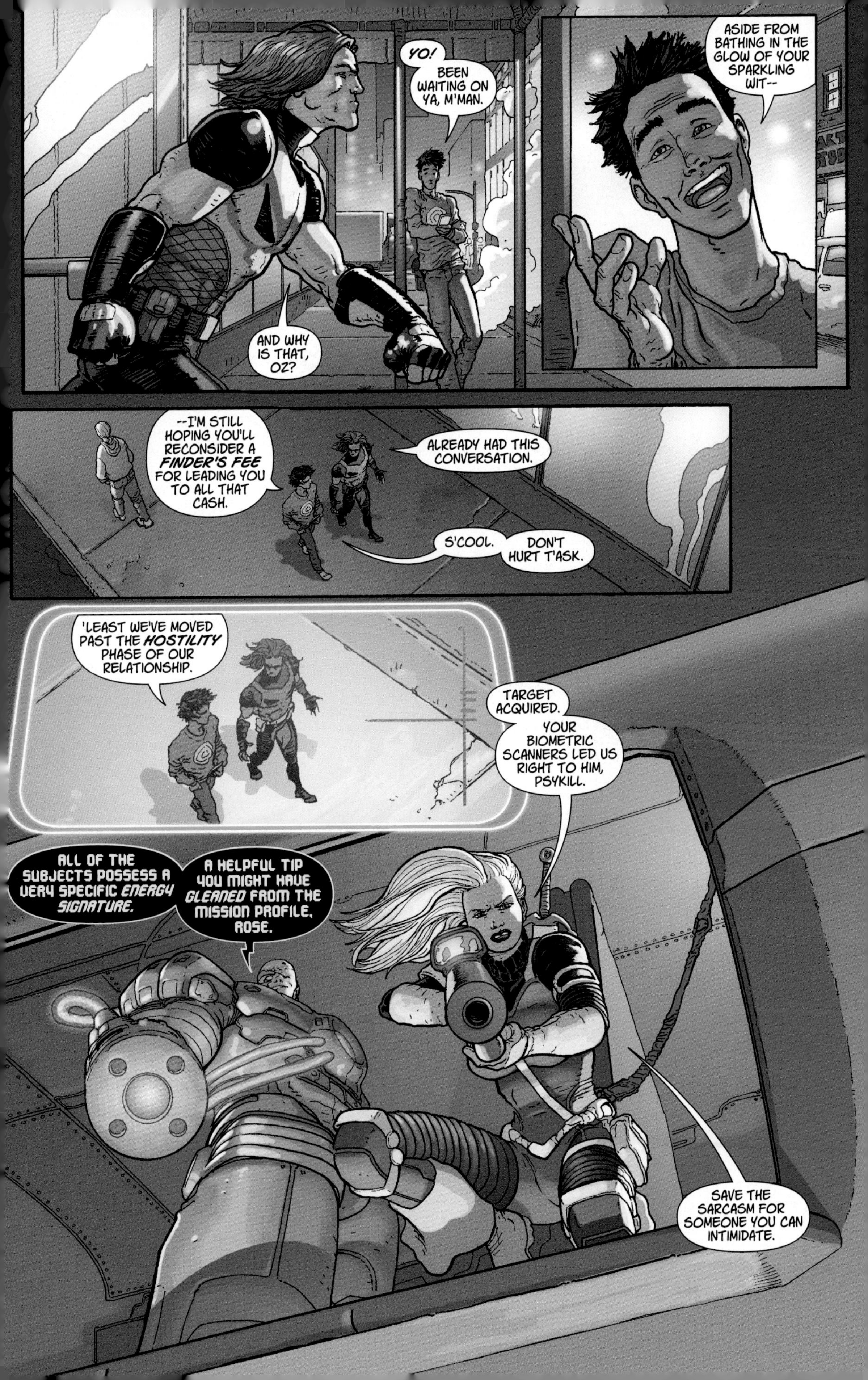
YO!
BEEN WAITING ON YA, M'MAN.
AND WHY IS THAT, OZ?
ASIDE FROM BATHING IN THE GLOW OF YOUR SPARKLING WIT--
--I'M STILL HOPING YOU'LL RECONSIDER A FINDER'S FEE FOR LEADING YOU TO ALL THAT CASH.
ALREADY HAD THIS CONVERSATION.
S'COOL.
DON'T HURT T'ASK.
'LEAST WE'VE MOVED PAST THE HOSTILITY PHASE OF OUR RELATIONSHIP.
TARGET ACQUIRED.
YOUR BIOMETRIC SCANNERS LED US RIGHT TO HIM, PSYKILL.
ALL OF THE SUBJECTS POSSESS A VERY SPECIFIC ENERGY SIGNATURE.
A HELPFUL TIP YOU MIGHT HAVE GLEANED FROM THE MISSION PROFILE, ROSE.
SAVE THE SARCASM FOR SOMEONE YOU CAN INTIMIDATE.

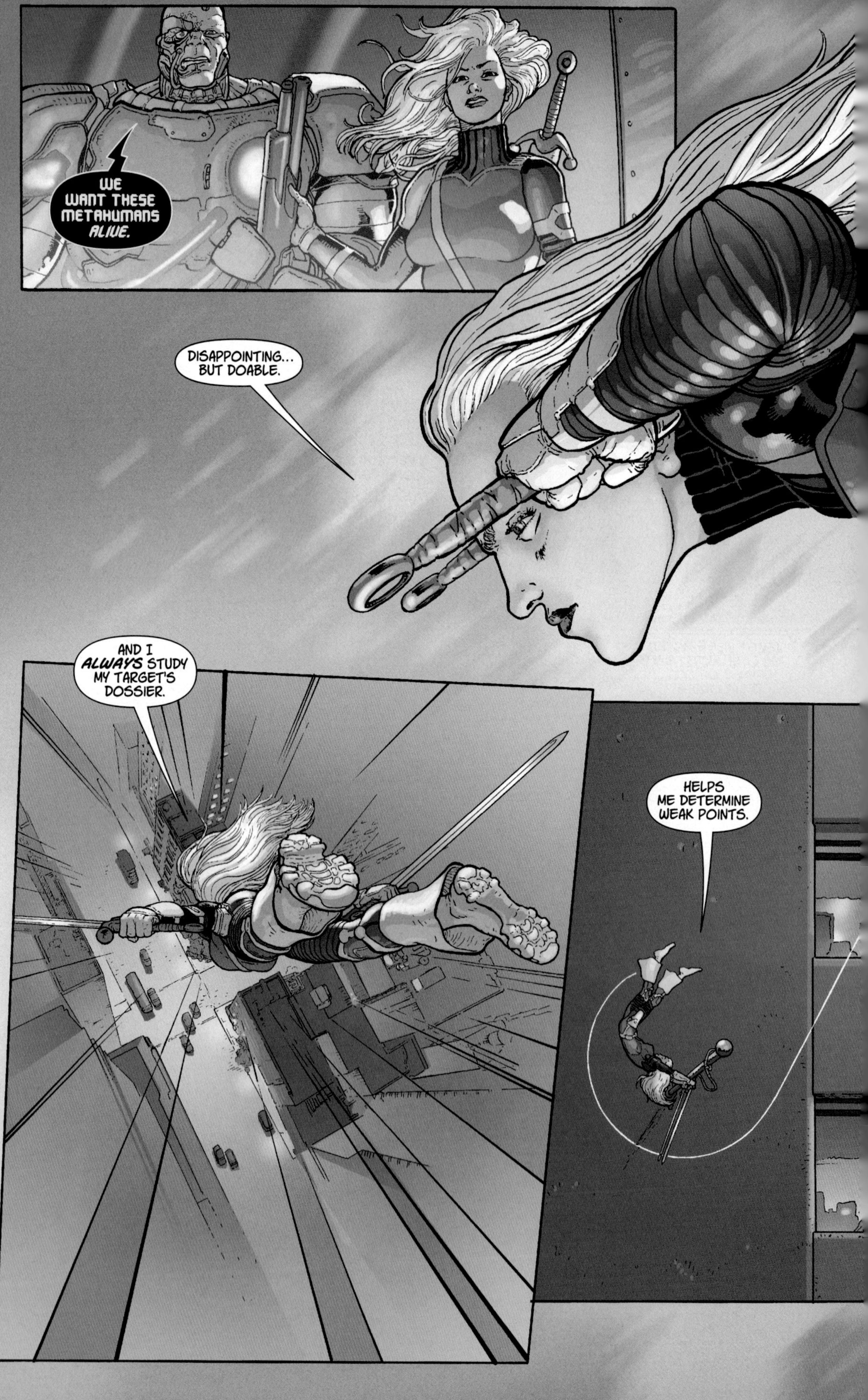
WE WANT THESE METAHUMANS ALIVE.
DISAPPOINTING... BUT DOABLE.
AND I ALWAYS STUDY MY TARGET'S DOSSIER.
HELPS ME DETERMINE WEAK POINTS.

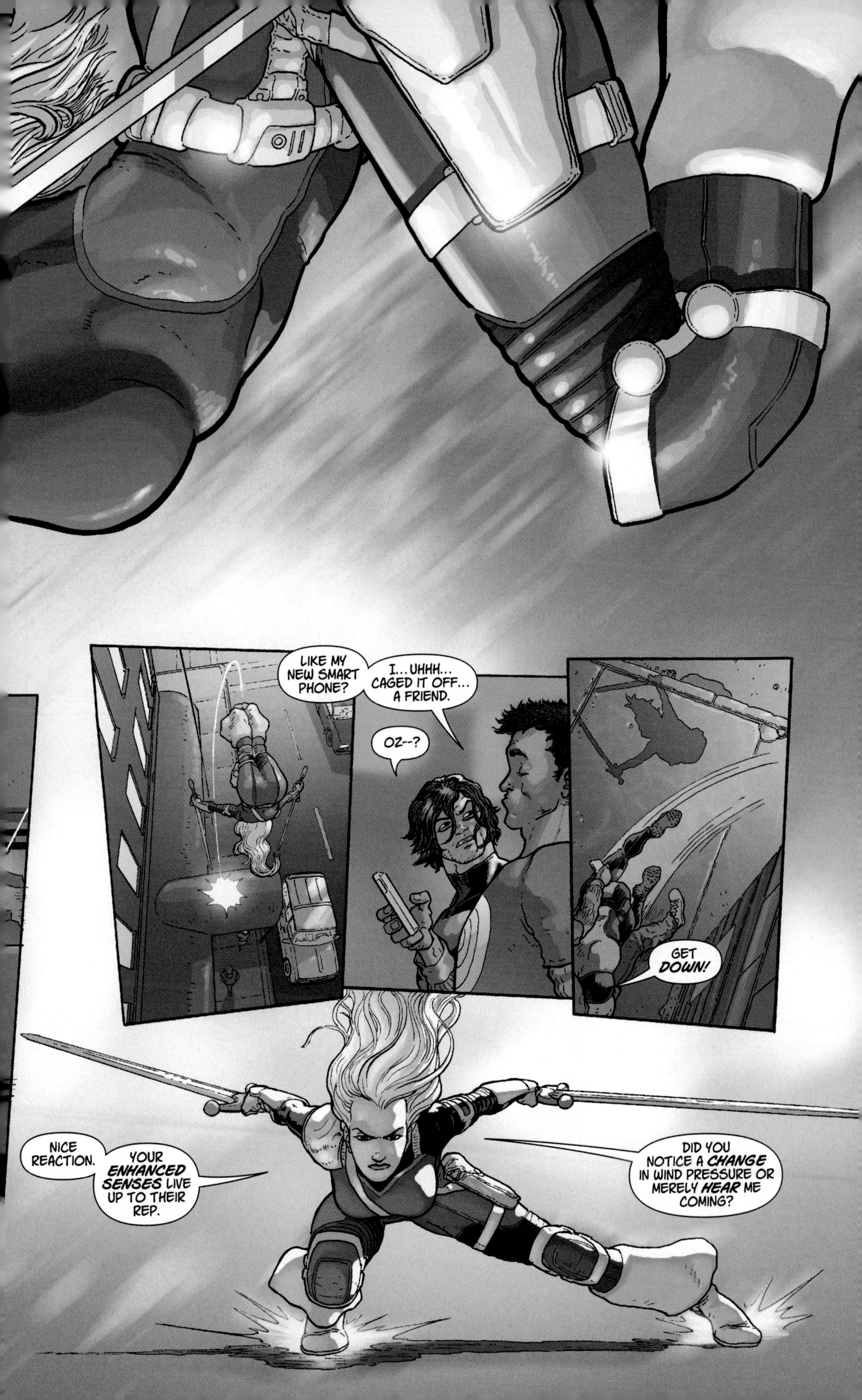
LIKE MY NEW SMART PHONE?
I... UHHH... CAGED IT OFF... A FRIEND.
OZ--?
GET DOWN!
NICE REACTION.
YOUR ENHANCED SENSES LIVE UP TO THEIR REP.
DID YOU NOTICE A CHANGE IN WIND PRESSURE OR MERELY HEAR ME COMING?

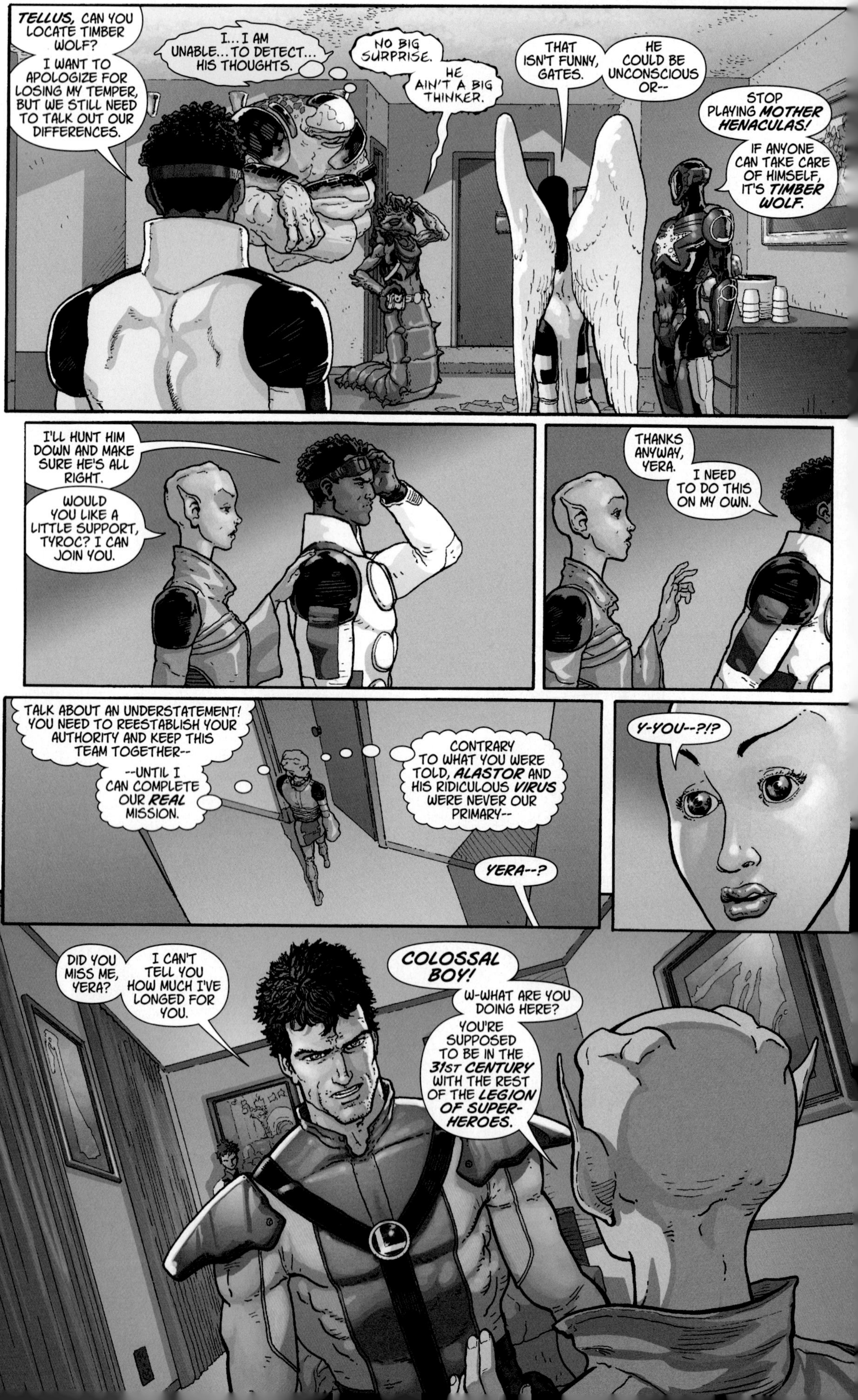
TELLUS, CAN YOU LOCATE TIMBER WOLF?
I WANT TO APOLOGIZE FOR LOSING MY TEMPER, BUT WE STILL NEED TO TALK OUT OUR DIFFERENCES.
I... I AM UNABLE... TO DETECT... HIS THOUGHTS.
NO BIG SURPRISE.
HE AIN'T A BIG THINKER.
THAT ISN'T FUNNY, GATES.
HE COULD BE UNCONSCIOUS OR--
STOP PLAYING MOTHER HENACULAS!
IF ANYONE CAN TAKE CARE OF HIMSELF, IT'S TIMBER WOLF.
I'LL HUNT HIM DOWN AND MAKE SURE HE'S ALL RIGHT.
WOULD YOU LIKE A LITTLE SUPPORT, TYROC? I CAN JOIN YOU.
THANKS ANYWAY, YERA.
I NEED TO DO THIS ON MY OWN.
TALK ABOUT AN UNDERSTATEMENT! YOU NEED TO REESTABLISH YOUR AUTHORITY AND KEEP THIS TEAM TOGETHER--
--UNTIL I CAN COMPLETE OUR REAL MISSION.
CONTRARY TO WHAT YOU WERE TOLD, ALASTOR AND HIS RIDICULOUS VIRUS WERE NEVER OUR PRIMARY--
YERA--?
Y-YOU--?!?
DID YOU MISS ME, YERA?
I CAN'T TELL YOU HOW MUCH I'VE LONGED FOR YOU.
COLOSSAL BOY!
W-WHAT ARE YOU DOING HERE?
YOU'RE SUPPOSED TO BE IN THE 31ST CENTURY WITH THE REST OF THE LEGION OF SUPER-HEROES.

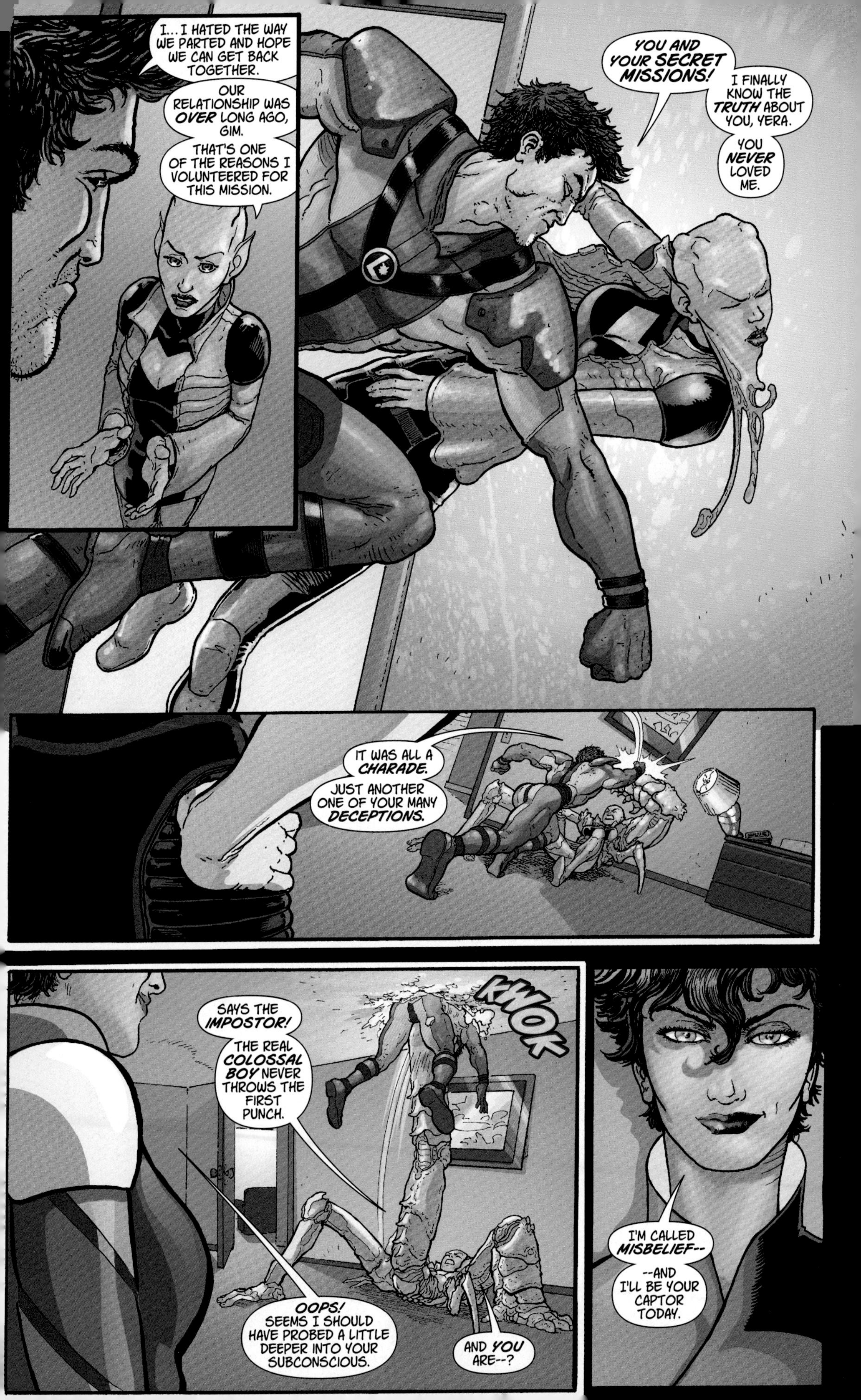
I... I HATED THE WAY WE PARTED AND HOPE WE CAN GET BACK TOGETHER.
OUR RELATIONSHIP WAS OVER LONG AGO, GIM.
THAT'S ONE OF THE REASONS I VOLUNTEERED FOR THIS MISSION.
YOU AND YOUR SECRET MISSIONS!
I FINALLY KNOW THE TRUTH ABOUT YOU, YERA.
YOU NEVER LOVED ME.
IT WAS ALL A CHARADE.
JUST ANOTHER ONE OF YOUR MANY DECEPTIONS.
KWOK
SAYS THE IMPOSTOR!
THE REAL COLOSSAL BOY NEVER THROWS THE FIRST PUNCH.
OOPS! SEEMS I SHOULD HAVE PROBED A LITTLE DEEPER INTO YOUR SUBCONSCIOUS.
AND YOU ARE--?
I'M CALLED MISBELIEF--
--AND I'LL BE YOUR CAPTOR TODAY.

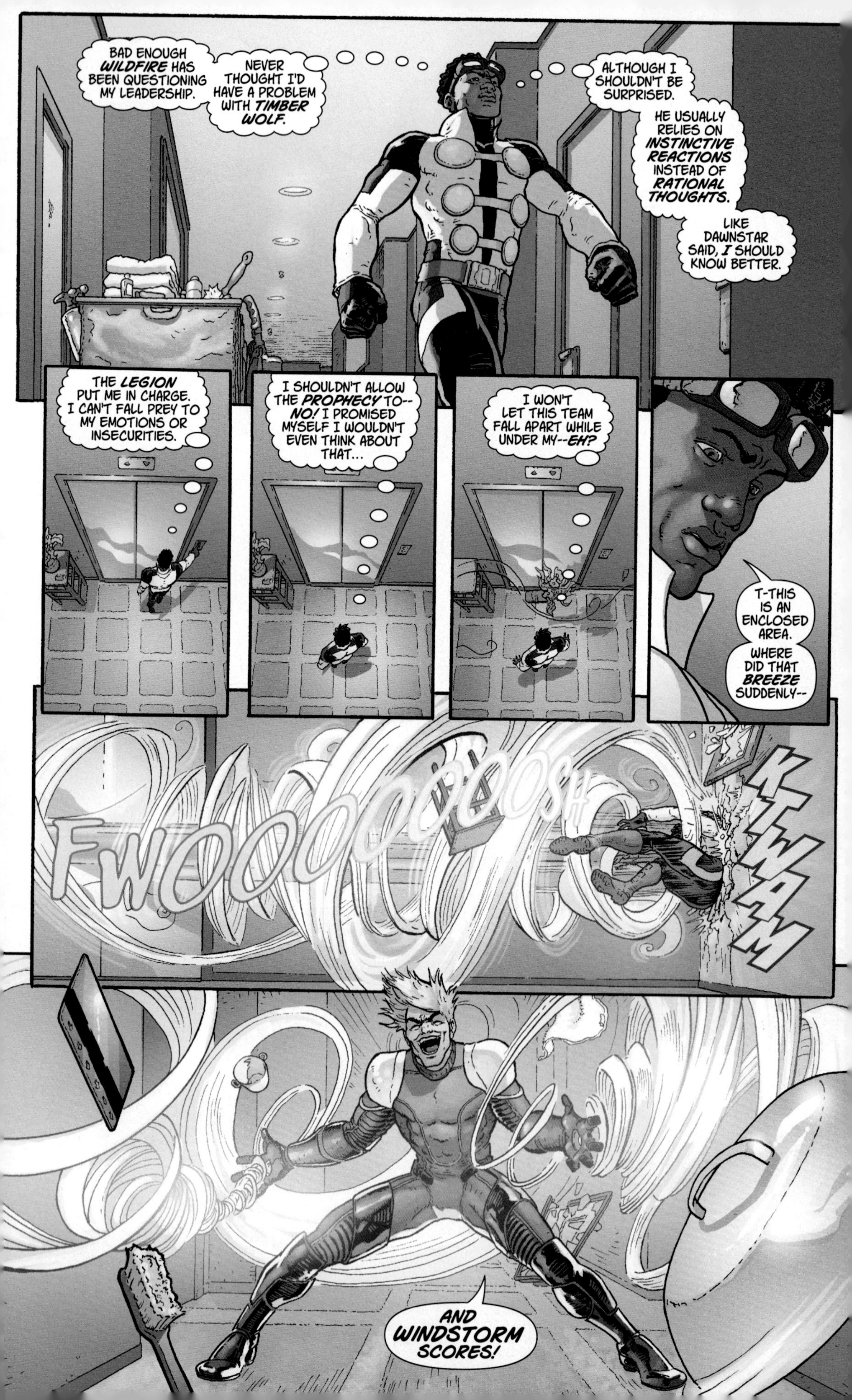
BAD ENOUGH WILDFIRE HAS BEEN QUESTIONING MY LEADERSHIP.
NEVER THOUGHT I'D HAVE A PROBLEM WITH TIMBER WOLF.
ALTHOUGH I SHOULDN'T BE SURPRISED.
HE USUALLY RELIES ON INSTINCTIVE REACTIONS INSTEAD OF RATIONAL THOUGHTS.
LIKE DAWNSTAR SAID, I SHOULD KNOW BETTER.
THE LEGION PUT ME IN CHARGE. I CAN'T FALL PREY TO MY EMOTIONS OR INSECURITIES.
I SHOULDN'T ALLOW THE PROPHECY TO-- NO! I PROMISED MYSELF I WOULDN'T EVEN THINK ABOUT THAT...
I WON'T LET THIS TEAM FALL APART WHILE UNDER MY--EH?
T-THIS IS AN ENCLOSED AREA.
WHERE DID THAT BREEZE SUDDENLY--
FWOOOOOOOOSH
KWAM
AND WINDSTORM SCORES!

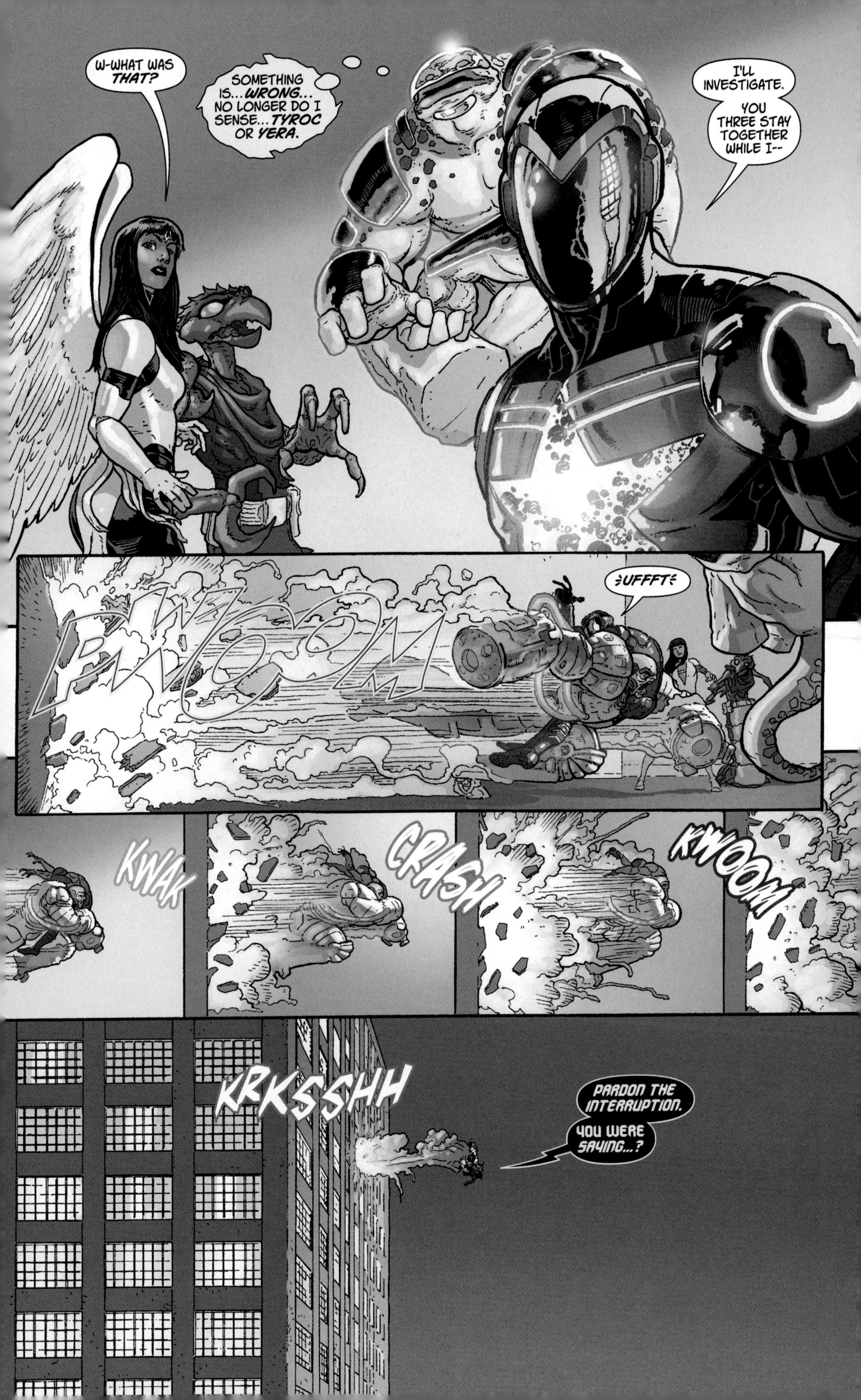
W-WHAT WAS *THAT?*
SOMETHING IS... *WRONG*... NO LONGER DO I SENSE... *TYROC* OR *YERA.*
I'LL INVESTIGATE.
YOU THREE STAY TOGETHER WHILE I--
PWOOOM
UFFFT
KWAK
CRASH
KWOOM
KRKSSHH
PARDON THE INTERRUPTION.
YOU WERE SAYING...?

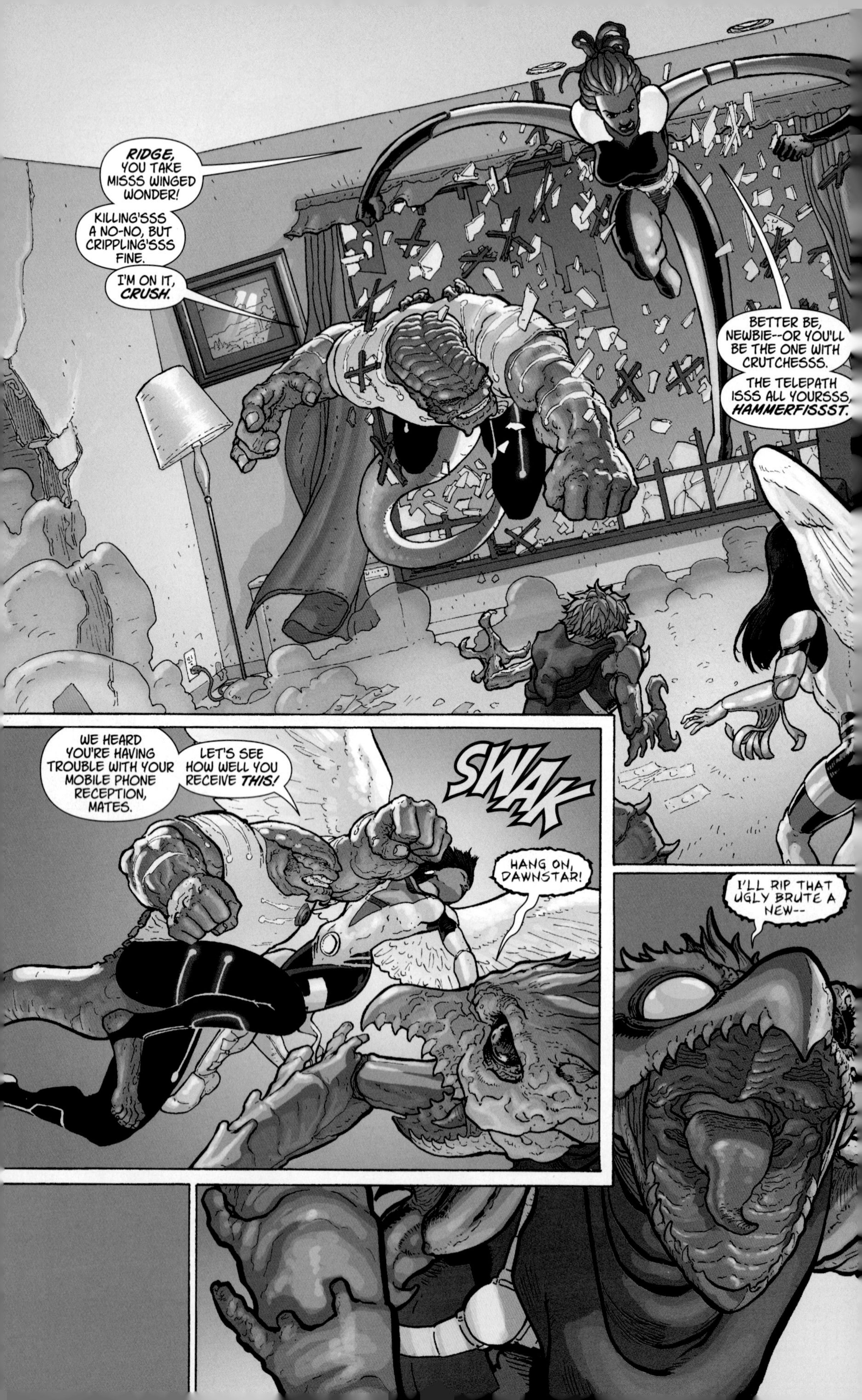
RIDGE, YOU TAKE MISSS WINGED WONDER!
KILLING'SSS A NO-NO, BUT CRIPPLING'SSS FINE.
I'M ON IT, CRUSH.
BETTER BE, NEWBIE--OR YOU'LL BE THE ONE WITH CRUTCHESSS.
THE TELEPATH ISSS ALL YOURSSS, HAMMERFISSST.
WE HEARD YOU'RE HAVING TROUBLE WITH YOUR MOBILE PHONE RECEPTION, MATES.
LET'S SEE HOW WELL YOU RECEIVE THIS!
SWAK
HANG ON, DAWNSTAR!
I'LL RIP THAT UGLY BRUTE A NEW--

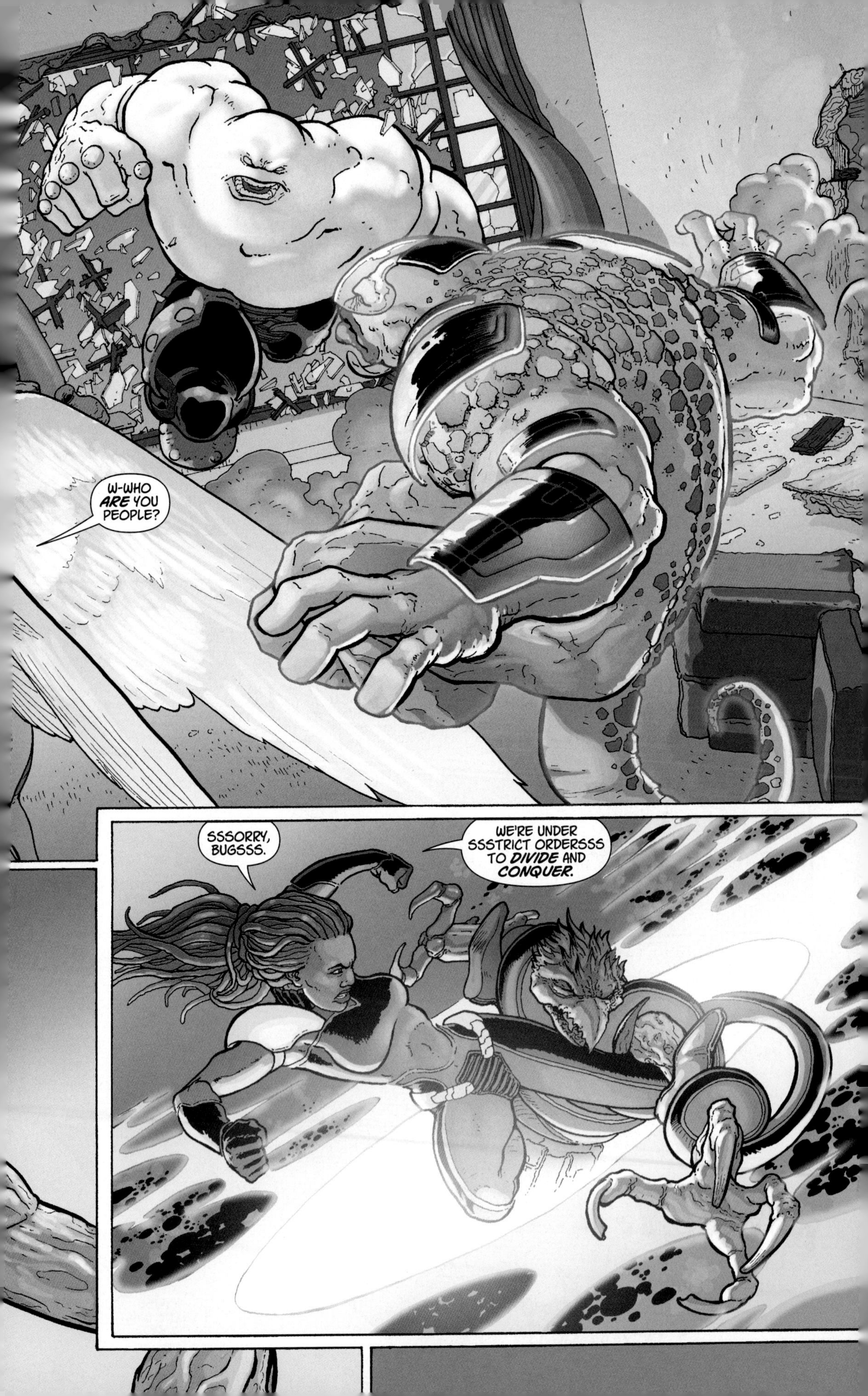
W-WHO *ARE* YOU PEOPLE?
SSSORRY, BUGSSS.
WE'RE UNDER SSSTRICT ORDERSSS TO *DIVIDE* AND *CONQUER.*

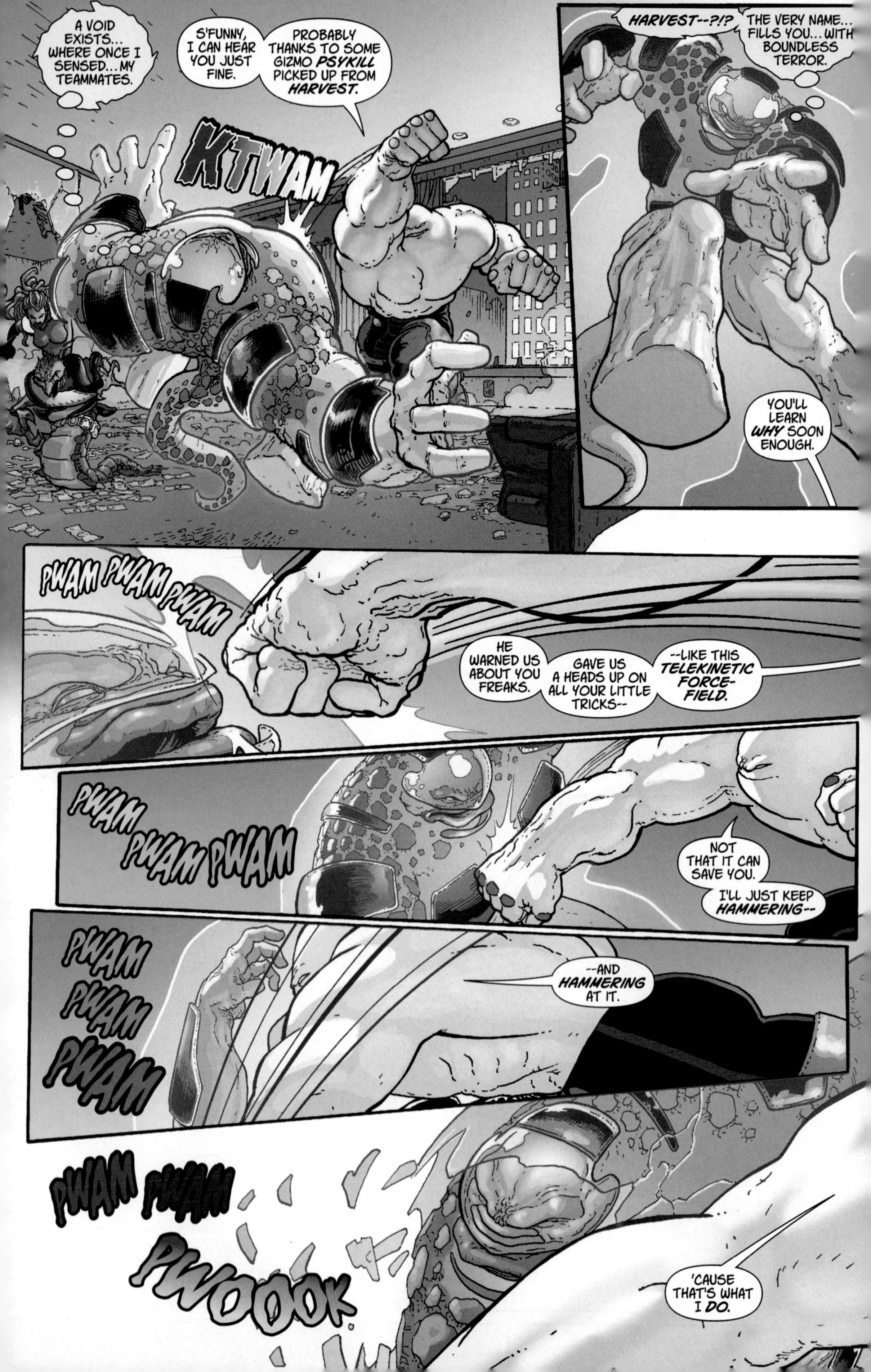
A VOID EXISTS... WHERE ONCE I SENSED... MY TEAMMATES.
S'FUNNY, I CAN HEAR YOU JUST FINE.
PROBABLY THANKS TO SOME GIZMO PSYKILL PICKED UP FROM HARVEST.
KTWAM
HARVEST--?!?
THE VERY NAME... FILLS YOU... WITH BOUNDLESS TERROR.
YOU'LL LEARN WHY SOON ENOUGH.
PWAM PWAM PWAM
HE WARNED US ABOUT YOU FREAKS.
GAVE US A HEADS UP ON ALL YOUR LITTLE TRICKS--
--LIKE THIS TELEKINETIC FORCE-FIELD.
PWAM PWAM PWAM
NOT THAT IT CAN SAVE YOU.
I'LL JUST KEEP HAMMERING--
PWAM PWAM PWAM
--AND HAMMERING AT IT.
PWAM PWAM
PWOOOK
'CAUSE THAT'S WHAT I DO.

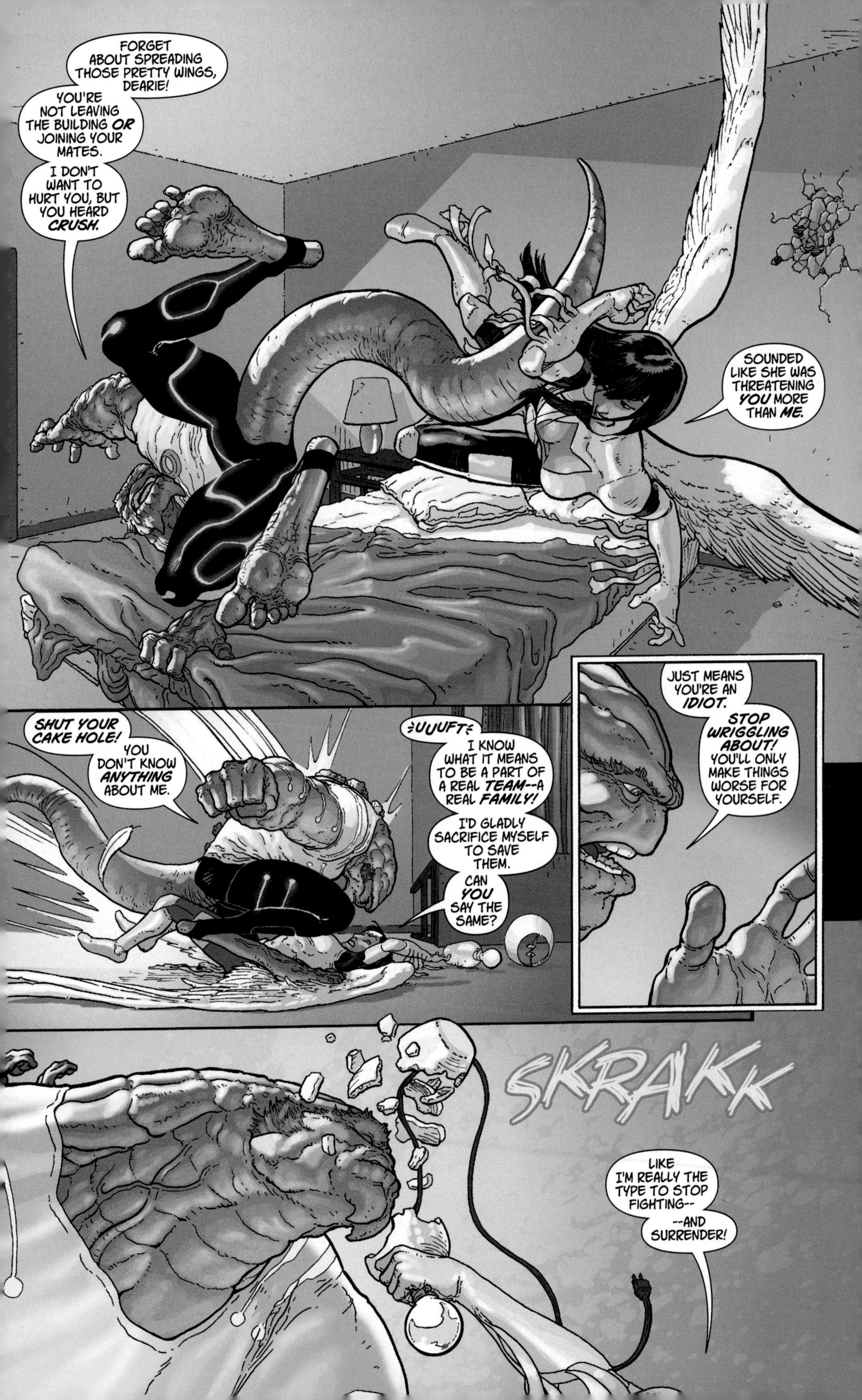
FORGET ABOUT SPREADING THOSE PRETTY WINGS, DEARIE!
YOU'RE NOT LEAVING THE BUILDING OR JOINING YOUR MATES.
I DON'T WANT TO HURT YOU, BUT YOU HEARD CRUSH.
SOUNDED LIKE SHE WAS THREATENING YOU MORE THAN ME.
JUST MEANS YOU'RE AN IDIOT.
STOP WRIGGLING ABOUT! YOU'LL ONLY MAKE THINGS WORSE FOR YOURSELF.
SHUT YOUR CAKE HOLE!
YOU DON'T KNOW ANYTHING ABOUT ME.
UUUFT
I KNOW WHAT IT MEANS TO BE A PART OF A REAL TEAM--A REAL FAMILY!
I'D GLADLY SACRIFICE MYSELF TO SAVE THEM.
CAN YOU SAY THE SAME?
SKRAKK
LIKE I'M REALLY THE TYPE TO STOP FIGHTING--
--AND SURRENDER!

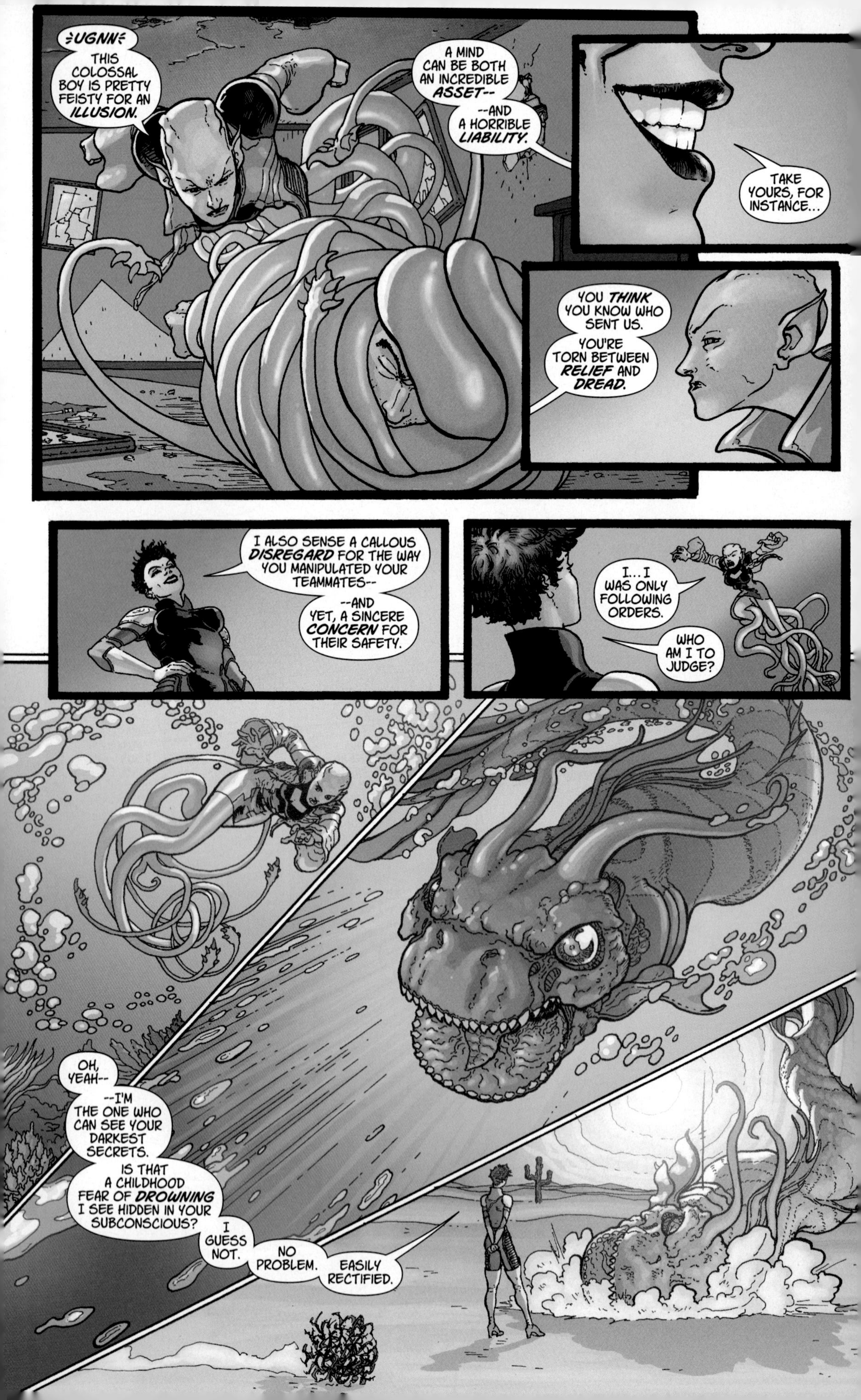

UGNN
THIS COLOSSAL BOY IS PRETTY FEISTY FOR AN ILLUSION.
A MIND CAN BE BOTH AN INCREDIBLE ASSET--
--AND A HORRIBLE LIABILITY.
TAKE YOURS, FOR INSTANCE...
YOU THINK YOU KNOW WHO SENT US.
YOU'RE TORN BETWEEN RELIEF AND DREAD.
I ALSO SENSE A CALLOUS DISREGARD FOR THE WAY YOU MANIPULATED YOUR TEAMMATES--
--AND YET, A SINCERE CONCERN FOR THEIR SAFETY.
I... I WAS ONLY FOLLOWING ORDERS.
WHO AM I TO JUDGE?
OH, YEAH--
--I'M THE ONE WHO CAN SEE YOUR DARKEST SECRETS.
IS THAT A CHILDHOOD FEAR OF DROWNING I SEE HIDDEN IN YOUR SUBCONSCIOUS?
I GUESS NOT.
NO PROBLEM.
EASILY RECTIFIED.

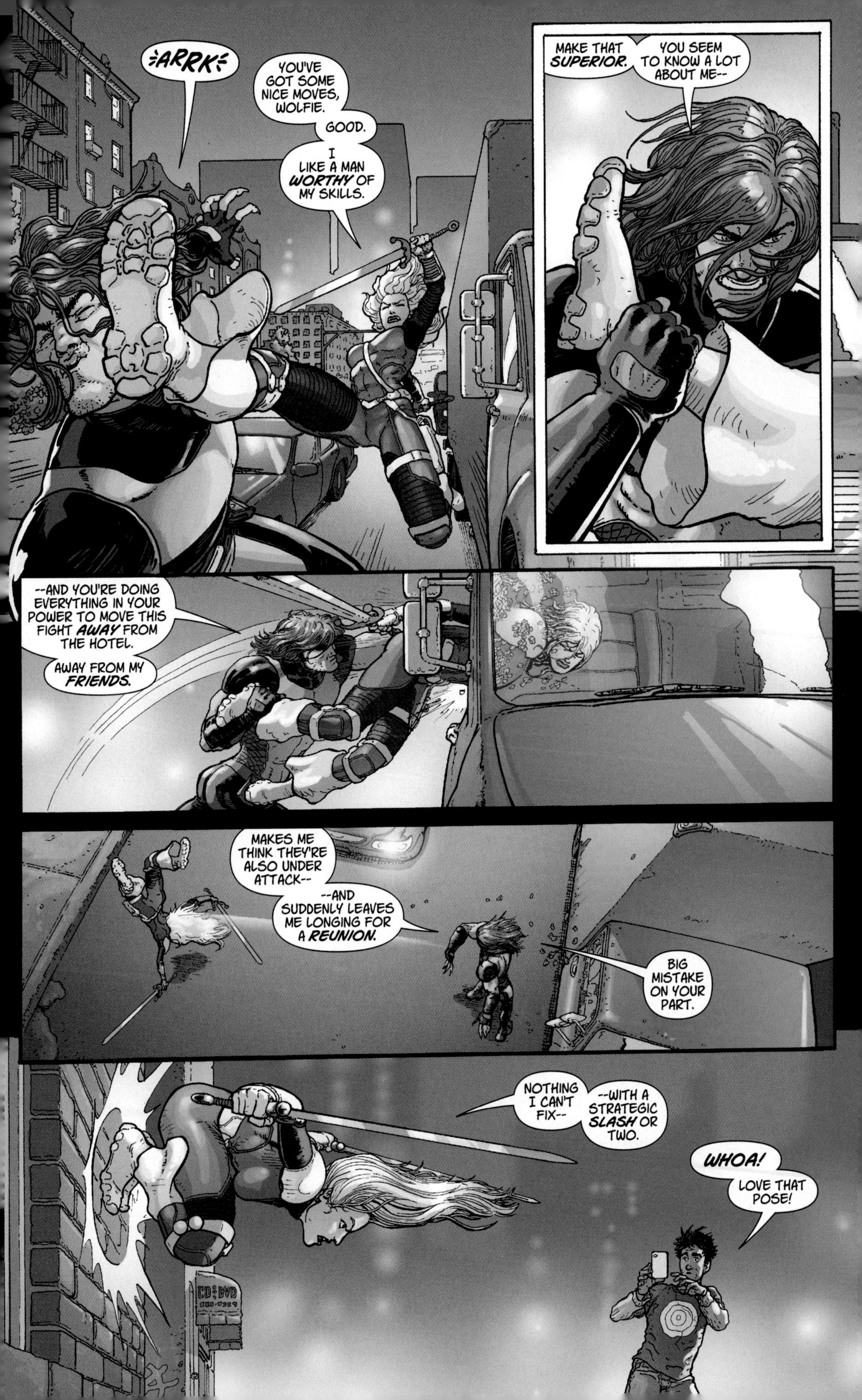
ARRK
YOU'VE GOT SOME NICE MOVES, WOLFIE.
GOOD.
I LIKE A MAN WORTHY OF MY SKILLS.
MAKE THAT SUPERIOR.
YOU SEEM TO KNOW A LOT ABOUT ME--
--AND YOU'RE DOING EVERYTHING IN YOUR POWER TO MOVE THIS FIGHT AWAY FROM THE HOTEL.
AWAY FROM MY FRIENDS.
MAKES ME THINK THEY'RE ALSO UNDER ATTACK--
--AND SUDDENLY LEAVES ME LONGING FOR A REUNION.
BIG MISTAKE ON YOUR PART.
NOTHING I CAN'T FIX--
--WITH A STRATEGIC SLASH OR TWO.
WHOA!
LOVE THAT POSE!
CD DVD

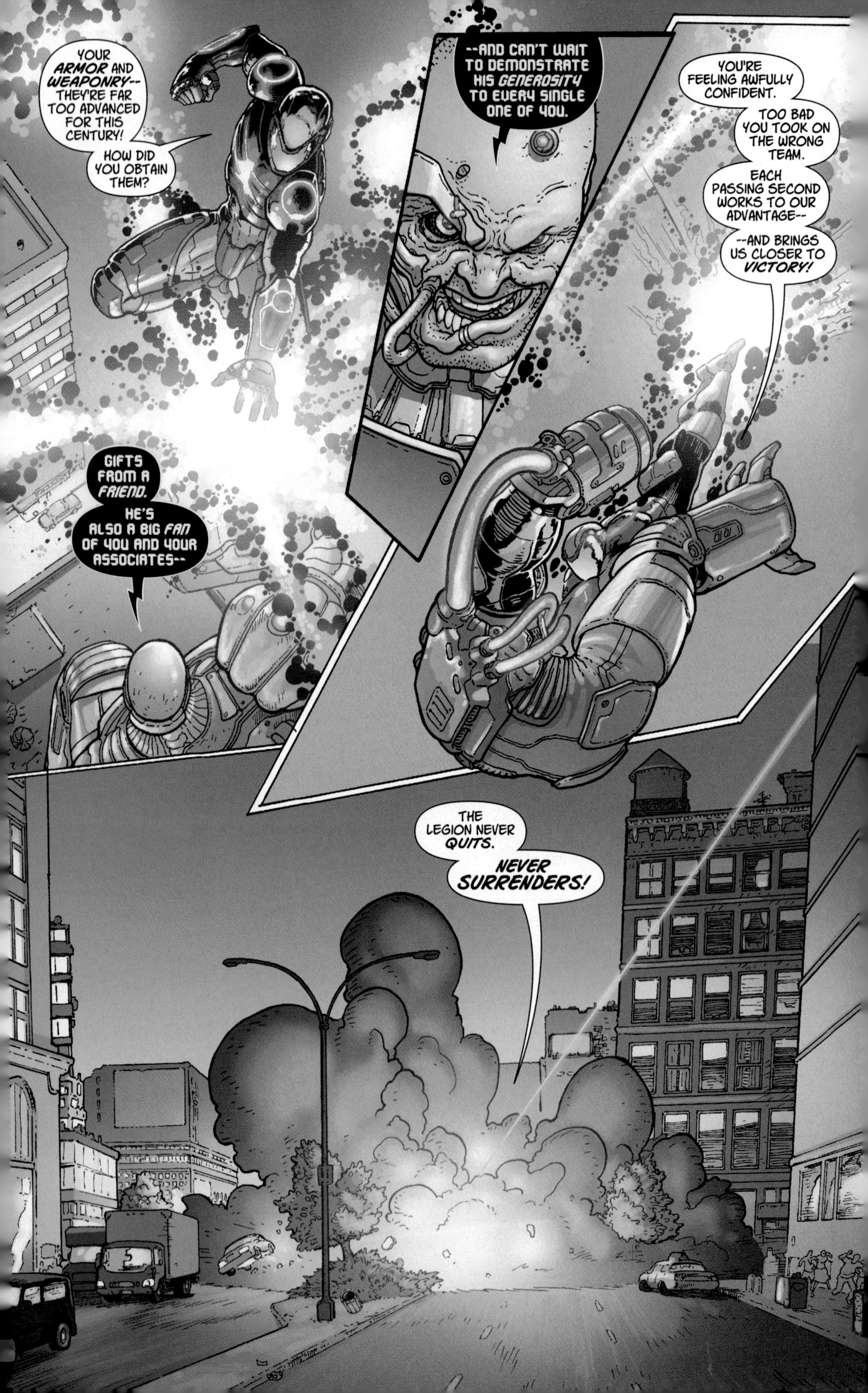
YOUR ARMOR AND WEAPONRY--THEY'RE FAR TOO ADVANCED FOR THIS CENTURY!
HOW DID YOU OBTAIN THEM?
GIFTS FROM A FRIEND.
HE'S ALSO A BIG FAN OF YOU AND YOUR ASSOCIATES--
--AND CAN'T WAIT TO DEMONSTRATE HIS GENEROSITY TO EVERY SINGLE ONE OF YOU.
YOU'RE FEELING AWFULLY CONFIDENT.
TOO BAD YOU TOOK ON THE WRONG TEAM.
EACH PASSING SECOND WORKS TO OUR ADVANTAGE--
--AND BRINGS US CLOSER TO VICTORY!
THE LEGION NEVER QUITS.
NEVER SURRENDERS!

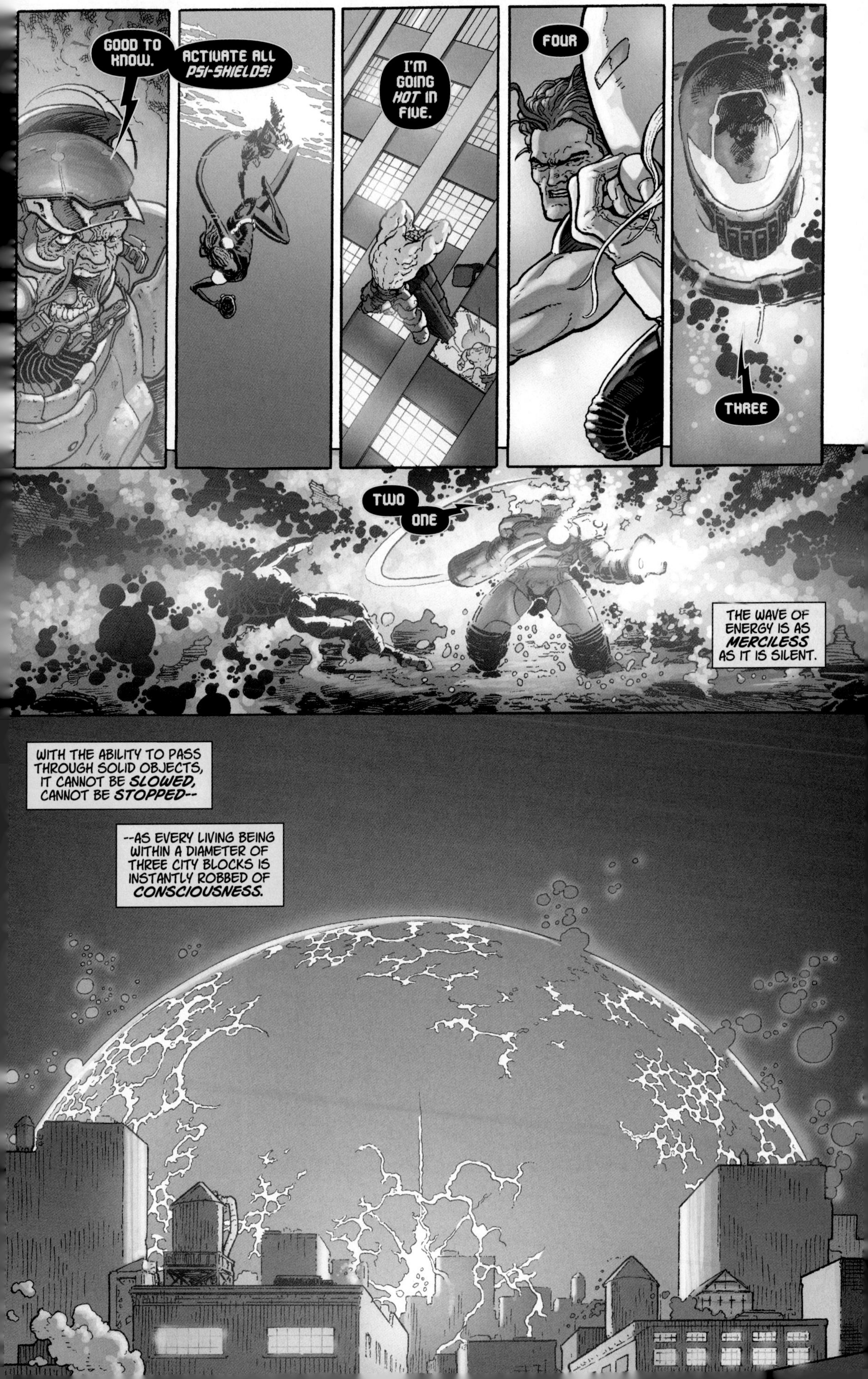
GOOD TO KNOW.
ACTIVATE ALL PSI-SHIELDS!
I'M GOING HOT IN FIVE.
FOUR
THREE
TWO
ONE
THE WAVE OF ENERGY IS AS MERCILESS AS IT IS SILENT.
WITH THE ABILITY TO PASS THROUGH SOLID OBJECTS, IT CANNOT BE SLOWED, CANNOT BE STOPPED--
--AS EVERY LIVING BEING WITHIN A DIAMETER OF THREE CITY BLOCKS IS INSTANTLY ROBBED OF CONSCIOUSNESS.

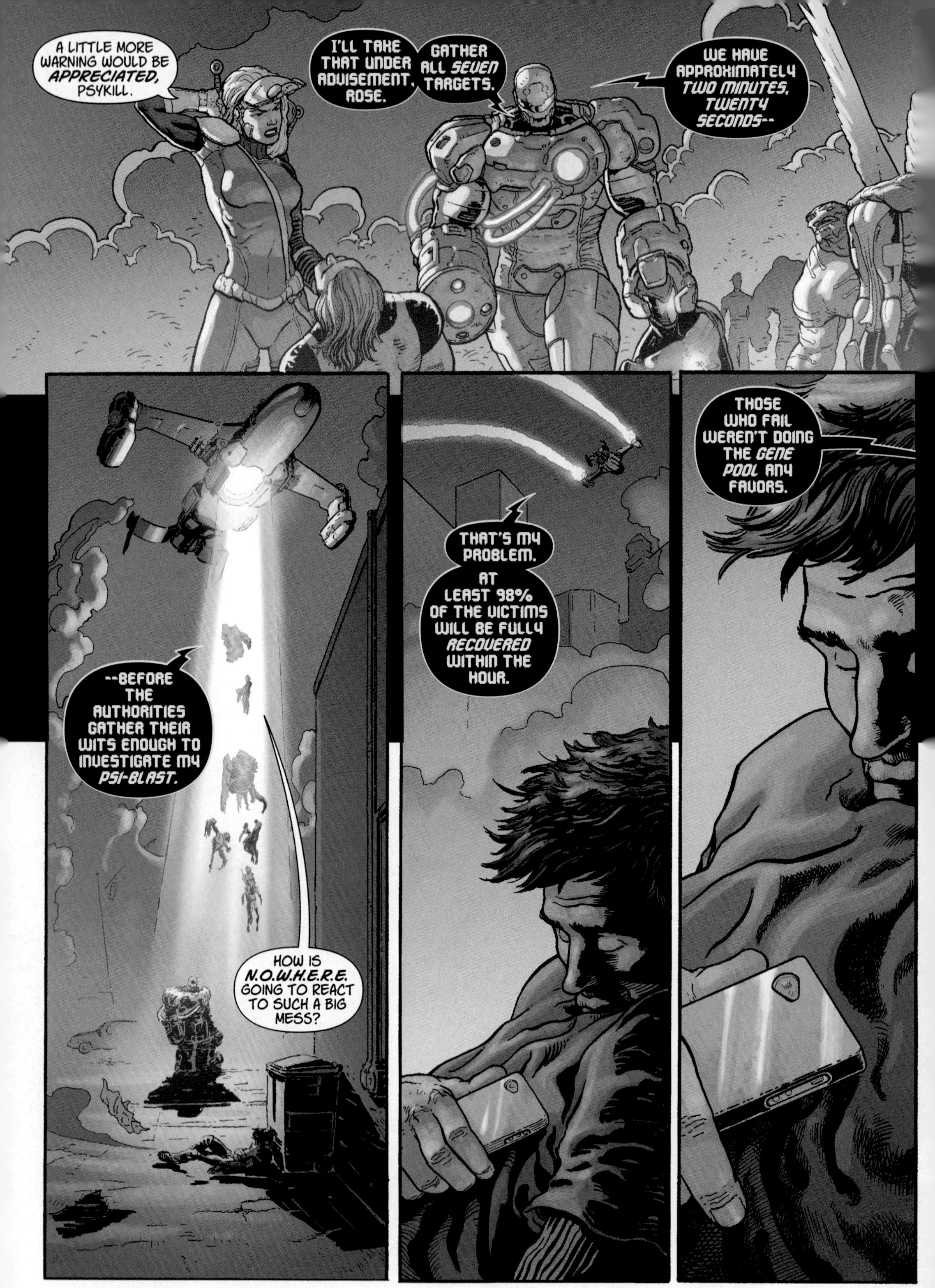
A LITTLE MORE WARNING WOULD BE *APPRECIATED,* PSYKILL.
I'LL TAKE THAT UNDER ADVISEMENT, ROSE.
GATHER ALL *SEVEN* TARGETS.
WE HAVE APPROXIMATELY *TWO MINUTES, TWENTY SECONDS--*
--BEFORE THE AUTHORITIES GATHER THEIR WITS ENOUGH TO INVESTIGATE MY *PSI-BLAST.*
HOW IS *N.O.W.H.E.R.E.* GOING TO REACT TO SUCH A BIG MESS?
THAT'S MY PROBLEM.
AT LEAST 98% OF THE VICTIMS WILL BE FULLY *RECOVERED* WITHIN THE HOUR.
THOSE WHO FAIL WEREN'T DOING THE *GENE POOL* ANY FAVORS.

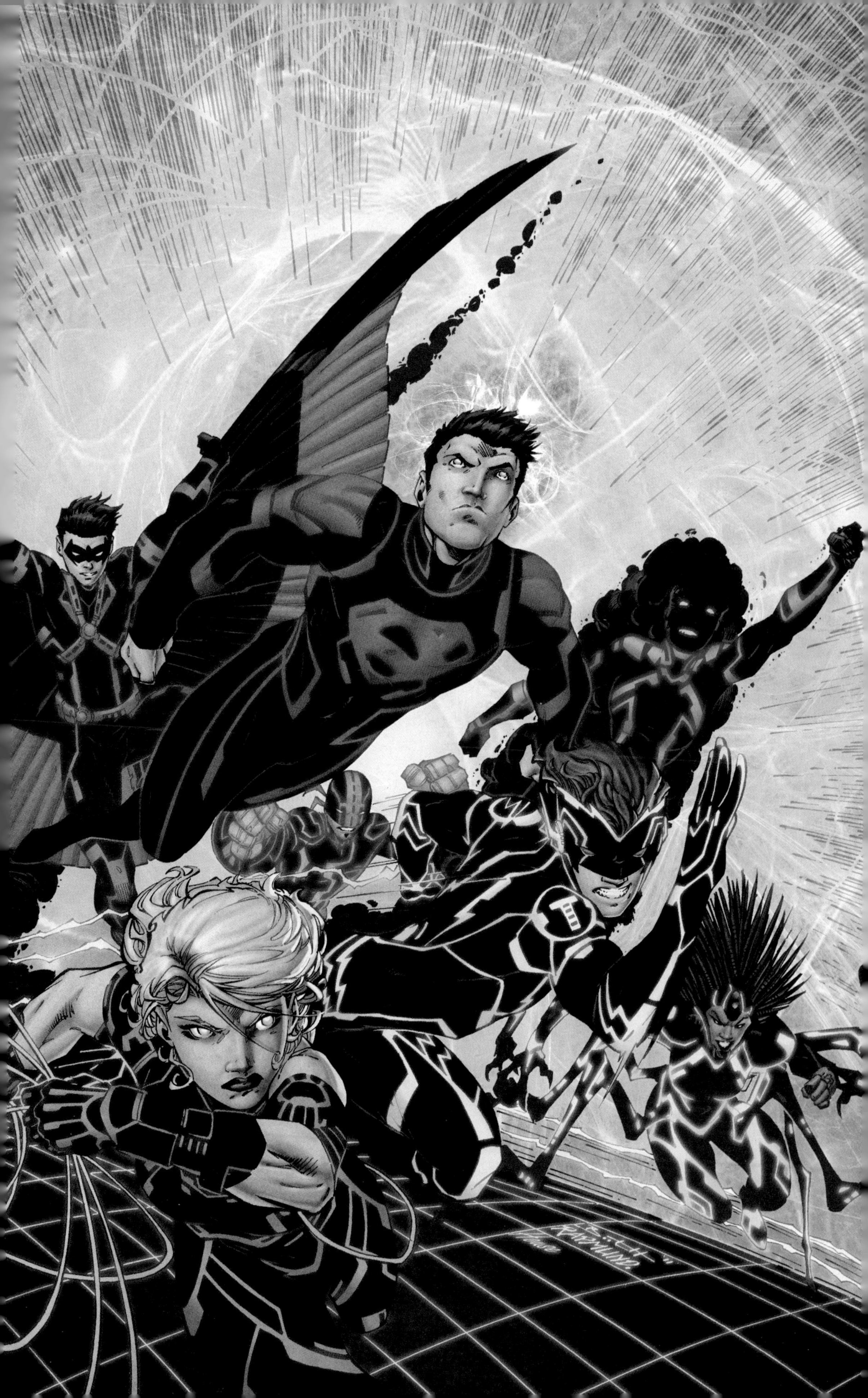

PRELUDE PART THREE: A DARK OMEN!
SCOTT LOBDELL writer IG GUARA penciller JP MAYER inker
cover art by BRETT BOOTH, NORM RAPMUND & ANDREW DALHOUSE

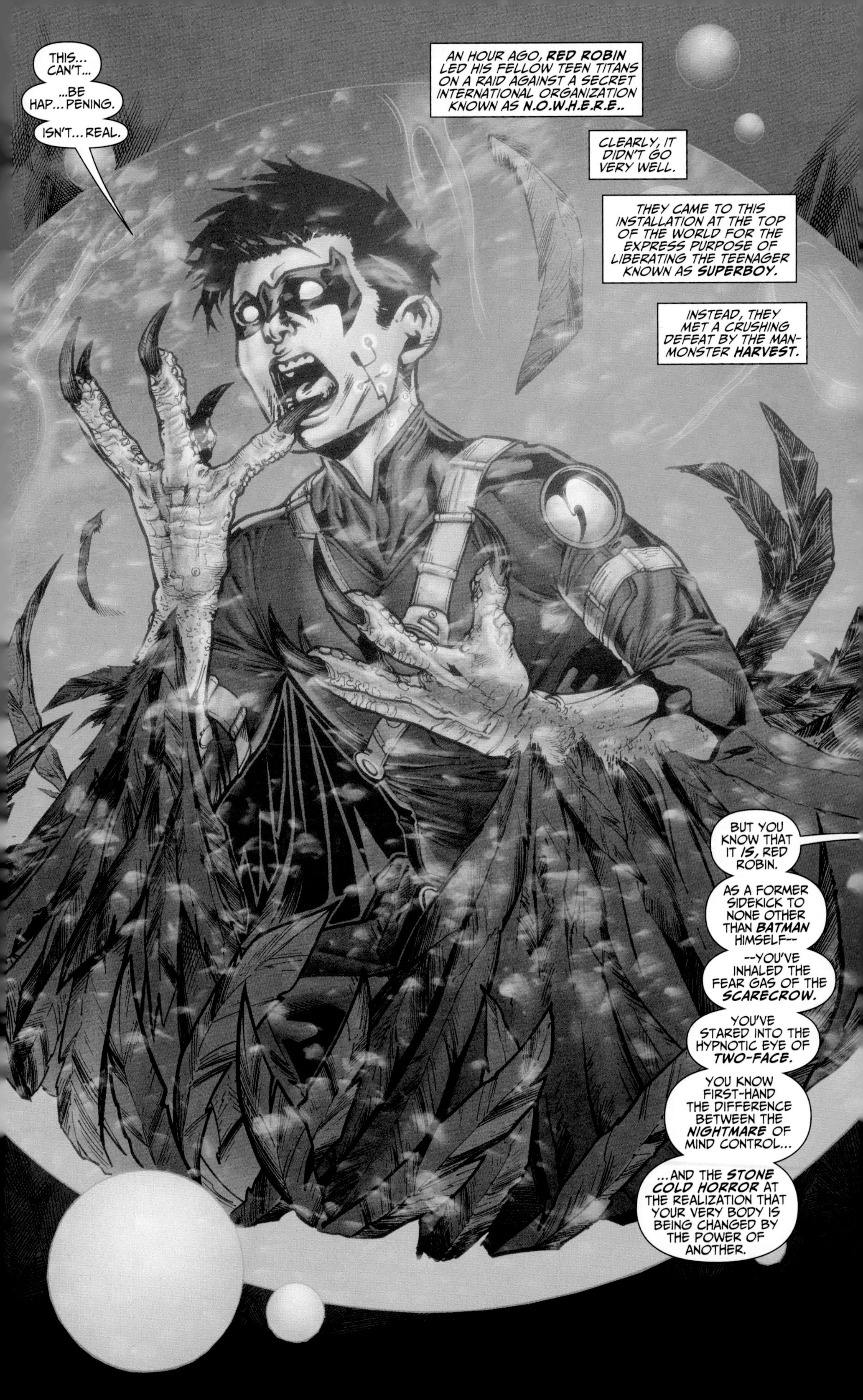

THIS... CAN'T...
...BE HAP...PENING.
ISN'T...REAL.
AN HOUR AGO, RED ROBIN LED HIS FELLOW TEEN TITANS ON A RAID AGAINST A SECRET INTERNATIONAL ORGANIZATION KNOWN AS N.O.W.H.E.R.E..
CLEARLY, IT DIDN'T GO VERY WELL.
THEY CAME TO THIS INSTALLATION AT THE TOP OF THE WORLD FOR THE EXPRESS PURPOSE OF LIBERATING THE TEENAGER KNOWN AS SUPERBOY.
INSTEAD, THEY MET A CRUSHING DEFEAT BY THE MAN-MONSTER HARVEST.
BUT YOU KNOW THAT IT IS, RED ROBIN.
AS A FORMER SIDEKICK TO NONE OTHER THAN BATMAN HIMSELF--
--YOU'VE INHALED THE FEAR GAS OF THE SCARECROW.
YOU'VE STARED INTO THE HYPNOTIC EYE OF TWO-FACE.
YOU KNOW FIRST-HAND THE DIFFERENCE BETWEEN THE NIGHTMARE OF MIND CONTROL...
...AND THE STONE COLD HORROR AT THE REALIZATION THAT YOUR VERY BODY IS BEING CHANGED BY THE POWER OF ANOTHER.

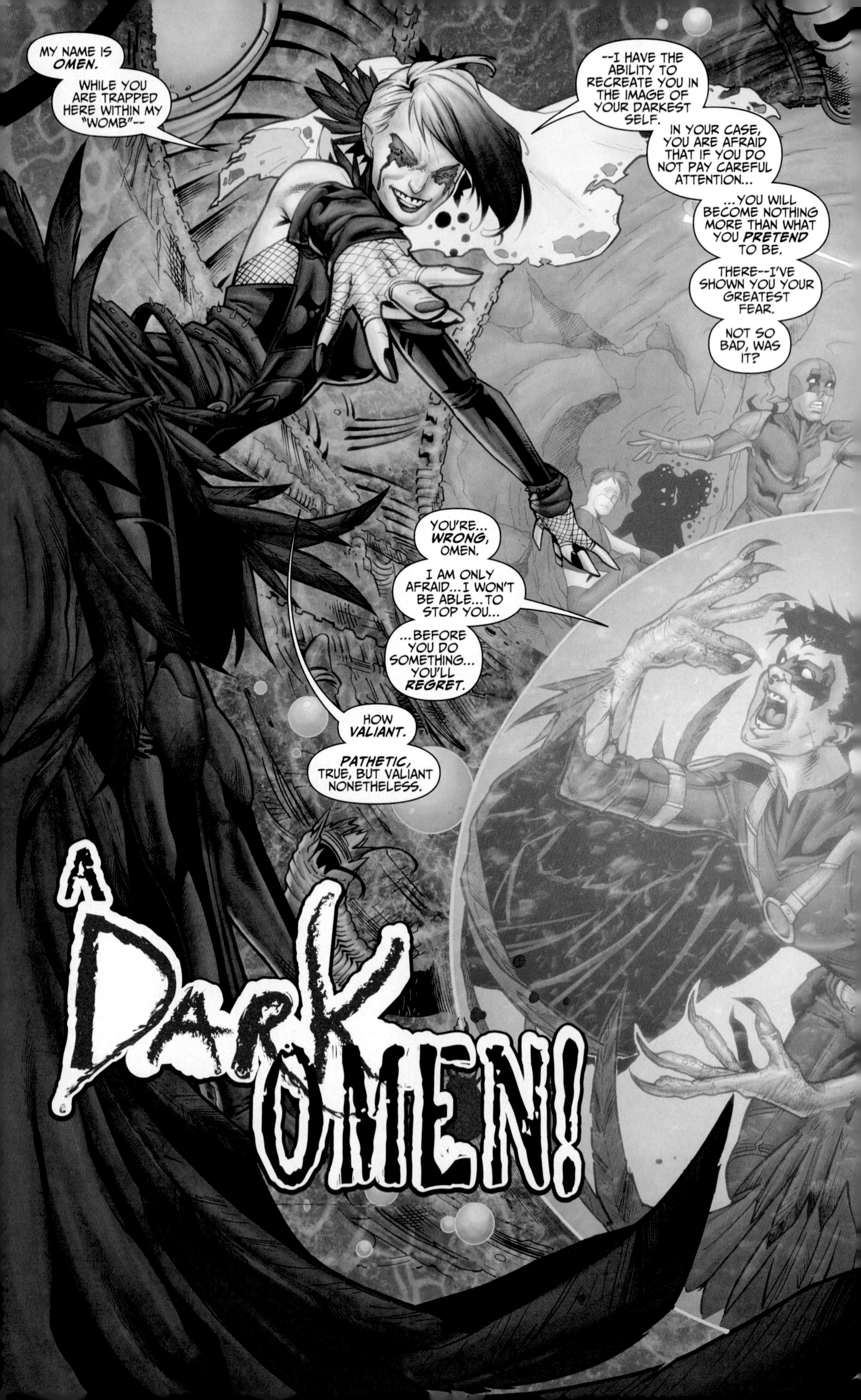
MY NAME IS OMEN.
WHILE YOU ARE TRAPPED HERE WITHIN MY "WOMB"--
--I HAVE THE ABILITY TO RECREATE YOU IN THE IMAGE OF YOUR DARKEST SELF.
IN YOUR CASE, YOU ARE AFRAID THAT IF YOU DO NOT PAY CAREFUL ATTENTION...
...YOU WILL BECOME NOTHING MORE THAN WHAT YOU PRETEND TO BE.
THERE--I'VE SHOWN YOU YOUR GREATEST FEAR.
NOT SO BAD, WAS IT?
YOU'RE... WRONG, OMEN.
I AM ONLY AFRAID...I WON'T BE ABLE...TO STOP YOU...
...BEFORE YOU DO SOMETHING... YOU'LL REGRET.
HOW VALIANT.
PATHETIC, TRUE, BUT VALIANT NONETHELESS.
A DARK OMEN!

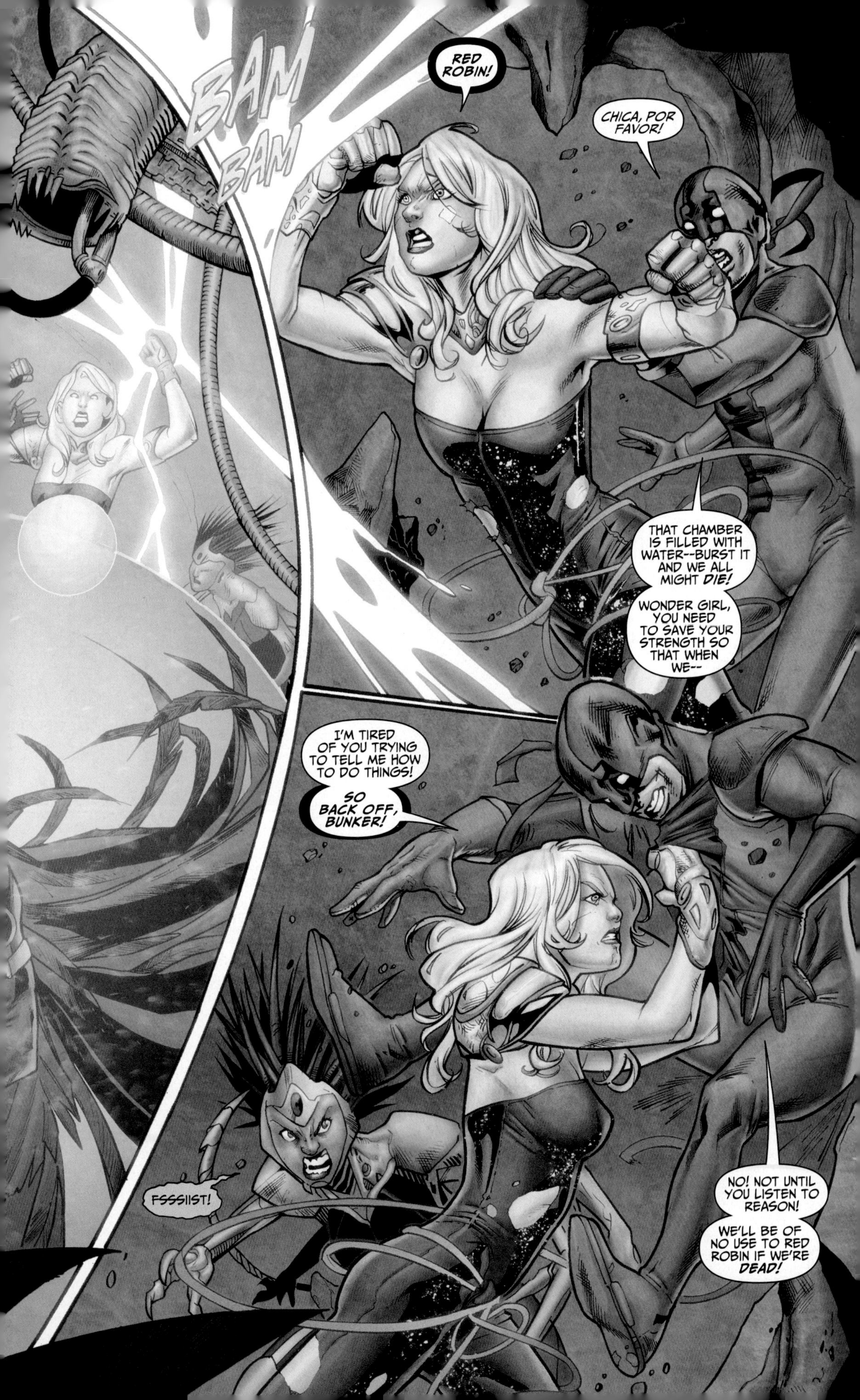
BAM
BAM
BAM
RED ROBIN!
CHICA, POR FAVOR!
THAT CHAMBER IS FILLED WITH WATER--BURST IT AND WE ALL MIGHT DIE!
WONDER GIRL, YOU NEED TO SAVE YOUR STRENGTH SO THAT WHEN WE--
I'M TIRED OF YOU TRYING TO TELL ME HOW TO DO THINGS!
SO BACK OFF, BUNKER!
FSSSIIST!
NO! NOT UNTIL YOU LISTEN TO REASON!
WE'LL BE OF NO USE TO RED ROBIN IF WE'RE DEAD!

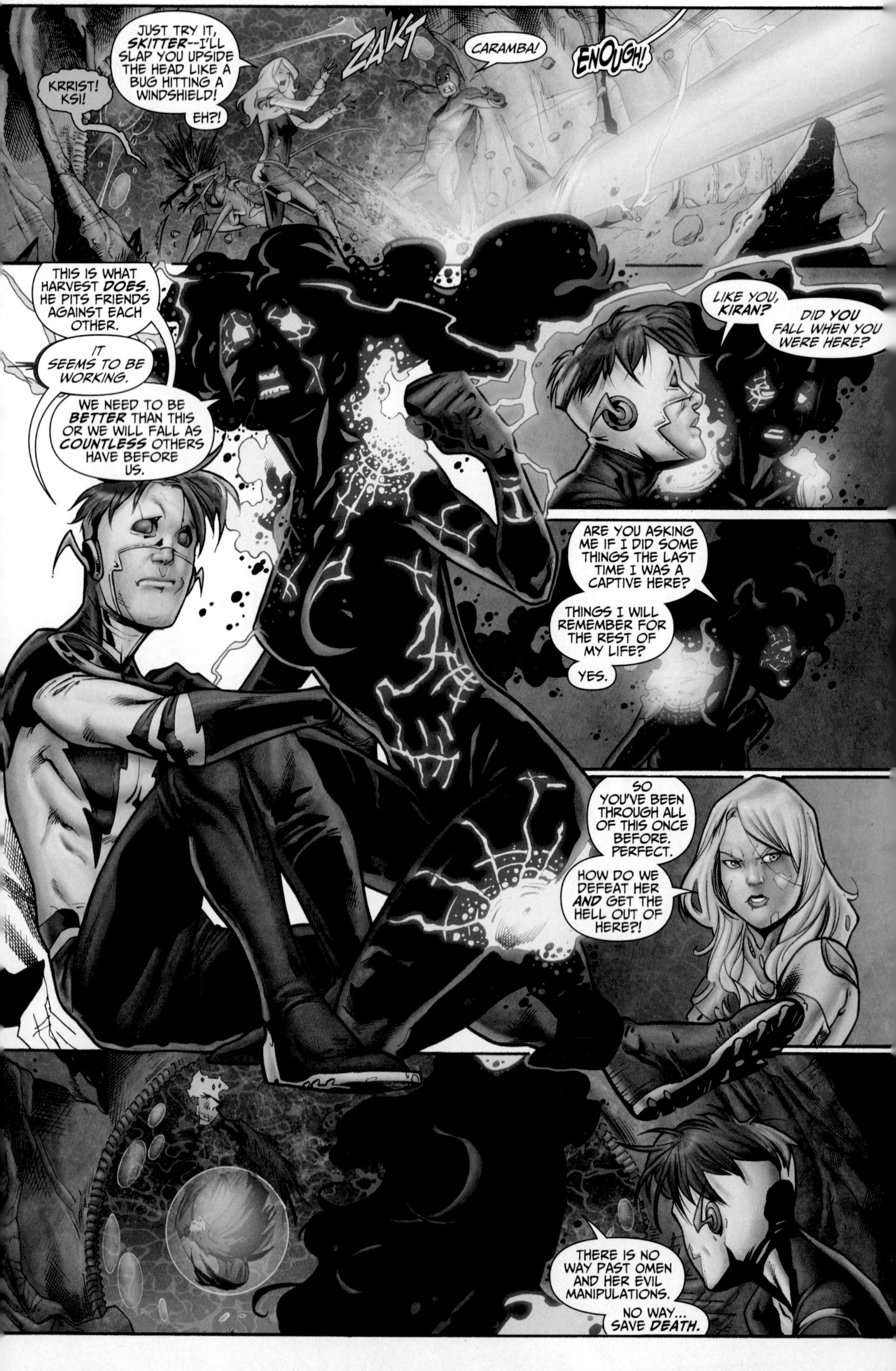

KRRIST! KSI!
JUST TRY IT, SKITTER--I'LL SLAP YOU UPSIDE THE HEAD LIKE A BUG HITTING A WINDSHIELD!
EH?!
ZAKT
CARAMBA!
ENOUGH!
THIS IS WHAT HARVEST DOES. HE PITS FRIENDS AGAINST EACH OTHER.
IT SEEMS TO BE WORKING.
WE NEED TO BE BETTER THAN THIS OR WE WILL FALL AS COUNTLESS OTHERS HAVE BEFORE US.
LIKE YOU, KIRAN?
DID YOU FALL WHEN YOU WERE HERE?
ARE YOU ASKING ME IF I DID SOME THINGS THE LAST TIME I WAS A CAPTIVE HERE?
THINGS I WILL REMEMBER FOR THE REST OF MY LIFE?
YES.
SO YOU'VE BEEN THROUGH ALL OF THIS ONCE BEFORE. PERFECT.
HOW DO WE DEFEAT HER AND GET THE HELL OUT OF HERE?!
THERE IS NO WAY PAST OMEN AND HER EVIL MANIPULATIONS.
NO WAY... SAVE DEATH.

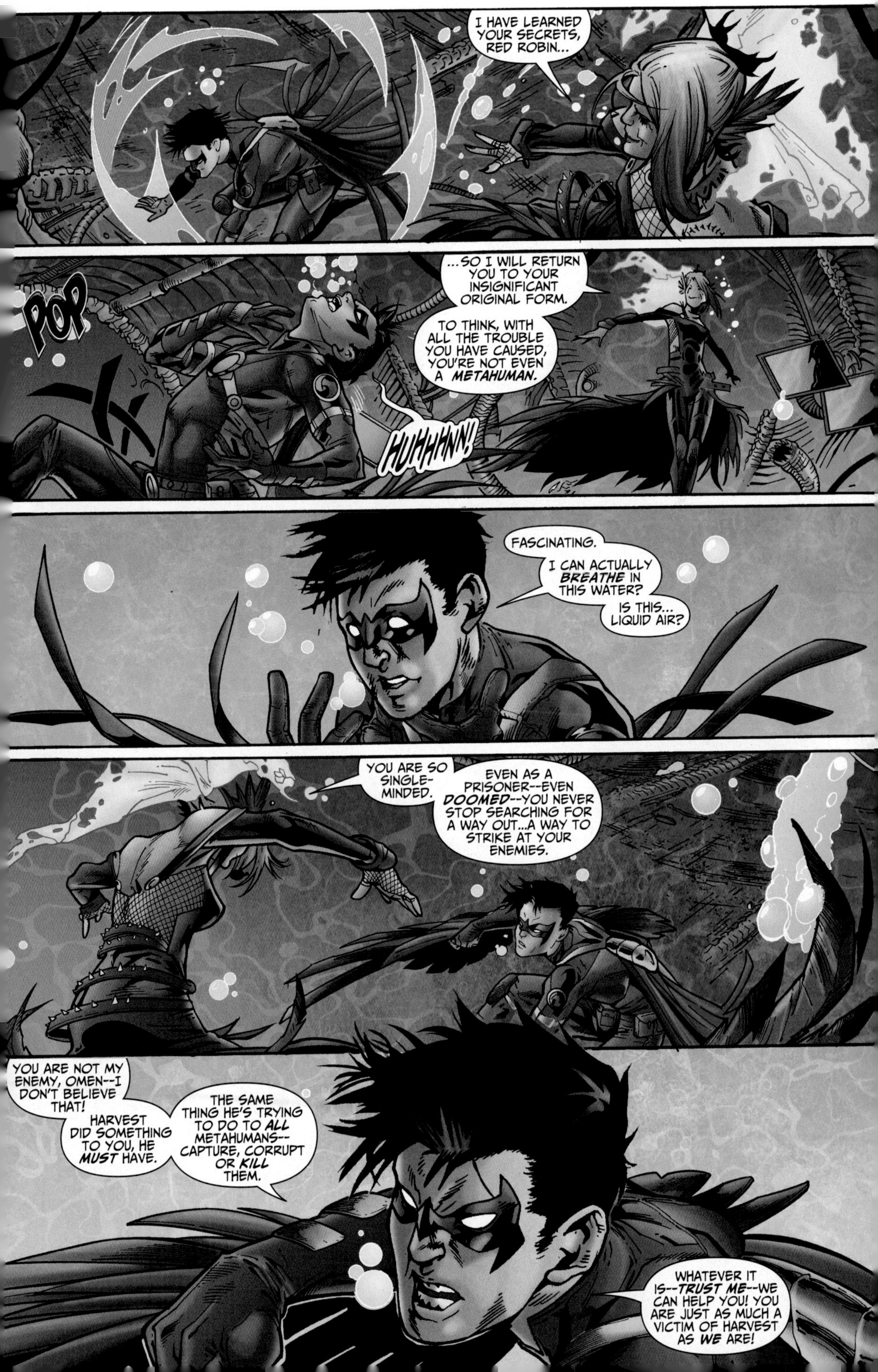

I HAVE LEARNED YOUR SECRETS, RED ROBIN...
...SO I WILL RETURN YOU TO YOUR INSIGNIFICANT ORIGINAL FORM.
TO THINK, WITH ALL THE TROUBLE YOU HAVE CAUSED, YOU'RE NOT EVEN A METAHUMAN.
POP
HUHHHNN!
FASCINATING.
I CAN ACTUALLY BREATHE IN THIS WATER?
IS THIS... LIQUID AIR?
YOU ARE SO SINGLE-MINDED.
EVEN AS A PRISONER--EVEN DOOMED--YOU NEVER STOP SEARCHING FOR A WAY OUT...A WAY TO STRIKE AT YOUR ENEMIES.
YOU ARE NOT MY ENEMY, OMEN--I DON'T BELIEVE THAT!
HARVEST DID SOMETHING TO YOU, HE MUST HAVE.
THE SAME THING HE'S TRYING TO DO TO ALL METAHUMANS--CAPTURE, CORRUPT OR KILL THEM.
WHATEVER IT IS--TRUST ME--WE CAN HELP YOU! YOU ARE JUST AS MUCH A VICTIM OF HARVEST AS WE ARE!

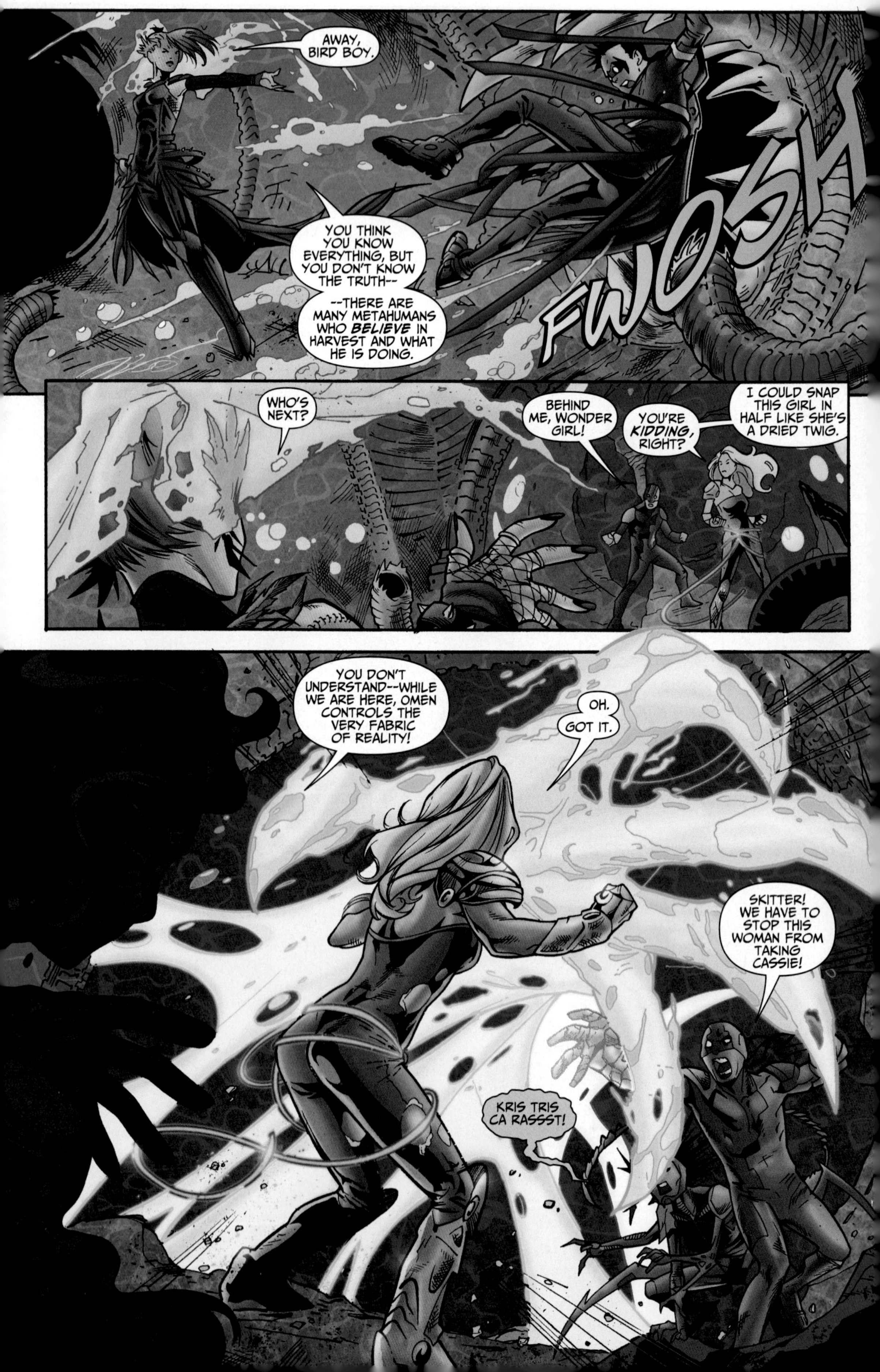
AWAY, BIRD BOY.
FWOOSH
YOU THINK YOU KNOW EVERYTHING, BUT YOU DON'T KNOW THE TRUTH--
--THERE ARE MANY METAHUMANS WHO BELIEVE IN HARVEST AND WHAT HE IS DOING.
WHO'S NEXT?
BEHIND ME, WONDER GIRL!
YOU'RE KIDDING, RIGHT?
I COULD SNAP THIS GIRL IN HALF LIKE SHE'S A DRIED TWIG.
YOU DON'T UNDERSTAND--WHILE WE ARE HERE, OMEN CONTROLS THE VERY FABRIC OF REALITY!
OH. GOT IT.
SKITTER! WE HAVE TO STOP THIS WOMAN FROM TAKING CASSIE!
KRIS TRIS CA RASSST!

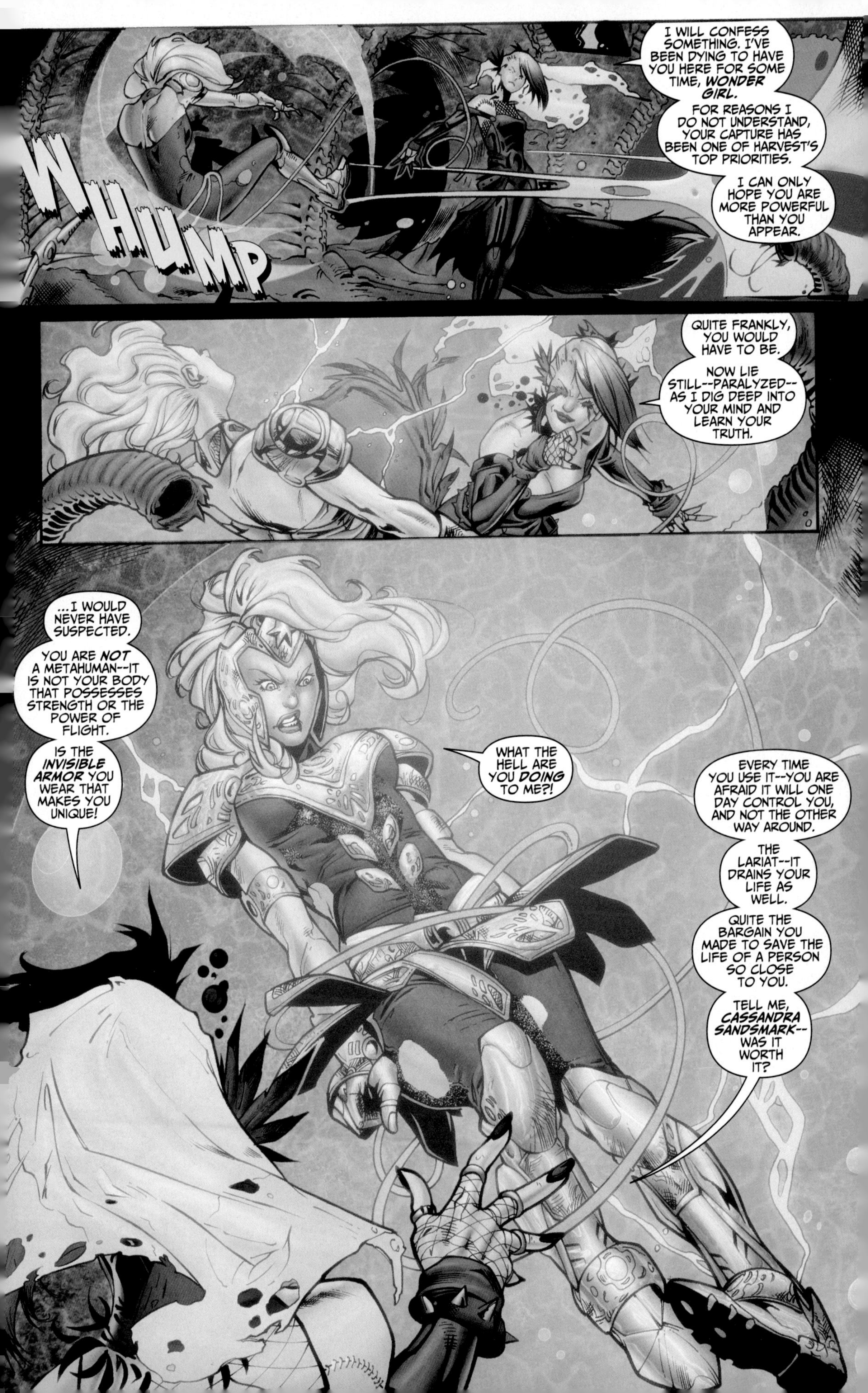

I WILL CONFESS SOMETHING. I'VE BEEN DYING TO HAVE YOU HERE FOR SOME TIME, WONDER GIRL.
FOR REASONS I DO NOT UNDERSTAND, YOUR CAPTURE HAS BEEN ONE OF HARVEST'S TOP PRIORITIES.
I CAN ONLY HOPE YOU ARE MORE POWERFUL THAN YOU APPEAR.
WHUMP
QUITE FRANKLY, YOU WOULD HAVE TO BE.
NOW LIE STILL--PARALYZED--AS I DIG DEEP INTO YOUR MIND AND LEARN YOUR TRUTH.
...I WOULD NEVER HAVE SUSPECTED.
YOU ARE NOT A METAHUMAN--IT IS NOT YOUR BODY THAT POSSESSES STRENGTH OR THE POWER OF FLIGHT.
IS THE INVISIBLE ARMOR YOU WEAR THAT MAKES YOU UNIQUE!
WHAT THE HELL ARE YOU DOING TO ME?!
EVERY TIME YOU USE IT--YOU ARE AFRAID IT WILL ONE DAY CONTROL YOU, AND NOT THE OTHER WAY AROUND.
THE LARIAT--IT DRAINS YOUR LIFE AS WELL.
QUITE THE BARGAIN YOU MADE TO SAVE THE LIFE OF A PERSON SO CLOSE TO YOU.
TELL ME, CASSANDRA SANDSMARK--WAS IT WORTH IT?

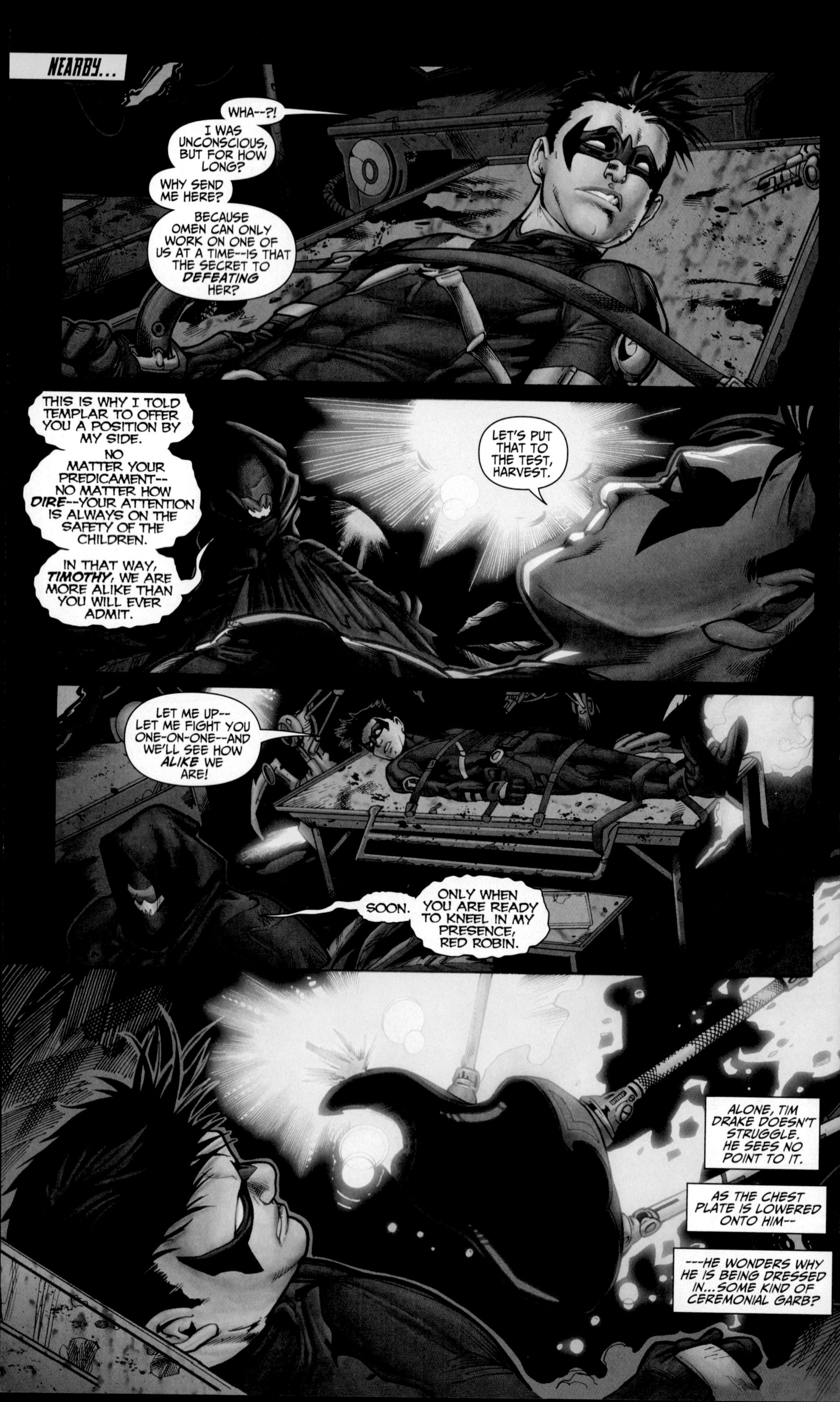
NEARBY...
WHA--?!
I WAS UNCONSCIOUS, BUT FOR HOW LONG?
WHY SEND ME HERE?
BECAUSE OMEN CAN ONLY WORK ON ONE OF US AT A TIME--IS THAT THE SECRET TO DEFEATING HER?
THIS IS WHY I TOLD TEMPLAR TO OFFER YOU A POSITION BY MY SIDE.
NO MATTER YOUR PREDICAMENT-- NO MATTER HOW DIRE--YOUR ATTENTION IS ALWAYS ON THE SAFETY OF THE CHILDREN.
IN THAT WAY, TIMOTHY, WE ARE MORE ALIKE THAN YOU WILL EVER ADMIT.
LET'S PUT THAT TO THE TEST, HARVEST.
LET ME UP-- LET ME FIGHT YOU ONE-ON-ONE--AND WE'LL SEE HOW ALIKE WE ARE!
SOON.
ONLY WHEN YOU ARE READY TO KNEEL IN MY PRESENCE, RED ROBIN.
ALONE, TIM DRAKE DOESN'T STRUGGLE. HE SEES NO POINT TO IT.
AS THE CHEST PLATE IS LOWERED ONTO HIM--
---HE WONDERS WHY HE IS BEING DRESSED IN...SOME KIND OF CEREMONIAL GARB?

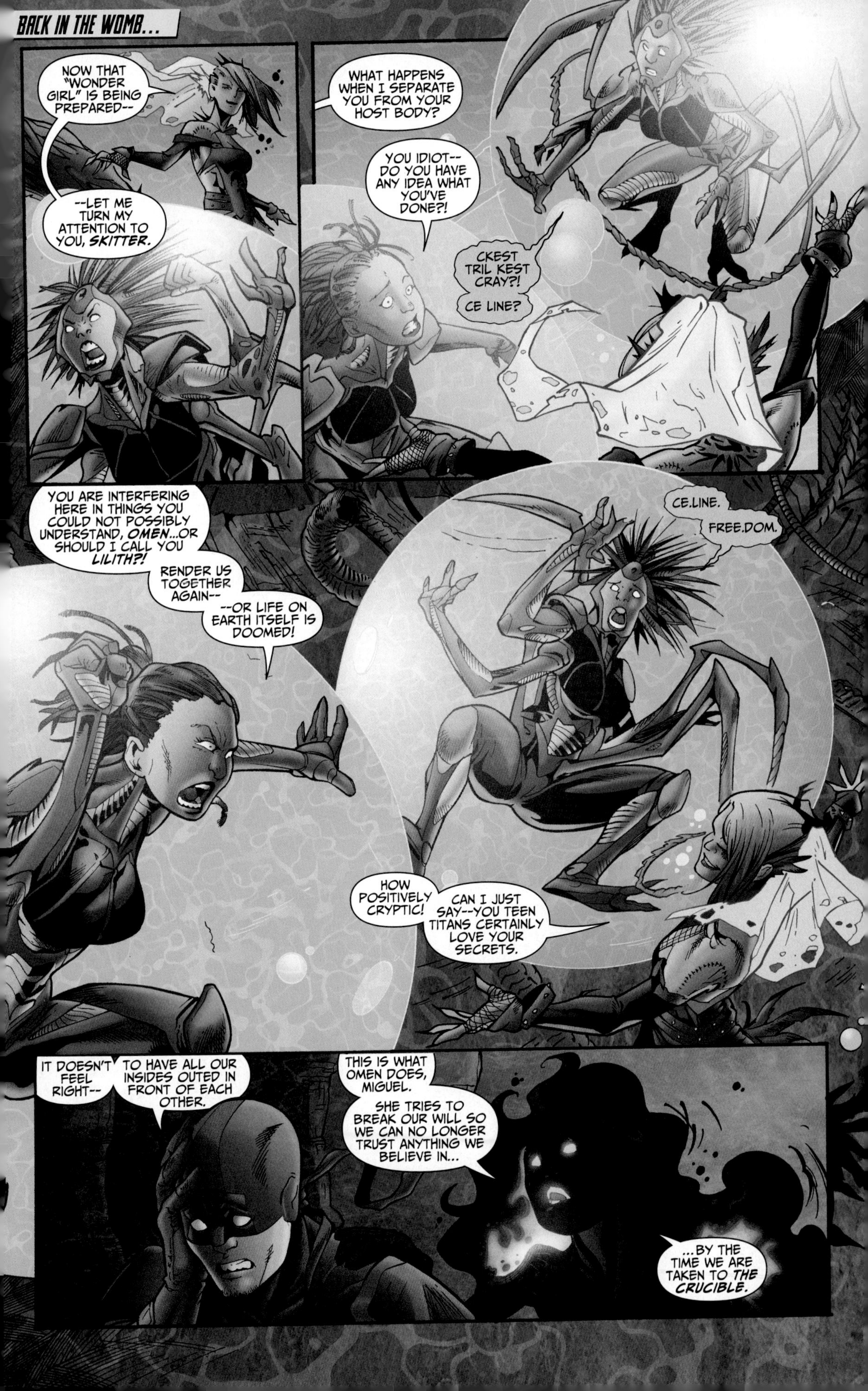
BACK IN THE WOMB...
NOW THAT "WONDER GIRL" IS BEING PREPARED--
--LET ME TURN MY ATTENTION TO YOU, SKITTER.
WHAT HAPPENS WHEN I SEPARATE YOU FROM YOUR HOST BODY?
YOU IDIOT-- DO YOU HAVE ANY IDEA WHAT YOU'VE DONE?!
CKEST TRIL KEST CRAY?!
CE LINE?
YOU ARE INTERFERING HERE IN THINGS YOU COULD NOT POSSIBLY UNDERSTAND, OMEN...OR SHOULD I CALL YOU LILITH?!
RENDER US TOGETHER AGAIN--
--OR LIFE ON EARTH ITSELF IS DOOMED!
CE.LINE.
FREE.DOM.
HOW POSITIVELY CRYPTIC!
CAN I JUST SAY--YOU TEEN TITANS CERTAINLY LOVE YOUR SECRETS.
IT DOESN'T FEEL RIGHT--
TO HAVE ALL OUR INSIDES OUTED IN FRONT OF EACH OTHER.
THIS IS WHAT OMEN DOES, MIGUEL.
SHE TRIES TO BREAK OUR WILL SO WE CAN NO LONGER TRUST ANYTHING WE BELIEVE IN...
...BY THE TIME WE ARE TAKEN TO THE CRUCIBLE.

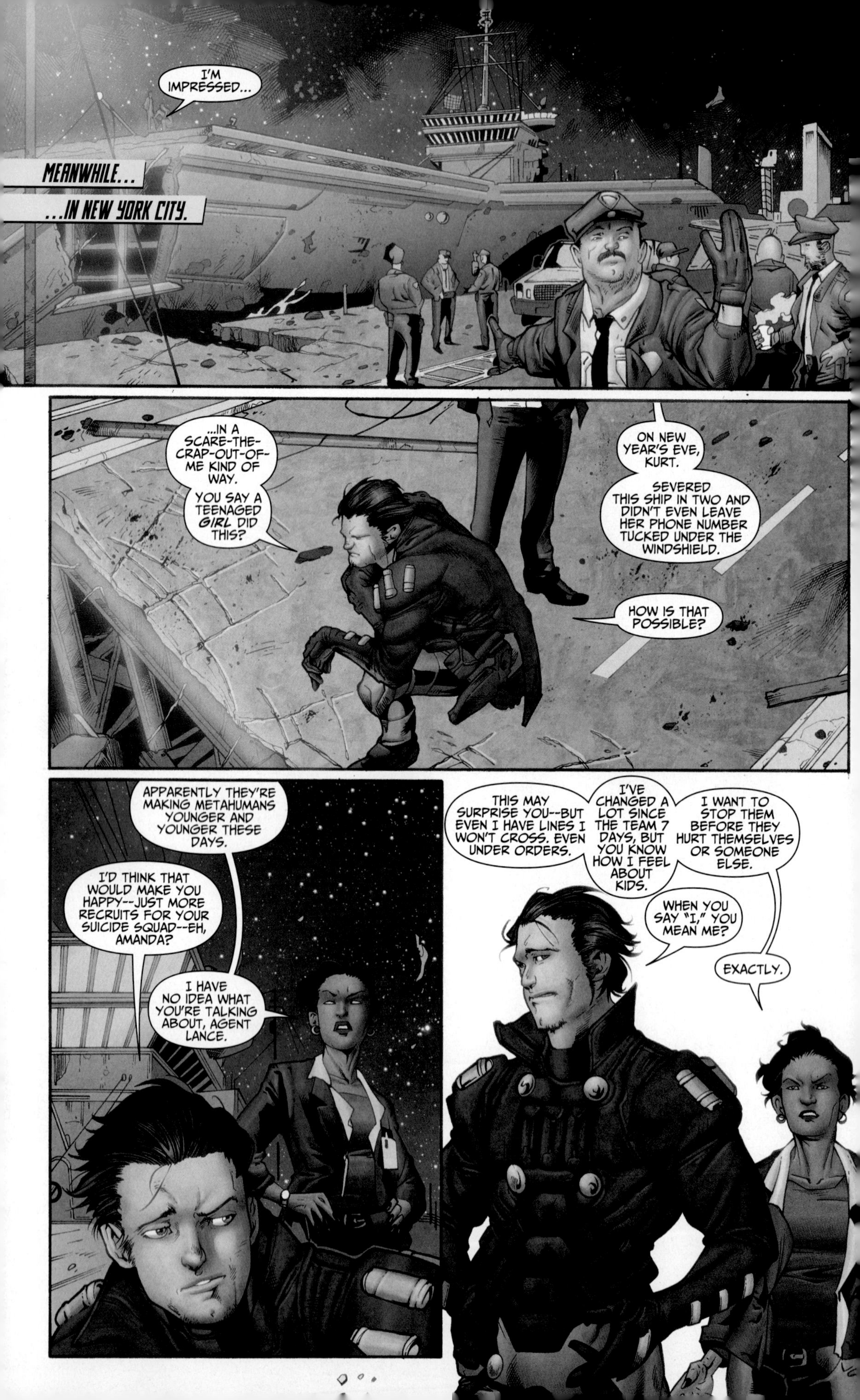
I'M IMPRESSED...
MEANWHILE...
...IN NEW YORK CITY.
...IN A SCARE-THE-CRAP-OUT-OF-ME KIND OF WAY.
YOU SAY A TEENAGED GIRL DID THIS?
ON NEW YEAR'S EVE, KURT.
SEVERED THIS SHIP IN TWO AND DIDN'T EVEN LEAVE HER PHONE NUMBER TUCKED UNDER THE WINDSHIELD.
HOW IS THAT POSSIBLE?
APPARENTLY THEY'RE MAKING METAHUMANS YOUNGER AND YOUNGER THESE DAYS.
I'D THINK THAT WOULD MAKE YOU HAPPY--JUST MORE RECRUITS FOR YOUR SUICIDE SQUAD--EH, AMANDA?
I HAVE NO IDEA WHAT YOU'RE TALKING ABOUT, AGENT LANCE.
THIS MAY SURPRISE YOU--BUT EVEN I HAVE LINES I WON'T CROSS. EVEN UNDER ORDERS.
I'VE CHANGED A LOT SINCE THE TEAM 7 DAYS, BUT YOU KNOW HOW I FEEL ABOUT KIDS.
I WANT TO STOP THEM BEFORE THEY HURT THEMSELVES OR SOMEONE ELSE.
WHEN YOU SAY "I," YOU MEAN ME?
EXACTLY.

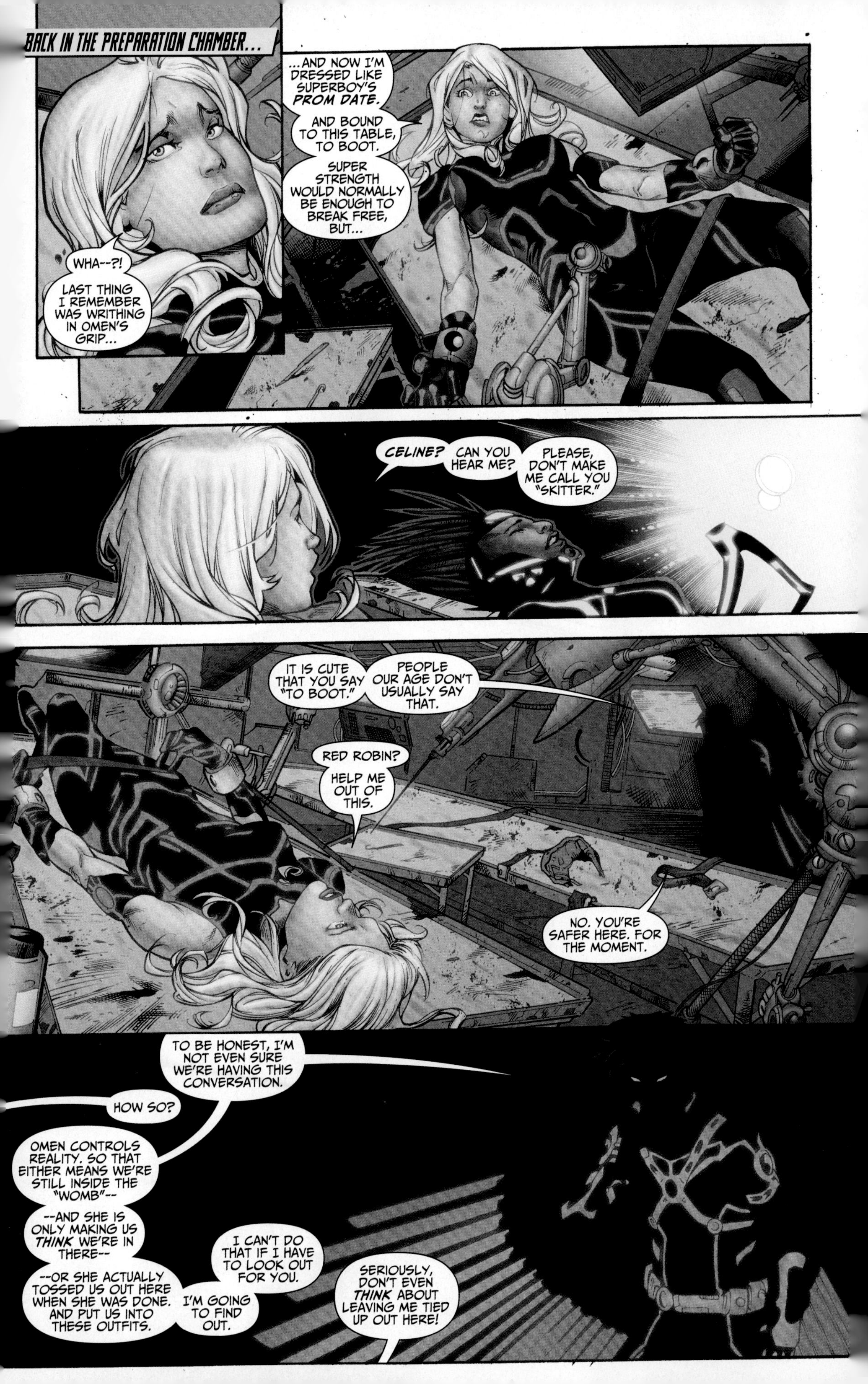

BACK IN THE PREPARATION CHAMBER...
WHA--?!
LAST THING I REMEMBER WAS WRITHING IN OMEN'S GRIP...
...AND NOW I'M DRESSED LIKE SUPERBOY'S PROM DATE.
AND BOUND TO THIS TABLE, TO BOOT.
SUPER STRENGTH WOULD NORMALLY BE ENOUGH TO BREAK FREE, BUT...
CELINE? CAN YOU HEAR ME?
PLEASE, DON'T MAKE ME CALL YOU "SKITTER."
IT IS CUTE THAT YOU SAY "TO BOOT."
PEOPLE OUR AGE DON'T USUALLY SAY THAT.
RED ROBIN?
HELP ME OUT OF THIS.
NO. YOU'RE SAFER HERE. FOR THE MOMENT.
TO BE HONEST, I'M NOT EVEN SURE WE'RE HAVING THIS CONVERSATION.
HOW SO?
OMEN CONTROLS REALITY. SO THAT EITHER MEANS WE'RE STILL INSIDE THE "WOMB"--
--AND SHE IS ONLY MAKING US THINK WE'RE IN THERE--
--OR SHE ACTUALLY TOSSED US OUT HERE WHEN SHE WAS DONE. AND PUT US INTO THESE OUTFITS.
I'M GOING TO FIND OUT.
I CAN'T DO THAT IF I HAVE TO LOOK OUT FOR YOU.
SERIOUSLY, DON'T EVEN THINK ABOUT LEAVING ME TIED UP OUT HERE!

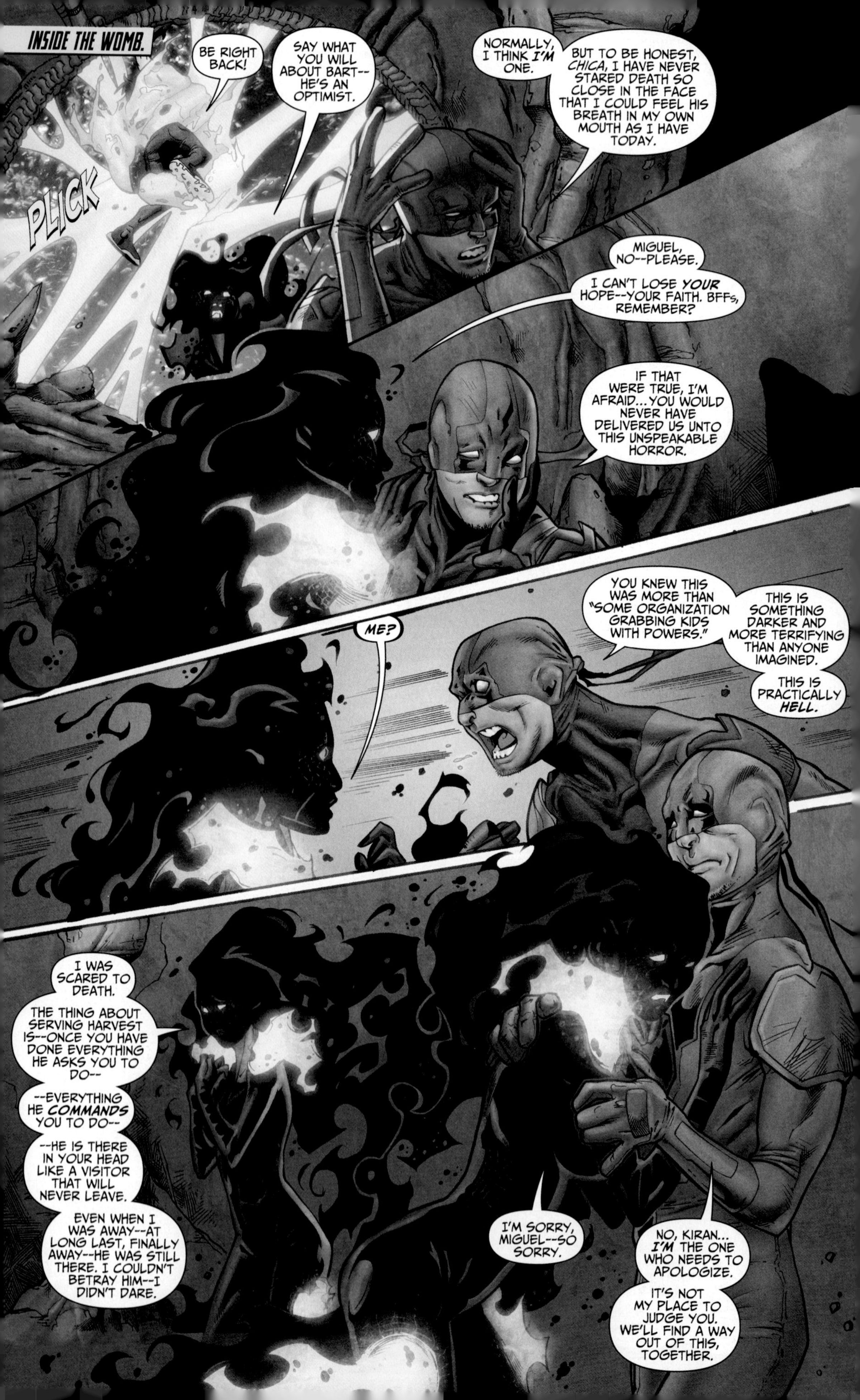
INSIDE THE WOMB.
BE RIGHT BACK!
SAY WHAT YOU WILL ABOUT BART--HE'S AN OPTIMIST.
NORMALLY, I THINK *I'M* ONE.
BUT TO BE HONEST, *CHICA*, I HAVE NEVER STARED DEATH SO CLOSE IN THE FACE THAT I COULD FEEL HIS BREATH IN MY OWN MOUTH AS I HAVE TODAY.
PLICK
MIGUEL, NO--PLEASE.
I CAN'T LOSE **YOUR** HOPE--YOUR FAITH. BFFs, REMEMBER?
IF THAT WERE TRUE, I'M AFRAID...YOU WOULD NEVER HAVE DELIVERED US UNTO THIS UNSPEAKABLE HORROR.
ME?
YOU KNEW THIS WAS MORE THAN "SOME ORGANIZATION GRABBING KIDS WITH POWERS."
THIS IS SOMETHING DARKER AND MORE TERRIFYING THAN ANYONE IMAGINED.
THIS IS PRACTICALLY **HELL.**
I WAS SCARED TO DEATH.
THE THING ABOUT SERVING HARVEST IS--ONCE YOU HAVE DONE EVERYTHING HE ASKS YOU TO DO--
--EVERYTHING HE **COMMANDS** YOU TO DO--
--HE IS THERE IN YOUR HEAD LIKE A VISITOR THAT WILL NEVER LEAVE.
EVEN WHEN I WAS AWAY--AT LONG LAST, FINALLY AWAY--HE WAS STILL THERE. I COULDN'T BETRAY HIM--I DIDN'T DARE.
I'M SORRY, MIGUEL--SO SORRY.
NO, KIRAN... ***I'M*** THE ONE WHO NEEDS TO APOLOGIZE.
IT'S NOT MY PLACE TO JUDGE YOU. WE'LL FIND A WAY OUT OF THIS, TOGETHER.

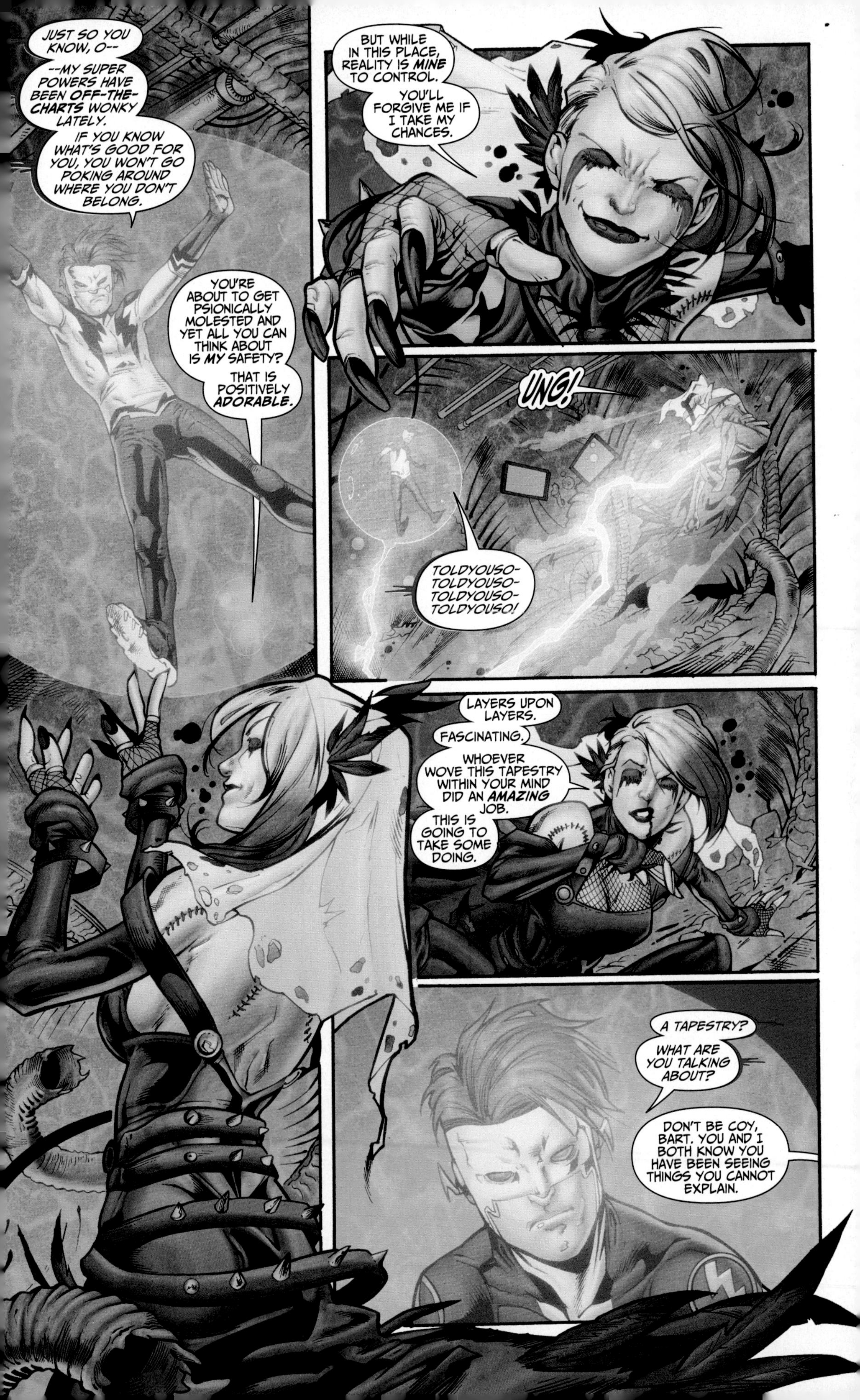
JUST SO YOU KNOW, O--
--MY SUPER POWERS HAVE BEEN OFF-THE-CHARTS WONKY LATELY.
IF YOU KNOW WHAT'S GOOD FOR YOU, YOU WON'T GO POKING AROUND WHERE YOU DON'T BELONG.
YOU'RE ABOUT TO GET PSIONICALLY MOLESTED AND YET ALL YOU CAN THINK ABOUT IS MY SAFETY?
THAT IS POSITIVELY ADORABLE.
BUT WHILE IN THIS PLACE, REALITY IS MINE TO CONTROL.
YOU'LL FORGIVE ME IF I TAKE MY CHANCES.
UNG!
TOLDYOUSO-TOLDYOUSO-TOLDYOUSO-TOLDYOUSO!
LAYERS UPON LAYERS.
FASCINATING.
WHOEVER WOVE THIS TAPESTRY WITHIN YOUR MIND DID AN AMAZING JOB.
THIS IS GOING TO TAKE SOME DOING.
A TAPESTRY?
WHAT ARE YOU TALKING ABOUT?
DON'T BE COY, BART. YOU AND I BOTH KNOW YOU HAVE BEEN SEEING THINGS YOU CANNOT EXPLAIN.

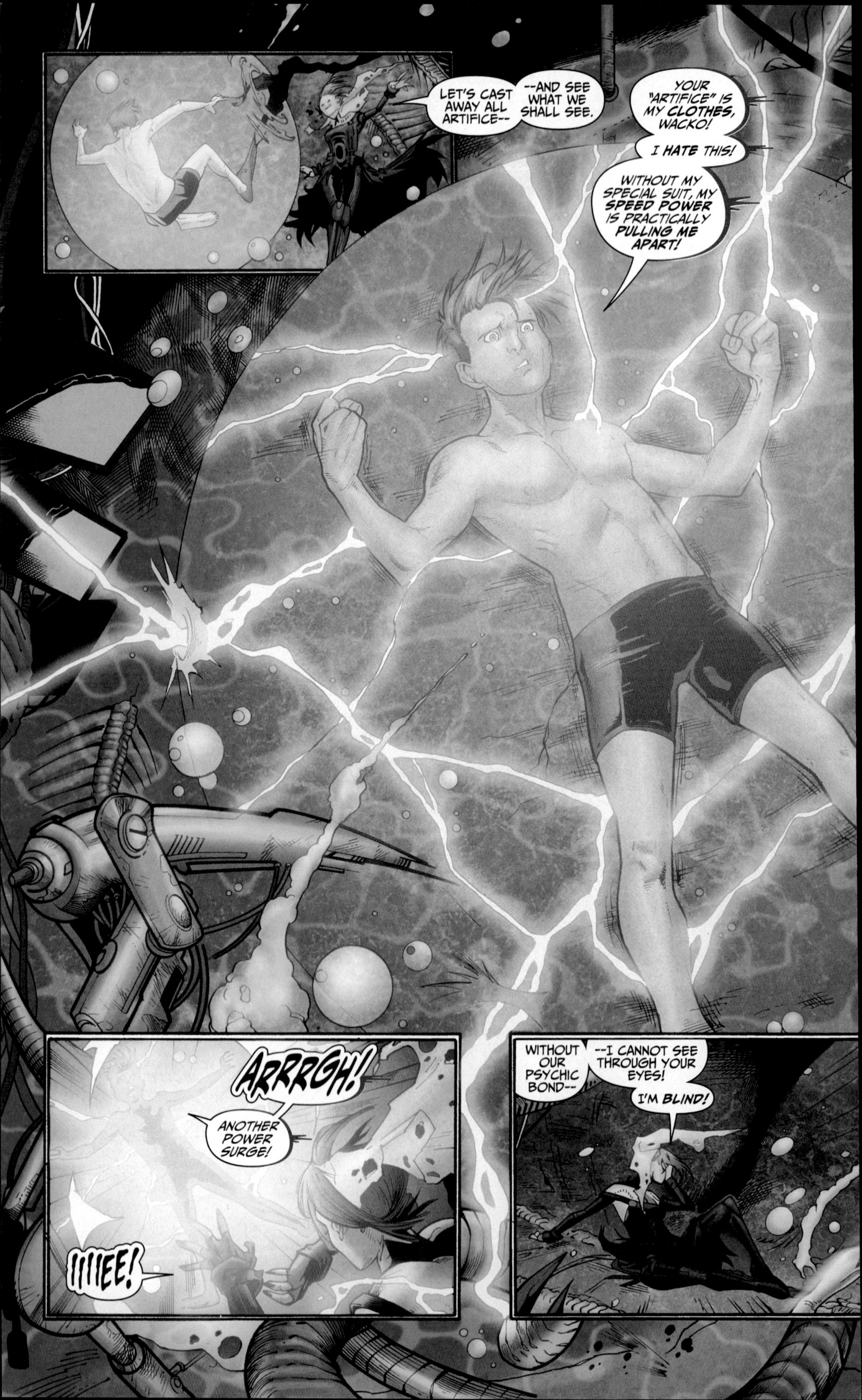
LET'S CAST AWAY ALL ARTIFICE--
--AND SEE WHAT WE SHALL SEE.
YOUR "ARTIFICE" IS MY CLOTHES, WACKO!
I HATE THIS!
WITHOUT MY SPECIAL SUIT, MY SPEED POWER IS PRACTICALLY PULLING ME APART!
ARRRGH!
ANOTHER POWER SURGE!
IIIIEE!
WITHOUT OUR PSYCHIC BOND--
--I CANNOT SEE THROUGH YOUR EYES!
I'M BLIND!

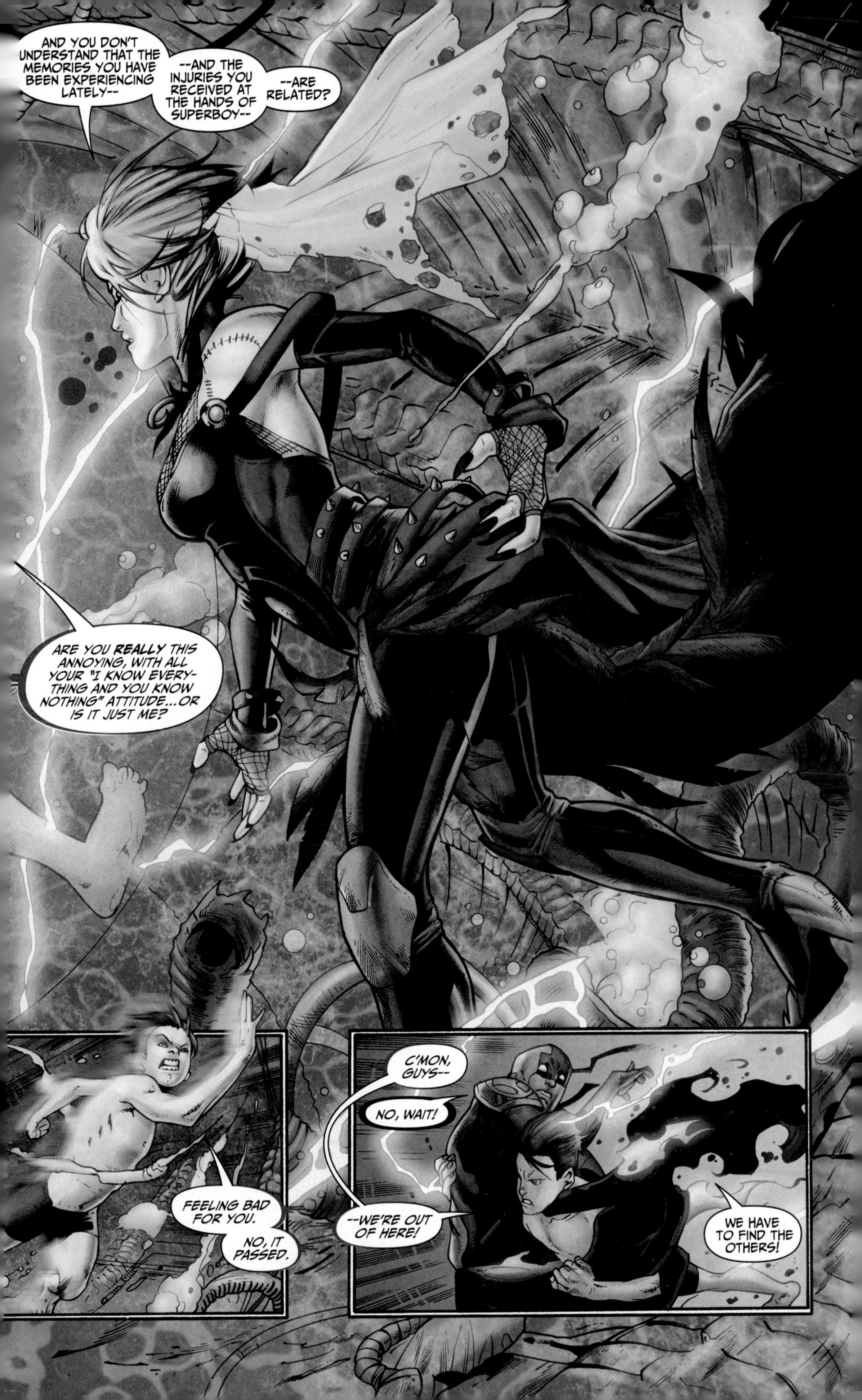
AND YOU DON'T UNDERSTAND THAT THE MEMORIES YOU HAVE BEEN EXPERIENCING LATELY--
--AND THE INJURIES YOU RECEIVED AT THE HANDS OF SUPERBOY--
--ARE RELATED?
ARE YOU REALLY THIS ANNOYING, WITH ALL YOUR "I KNOW EVERYTHING AND YOU KNOW NOTHING" ATTITUDE...OR IS IT JUST ME?
FEELING BAD FOR YOU.
NO, IT PASSED.
C'MON, GUYS--
NO, WAIT!
--WE'RE OUT OF HERE!
WE HAVE TO FIND THE OTHERS!

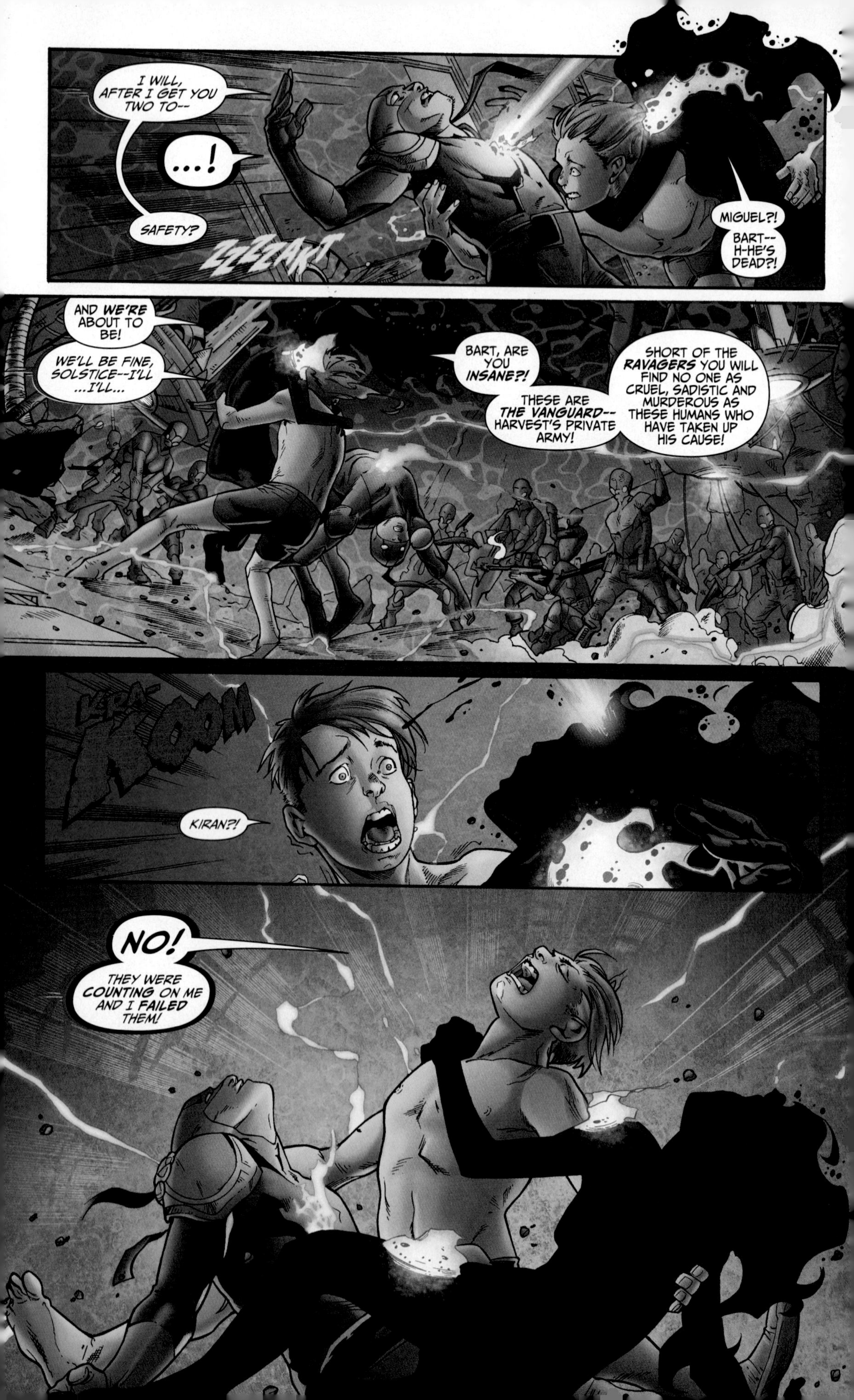
I WILL, AFTER I GET YOU TWO TO--
...!
SAFETY?
ZZZZAKT
MIGUEL?! BART-- H-HE'S DEAD?!
AND WE'RE ABOUT TO BE!
WE'LL BE FINE, SOLSTICE--I'LL ...I'LL...
BART, ARE YOU INSANE?!
THESE ARE THE VANGUARD-- HARVEST'S PRIVATE ARMY!
SHORT OF THE RAVAGERS YOU WILL FIND NO ONE AS CRUEL, SADISTIC AND MURDEROUS AS THESE HUMANS WHO HAVE TAKEN UP HIS CAUSE!
KRA-KOOOM
KIRAN?!
NO!
THEY WERE COUNTING ON ME AND I FAILED THEM!

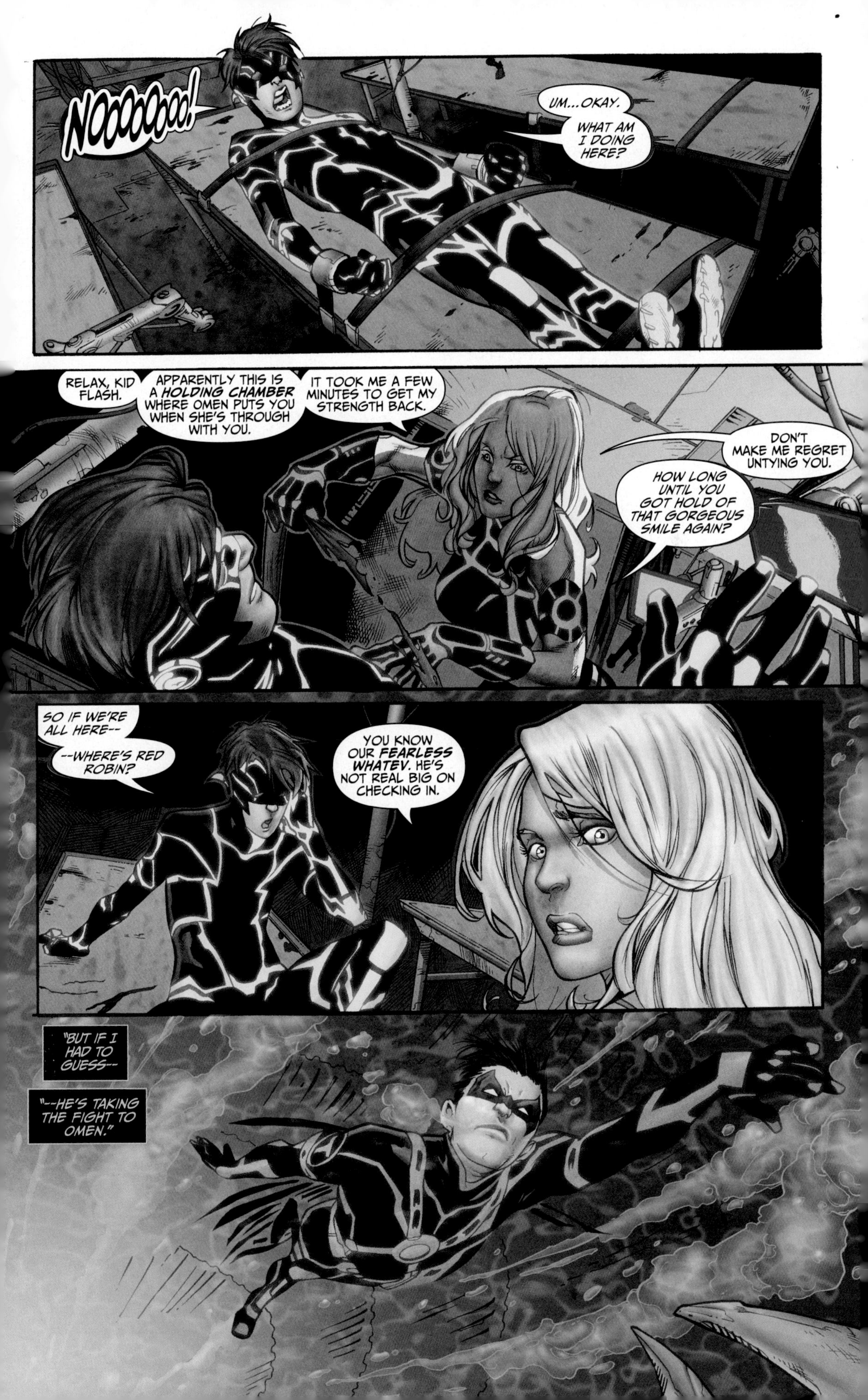
NOOOOOOO!
UM...OKAY.
WHAT AM I DOING HERE?
RELAX, KID FLASH.
APPARENTLY THIS IS A HOLDING CHAMBER WHERE OMEN PUTS YOU WHEN SHE'S THROUGH WITH YOU.
IT TOOK ME A FEW MINUTES TO GET MY STRENGTH BACK.
DON'T MAKE ME REGRET UNTYING YOU.
HOW LONG UNTIL YOU GOT HOLD OF THAT GORGEOUS SMILE AGAIN?
SO IF WE'RE ALL HERE--
--WHERE'S RED ROBIN?
YOU KNOW OUR FEARLESS WHATEV. HE'S NOT REAL BIG ON CHECKING IN.
"BUT IF I HAD TO GUESS--
"--HE'S TAKING THE FIGHT TO OMEN."

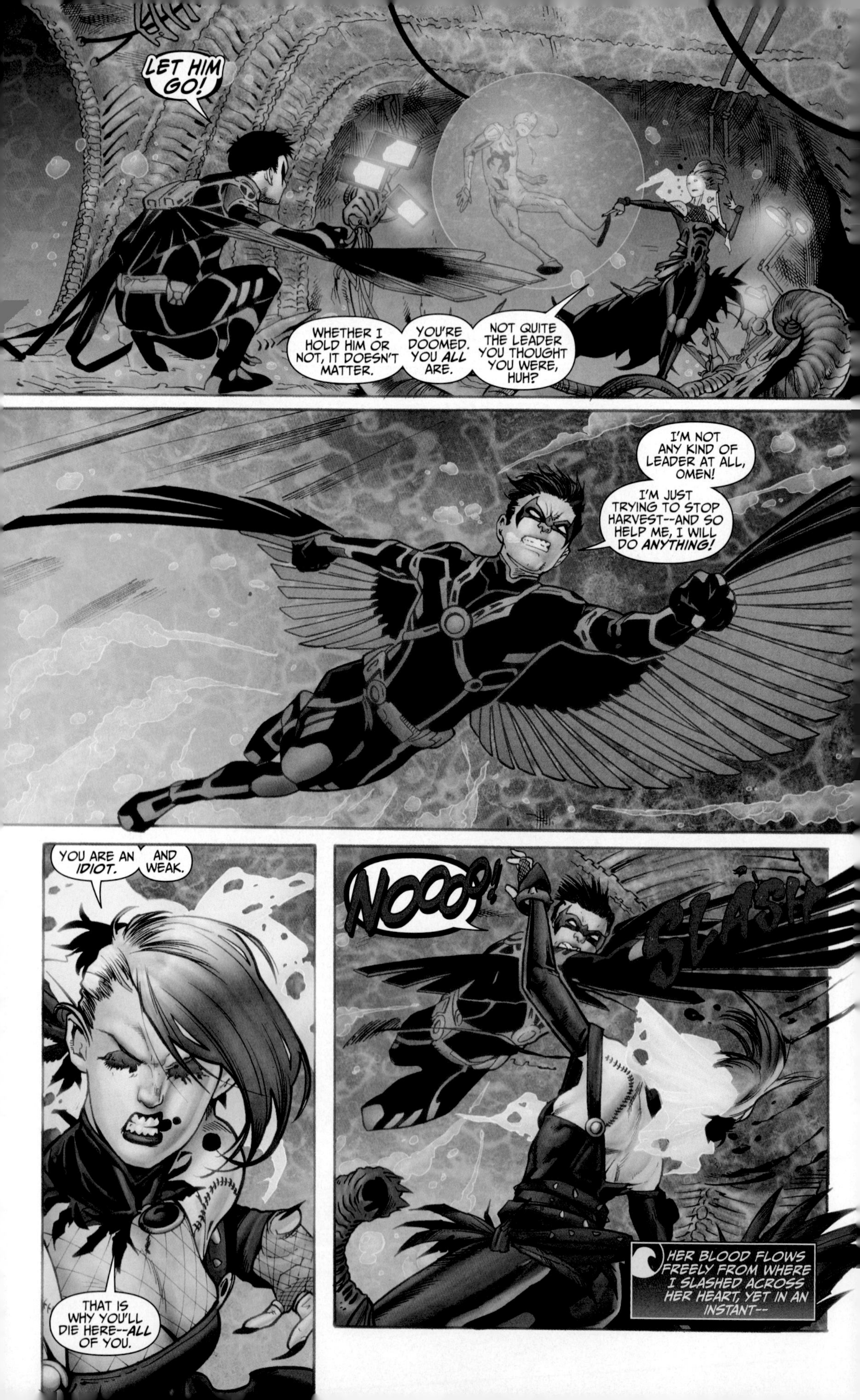
LET HIM GO!
WHETHER I HOLD HIM OR NOT, IT DOESN'T MATTER.
YOU'RE DOOMED. YOU ALL ARE.
NOT QUITE THE LEADER YOU THOUGHT YOU WERE, HUH?
I'M NOT ANY KIND OF LEADER AT ALL, OMEN!
I'M JUST TRYING TO STOP HARVEST--AND SO HELP ME, I WILL DO ANYTHING!
YOU ARE AN IDIOT.
AND WEAK.
THAT IS WHY YOU'LL DIE HERE--ALL OF YOU.
NOOOO!
SLASH
HER BLOOD FLOWS FREELY FROM WHERE I SLASHED ACROSS HER HEART, YET IN AN INSTANT--

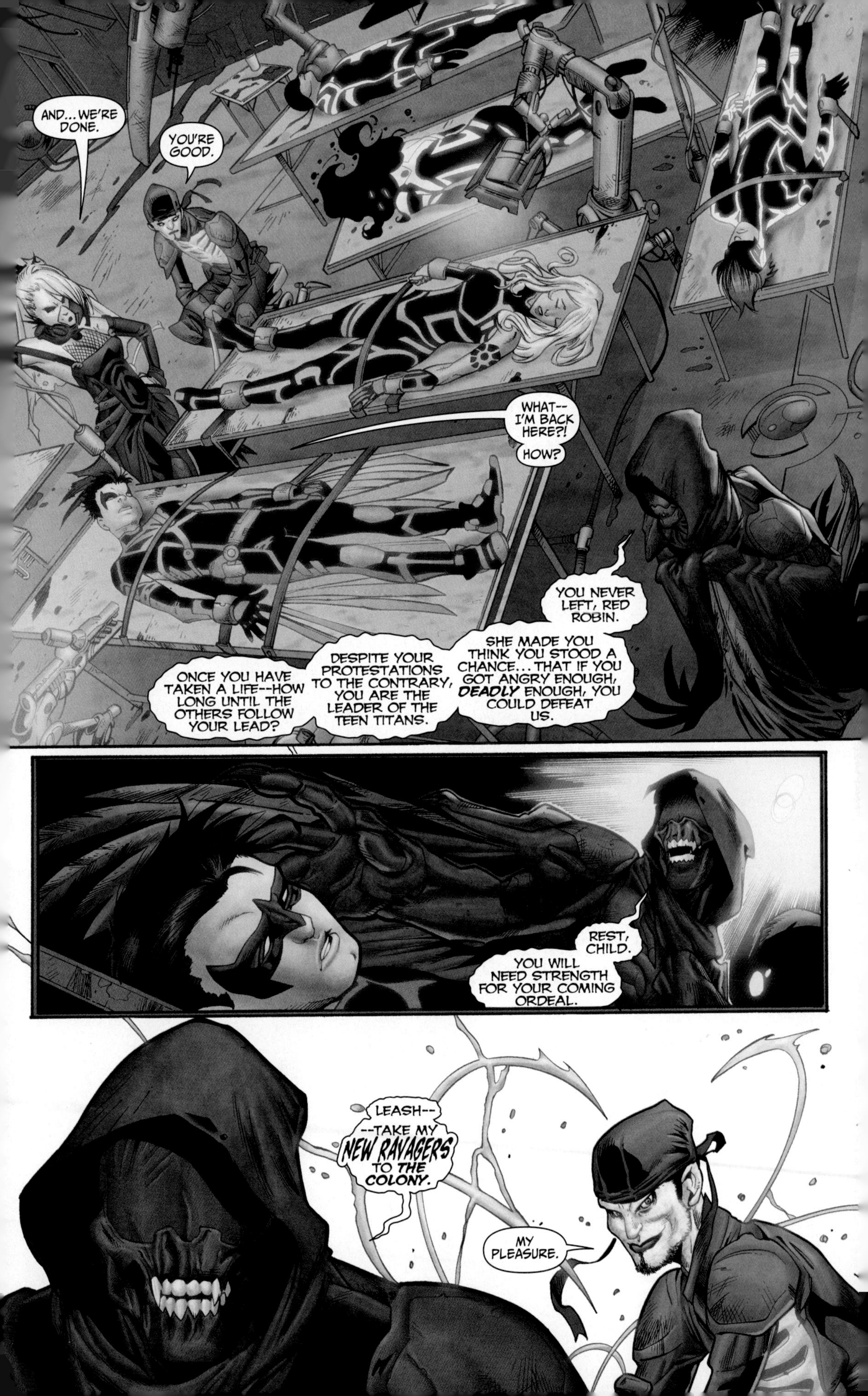
AND... WE'RE DONE.
YOU'RE GOOD.
WHAT-- I'M BACK HERE?!
HOW?
YOU NEVER LEFT, RED ROBIN.
SHE MADE YOU THINK YOU STOOD A CHANCE... THAT IF YOU GOT ANGRY ENOUGH, DEADLY ENOUGH, YOU COULD DEFEAT US.
DESPITE YOUR PROTESTATIONS TO THE CONTRARY, YOU ARE THE LEADER OF THE TEEN TITANS.
ONCE YOU HAVE TAKEN A LIFE--HOW LONG UNTIL THE OTHERS FOLLOW YOUR LEAD?
REST, CHILD.
YOU WILL NEED STRENGTH FOR YOUR COMING ORDEAL.
LEASH--
--TAKE MY NEW RAVAGERS TO THE COLONY.
MY PLEASURE.

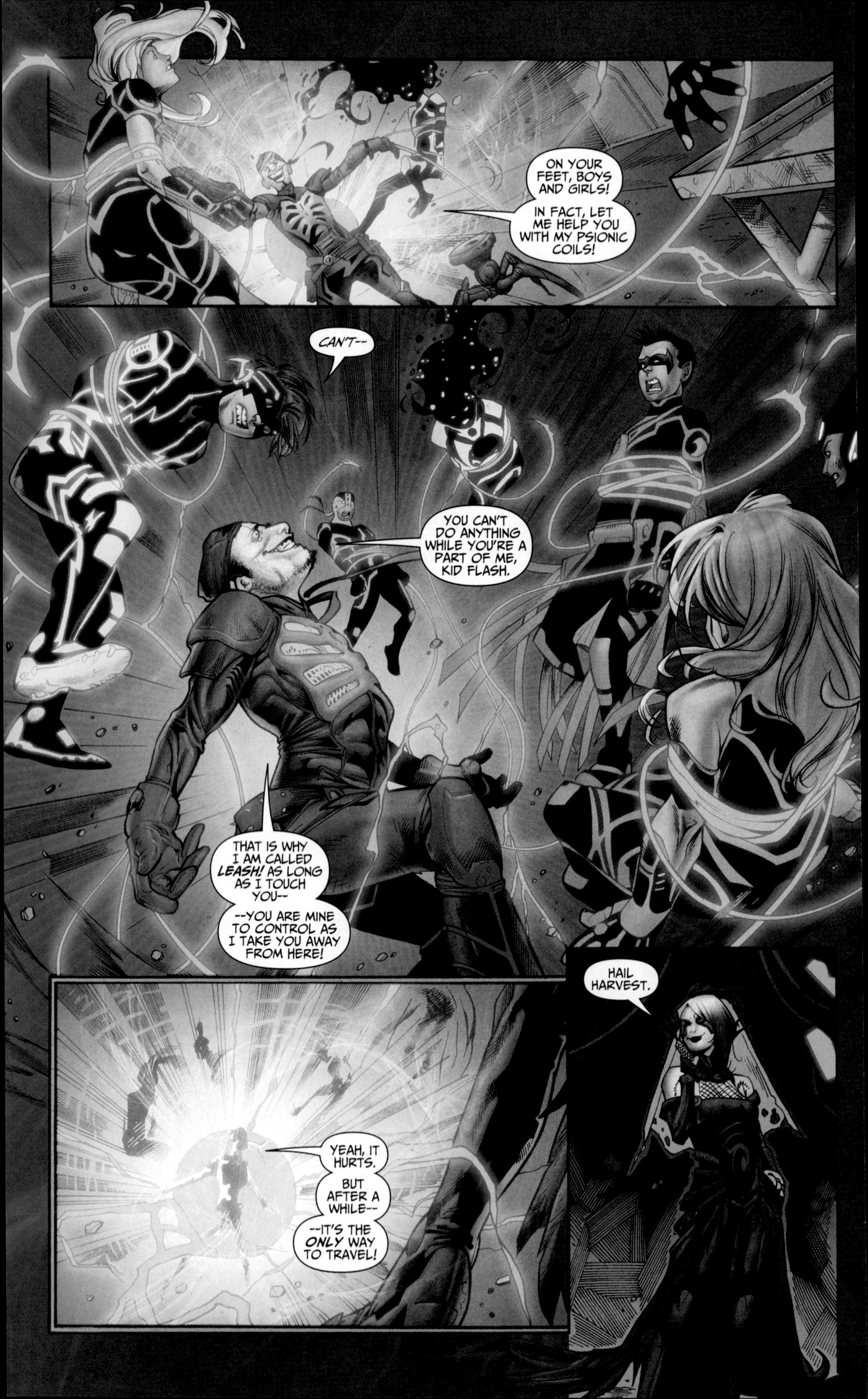
ON YOUR FEET, BOYS AND GIRLS!
IN FACT, LET ME HELP YOU WITH MY PSIONIC COILS!
CAN'T--
YOU CAN'T DO ANYTHING WHILE YOU'RE A PART OF ME, KID FLASH.
THAT IS WHY I AM CALLED *LEASH!* AS LONG AS I TOUCH YOU--
--YOU ARE MINE TO CONTROL AS I TAKE YOU AWAY FROM HERE!
HAIL HARVEST.
YEAH, IT HURTS.
BUT AFTER A WHILE--
--IT'S THE *ONLY* WAY TO TRAVEL!

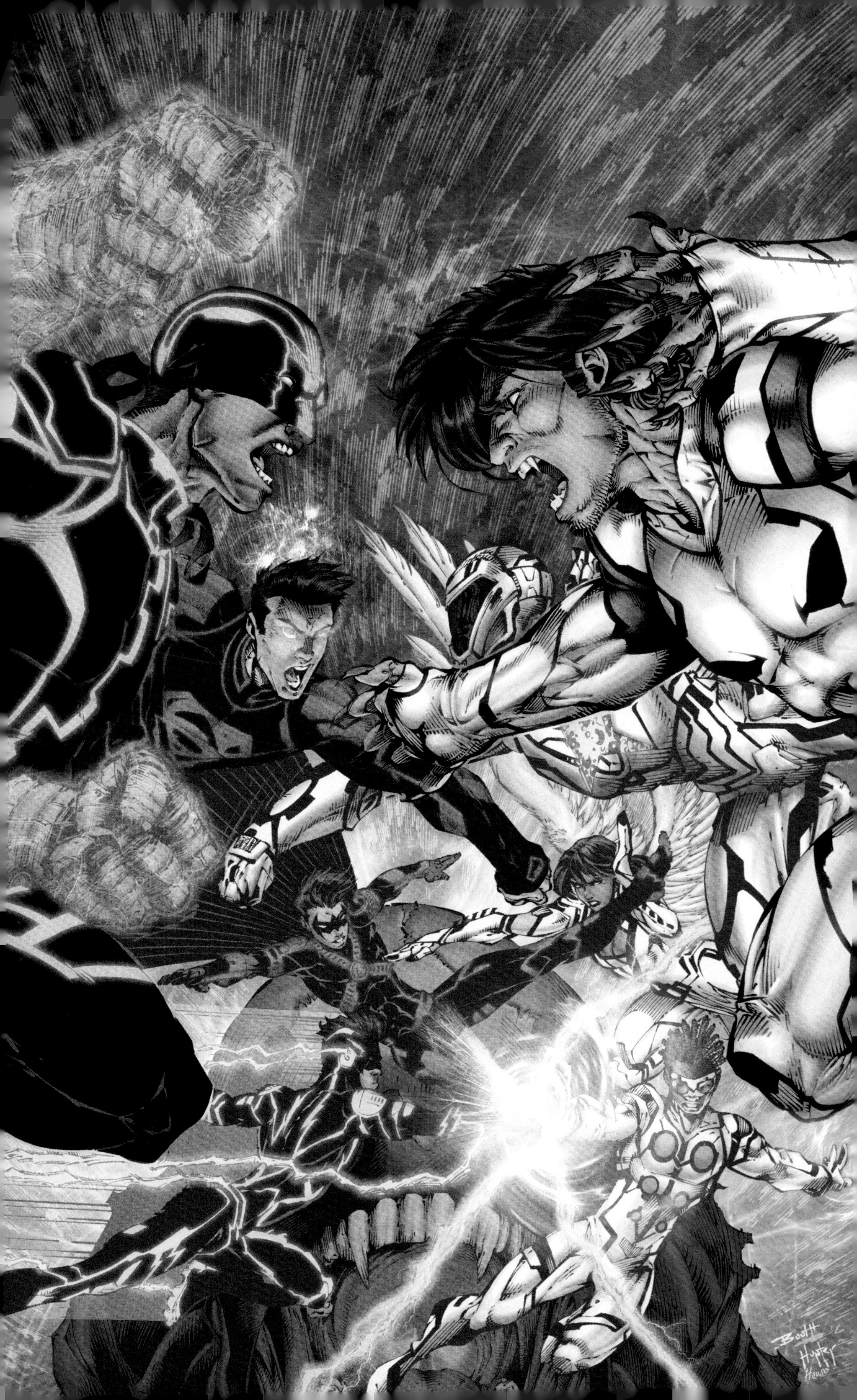

THE CULLING PART ONE

TOM DEFALCO SCOTT LOBDELL writers BRETT BOOTH penciller
NORM RAPMUND, SAL REGLA, MARLO ALQUIZA & JOHN LIVESAY inkers
cover art by BRETT BOOTH, ROB HUNTER & ANDREW DALHOUSE

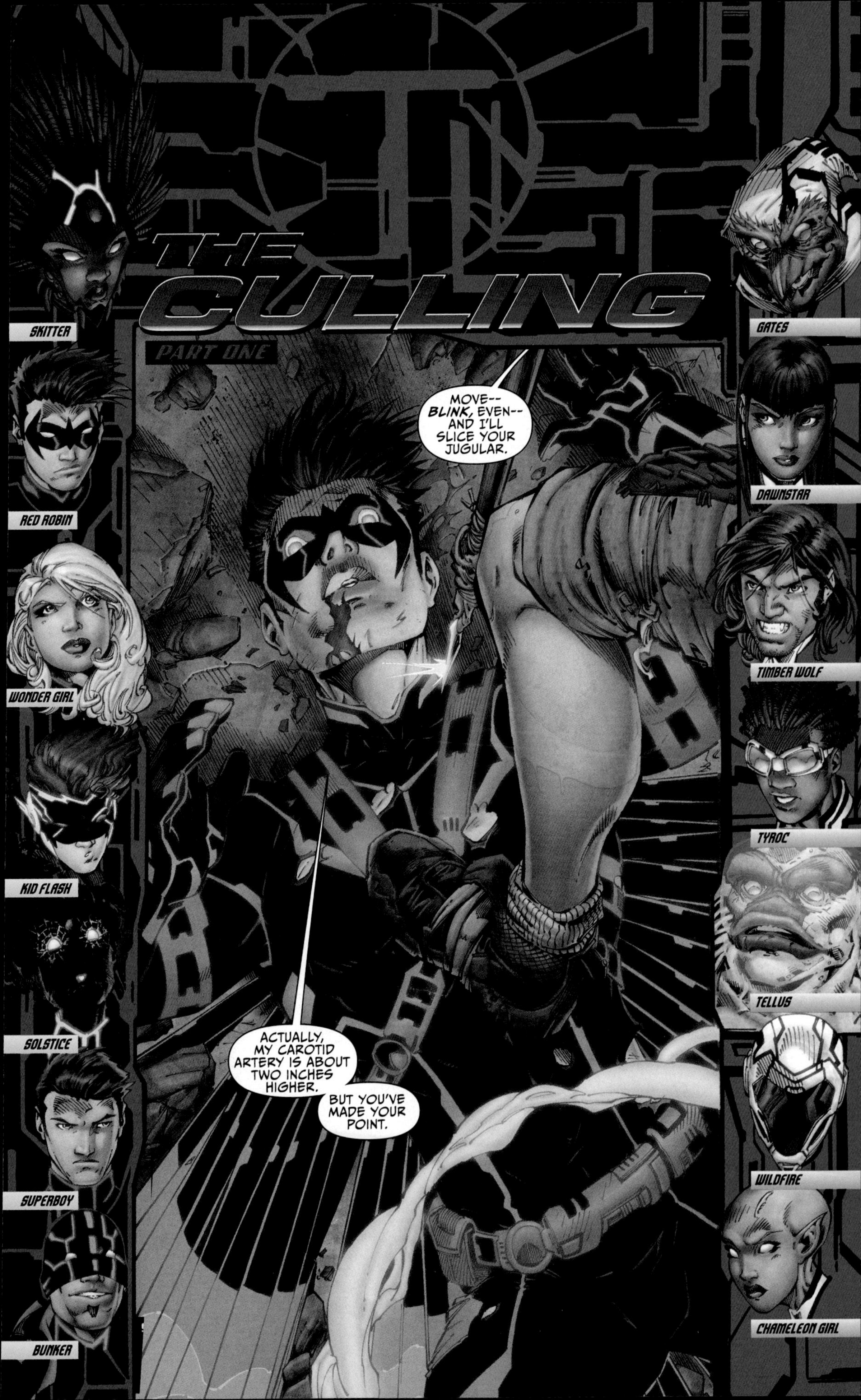
THE CULLING
PART ONE
SKITTER
RED ROBIN
WONDER GIRL
KID FLASH
SOLSTICE
SUPERBOY
BUNKER
GATES
DAWNSTAR
TIMBER WOLF
TYROC
TELLUS
WILDFIRE
CHAMELEON GIRL
MOVE-- BLINK, EVEN-- AND I'LL SLICE YOUR JUGULAR.
ACTUALLY, MY CAROTID ARTERY IS ABOUT TWO INCHES HIGHER.
BUT YOU'VE MADE YOUR POINT.

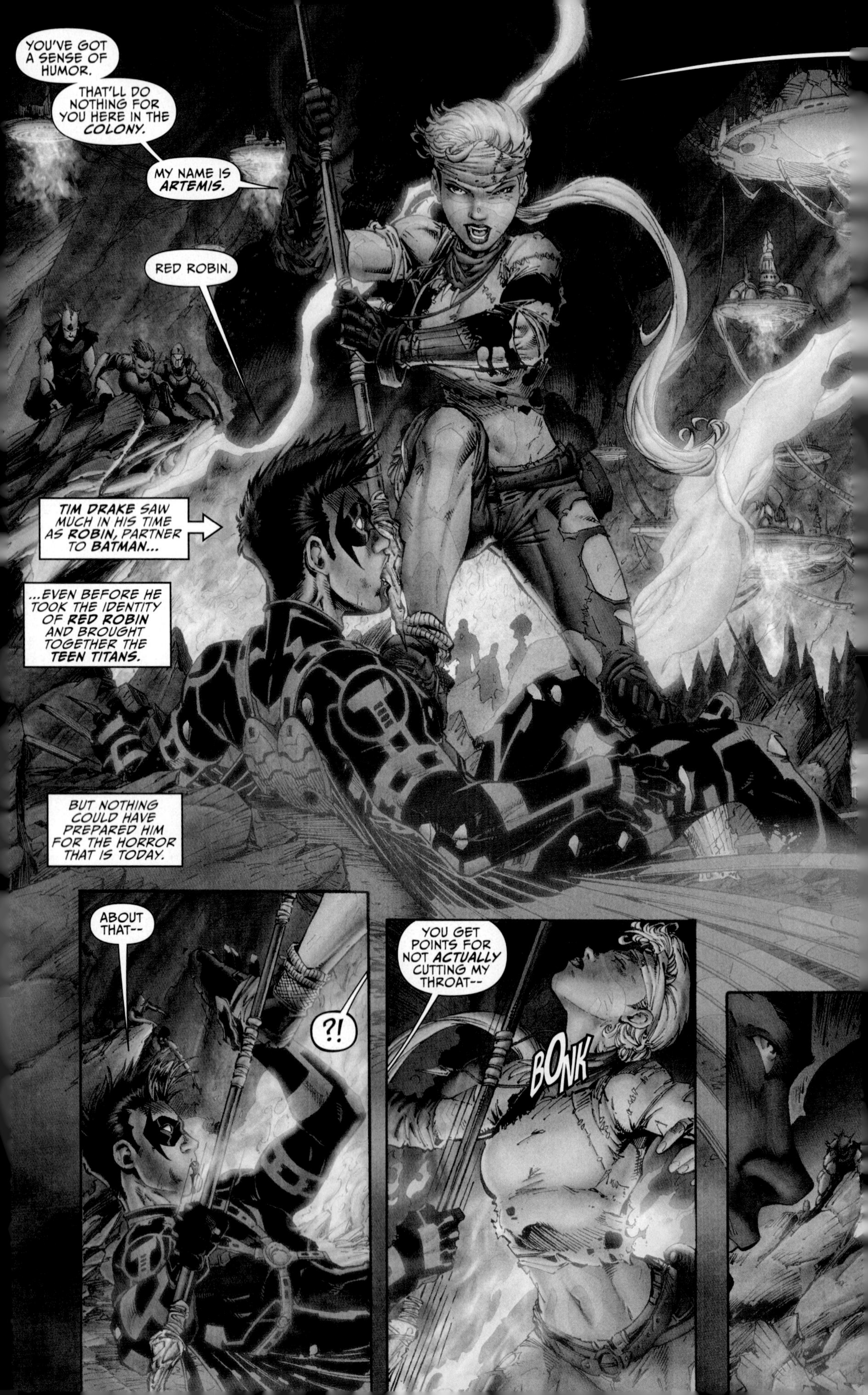

YOU'VE GOT A SENSE OF HUMOR.
THAT'LL DO NOTHING FOR YOU HERE IN THE COLONY.
MY NAME IS ARTEMIS.
RED ROBIN.
TIM DRAKE SAW MUCH IN HIS TIME AS ROBIN, PARTNER TO BATMAN...
...EVEN BEFORE HE TOOK THE IDENTITY OF RED ROBIN AND BROUGHT TOGETHER THE TEEN TITANS.
BUT NOTHING COULD HAVE PREPARED HIM FOR THE HORROR THAT IS TODAY.
ABOUT THAT--
?!
YOU GET POINTS FOR NOT ACTUALLY CUTTING MY THROAT--
BONK

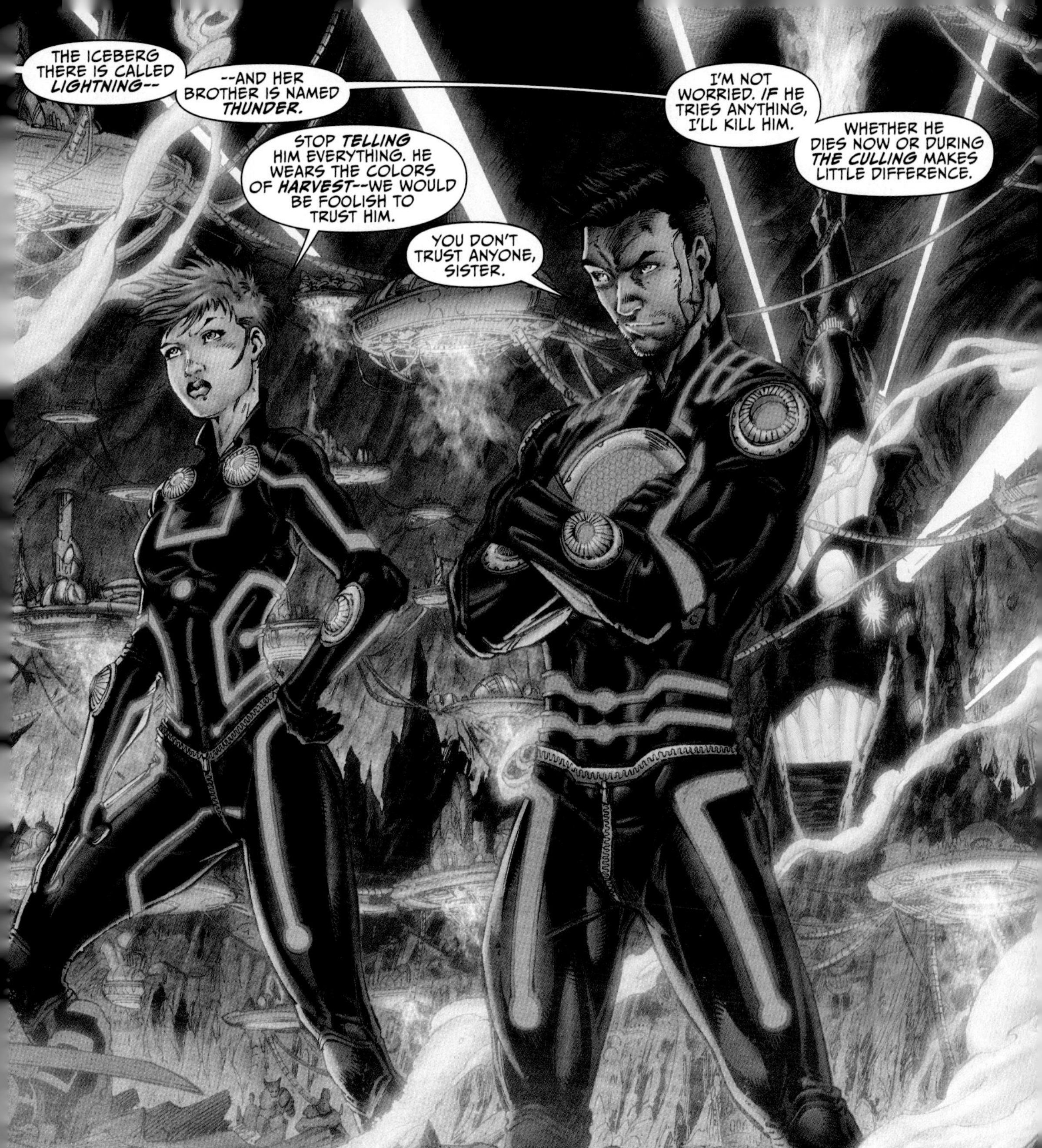
THE ICEBERG THERE IS CALLED LIGHTNING--
--AND HER BROTHER IS NAMED THUNDER.
STOP TELLING HIM EVERYTHING. HE WEARS THE COLORS OF HARVEST--WE WOULD BE FOOLISH TO TRUST HIM.
YOU DON'T TRUST ANYONE, SISTER.
I'M NOT WORRIED. IF HE TRIES ANYTHING, I'LL KILL HIM.
WHETHER HE DIES NOW OR DURING THE CULLING MAKES LITTLE DIFFERENCE.

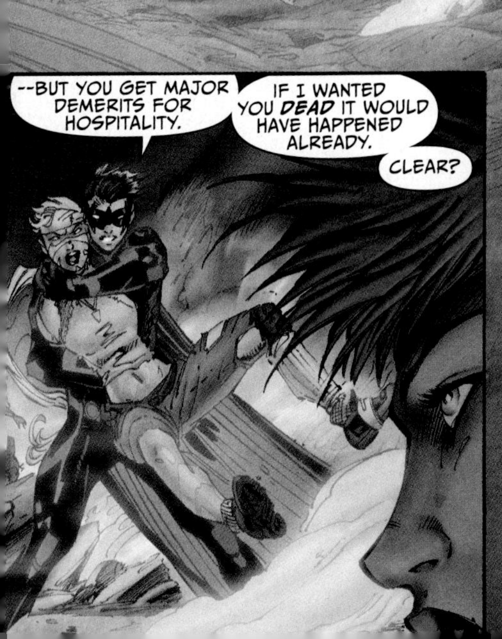
--BUT YOU GET MAJOR DEMERITS FOR HOSPITALITY.
IF I WANTED YOU DEAD IT WOULD HAVE HAPPENED ALREADY.
CLEAR?

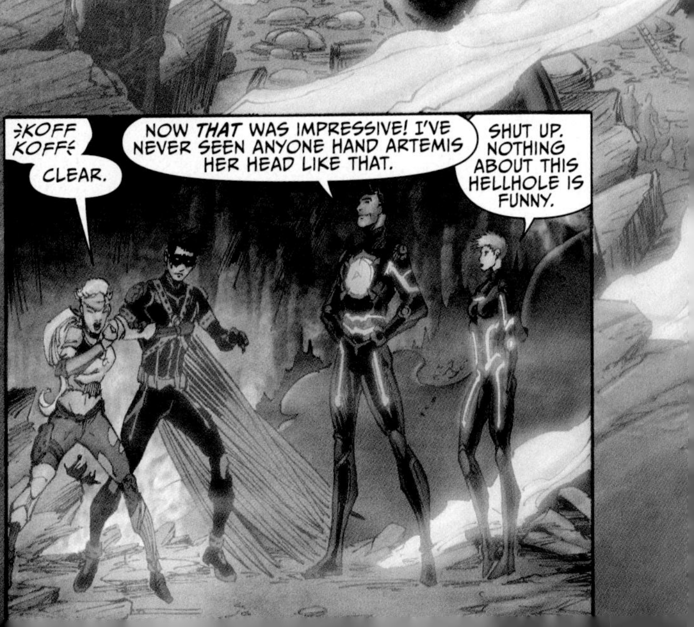
KOFF KOFF
CLEAR.
NOW THAT WAS IMPRESSIVE! I'VE NEVER SEEN ANYONE HAND ARTEMIS HER HEAD LIKE THAT.
SHUT UP. NOTHING ABOUT THIS HELLHOLE IS FUNNY.

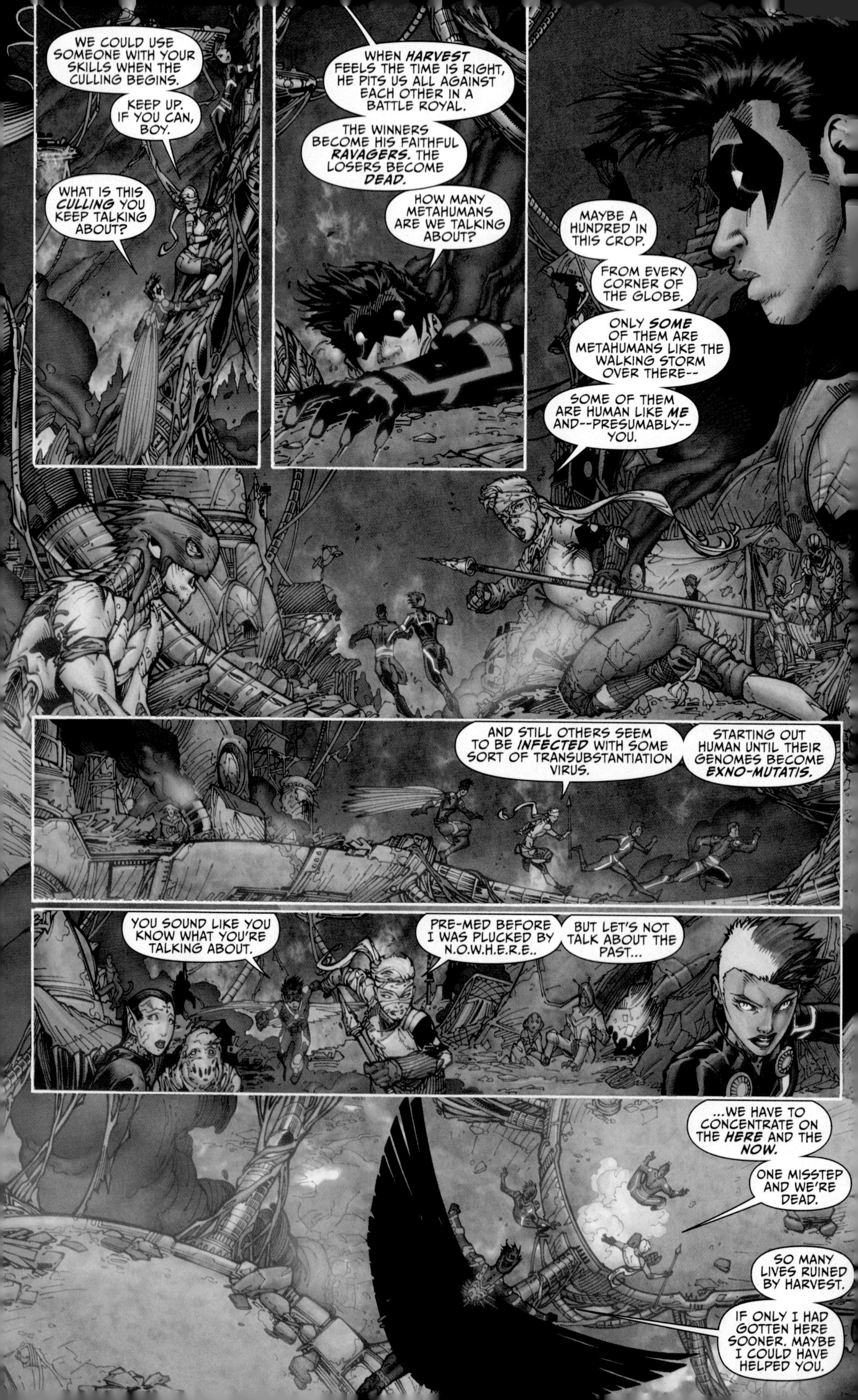
WE COULD USE SOMEONE WITH YOUR SKILLS WHEN THE CULLING BEGINS.
KEEP UP. IF YOU CAN, BOY.
WHAT IS THIS CULLING YOU KEEP TALKING ABOUT?
WHEN HARVEST FEELS THE TIME IS RIGHT, HE PITS US ALL AGAINST EACH OTHER IN A BATTLE ROYAL.
THE WINNERS BECOME HIS FAITHFUL RAVAGERS. THE LOSERS BECOME DEAD.
HOW MANY METAHUMANS ARE WE TALKING ABOUT?
MAYBE A HUNDRED IN THIS CROP.
FROM EVERY CORNER OF THE GLOBE.
ONLY SOME OF THEM ARE METAHUMANS LIKE THE WALKING STORM OVER THERE--
SOME OF THEM ARE HUMAN LIKE ME AND--PRESUMABLY--YOU.
AND STILL OTHERS SEEM TO BE INFECTED WITH SOME SORT OF TRANSUBSTANTIATION VIRUS.
STARTING OUT HUMAN UNTIL THEIR GENOMES BECOME EXNO-MUTATIS.
YOU SOUND LIKE YOU KNOW WHAT YOU'RE TALKING ABOUT.
PRE-MED BEFORE I WAS PLUCKED BY N.O.W.H.E.R.E..
BUT LET'S NOT TALK ABOUT THE PAST...
...WE HAVE TO CONCENTRATE ON THE HERE AND THE NOW.
ONE MISSTEP AND WE'RE DEAD.
SO MANY LIVES RUINED BY HARVEST.
IF ONLY I HAD GOTTEN HERE SOONER. MAYBE I COULD HAVE HELPED YOU.

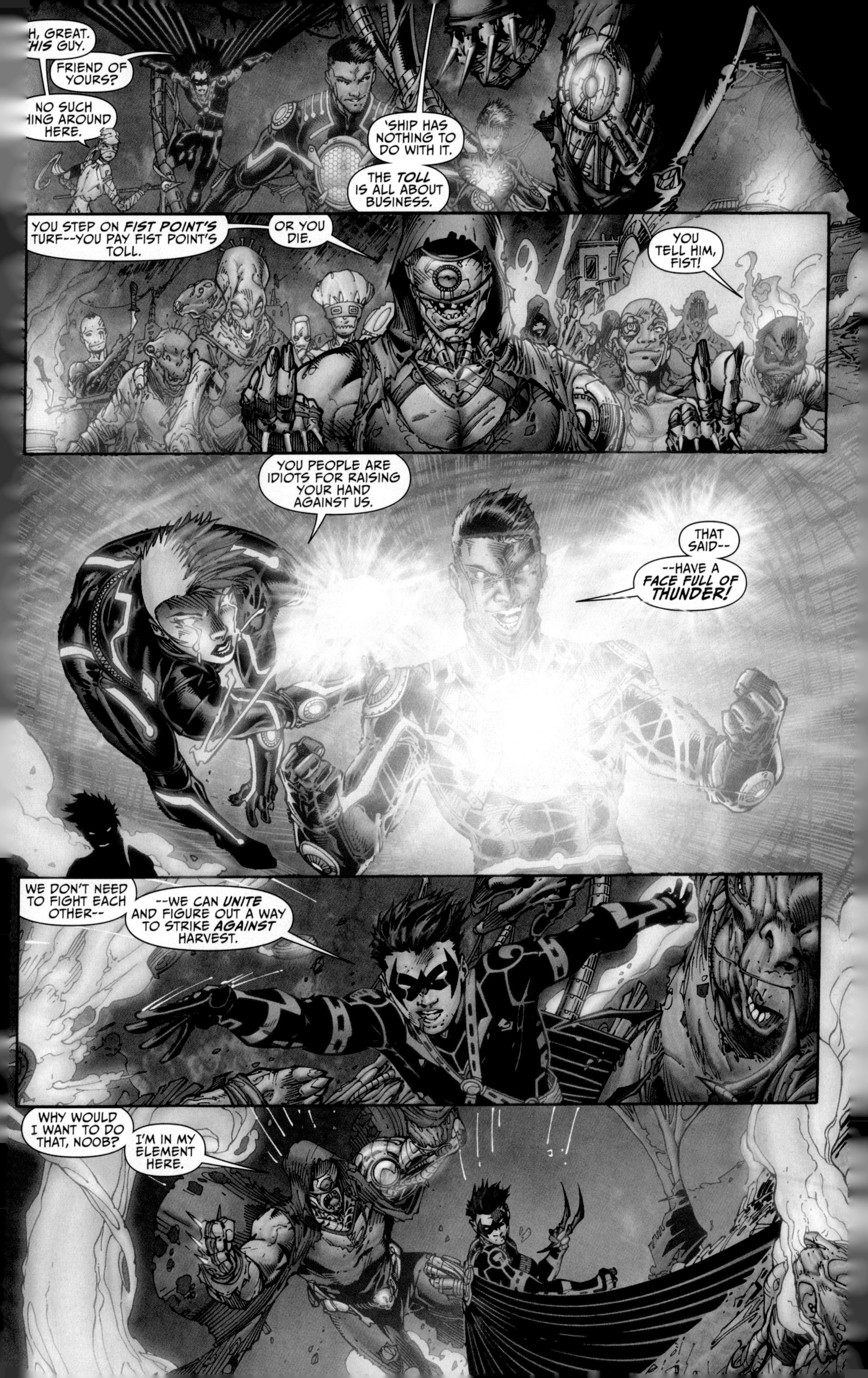

H, GREAT. THIS GUY.
FRIEND OF YOURS?
NO SUCH HING AROUND HERE.
'SHIP HAS NOTHING TO DO WITH IT.
THE TOLL IS ALL ABOUT BUSINESS.
YOU STEP ON FIST POINT'S TURF--YOU PAY FIST POINT'S TOLL.
OR YOU DIE.
YOU TELL HIM, FIST!
YOU PEOPLE ARE IDIOTS FOR RAISING YOUR HAND AGAINST US.
THAT SAID--
--HAVE A FACE FULL OF THUNDER!
WE DON'T NEED TO FIGHT EACH OTHER--
--WE CAN UNITE AND FIGURE OUT A WAY TO STRIKE AGAINST HARVEST.
WHY WOULD I WANT TO DO THAT, NOOB?
I'M IN MY ELEMENT HERE.

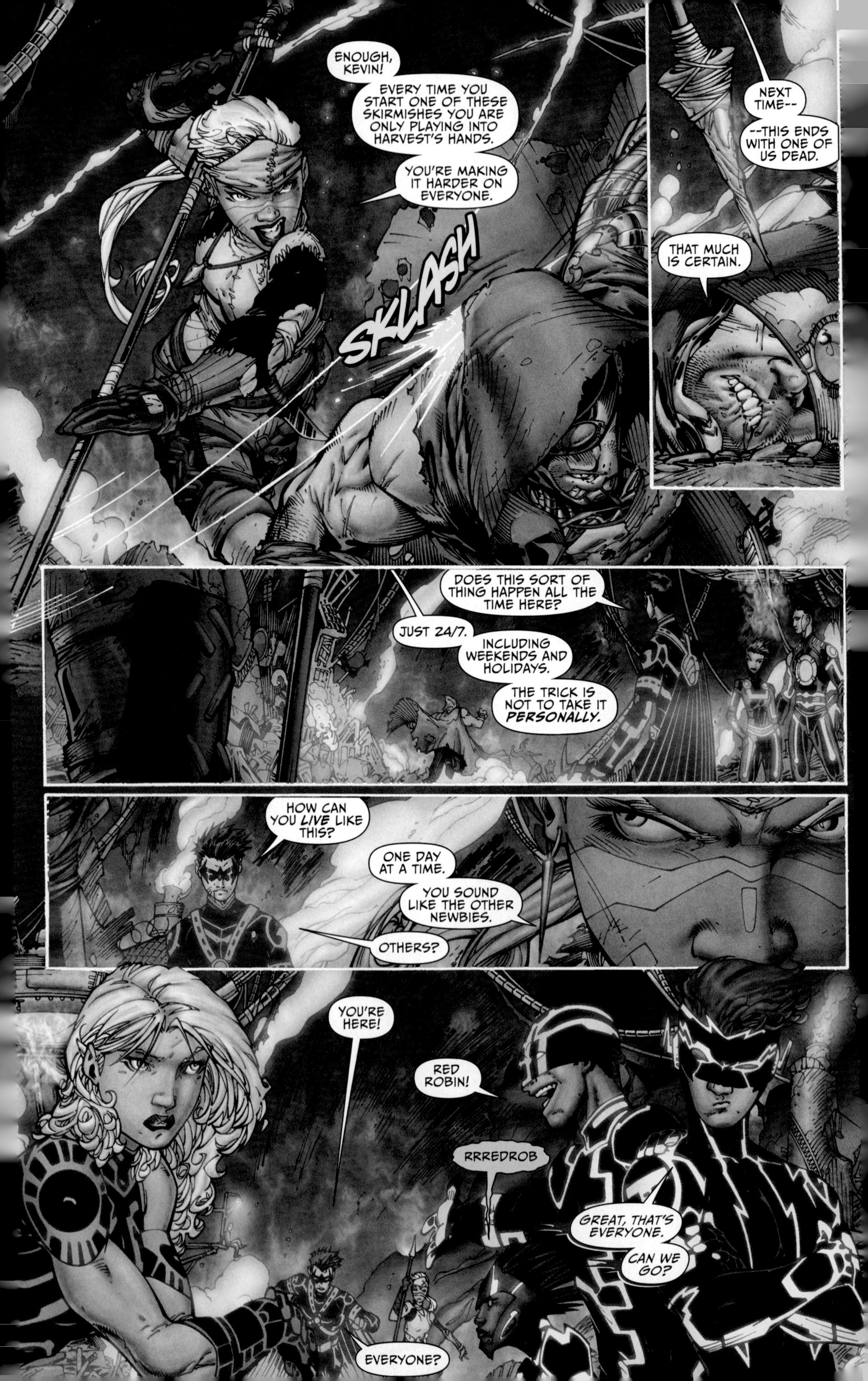

ENOUGH, KEVIN!
EVERY TIME YOU START ONE OF THESE SKIRMISHES YOU ARE ONLY PLAYING INTO HARVEST'S HANDS.
YOU'RE MAKING IT HARDER ON EVERYONE.
SKLASH
NEXT TIME--
--THIS ENDS WITH ONE OF US DEAD.
THAT MUCH IS CERTAIN.
DOES THIS SORT OF THING HAPPEN ALL THE TIME HERE?
JUST 24/7.
INCLUDING WEEKENDS AND HOLIDAYS.
THE TRICK IS NOT TO TAKE IT PERSONALLY.
HOW CAN YOU LIVE LIKE THIS?
ONE DAY AT A TIME.
YOU SOUND LIKE THE OTHER NEWBIES.
OTHERS?
YOU'RE HERE!
RED ROBIN!
RRREDROB
GREAT, THAT'S EVERYONE.
CAN WE GO?
EVERYONE?

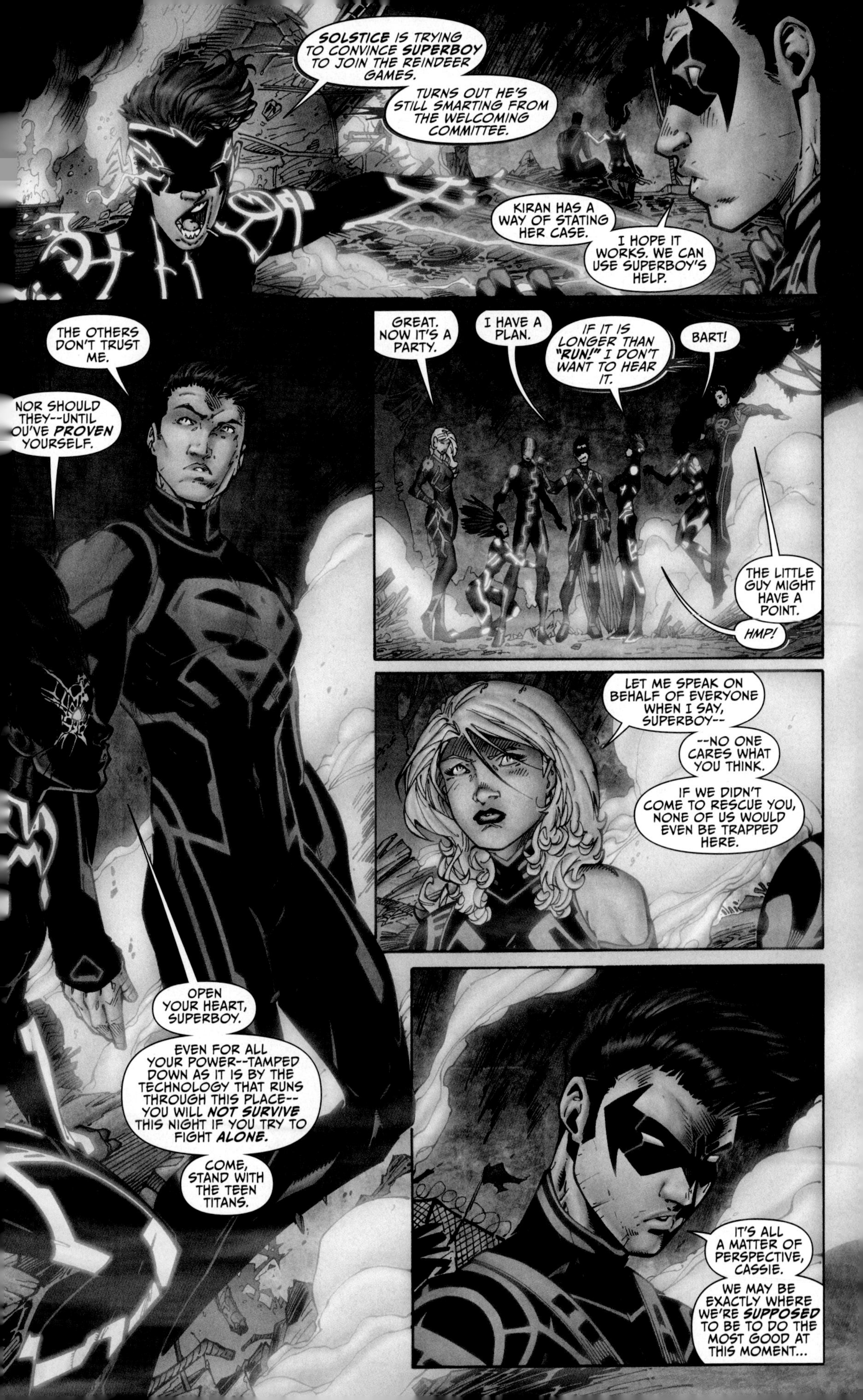
SOLSTICE IS TRYING TO CONVINCE SUPERBOY TO JOIN THE REINDEER GAMES.
TURNS OUT HE'S STILL SMARTING FROM THE WELCOMING COMMITTEE.
KIRAN HAS A WAY OF STATING HER CASE.
I HOPE IT WORKS. WE CAN USE SUPERBOY'S HELP.
THE OTHERS DON'T TRUST ME.
NOR SHOULD THEY--UNTIL OU'VE PROVEN YOURSELF.
GREAT. NOW IT'S A PARTY.
I HAVE A PLAN.
IF IT IS LONGER THAN "RUN!" I DON'T WANT TO HEAR IT.
BART!
THE LITTLE GUY MIGHT HAVE A POINT.
HMP!
LET ME SPEAK ON BEHALF OF EVERYONE WHEN I SAY, SUPERBOY--
--NO ONE CARES WHAT YOU THINK.
IF WE DIDN'T COME TO RESCUE YOU, NONE OF US WOULD EVEN BE TRAPPED HERE.
OPEN YOUR HEART, SUPERBOY.
EVEN FOR ALL YOUR POWER--TAMPED DOWN AS IT IS BY THE TECHNOLOGY THAT RUNS THROUGH THIS PLACE--YOU WILL NOT SURVIVE THIS NIGHT IF YOU TRY TO FIGHT ALONE.
COME, STAND WITH THE TEEN TITANS.
IT'S ALL A MATTER OF PERSPECTIVE, CASSIE.
WE MAY BE EXACTLY WHERE WE'RE SUPPOSED TO BE TO DO THE MOST GOOD AT THIS MOMENT...

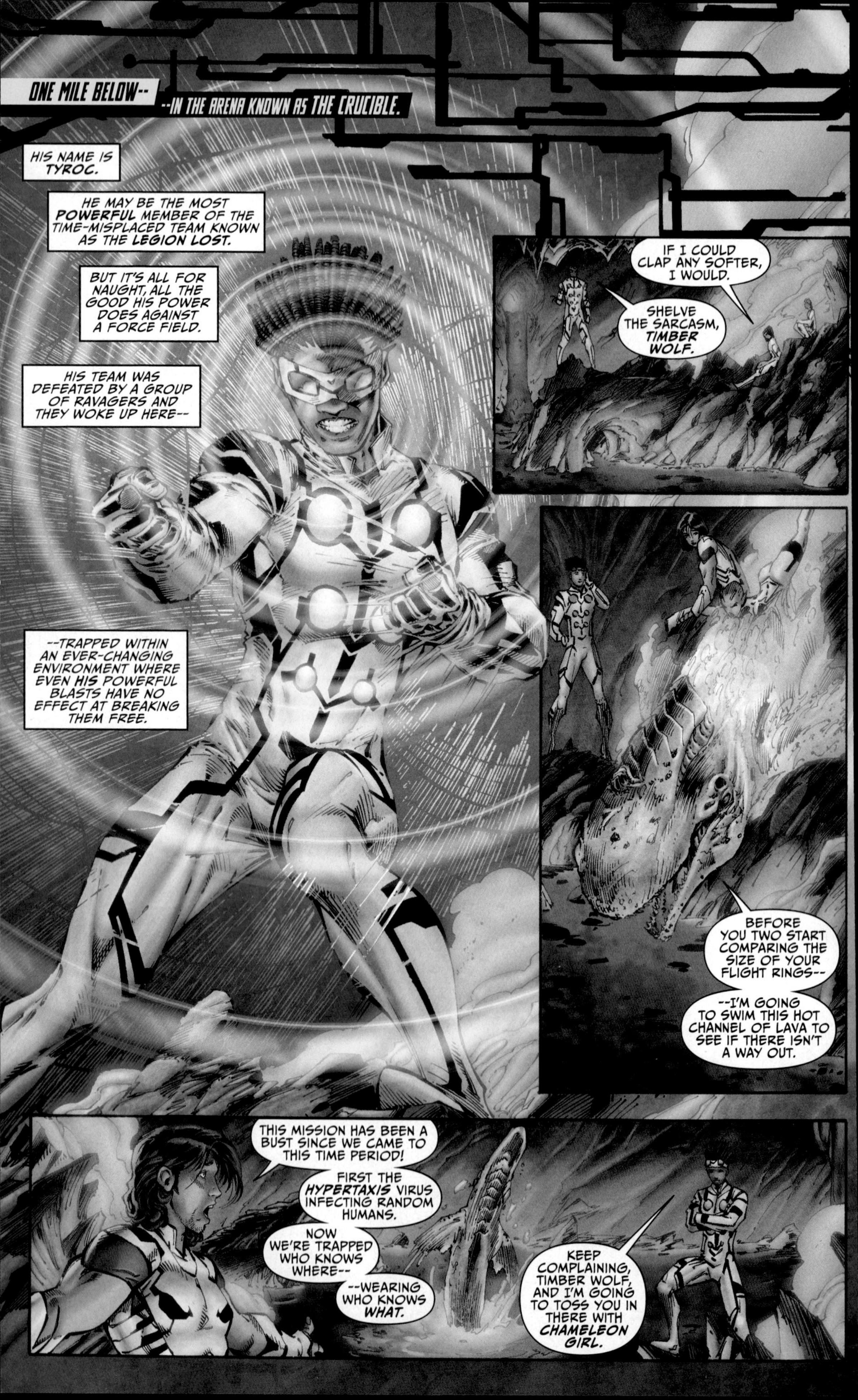
ONE MILE BELOW--
--IN THE ARENA KNOWN AS THE CRUCIBLE.
HIS NAME IS TYROC.
HE MAY BE THE MOST POWERFUL MEMBER OF THE TIME-MISPLACED TEAM KNOWN AS THE LEGION LOST.
BUT IT'S ALL FOR NAUGHT, ALL THE GOOD HIS POWER DOES AGAINST A FORCE FIELD.
HIS TEAM WAS DEFEATED BY A GROUP OF RAVAGERS AND THEY WOKE UP HERE--
--TRAPPED WITHIN AN EVER-CHANGING ENVIRONMENT WHERE EVEN HIS POWERFUL BLASTS HAVE NO EFFECT AT BREAKING THEM FREE.
IF I COULD CLAP ANY SOFTER, I WOULD.
SHELVE THE SARCASM, TIMBER WOLF.
BEFORE YOU TWO START COMPARING THE SIZE OF YOUR FLIGHT RINGS--
--I'M GOING TO SWIM THIS HOT CHANNEL OF LAVA TO SEE IF THERE ISN'T A WAY OUT.
THIS MISSION HAS BEEN A BUST SINCE WE CAME TO THIS TIME PERIOD!
FIRST THE HYPERTAXIS VIRUS INFECTING RANDOM HUMANS.
NOW WE'RE TRAPPED WHO KNOWS WHERE--
--WEARING WHO KNOWS WHAT.
KEEP COMPLAINING, TIMBER WOLF, AND I'M GOING TO TOSS YOU IN THERE WITH CHAMELEON GIRL.

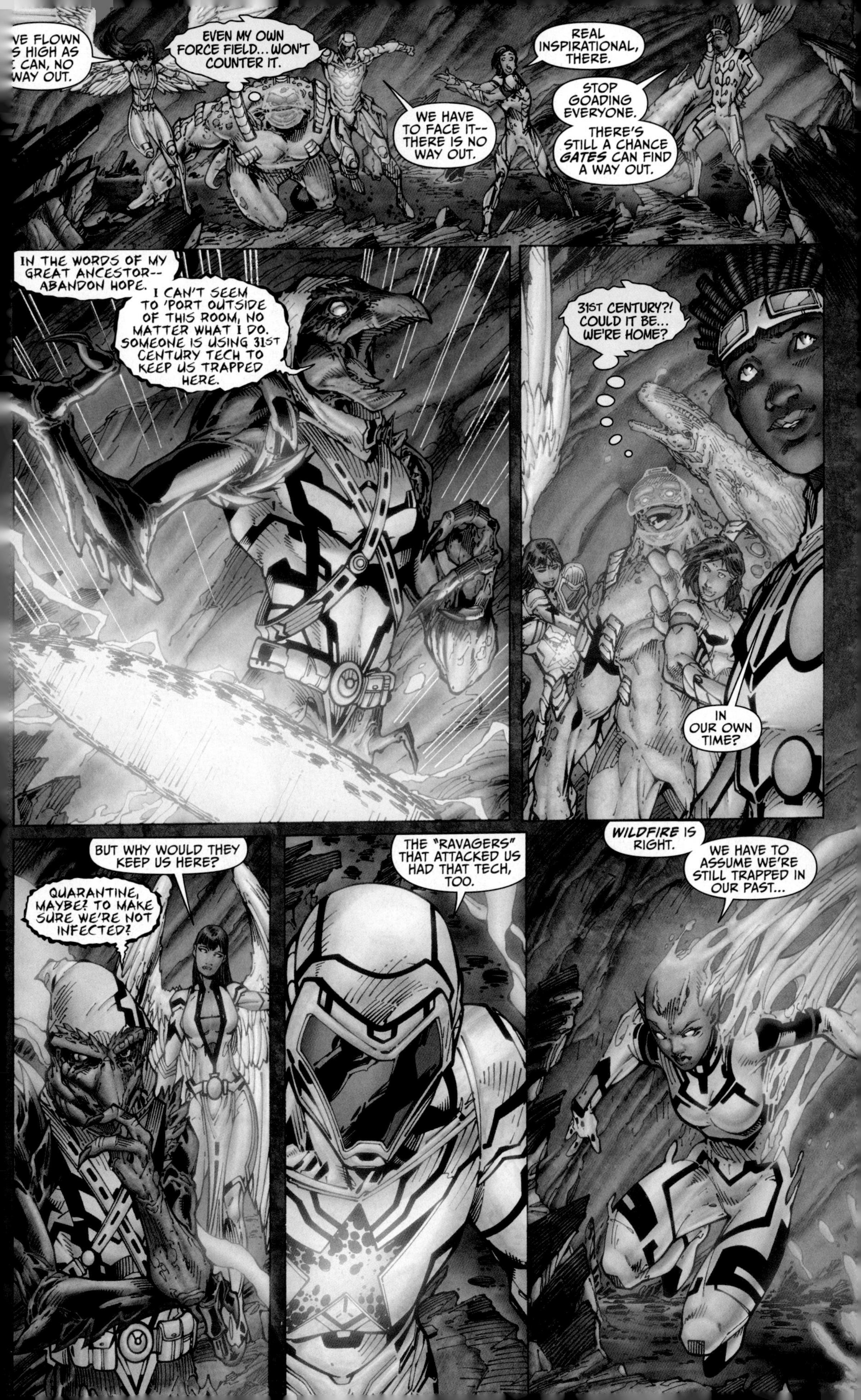

VE FLOWN S HIGH AS E CAN, NO WAY OUT.
EVEN MY OWN FORCE FIELD... WON'T COUNTER IT.
WE HAVE TO FACE IT-- THERE IS NO WAY OUT.
REAL INSPIRATIONAL, THERE.
STOP GOADING EVERYONE.
THERE'S STILL A CHANCE GATES CAN FIND A WAY OUT.
IN THE WORDS OF MY GREAT ANCESTOR-- ABANDON HOPE.
I CAN'T SEEM TO 'PORT OUTSIDE OF THIS ROOM, NO MATTER WHAT I DO. SOMEONE IS USING 31ST CENTURY TECH TO KEEP US TRAPPED HERE.
31ST CENTURY?! COULD IT BE... WE'RE HOME?
IN OUR OWN TIME?
BUT WHY WOULD THEY KEEP US HERE?
QUARANTINE, MAYBE? TO MAKE SURE WE'RE NOT INFECTED?
THE "RAVAGERS" THAT ATTACKED US HAD THAT TECH, TOO.
WILDFIRE IS RIGHT.
WE HAVE TO ASSUME WE'RE STILL TRAPPED IN OUR PAST...

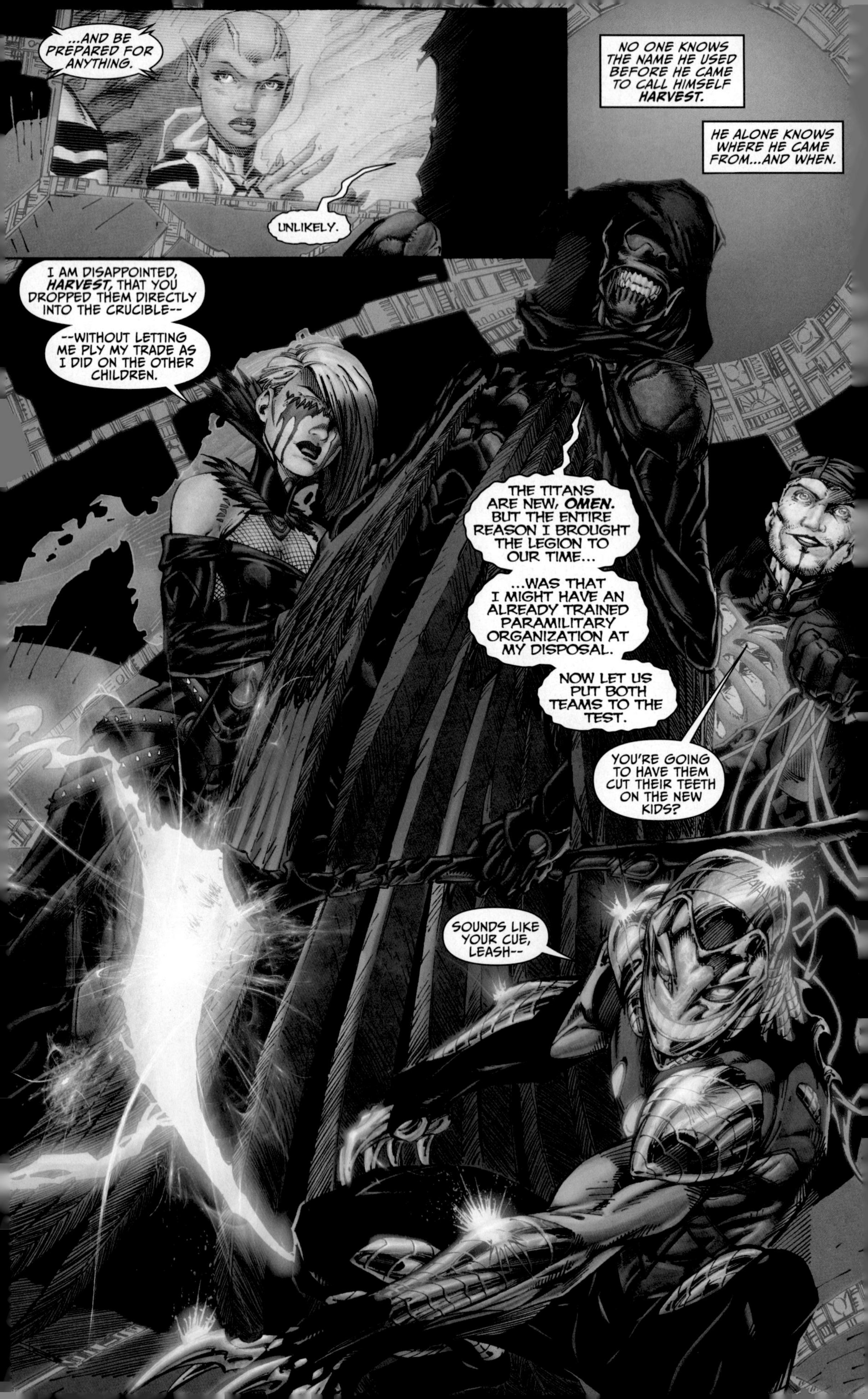
...AND BE PREPARED FOR ANYTHING.
NO ONE KNOWS THE NAME HE USED BEFORE HE CAME TO CALL HIMSELF HARVEST.
HE ALONE KNOWS WHERE HE CAME FROM...AND WHEN.
UNLIKELY.
I AM DISAPPOINTED, HARVEST, THAT YOU DROPPED THEM DIRECTLY INTO THE CRUCIBLE--
--WITHOUT LETTING ME PLY MY TRADE AS I DID ON THE OTHER CHILDREN.
THE TITANS ARE NEW, OMEN. BUT THE ENTIRE REASON I BROUGHT THE LEGION TO OUR TIME...
...WAS THAT I MIGHT HAVE AN ALREADY TRAINED PARAMILITARY ORGANIZATION AT MY DISPOSAL.
NOW LET US PUT BOTH TEAMS TO THE TEST.
YOU'RE GOING TO HAVE THEM CUT THEIR TEETH ON THE NEW KIDS?
SOUNDS LIKE YOUR CUE, LEASH--

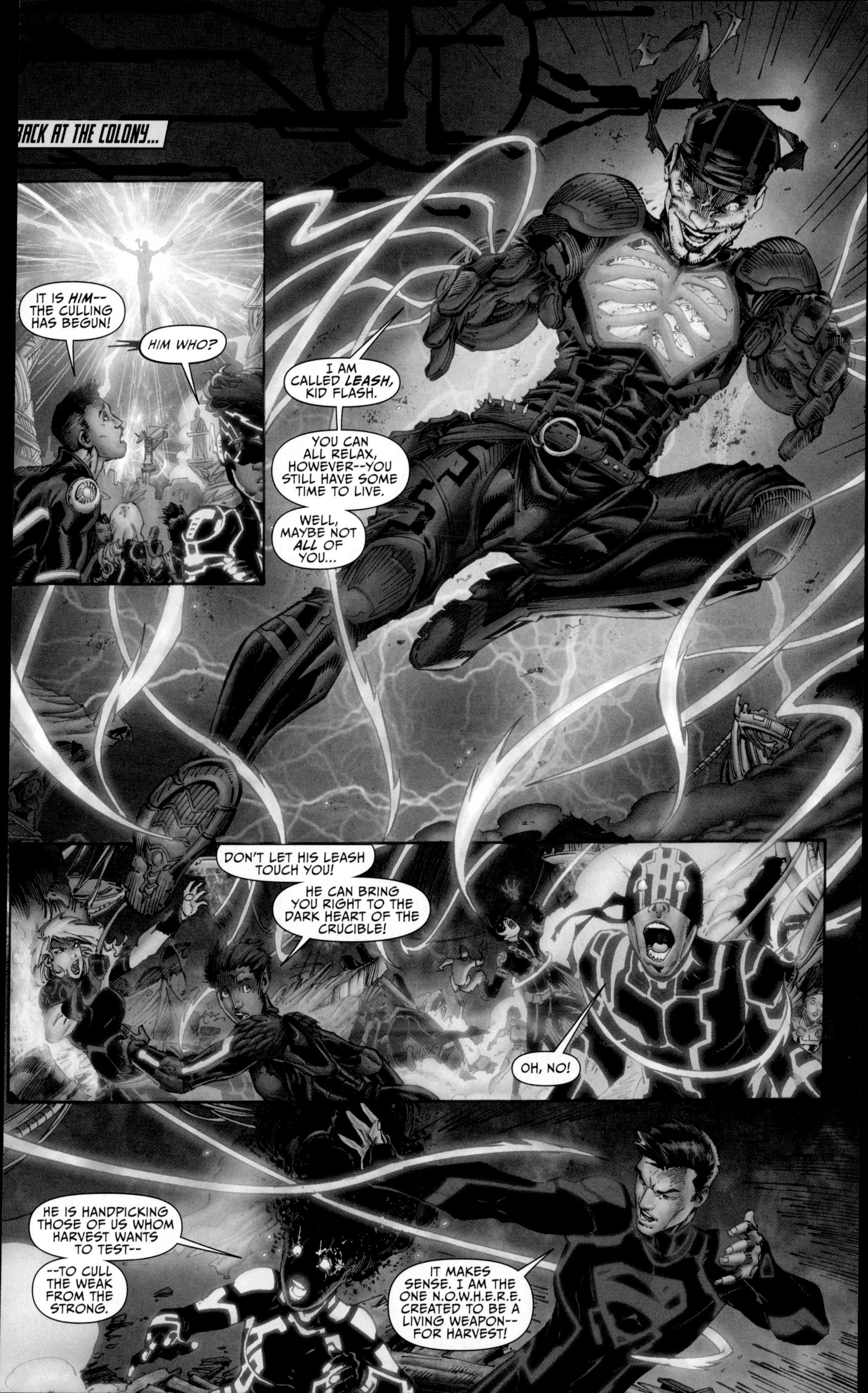
BACK AT THE COLONY...
IT IS HIM-- THE CULLING HAS BEGUN!
HIM WHO?
I AM CALLED LEASH, KID FLASH.
YOU CAN ALL RELAX, HOWEVER--YOU STILL HAVE SOME TIME TO LIVE.
WELL, MAYBE NOT ALL OF YOU...
DON'T LET HIS LEASH TOUCH YOU!
HE CAN BRING YOU RIGHT TO THE DARK HEART OF THE CRUCIBLE!
OH, NO!
HE IS HANDPICKING THOSE OF US WHOM HARVEST WANTS TO TEST--
--TO CULL THE WEAK FROM THE STRONG.
IT MAKES SENSE. I AM THE ONE N.O.W.H.E.R.E. CREATED TO BE A LIVING WEAPON-- FOR HARVEST!

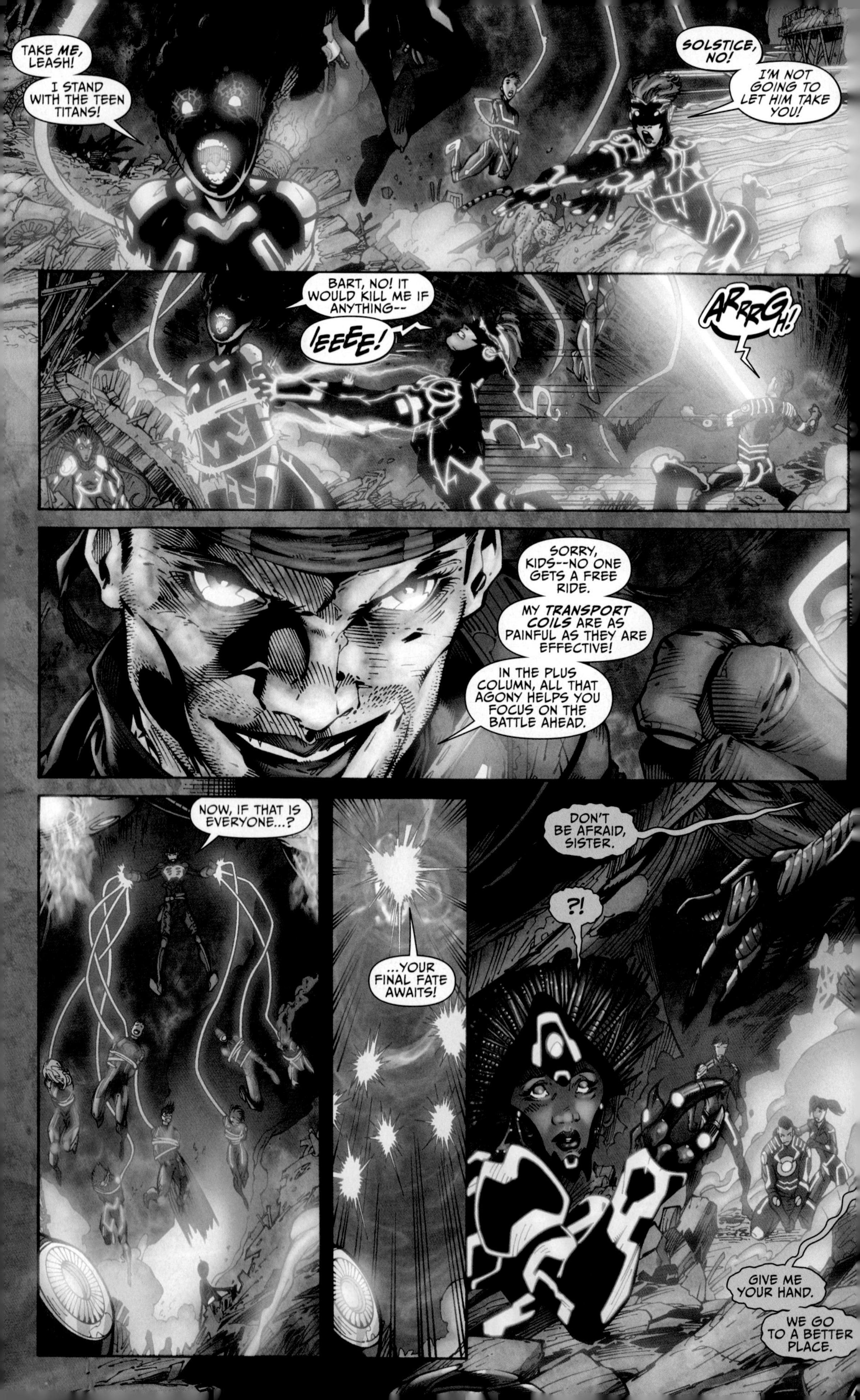
TAKE ME, LEASH!
I STAND WITH THE TEEN TITANS!
SOLSTICE, NO!
I'M NOT GOING TO LET HIM TAKE YOU!
BART, NO! IT WOULD KILL ME IF ANYTHING--
IEEEE!
ARRRGH!
SORRY, KIDS--NO ONE GETS A FREE RIDE.
MY TRANSPORT COILS ARE AS PAINFUL AS THEY ARE EFFECTIVE!
IN THE PLUS COLUMN, ALL THAT AGONY HELPS YOU FOCUS ON THE BATTLE AHEAD.
NOW, IF THAT IS EVERYONE...?
...YOUR FINAL FATE AWAITS!
DON'T BE AFRAID, SISTER.
?!
GIVE ME YOUR HAND.
WE GO TO A BETTER PLACE.

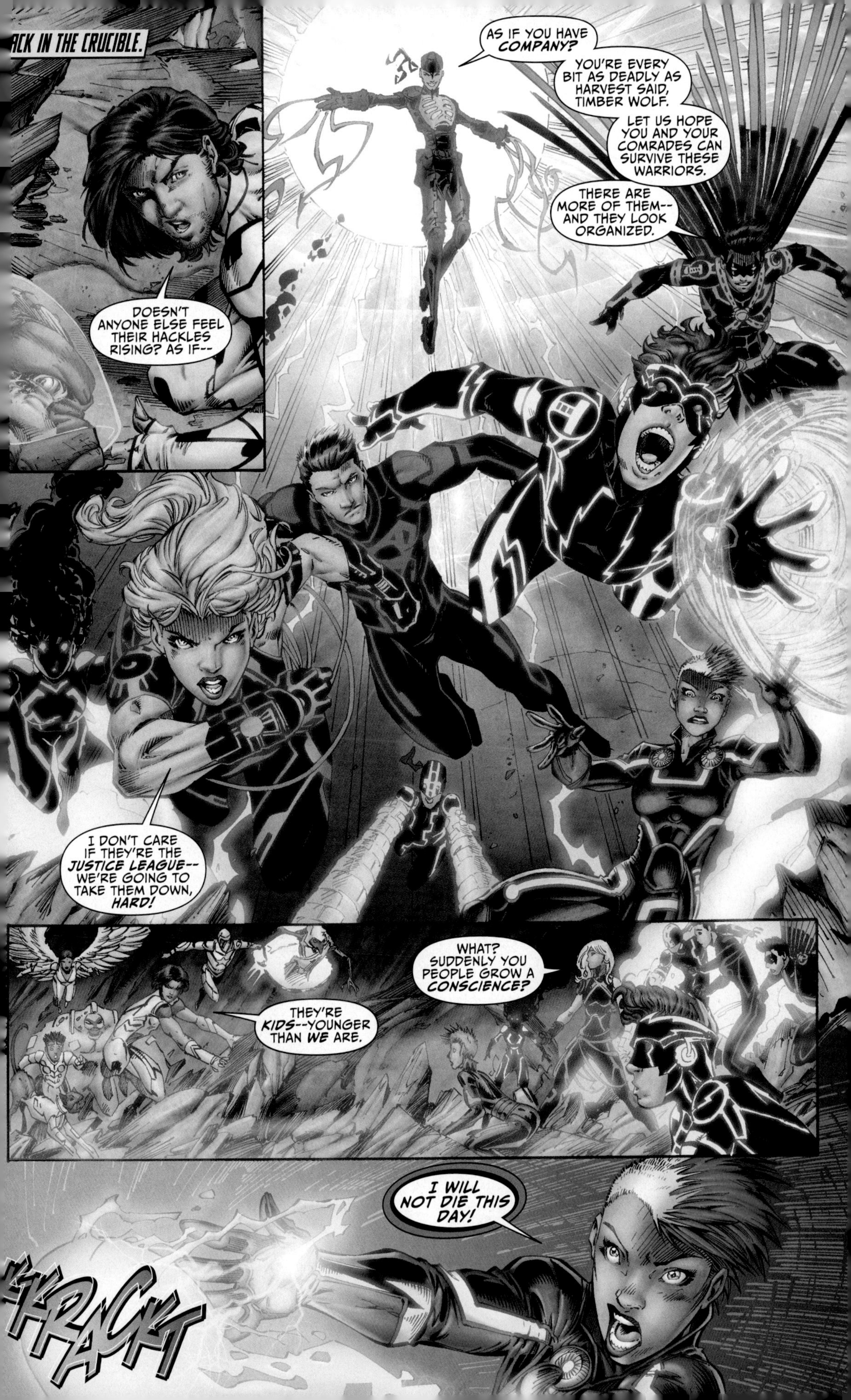

ACK IN THE CRUCIBLE.
DOESN'T ANYONE ELSE FEEL THEIR HACKLES RISING? AS IF--
AS IF YOU HAVE COMPANY?
YOU'RE EVERY BIT AS DEADLY AS HARVEST SAID, TIMBER WOLF.
LET US HOPE YOU AND YOUR COMRADES CAN SURVIVE THESE WARRIORS.
THERE ARE MORE OF THEM-- AND THEY LOOK ORGANIZED.
I DON'T CARE IF THEY'RE THE JUSTICE LEAGUE-- WE'RE GOING TO TAKE THEM DOWN, HARD!
THEY'RE KIDS--YOUNGER THAN WE ARE.
WHAT? SUDDENLY YOU PEOPLE GROW A CONSCIENCE?
I WILL NOT DIE THIS DAY!
KRACKT

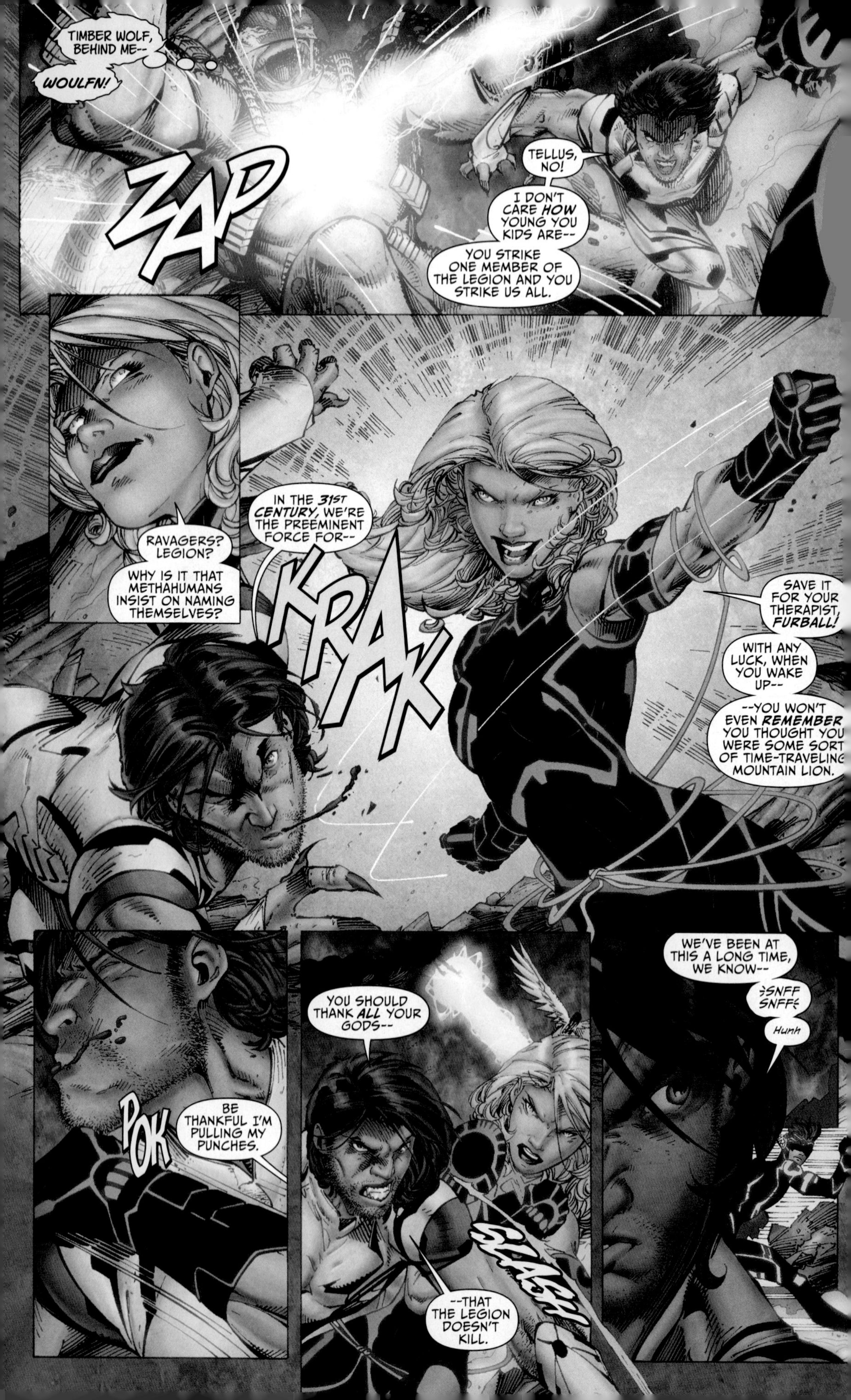

TIMBER WOLF, BEHIND ME--
WOULFN!
ZAP
TELLUS, NO!
I DON'T CARE HOW YOUNG YOU KIDS ARE--
YOU STRIKE ONE MEMBER OF THE LEGION AND YOU STRIKE US ALL.
RAVAGERS? LEGION?
WHY IS IT THAT METHAHUMANS INSIST ON NAMING THEMSELVES?
IN THE 31ST CENTURY, WE'RE THE PREEMINENT FORCE FOR--
KRAAK
SAVE IT FOR YOUR THERAPIST, FURBALL!
WITH ANY LUCK, WHEN YOU WAKE UP--
--YOU WON'T EVEN REMEMBER YOU THOUGHT YOU WERE SOME SORT OF TIME-TRAVELING MOUNTAIN LION.
POK
BE THANKFUL I'M PULLING MY PUNCHES.
YOU SHOULD THANK ALL YOUR GODS--
--THAT THE LEGION DOESN'T KILL.
SLASH
WE'VE BEEN AT THIS A LONG TIME, WE KNOW--
SNFF SNFF
Hunh

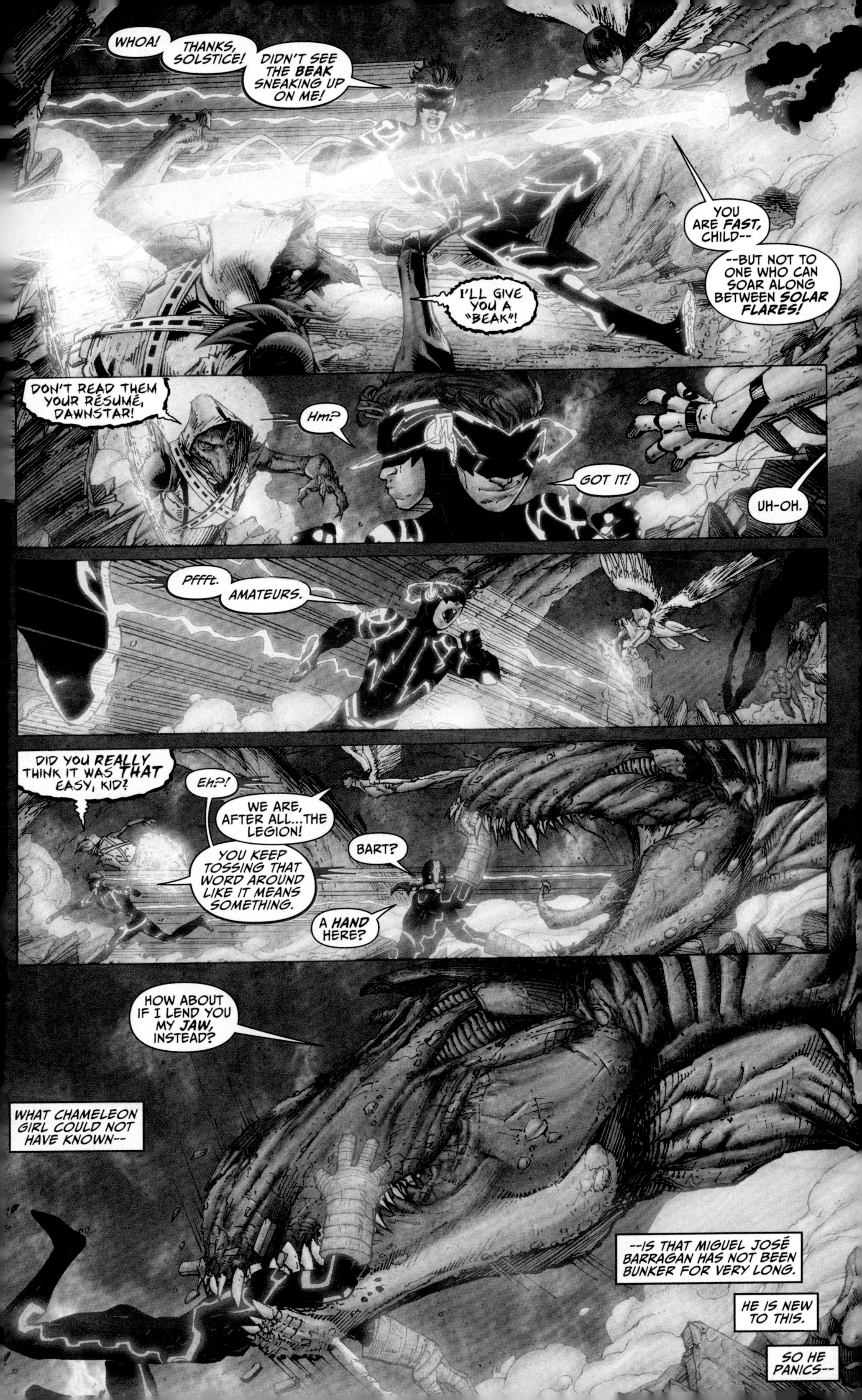
WHOA!
THANKS, SOLSTICE!
DIDN'T SEE THE BEAK SNEAKING UP ON ME!
YOU ARE FAST, CHILD--
--BUT NOT TO ONE WHO CAN SOAR ALONG BETWEEN SOLAR FLARES!
I'LL GIVE YOU A "BEAK"!
DON'T READ THEM YOUR RÉSUMÉ, DAWNSTAR!
Hm?
GOT IT!
UH-OH.
Pffft.
AMATEURS.
DID YOU REALLY THINK IT WAS THAT EASY, KID?
Eh?!
WE ARE, AFTER ALL...THE LEGION!
YOU KEEP TOSSING THAT WORD AROUND LIKE IT MEANS SOMETHING.
BART?
A HAND HERE?
HOW ABOUT IF I LEND YOU MY JAW, INSTEAD?
WHAT CHAMELEON GIRL COULD NOT HAVE KNOWN--
--IS THAT MIGUEL JOSÉ BARRAGAN HAS NOT BEEN BUNKER FOR VERY LONG.
HE IS NEW TO THIS.
SO HE PANICS--

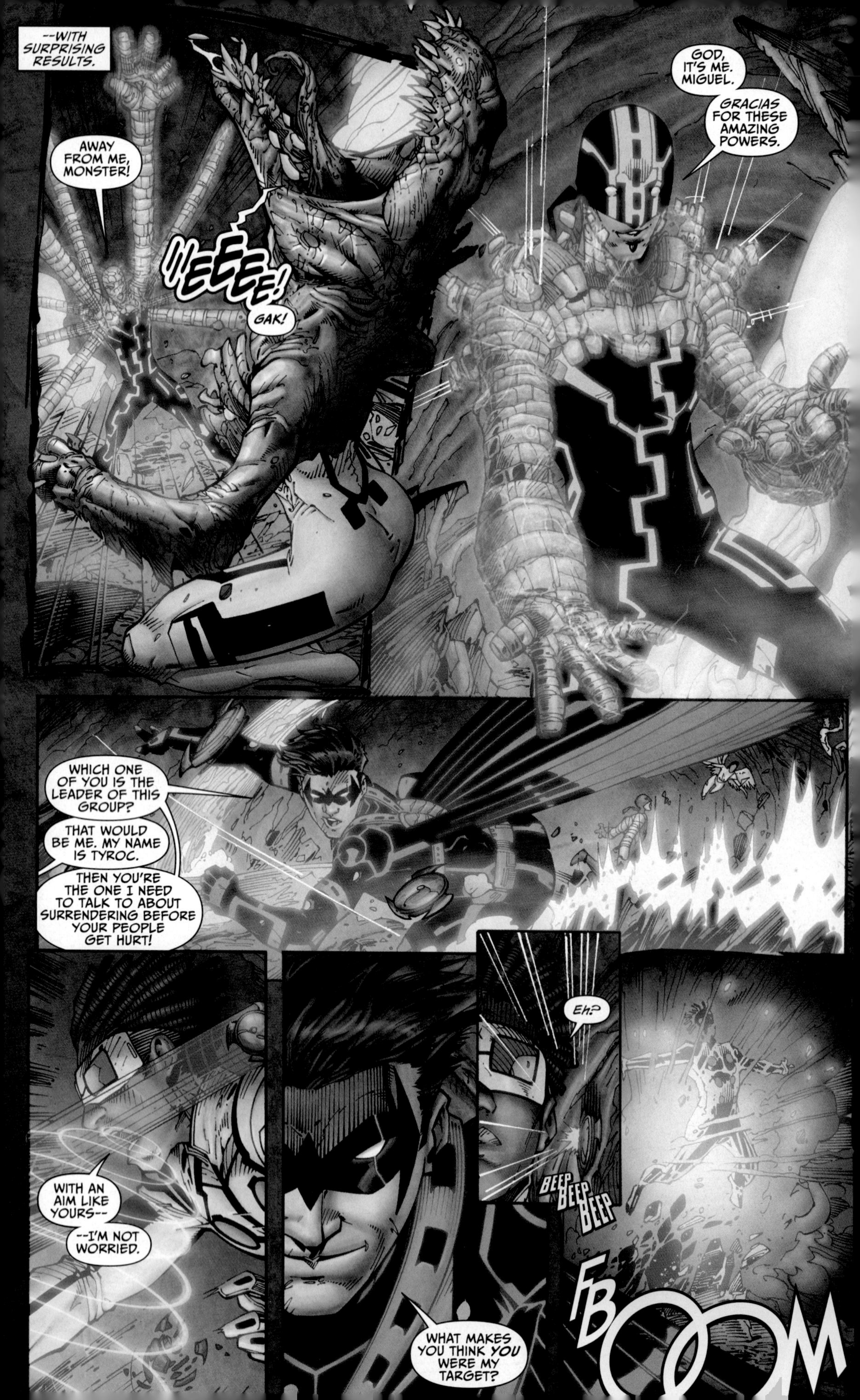
--WITH SURPRISING RESULTS.
AWAY FROM ME, MONSTER!
EEEEE!
GAK!
GOD, IT'S ME. MIGUEL.
GRACIAS FOR THESE AMAZING POWERS.
WHICH ONE OF YOU IS THE LEADER OF THIS GROUP?
THAT WOULD BE ME. MY NAME IS TYROC.
THEN YOU'RE THE ONE I NEED TO TALK TO ABOUT SURRENDERING BEFORE YOUR PEOPLE GET HURT!
WITH AN AIM LIKE YOURS--
--I'M NOT WORRIED.
WHAT MAKES YOU THINK YOU WERE MY TARGET?
Eh?
BEEP BEEP BEEP
FBOOM

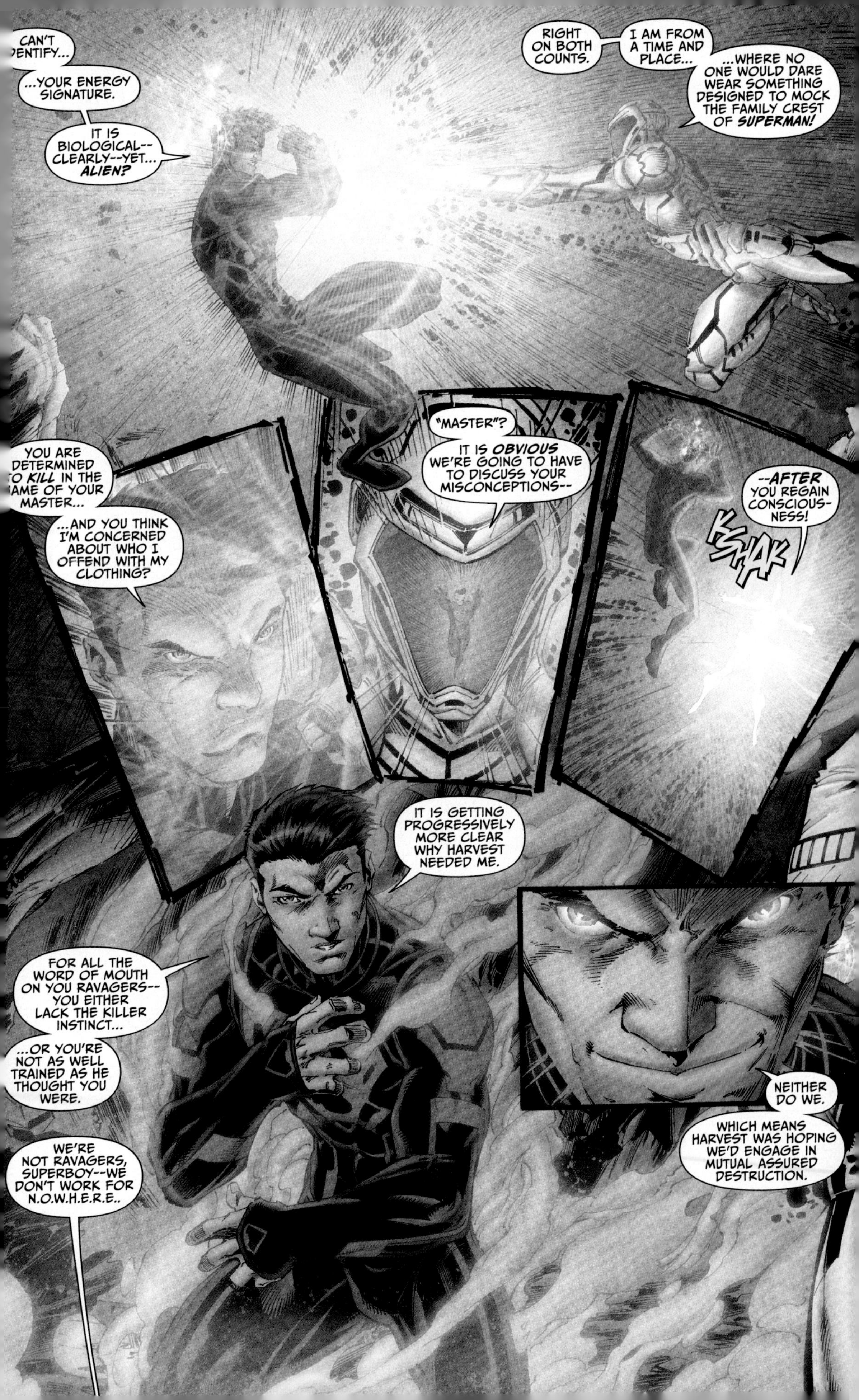
CAN'T
DENTIFY...
...YOUR ENERGY SIGNATURE.
IT IS BIOLOGICAL-- CLEARLY--YET... ALIEN?
RIGHT ON BOTH COUNTS.
I AM FROM A TIME AND PLACE...
...WHERE NO ONE WOULD DARE WEAR SOMETHING DESIGNED TO MOCK THE FAMILY CREST OF SUPERMAN!
YOU ARE DETERMINED TO KILL IN THE AME OF YOUR MASTER...
...AND YOU THINK I'M CONCERNED ABOUT WHO I OFFEND WITH MY CLOTHING?
"MASTER"?
IT IS OBVIOUS WE'RE GOING TO HAVE TO DISCUSS YOUR MISCONCEPTIONS--
--AFTER YOU REGAIN CONSCIOUS-NESS!
KSHAK
IT IS GETTING PROGRESSIVELY MORE CLEAR WHY HARVEST NEEDED ME.
FOR ALL THE WORD OF MOUTH ON YOU RAVAGERS-- YOU EITHER LACK THE KILLER INSTINCT...
...OR YOU'RE NOT AS WELL TRAINED AS HE THOUGHT YOU WERE.
WE'RE NOT RAVAGERS, SUPERBOY--WE DON'T WORK FOR N.O.W.H.E.R.E..
NEITHER DO WE.
WHICH MEANS HARVEST WAS HOPING WE'D ENGAGE IN MUTUAL ASSURED DESTRUCTION.

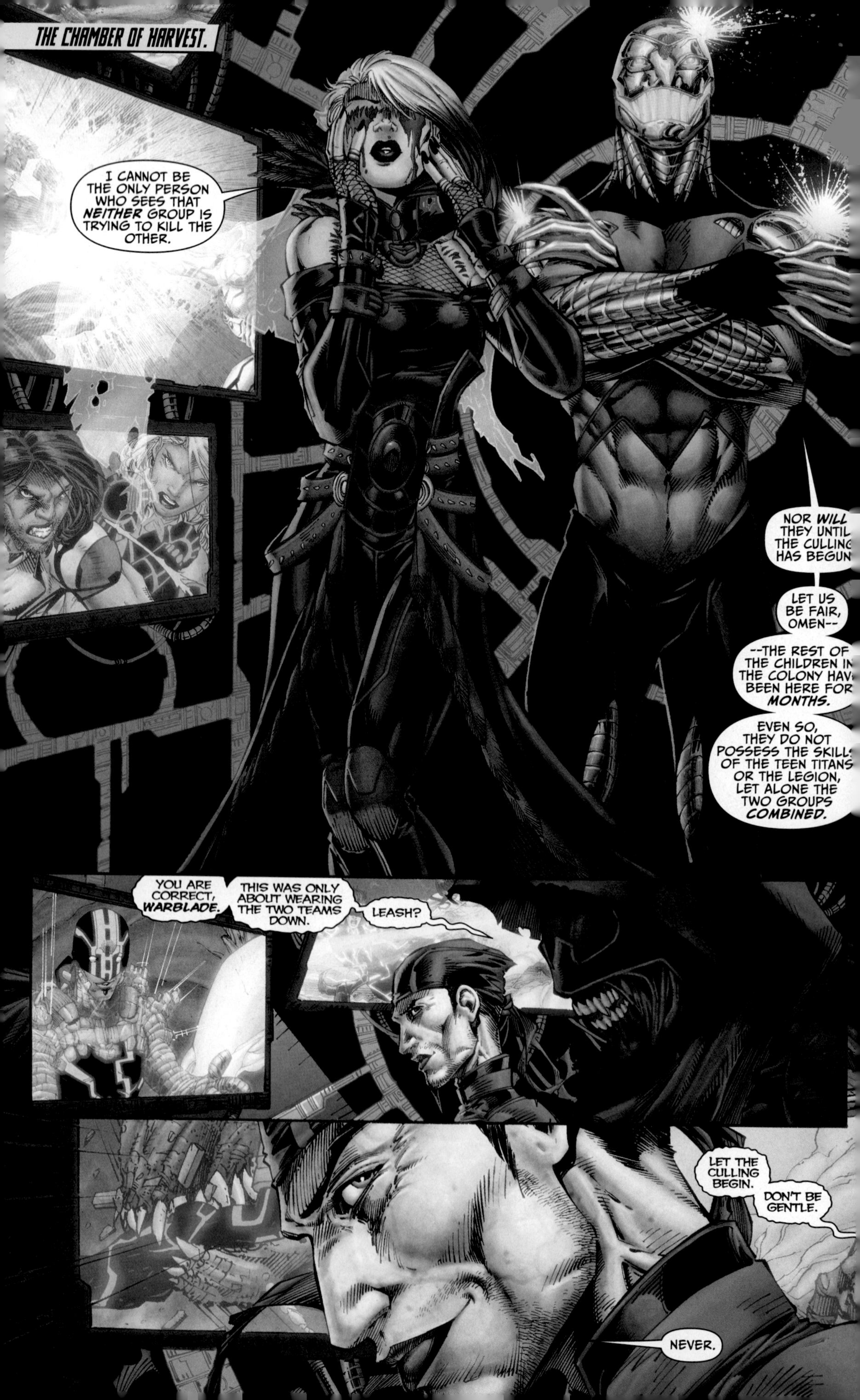
THE CHAMBER OF HARVEST.
I CANNOT BE THE ONLY PERSON WHO SEES THAT NEITHER GROUP IS TRYING TO KILL THE OTHER.
NOR WILL THEY UNTIL THE CULLING HAS BEGUN
LET US BE FAIR, OMEN--
--THE REST OF THE CHILDREN IN THE COLONY HAV BEEN HERE FOR MONTHS.
EVEN SO, THEY DO NOT POSSESS THE SKILLS OF THE TEEN TITANS OR THE LEGION, LET ALONE THE TWO GROUPS COMBINED.
YOU ARE CORRECT, WARBLADE.
THIS WAS ONLY ABOUT WEARING THE TWO TEAMS DOWN.
LEASH?
LET THE CULLING BEGIN.
DON'T BE GENTLE.
NEVER.

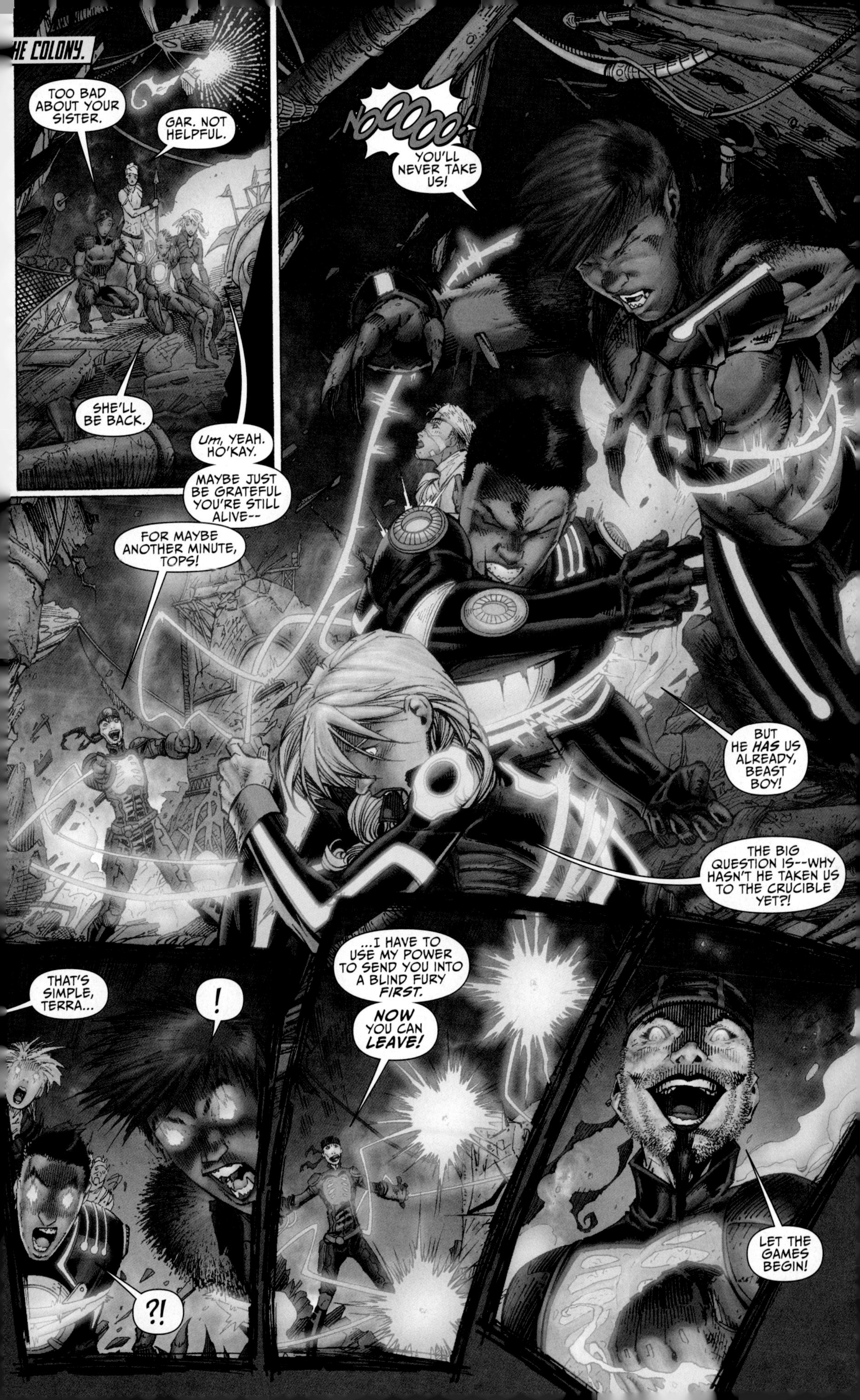
HE COLONY.
TOO BAD ABOUT YOUR SISTER.
GAR. NOT HELPFUL.
SHE'LL BE BACK.
Um, YEAH. HO'KAY.
MAYBE JUST BE GRATEFUL YOU'RE STILL ALIVE--
FOR MAYBE ANOTHER MINUTE, TOPS!
NOOOOOO!
YOU'LL NEVER TAKE US!
BUT HE HAS US ALREADY, BEAST BOY!
THE BIG QUESTION IS--WHY HASN'T HE TAKEN US TO THE CRUCIBLE YET?!
THAT'S SIMPLE, TERRA...
!
?!
...I HAVE TO USE MY POWER TO SEND YOU INTO A BLIND FURY FIRST.
NOW YOU CAN LEAVE!
LET THE GAMES BEGIN!

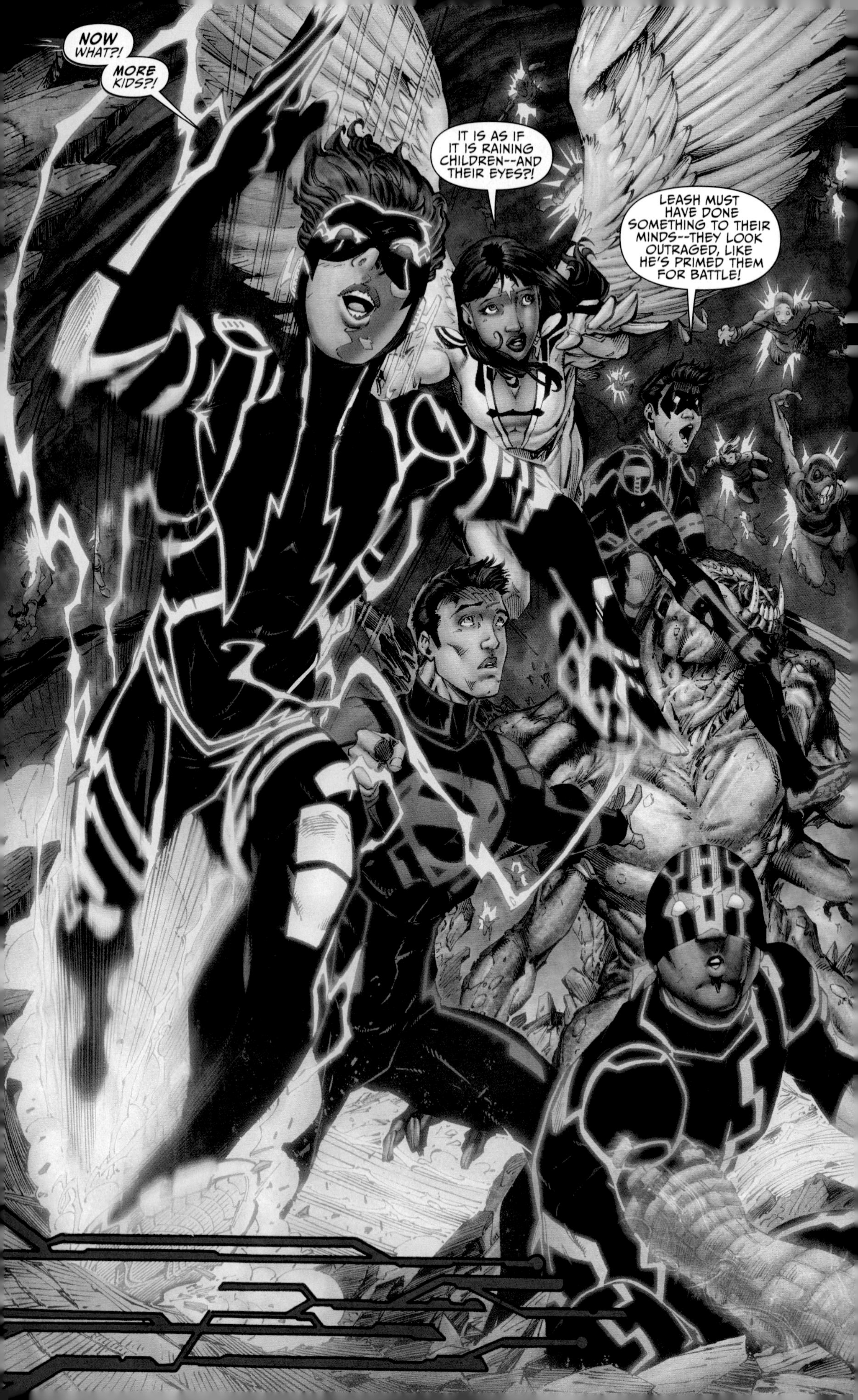
NOW WHAT?!
MORE KIDS?!
IT IS AS IF IT IS RAINING CHILDREN--AND THEIR EYES?!
LEASH MUST HAVE DONE SOMETHING TO THEIR MINDS--THEY LOOK OUTRAGED, LIKE HE'S PRIMED THEM FOR BATTLE!

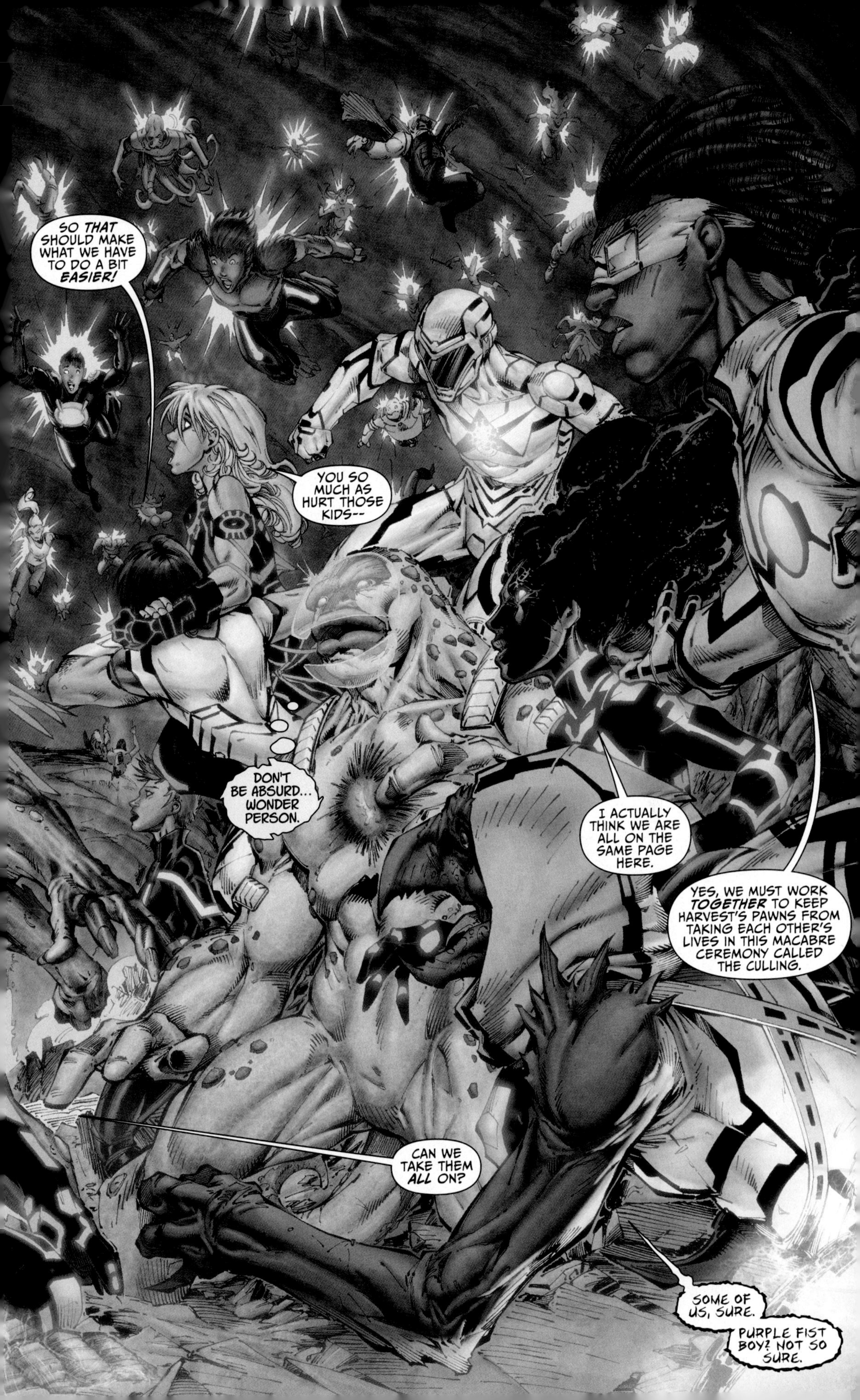
SO THAT SHOULD MAKE WHAT WE HAVE TO DO A BIT EASIER!
YOU SO MUCH AS HURT THOSE KIDS--
DON'T BE ABSURD... WONDER PERSON.
I ACTUALLY THINK WE ARE ALL ON THE SAME PAGE HERE.
YES, WE MUST WORK TOGETHER TO KEEP HARVEST'S PAWNS FROM TAKING EACH OTHER'S LIVES IN THIS MACABRE CEREMONY CALLED THE CULLING.
CAN WE TAKE THEM ALL ON?
SOME OF US, SURE.
PURPLE FIST BOY? NOT SO SURE.

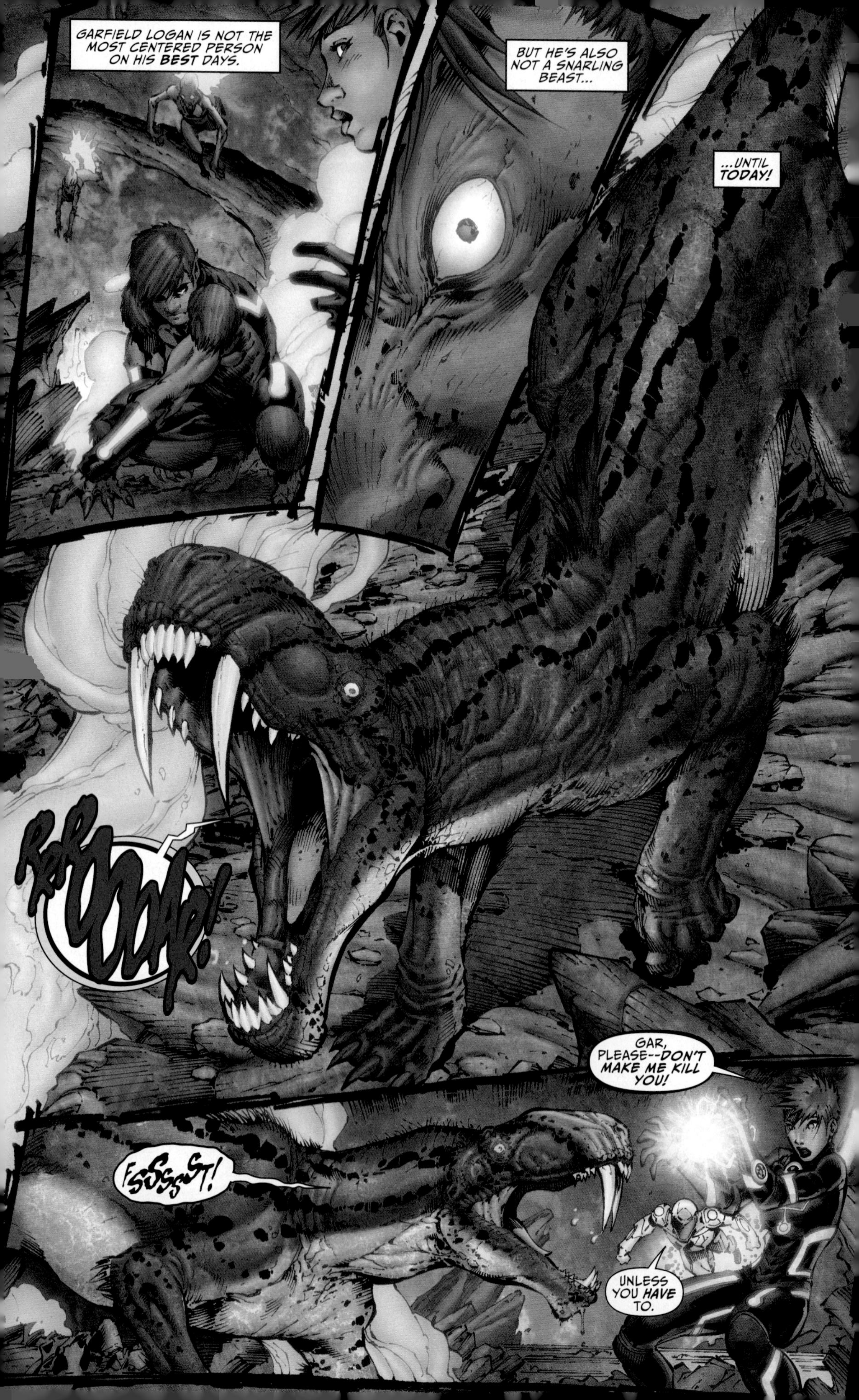
GARFIELD LOGAN IS NOT THE MOST CENTERED PERSON ON HIS BEST DAYS.
BUT HE'S ALSO NOT A SNARLING BEAST...
...UNTIL TODAY!
RRROOOAR!
GAR, PLEASE--DON'T MAKE ME KILL YOU!
FSSSSST!
UNLESS YOU HAVE TO.

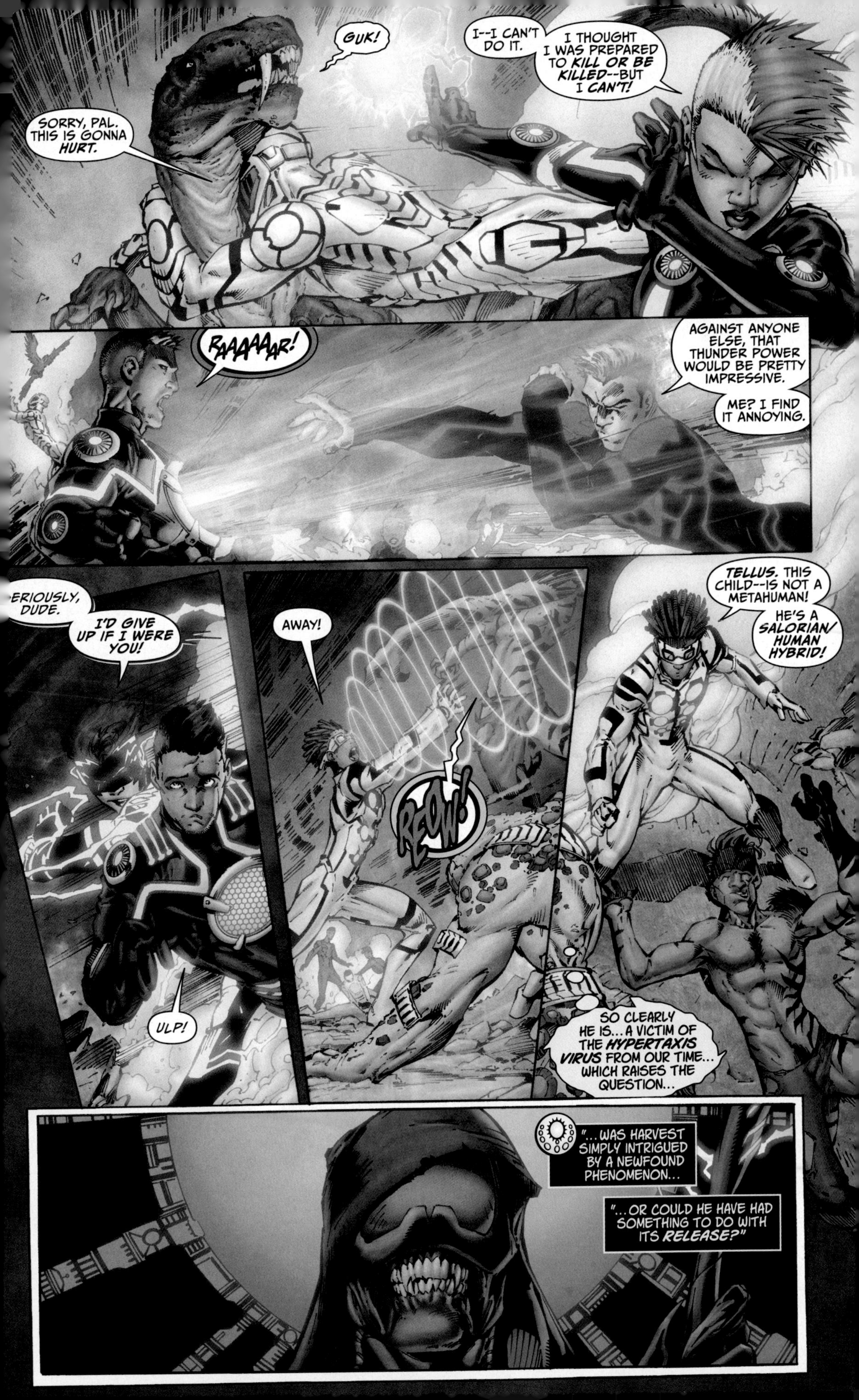
SORRY, PAL. THIS IS GONNA HURT.
GUK!
I--I CAN'T DO IT.
I THOUGHT I WAS PREPARED TO KILL OR BE KILLED--BUT I CAN'T!
RAAAAAAR!
AGAINST ANYONE ELSE, THAT THUNDER POWER WOULD BE PRETTY IMPRESSIVE.
ME? I FIND IT ANNOYING.
ERIOUSLY, DUDE.
I'D GIVE UP IF I WERE YOU!
ULP!
AWAY!
REOW!
TELLUS. THIS CHILD--IS NOT A METAHUMAN!
HE'S A SALORIAN/ HUMAN HYBRID!
SO CLEARLY HE IS... A VICTIM OF THE HYPERTAXIS VIRUS FROM OUR TIME... WHICH RAISES THE QUESTION...
"...WAS HARVEST SIMPLY INTRIGUED BY A NEWFOUND PHENOMENON...
"...OR COULD HE HAVE HAD SOMETHING TO DO WITH ITS RELEASE?"

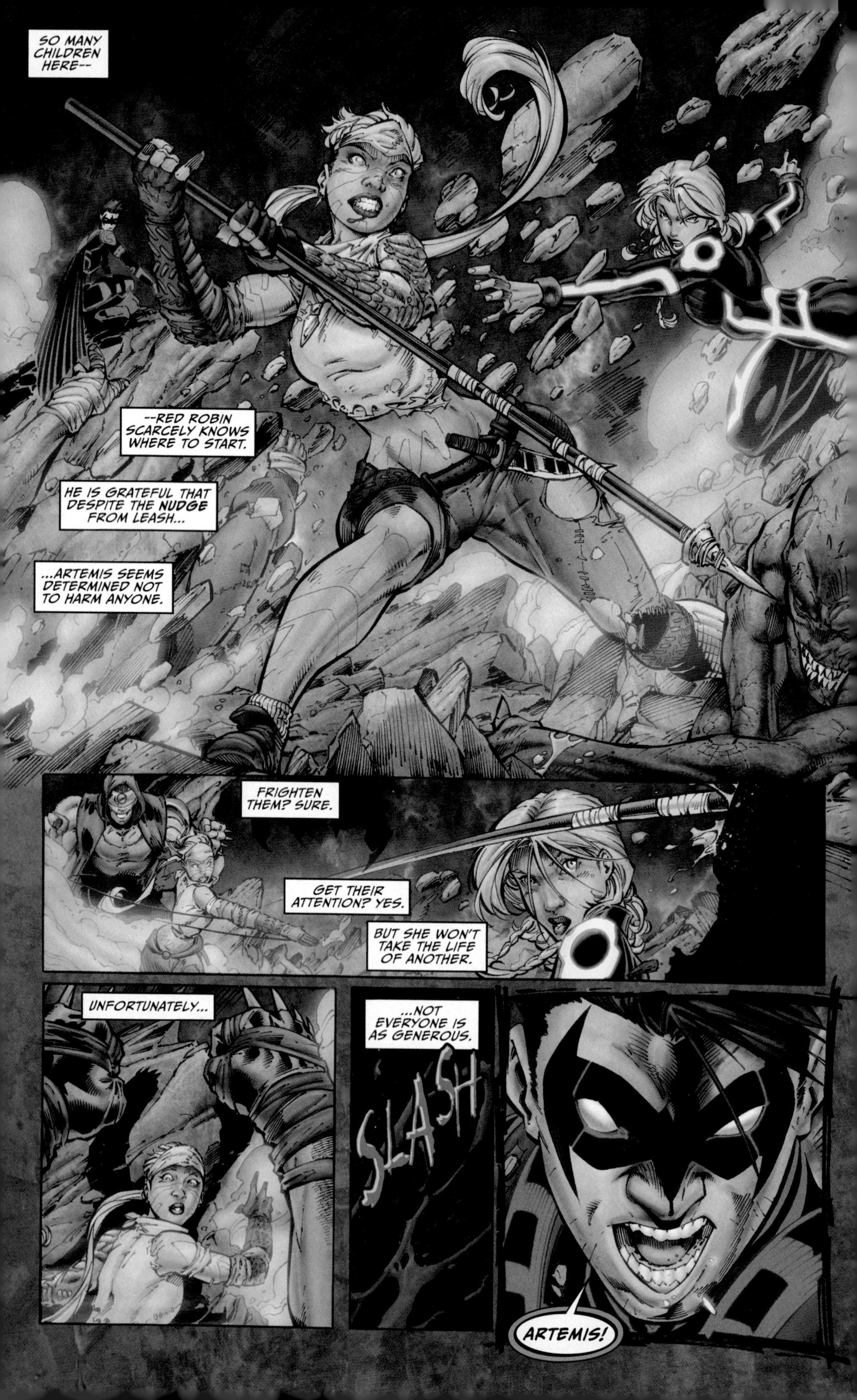
SO MANY CHILDREN HERE--
--RED ROBIN SCARCELY KNOWS WHERE TO START.
HE IS GRATEFUL THAT DESPITE THE NUDGE FROM LEASH...
...ARTEMIS SEEMS DETERMINED NOT TO HARM ANYONE.
FRIGHTEN THEM? SURE.
GET THEIR ATTENTION? YES.
BUT SHE WON'T TAKE THE LIFE OF ANOTHER.
UNFORTUNATELY...
...NOT EVERYONE IS AS GENEROUS.
SLASH
ARTEMIS!

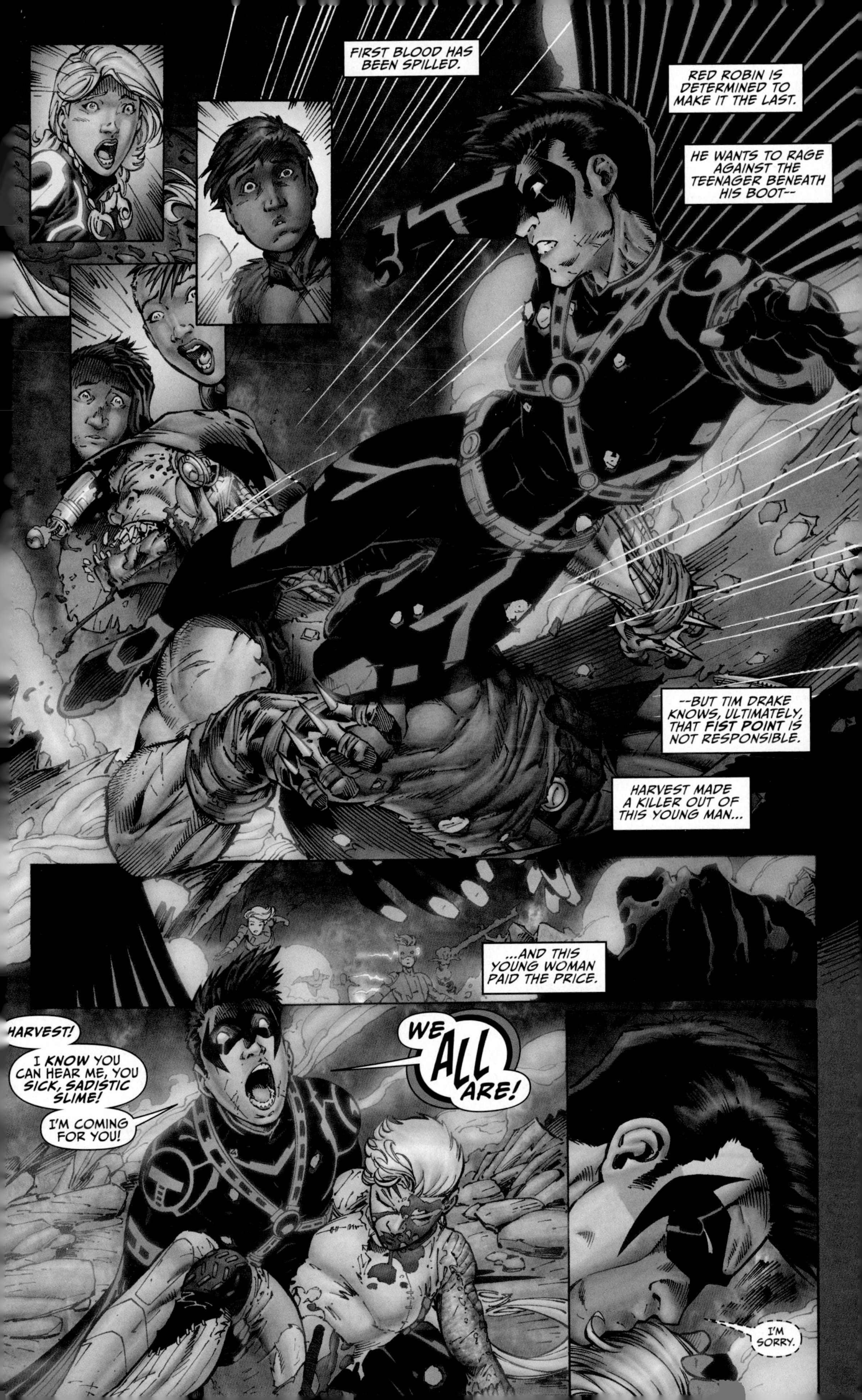
FIRST BLOOD HAS BEEN SPILLED.
RED ROBIN IS DETERMINED TO MAKE IT THE LAST.
HE WANTS TO RAGE AGAINST THE TEENAGER BENEATH HIS BOOT--
--BUT TIM DRAKE KNOWS, ULTIMATELY, THAT FIST POINT IS NOT RESPONSIBLE.
HARVEST MADE A KILLER OUT OF THIS YOUNG MAN...
...AND THIS YOUNG WOMAN PAID THE PRICE.
HARVEST!
I KNOW YOU CAN HEAR ME, YOU SICK, SADISTIC SLIME!
I'M COMING FOR YOU!
WE ALL ARE!
I'M SORRY.

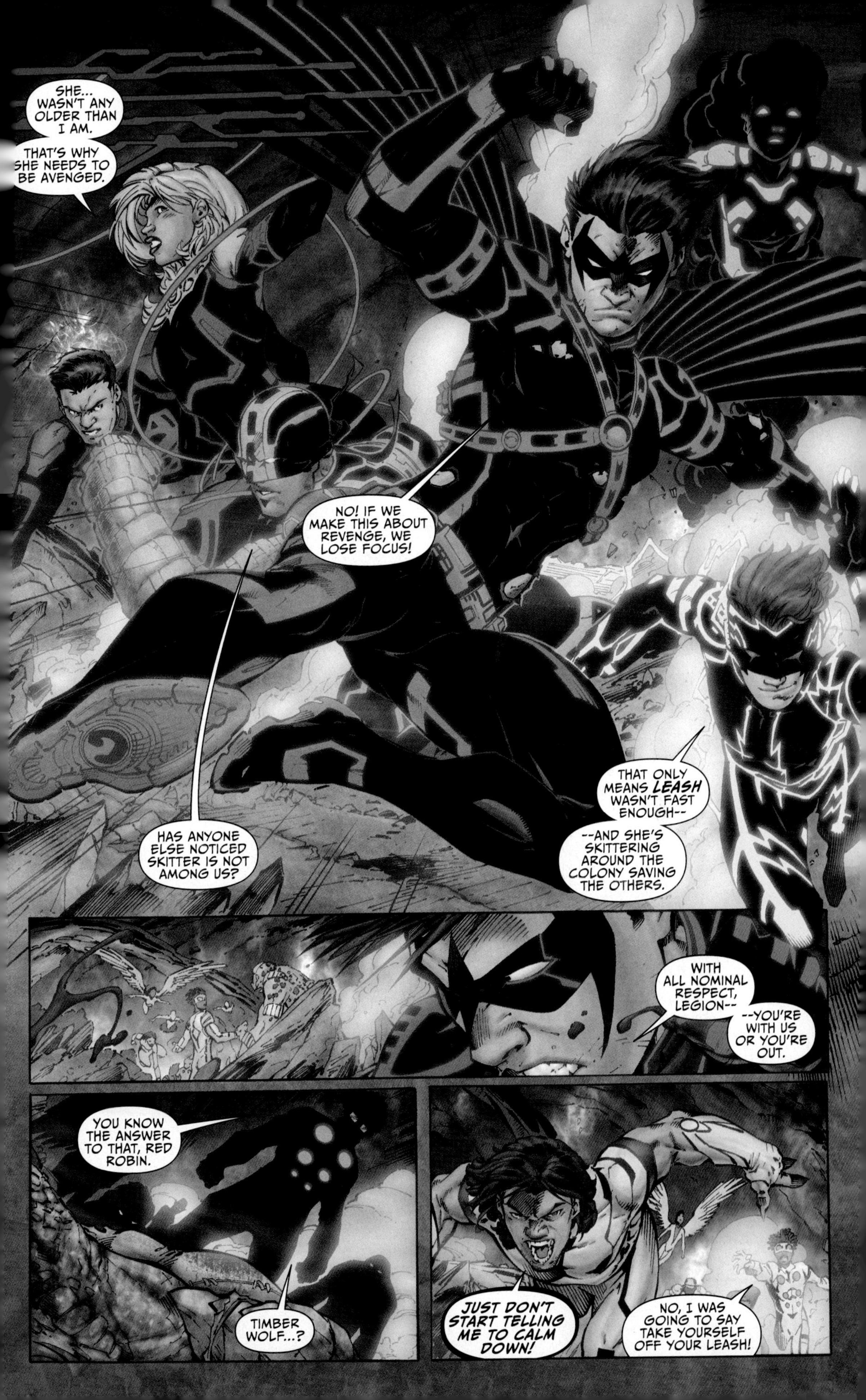
SHE... WASN'T ANY OLDER THAN I AM.
THAT'S WHY SHE NEEDS TO BE AVENGED.
NO! IF WE MAKE THIS ABOUT REVENGE, WE LOSE FOCUS!
HAS ANYONE ELSE NOTICED SKITTER IS NOT AMONG US?
THAT ONLY MEANS LEASH WASN'T FAST ENOUGH--
--AND SHE'S SKITTERING AROUND THE COLONY SAVING THE OTHERS.
WITH ALL NOMINAL RESPECT, LEGION--
--YOU'RE WITH US OR YOU'RE OUT.
YOU KNOW THE ANSWER TO THAT, RED ROBIN.
TIMBER WOLF...?
JUST DON'T START TELLING ME TO CALM DOWN!
NO, I WAS GOING TO SAY TAKE YOURSELF OFF YOUR LEASH!

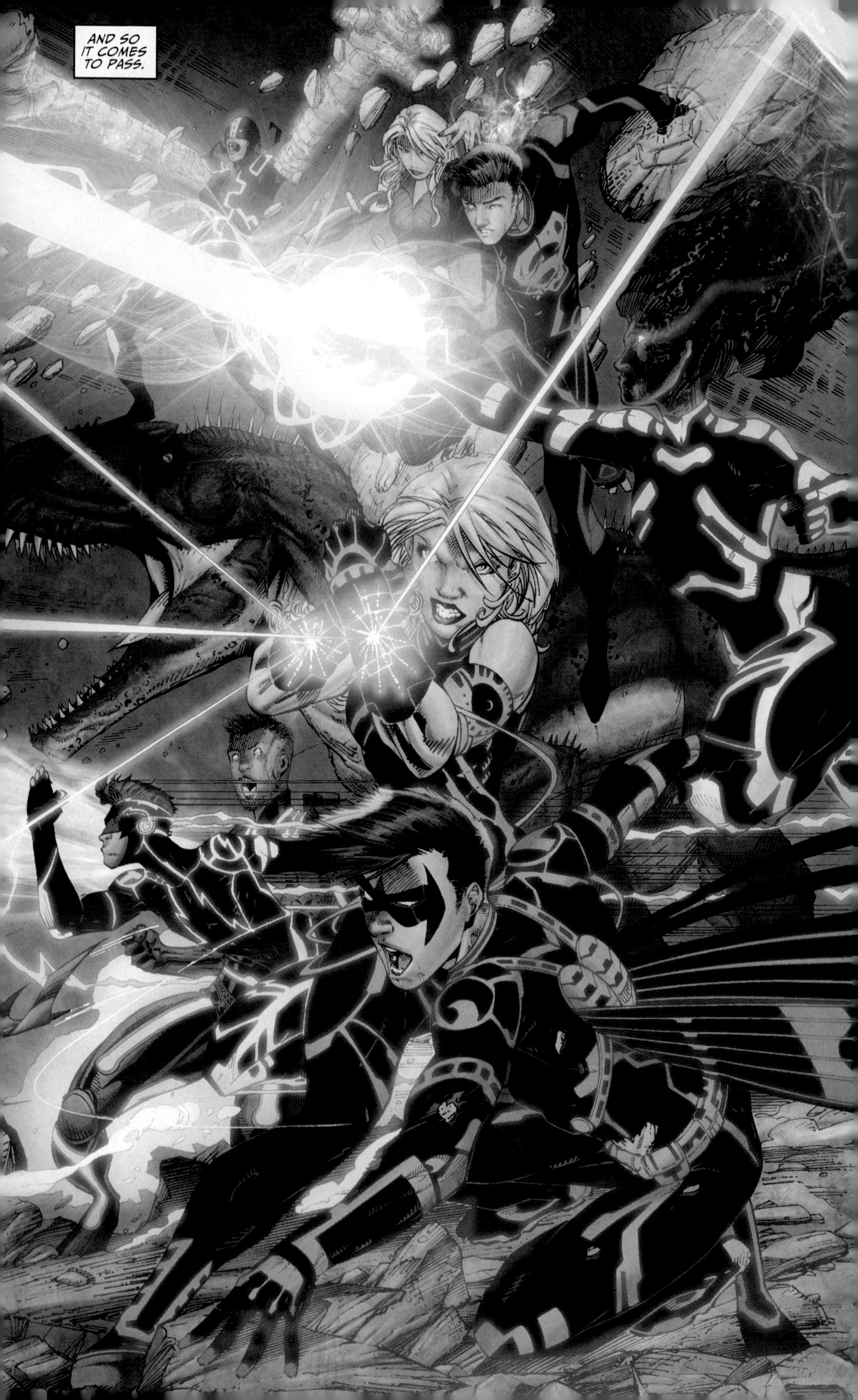
AND SO IT COMES TO PASS.

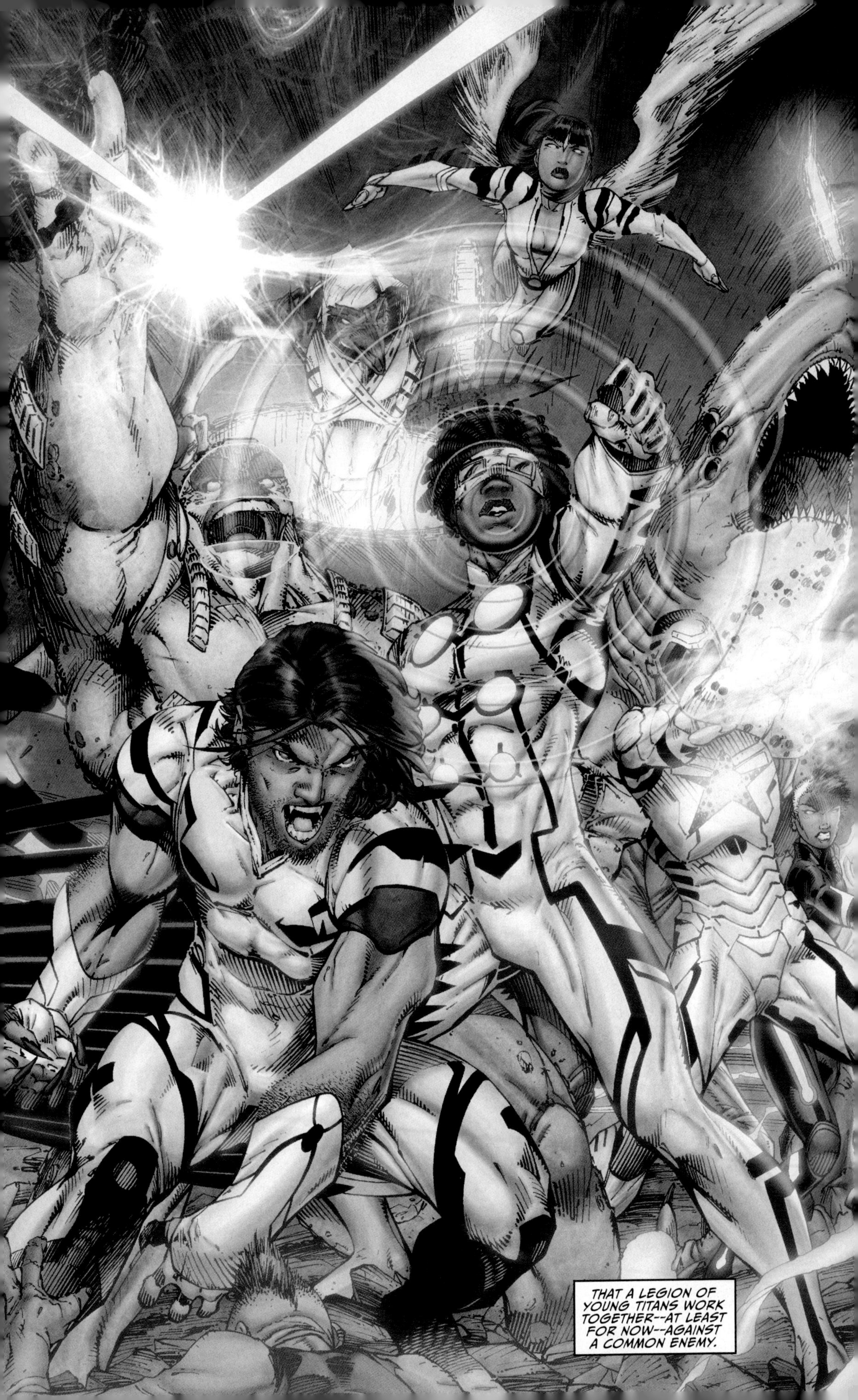
THAT A LEGION OF YOUNG TITANS WORK TOGETHER--AT LEAST FOR NOW--AGAINST A COMMON ENEMY.

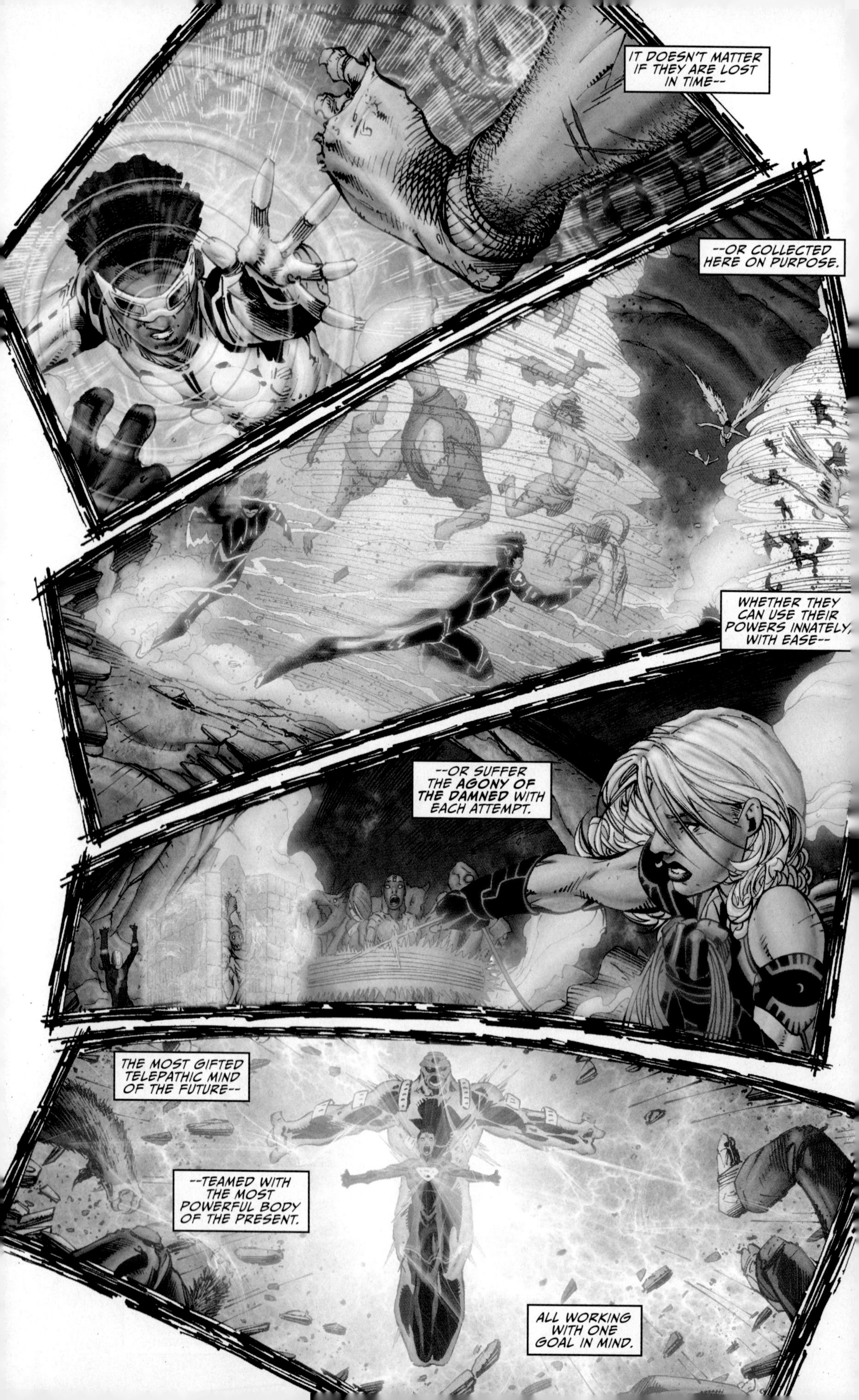
IT DOESN'T MATTER IF THEY ARE LOST IN TIME--
--OR COLLECTED HERE ON PURPOSE.
WHETHER THEY CAN USE THEIR POWERS INNATELY, WITH EASE--
--OR SUFFER THE AGONY OF THE DAMNED WITH EACH ATTEMPT.
THE MOST GIFTED TELEPATHIC MIND OF THE FUTURE--
--TEAMED WITH THE MOST POWERFUL BODY OF THE PRESENT.
ALL WORKING WITH ONE GOAL IN MIND.

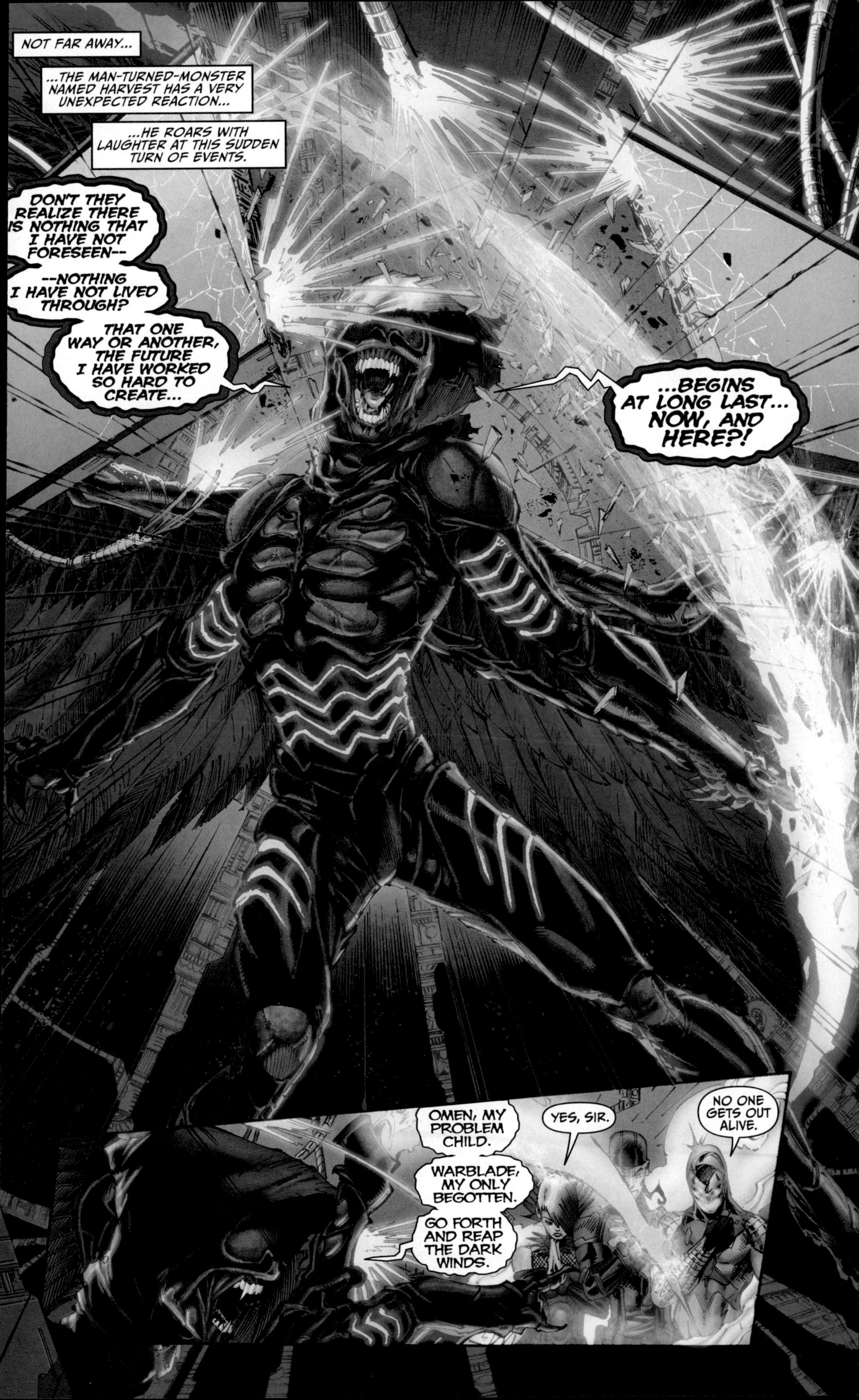
NOT FAR AWAY...
...THE MAN-TURNED-MONSTER NAMED HARVEST HAS A VERY UNEXPECTED REACTION...
...HE ROARS WITH LAUGHTER AT THIS SUDDEN TURN OF EVENTS.
DON'T THEY REALIZE THERE IS NOTHING THAT I HAVE NOT FORESEEN--
--NOTHING I HAVE NOT LIVED THROUGH?
THAT ONE WAY OR ANOTHER, THE FUTURE I HAVE WORKED SO HARD TO CREATE...
...BEGINS AT LONG LAST... NOW, AND HERE?!
OMEN, MY PROBLEM CHILD.
WARBLADE, MY ONLY BEGOTTEN.
GO FORTH AND REAP THE DARK WINDS.
YES, SIR.
NO ONE GETS OUT ALIVE.

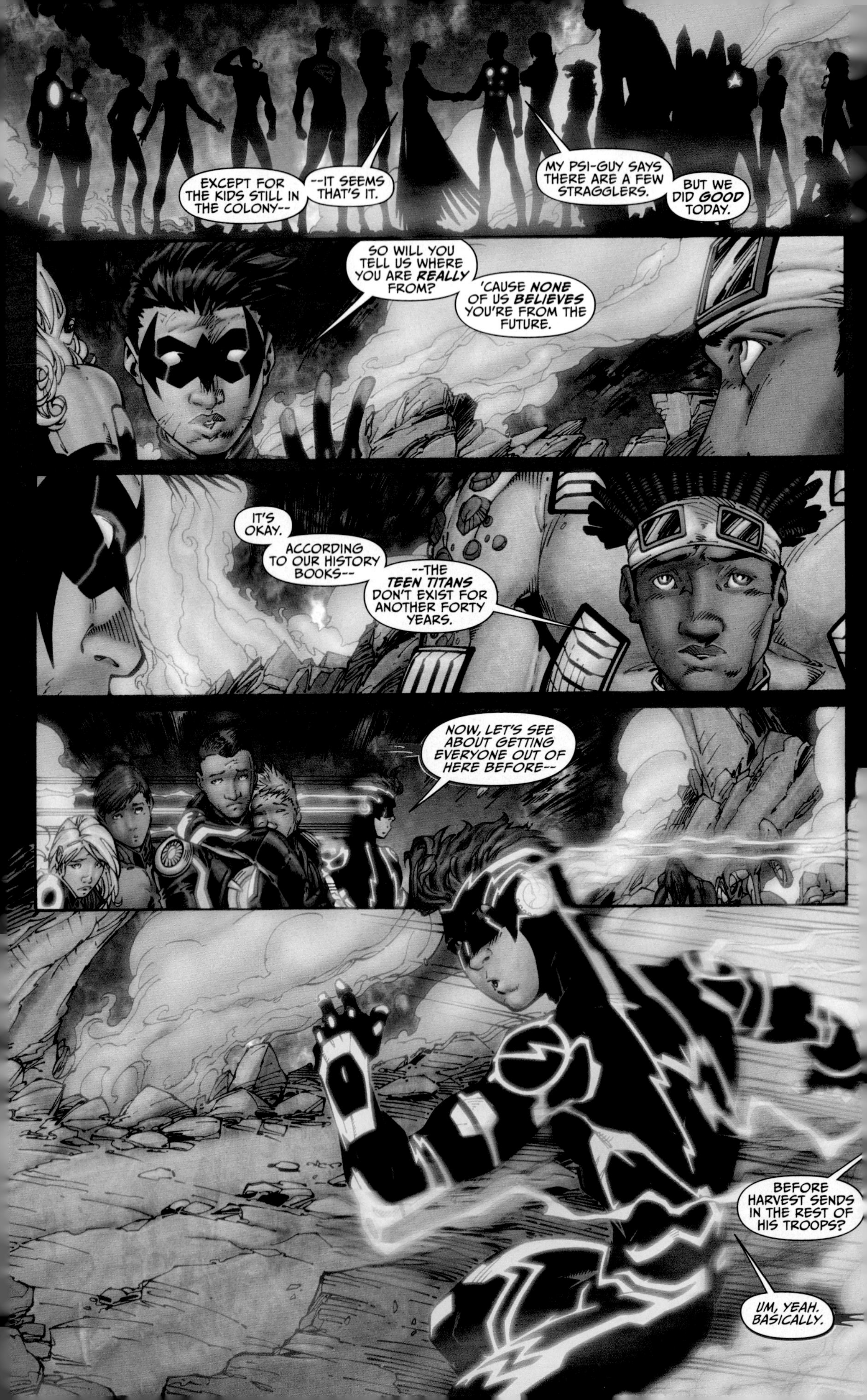
EXCEPT FOR THE KIDS STILL IN THE COLONY--
--IT SEEMS THAT'S IT.
MY PSI-GUY SAYS THERE ARE A FEW STRAGGLERS.
BUT WE DID GOOD TODAY.
SO WILL YOU TELL US WHERE YOU ARE REALLY FROM?
'CAUSE NONE OF US BELIEVES YOU'RE FROM THE FUTURE.
IT'S OKAY.
ACCORDING TO OUR HISTORY BOOKS--
--THE TEEN TITANS DON'T EXIST FOR ANOTHER FORTY YEARS.
NOW, LET'S SEE ABOUT GETTING EVERYONE OUT OF HERE BEFORE--
BEFORE HARVEST SENDS IN THE REST OF HIS TROOPS?
UM, YEAH. BASICALLY.

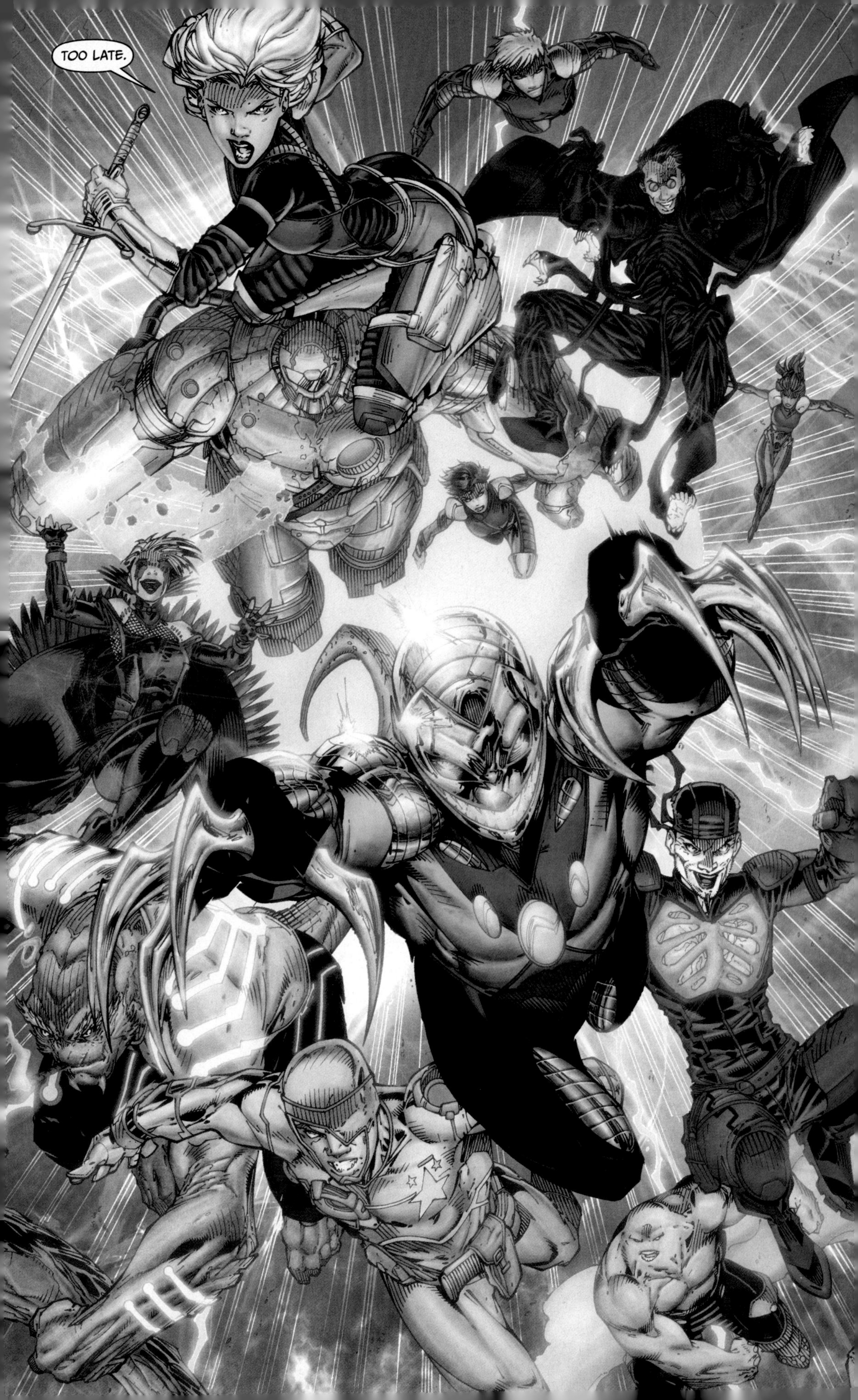
TOO LATE.

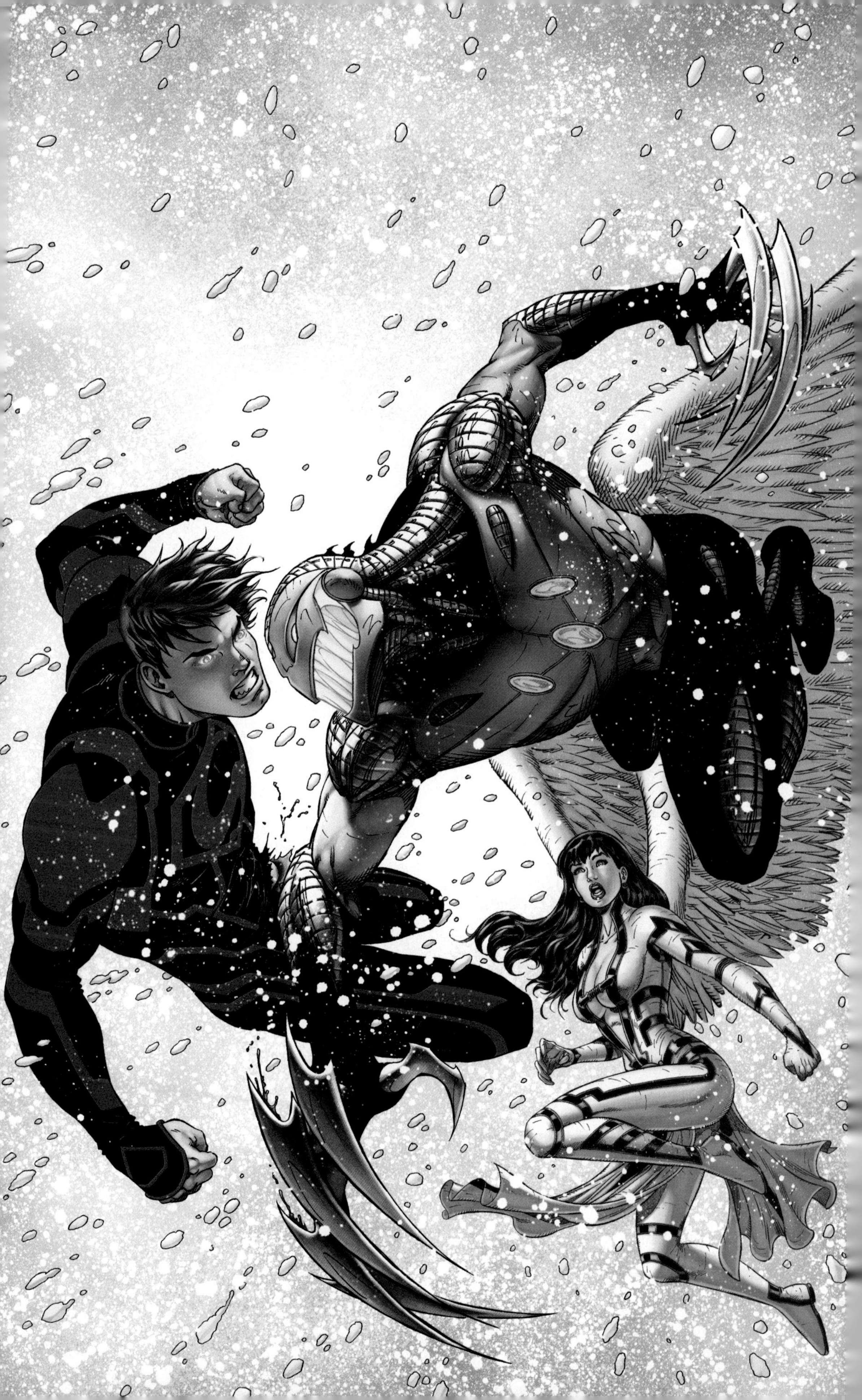

THE CULLING PART TWO: LOST CLAWS!

SCOTT LOBDELL & TOM DEFALCO writers R.B. SILVA penciller
ROB LEAN & IBAN COELLO inkers
cover art by IAN CHURCHILL & ALEX SOLLAZZO

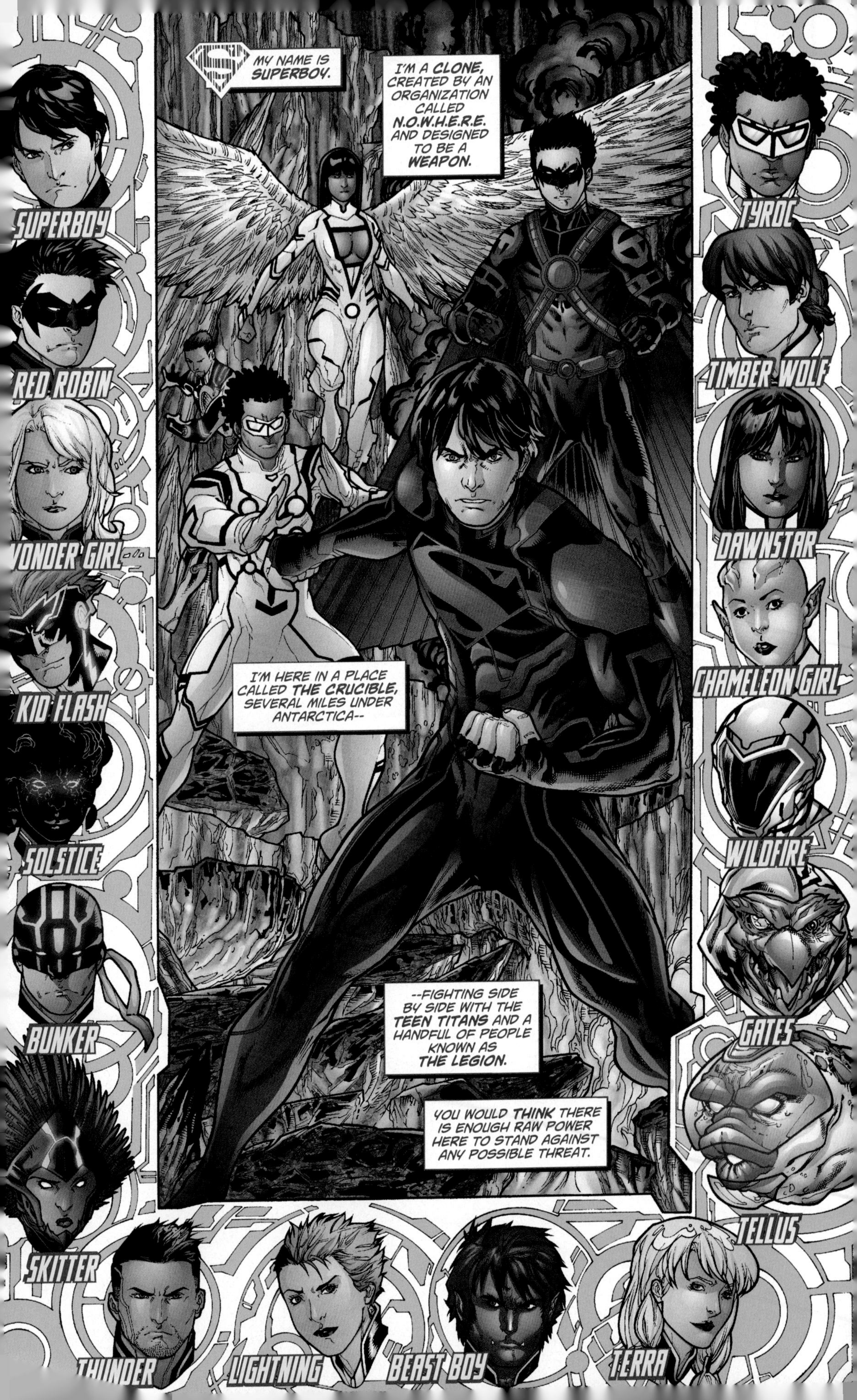
MY NAME IS SUPERBOY.
I'M A CLONE, CREATED BY AN ORGANIZATION CALLED N.O.W.H.E.R.E. AND DESIGNED TO BE A WEAPON.
I'M HERE IN A PLACE CALLED THE CRUCIBLE, SEVERAL MILES UNDER ANTARCTICA--
--FIGHTING SIDE BY SIDE WITH THE TEEN TITANS AND A HANDFUL OF PEOPLE KNOWN AS THE LEGION.
YOU WOULD THINK THERE IS ENOUGH RAW POWER HERE TO STAND AGAINST ANY POSSIBLE THREAT.
SUPERBOY
RED ROBIN
WONDER GIRL
KID FLASH
SOLSTICE
BUNKER
SKITTER
TYROC
TIMBER WOLF
DAWNSTAR
CHAMELEON GIRL
WILDFIRE
GATES
TELLUS
THUNDER
LIGHTNING
BEAST BOY
TERRA

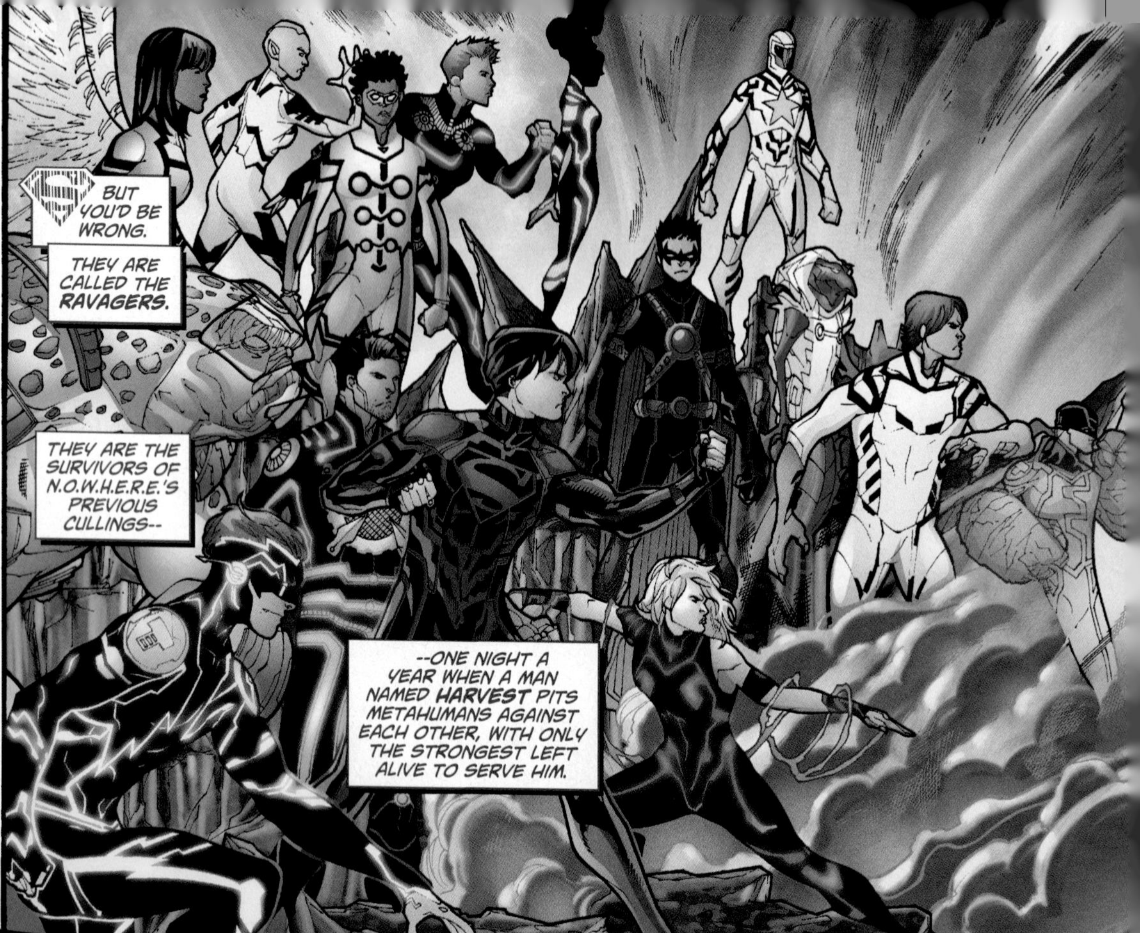
BUT YOU'D BE WRONG.
THEY ARE CALLED THE RAVAGERS.
THEY ARE THE SURVIVORS OF N.O.W.H.E.R.E.'S PREVIOUS CULLINGS--
--ONE NIGHT A YEAR WHEN A MAN NAMED HARVEST PITS METAHUMANS AGAINST EACH OTHER, WITH ONLY THE STRONGEST LEFT ALIVE TO SERVE HIM.

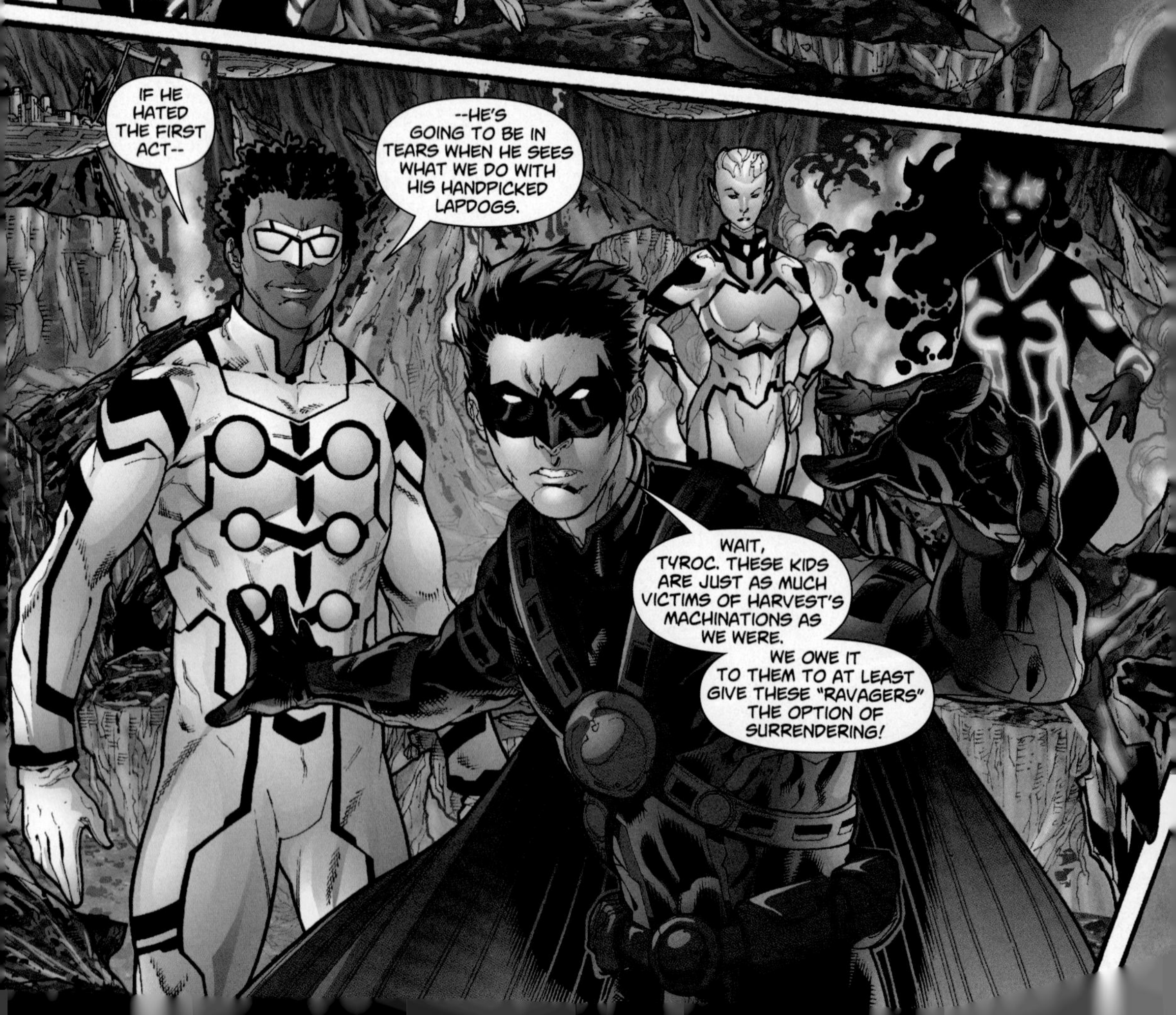
IF HE HATED THE FIRST ACT--
--HE'S GOING TO BE IN TEARS WHEN HE SEES WHAT WE DO WITH HIS HANDPICKED LAPDOGS.
WAIT, TYROC. THESE KIDS ARE JUST AS MUCH VICTIMS OF HARVEST'S MACHINATIONS AS WE WERE.
WE OWE IT TO THEM TO AT LEAST GIVE THESE "RAVAGERS" THE OPTION OF SURRENDERING!

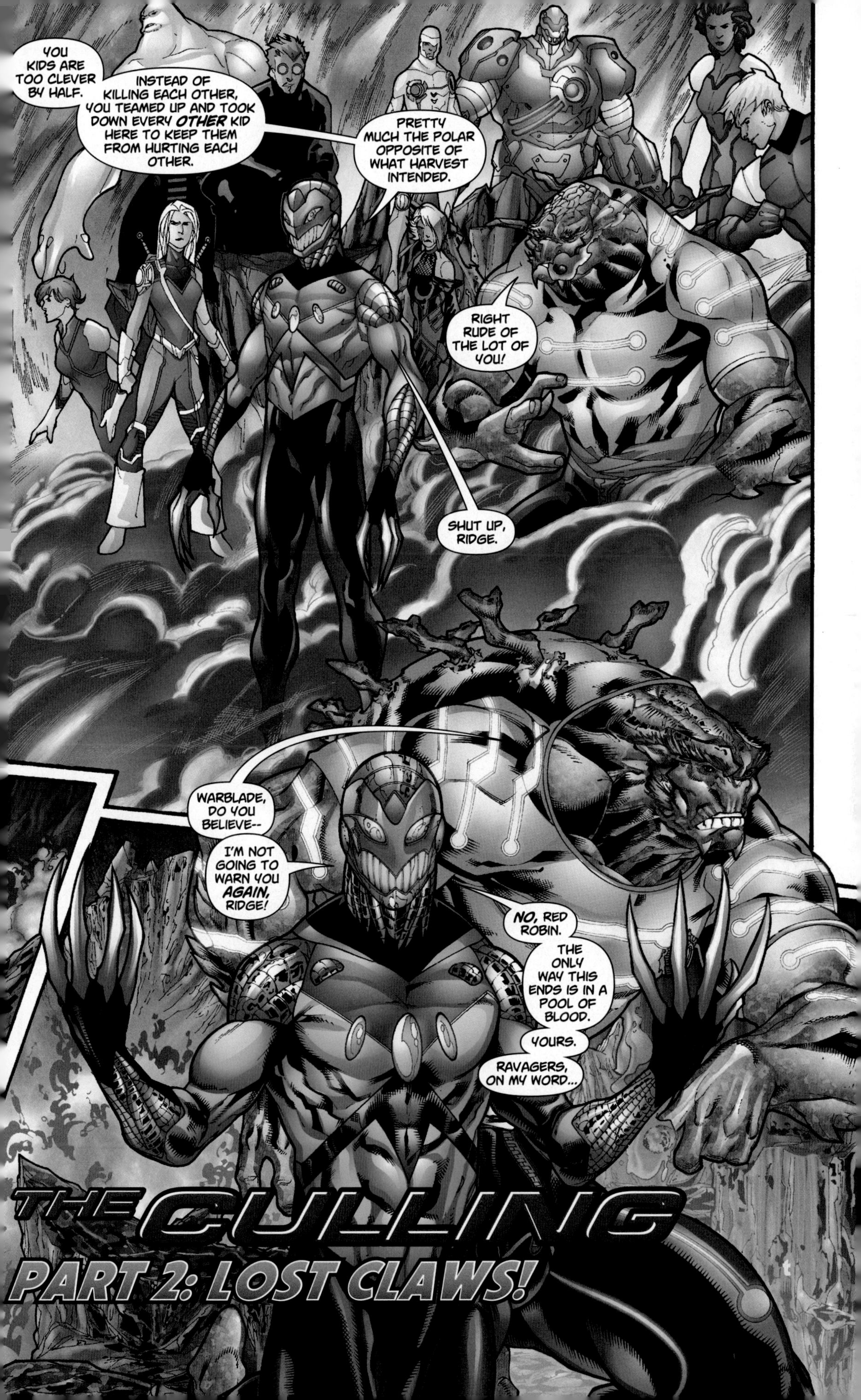
YOU KIDS ARE TOO CLEVER BY HALF.
INSTEAD OF KILLING EACH OTHER, YOU TEAMED UP AND TOOK DOWN EVERY OTHER KID HERE TO KEEP THEM FROM HURTING EACH OTHER.
PRETTY MUCH THE POLAR OPPOSITE OF WHAT HARVEST INTENDED.
RIGHT RUDE OF THE LOT OF YOU!
SHUT UP, RIDGE.
WARBLADE, DO YOU BELIEVE--
I'M NOT GOING TO WARN YOU AGAIN, RIDGE!
NO, RED ROBIN.
THE ONLY WAY THIS ENDS IS IN A POOL OF BLOOD.
YOURS.
RAVAGERS, ON MY WORD...
THE CULLING
PART 2: LOST CLAWS!

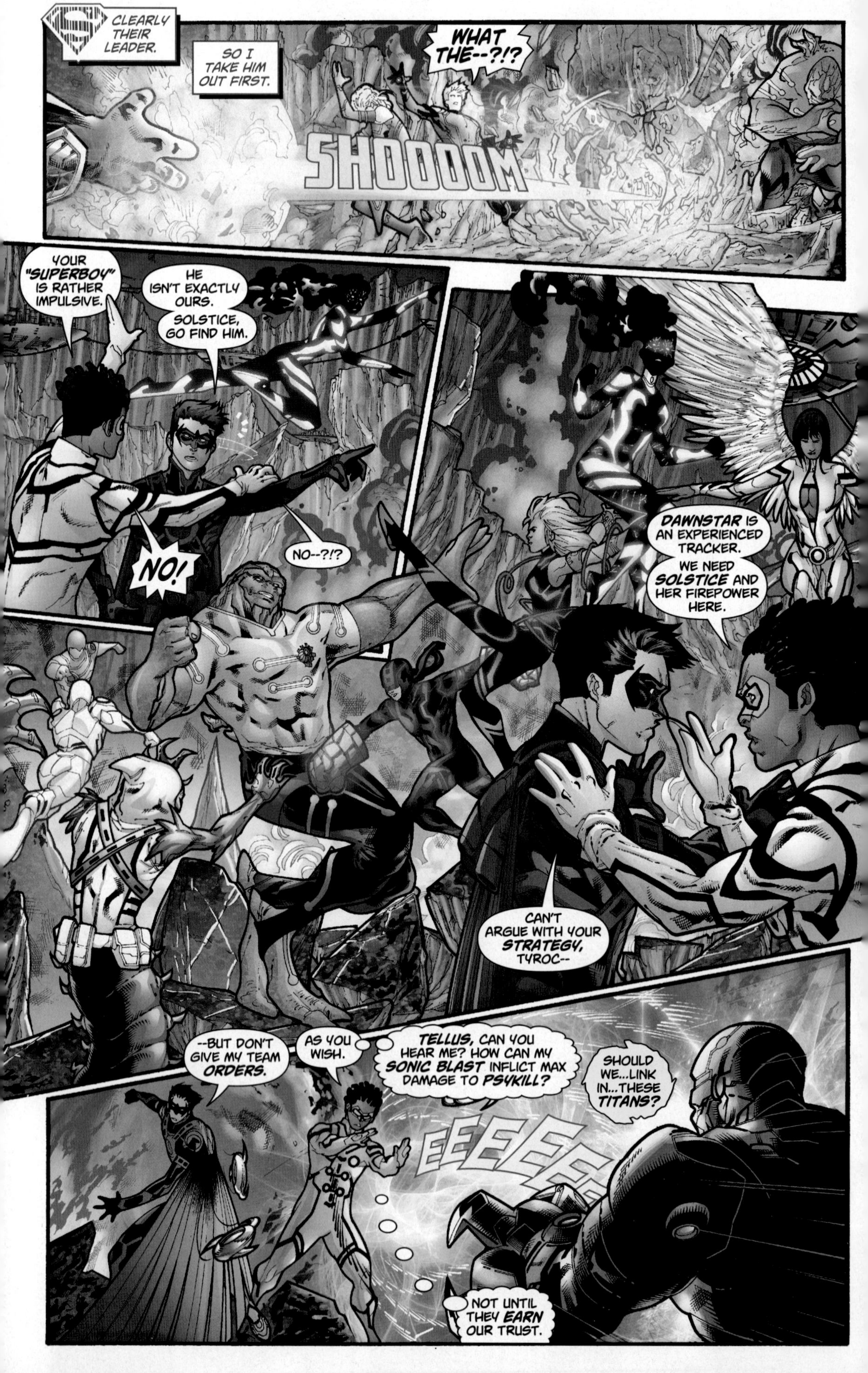
CLEARLY THEIR LEADER.
SO I TAKE HIM OUT FIRST.
WHAT THE--?!?
SHOOOOM
YOUR "SUPERBOY" IS RATHER IMPULSIVE.
HE ISN'T EXACTLY OURS.
SOLSTICE, GO FIND HIM.
NO!
NO--?!?
DAWNSTAR IS AN EXPERIENCED TRACKER.
WE NEED SOLSTICE AND HER FIREPOWER HERE.
CAN'T ARGUE WITH YOUR STRATEGY, TYROC--
--BUT DON'T GIVE MY TEAM ORDERS.
AS YOU WISH.
TELLUS, CAN YOU HEAR ME? HOW CAN MY SONIC BLAST INFLICT MAX DAMAGE TO PSYKILL?
SHOULD WE...LINK IN...THESE TITANS?
EEEEE
NOT UNTIL THEY EARN OUR TRUST.

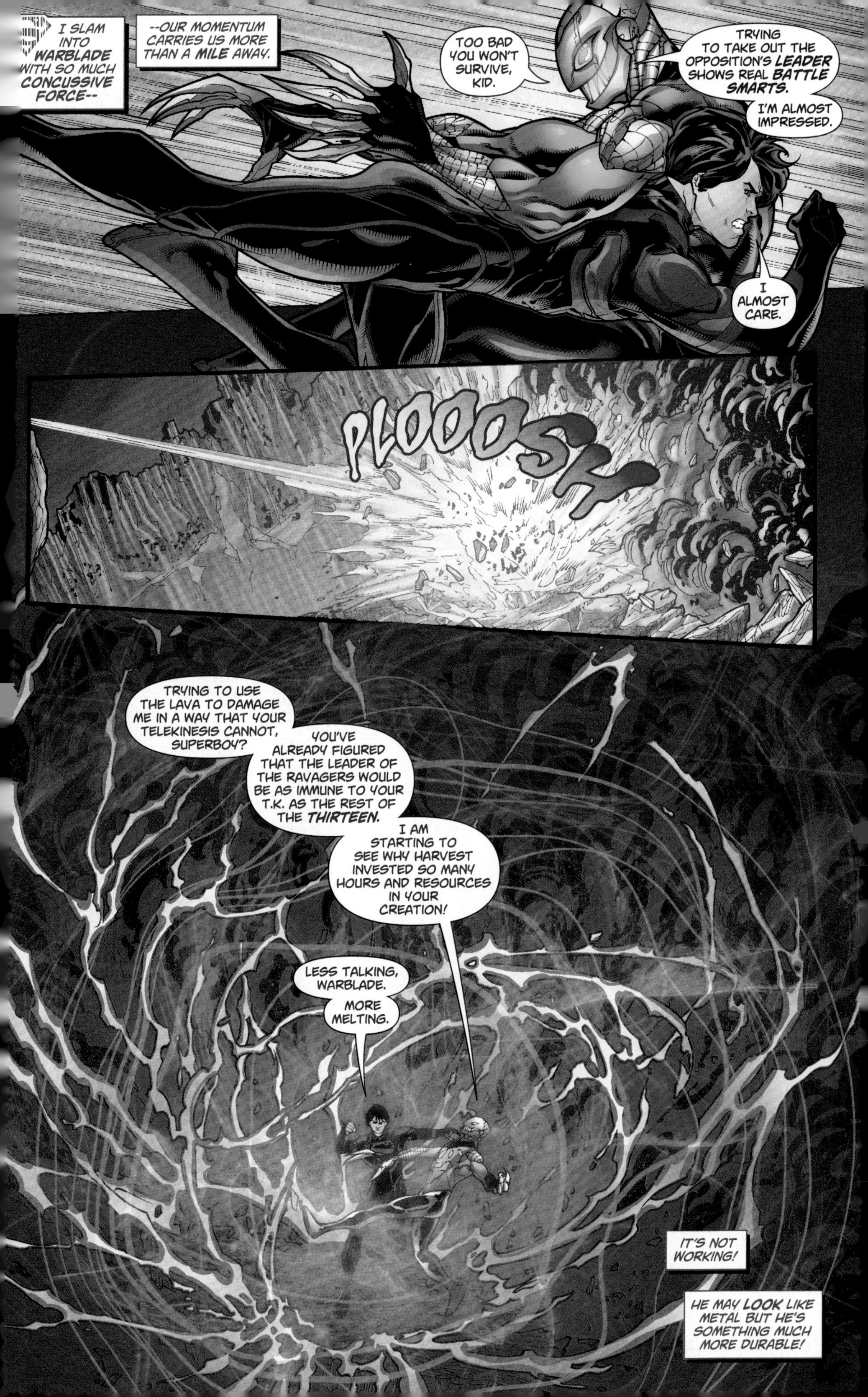
I SLAM INTO WARBLADE WITH SO MUCH CONCUSSIVE FORCE--
--OUR MOMENTUM CARRIES US MORE THAN A MILE AWAY.
TOO BAD YOU WON'T SURVIVE, KID.
TRYING TO TAKE OUT THE OPPOSITION'S LEADER SHOWS REAL BATTLE SMARTS.
I'M ALMOST IMPRESSED.
I ALMOST CARE.
PLOOOSH
TRYING TO USE THE LAVA TO DAMAGE ME IN A WAY THAT YOUR TELEKINESIS CANNOT, SUPERBOY?
YOU'VE ALREADY FIGURED THAT THE LEADER OF THE RAVAGERS WOULD BE AS IMMUNE TO YOUR T.K. AS THE REST OF THE THIRTEEN.
I AM STARTING TO SEE WHY HARVEST INVESTED SO MANY HOURS AND RESOURCES IN YOUR CREATION!
LESS TALKING, WARBLADE.
MORE MELTING.
IT'S NOT WORKING!
HE MAY LOOK LIKE METAL BUT HE'S SOMETHING MUCH MORE DURABLE!

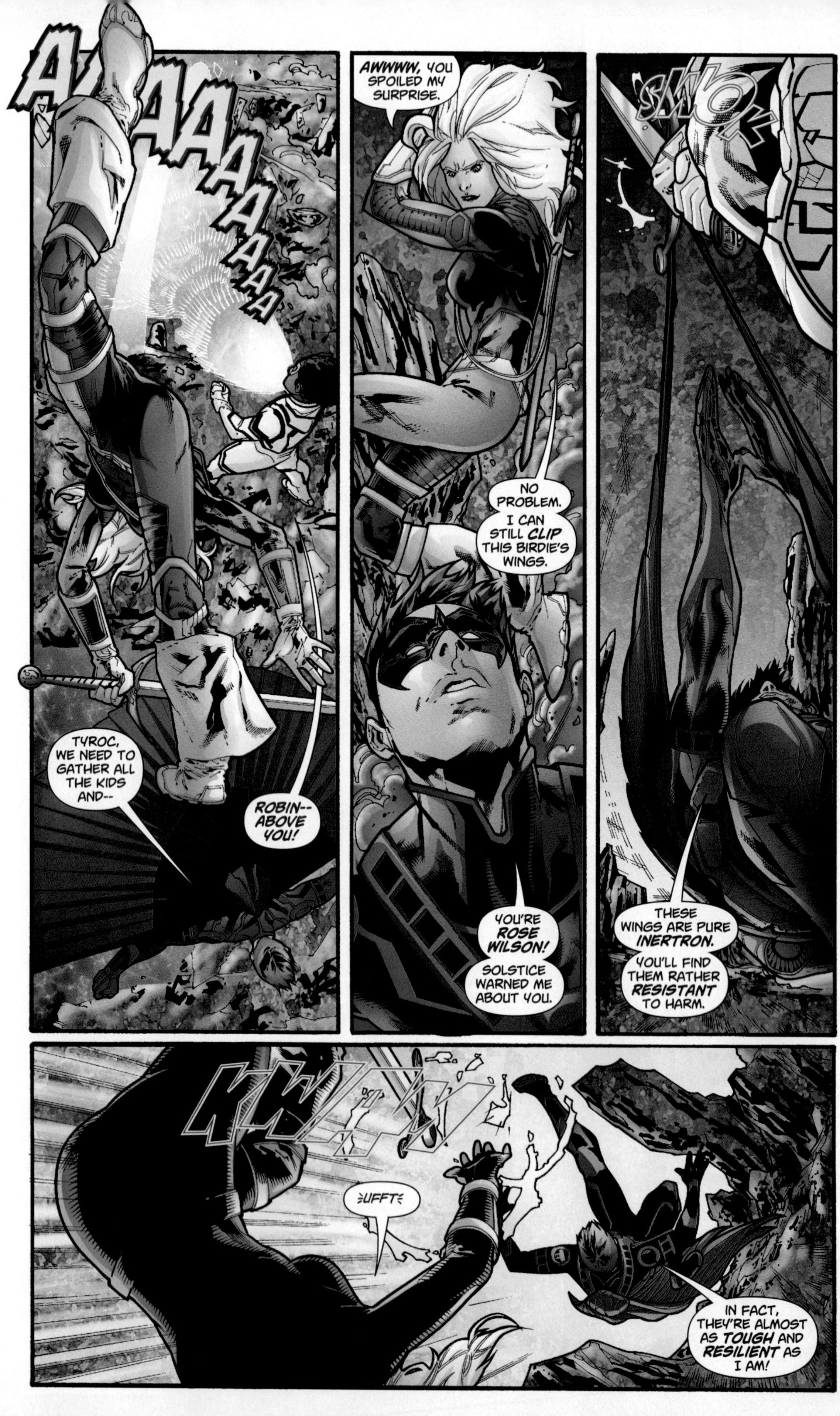
AAAAAAAAA
TYROC, WE NEED TO GATHER ALL THE KIDS AND--
ROBIN-- ABOVE YOU!
AWWWW, YOU SPOILED MY SURPRISE.
NO PROBLEM. I CAN STILL CLIP THIS BIRDIE'S WINGS.
YOU'RE ROSE WILSON!
SOLSTICE WARNED ME ABOUT YOU.
THESE WINGS ARE PURE INERTRON.
YOU'LL FIND THEM RATHER RESISTANT TO HARM.
UFFT
IN FACT, THEY'RE ALMOST AS TOUGH AND RESILIENT AS I AM!

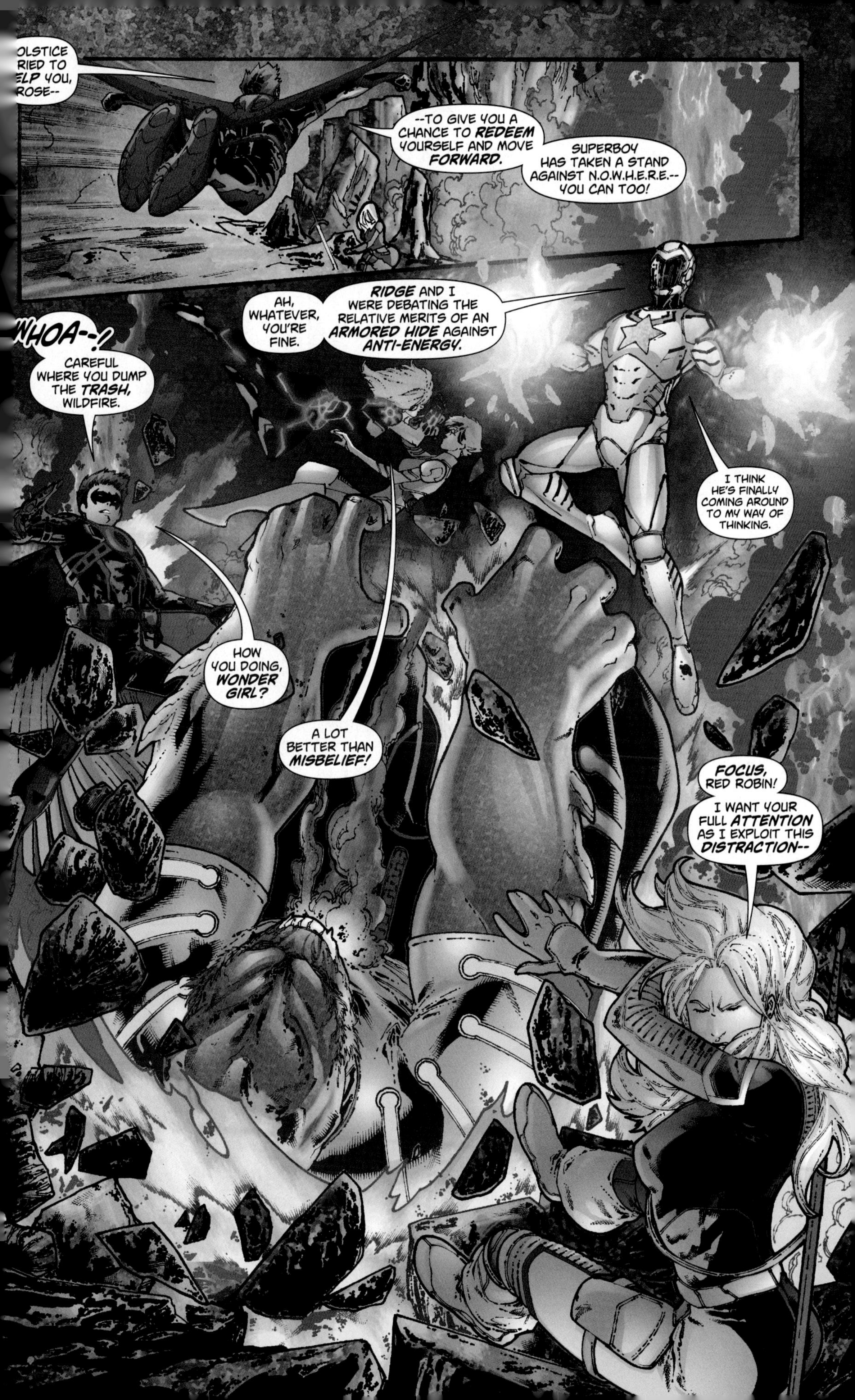

OLSTICE
RIED TO
ELP YOU,
ROSE--
--TO GIVE YOU A CHANCE TO REDEEM YOURSELF AND MOVE FORWARD.
SUPERBOY HAS TAKEN A STAND AGAINST N.O.W.H.E.R.E.-- YOU CAN TOO!
WHOA--!
CAREFUL WHERE YOU DUMP THE TRASH, WILDFIRE.
AH, WHATEVER, YOU'RE FINE.
RIDGE AND I WERE DEBATING THE RELATIVE MERITS OF AN ARMORED HIDE AGAINST ANTI-ENERGY.
I THINK HE'S FINALLY COMING AROUND TO MY WAY OF THINKING.
HOW YOU DOING, WONDER GIRL?
A LOT BETTER THAN MISBELIEF!
FOCUS, RED ROBIN!
I WANT YOUR FULL ATTENTION AS I EXPLOIT THIS DISTRACTION--

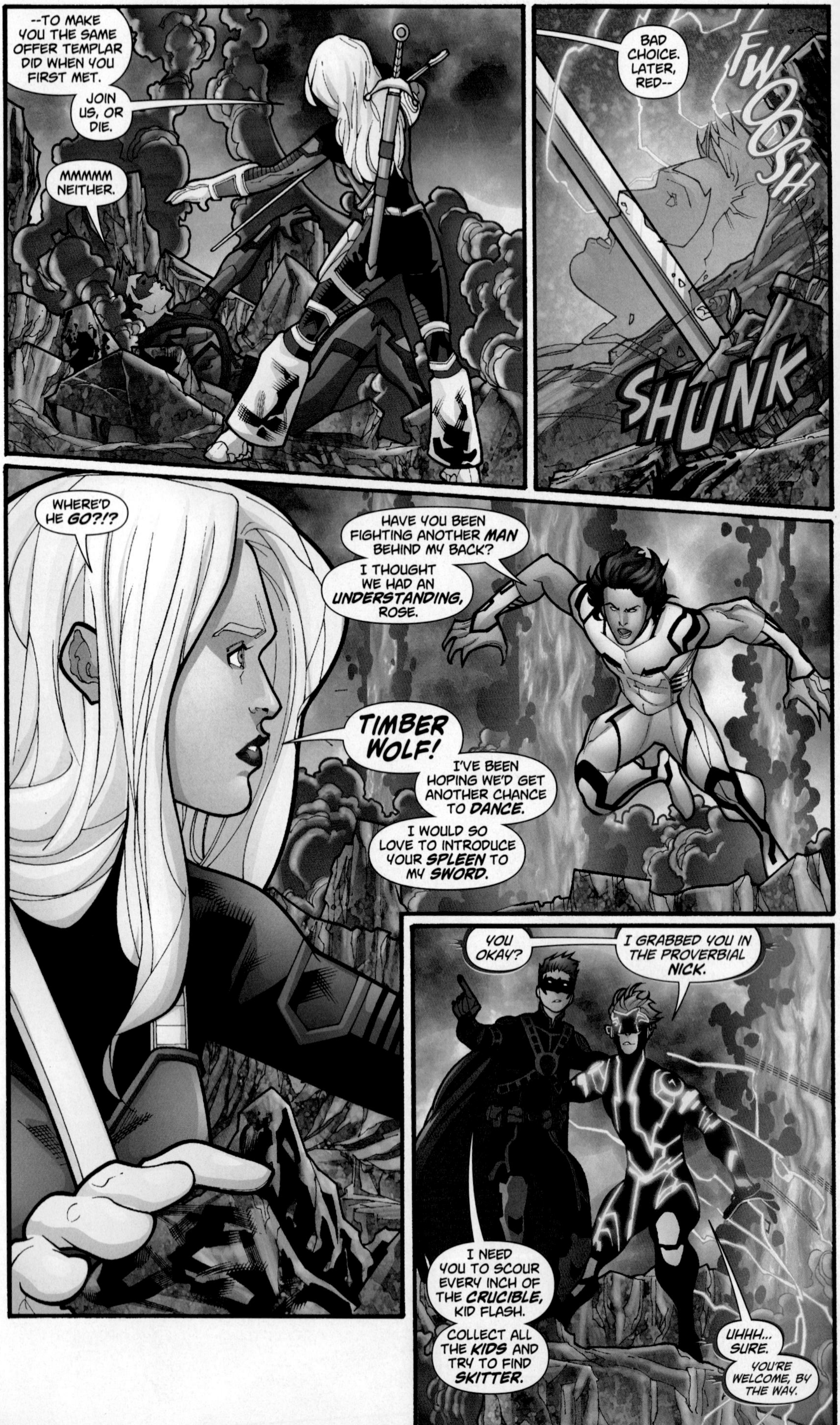
--TO MAKE YOU THE SAME OFFER TEMPLAR DID WHEN YOU FIRST MET.
JOIN US, OR DIE.
MMMMM NEITHER.
BAD CHOICE. LATER, RED--
FWOOSH
SHUNK
WHERE'D HE GO?!?
HAVE YOU BEEN FIGHTING ANOTHER MAN BEHIND MY BACK?
I THOUGHT WE HAD AN UNDERSTANDING, ROSE.
TIMBER WOLF!
I'VE BEEN HOPING WE'D GET ANOTHER CHANCE TO DANCE.
I WOULD SO LOVE TO INTRODUCE YOUR SPLEEN TO MY SWORD.
YOU OKAY?
I GRABBED YOU IN THE PROVERBIAL NICK.
I NEED YOU TO SCOUR EVERY INCH OF THE CRUCIBLE, KID FLASH.
COLLECT ALL THE KIDS AND TRY TO FIND SKITTER.
UHHH... SURE.
YOU'RE WELCOME, BY THE WAY.

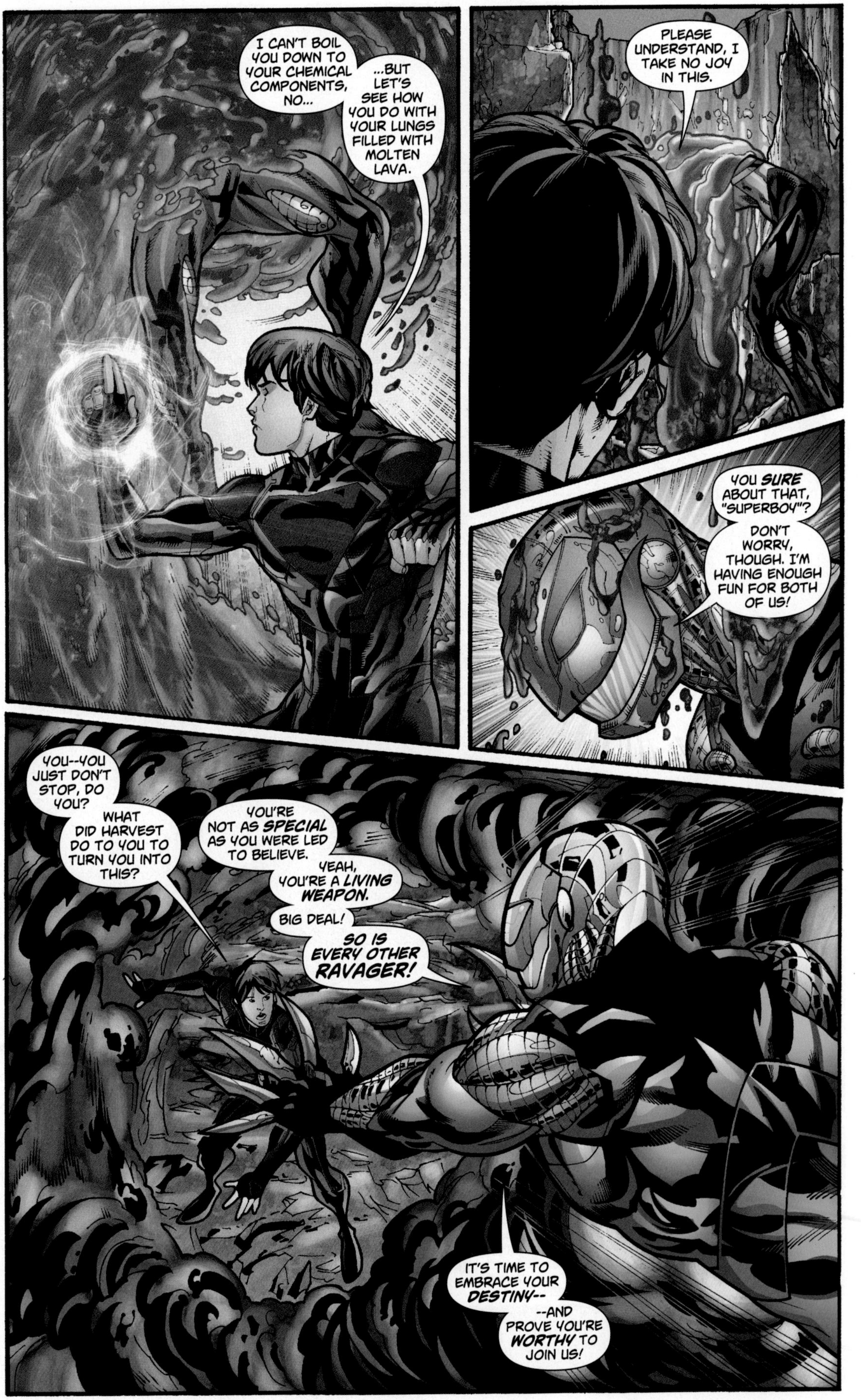
I CAN'T BOIL YOU DOWN TO YOUR CHEMICAL COMPONENTS, NO...
...BUT LET'S SEE HOW YOU DO WITH YOUR LUNGS FILLED WITH MOLTEN LAVA.
PLEASE UNDERSTAND, I TAKE NO JOY IN THIS.
YOU **SURE** ABOUT THAT, "SUPERBOY"?
DON'T WORRY, THOUGH. I'M HAVING ENOUGH FUN FOR BOTH OF US!
YOU--YOU JUST DON'T STOP, DO YOU?
WHAT DID HARVEST DO TO YOU TO TURN YOU INTO THIS?
YOU'RE NOT AS **SPECIAL** AS YOU WERE LED TO BELIEVE.
YEAH, YOU'RE A **LIVING WEAPON.**
BIG DEAL!
SO IS EVERY OTHER RAVAGER!
IT'S TIME TO EMBRACE YOUR **DESTINY**--
--AND PROVE YOU'RE **WORTHY** TO JOIN US!

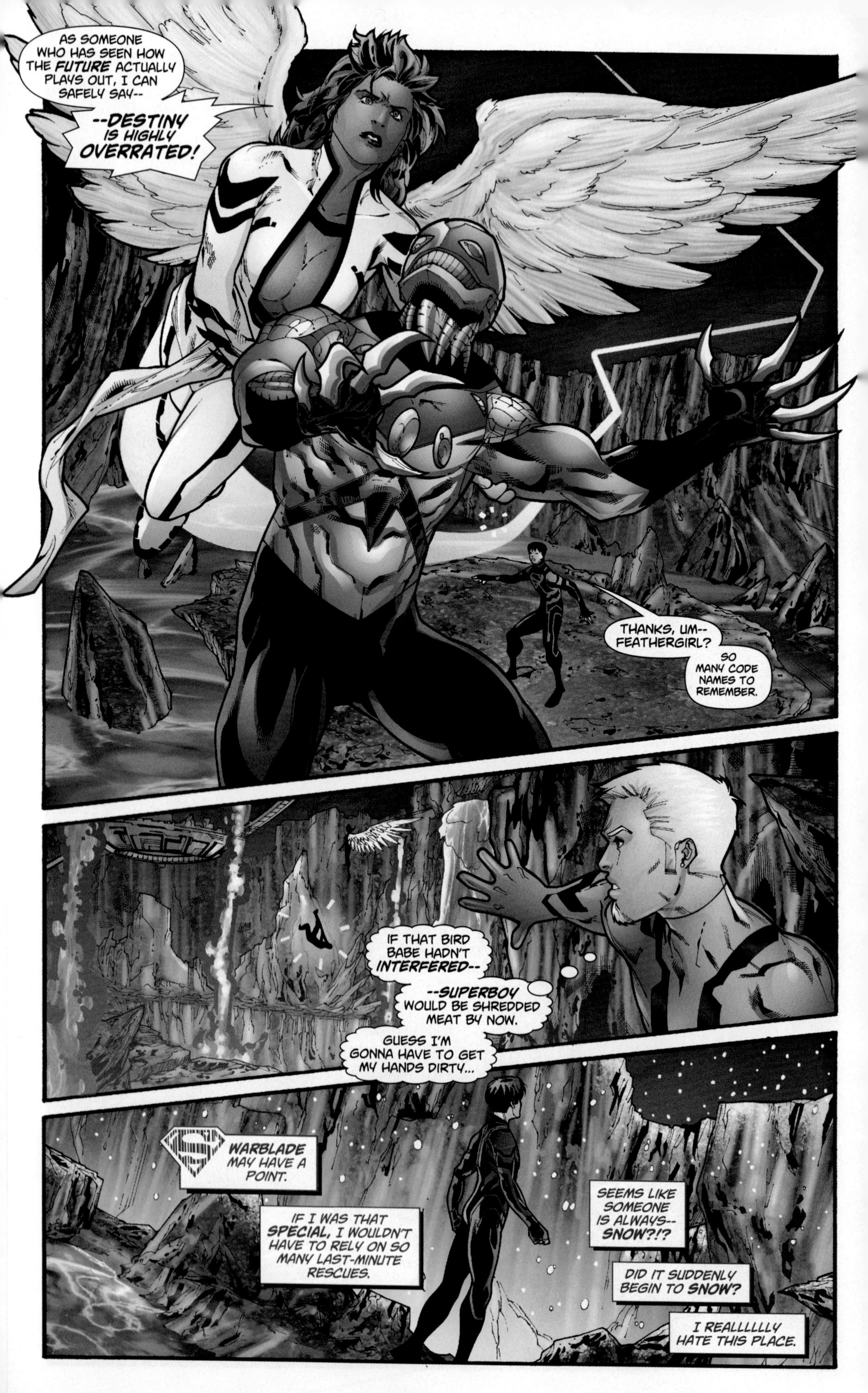
AS SOMEONE WHO HAS SEEN HOW THE FUTURE ACTUALLY PLAYS OUT, I CAN SAFELY SAY--
--DESTINY IS HIGHLY OVERRATED!
THANKS, UM-- FEATHERGIRL?
SO MANY CODE NAMES TO REMEMBER.
IF THAT BIRD BABE HADN'T INTERFERED--
--SUPERBOY WOULD BE SHREDDED MEAT BY NOW.
GUESS I'M GONNA HAVE TO GET MY HANDS DIRTY...
WARBLADE MAY HAVE A POINT.
IF I WAS THAT SPECIAL, I WOULDN'T HAVE TO RELY ON SO MANY LAST-MINUTE RESCUES.
SEEMS LIKE SOMEONE IS ALWAYS-- SNOW?!?
DID IT SUDDENLY BEGIN TO SNOW?
I REALLLLLLY HATE THIS PLACE.

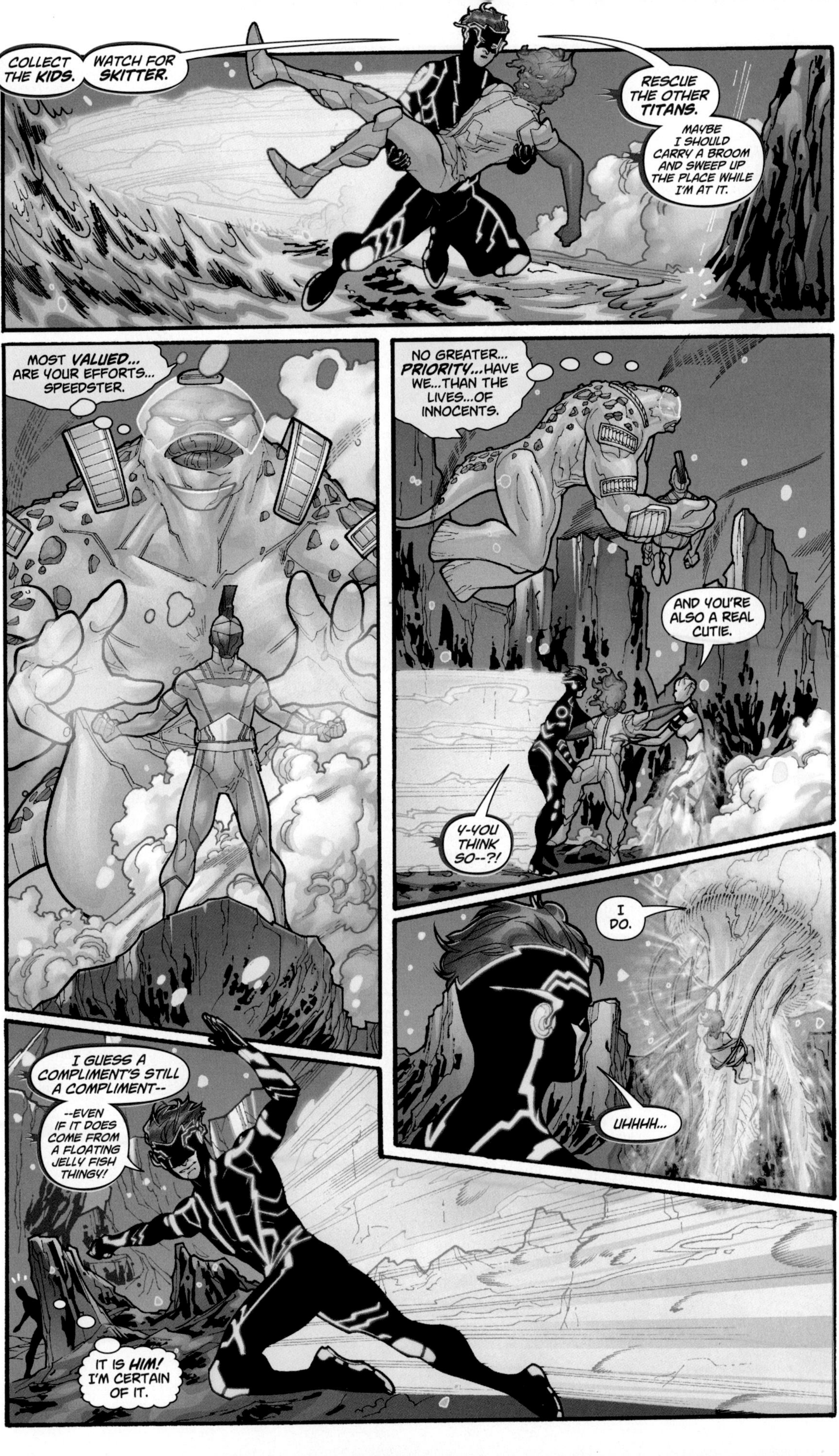

COLLECT THE KIDS.
WATCH FOR SKITTER.
RESCUE THE OTHER TITANS.
MAYBE I SHOULD CARRY A BROOM AND SWEEP UP THE PLACE WHILE I'M AT IT.
MOST VALUED... ARE YOUR EFFORTS... SPEEDSTER.
NO GREATER... PRIORITY...HAVE WE...THAN THE LIVES...OF INNOCENTS.
AND YOU'RE ALSO A REAL CUTIE.
Y-YOU THINK SO--?!
I DO.
UHHHH...
I GUESS A COMPLIMENT'S STILL A COMPLIMENT--
--EVEN IF IT DOES COME FROM A FLOATING JELLY FISH THINGY!
IT IS HIM! I'M CERTAIN OF IT.

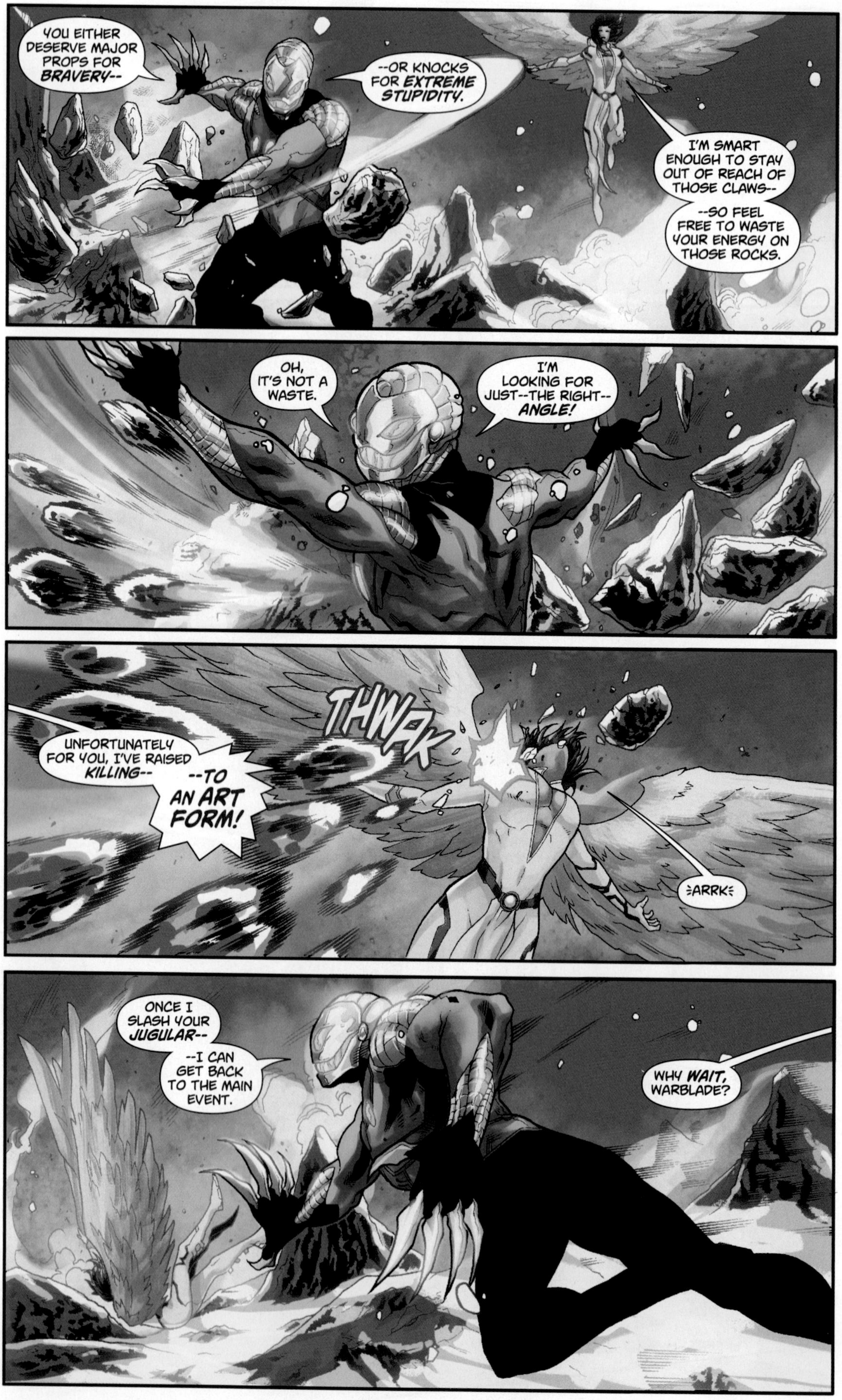
YOU EITHER DESERVE MAJOR PROPS FOR BRAVERY--
--OR KNOCKS FOR EXTREME STUPIDITY.
I'M SMART ENOUGH TO STAY OUT OF REACH OF THOSE CLAWS--
--SO FEEL FREE TO WASTE YOUR ENERGY ON THOSE ROCKS.
OH, IT'S NOT A WASTE.
I'M LOOKING FOR JUST--THE RIGHT-- ANGLE!
THWAK
UNFORTUNATELY FOR YOU, I'VE RAISED KILLING--
--TO AN ART FORM!
ARRK
ONCE I SLASH YOUR JUGULAR--
--I CAN GET BACK TO THE MAIN EVENT.
WHY WAIT, WARBLADE?

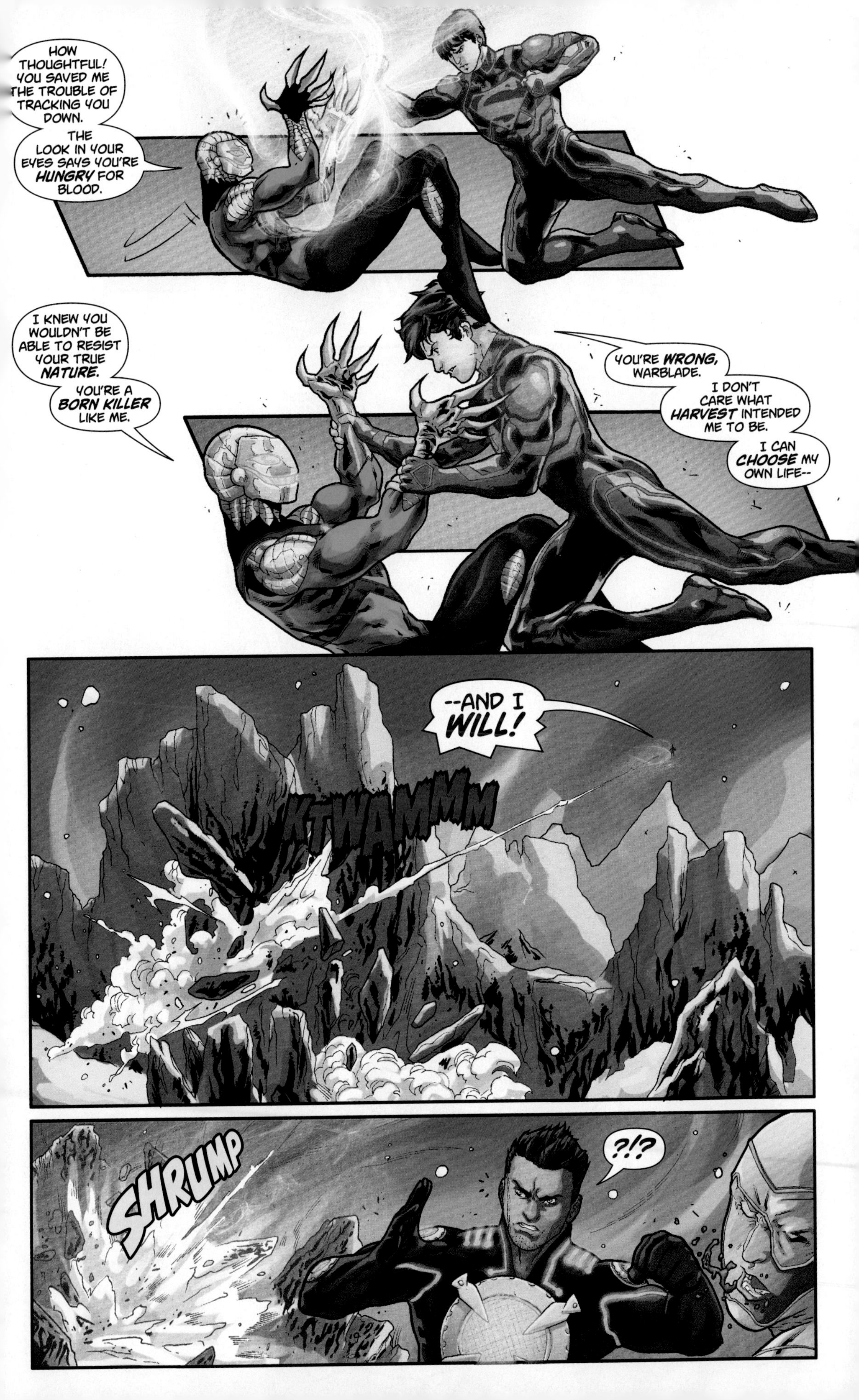
HOW THOUGHTFUL! YOU SAVED ME THE TROUBLE OF TRACKING YOU DOWN.
THE LOOK IN YOUR EYES SAYS YOU'RE HUNGRY FOR BLOOD.
I KNEW YOU WOULDN'T BE ABLE TO RESIST YOUR TRUE NATURE.
YOU'RE A BORN KILLER LIKE ME.
YOU'RE WRONG, WARBLADE.
I DON'T CARE WHAT HARVEST INTENDED ME TO BE.
I CAN CHOOSE MY OWN LIFE--
--AND I WILL!
KTWAMMMM
SHRUMP
?!?

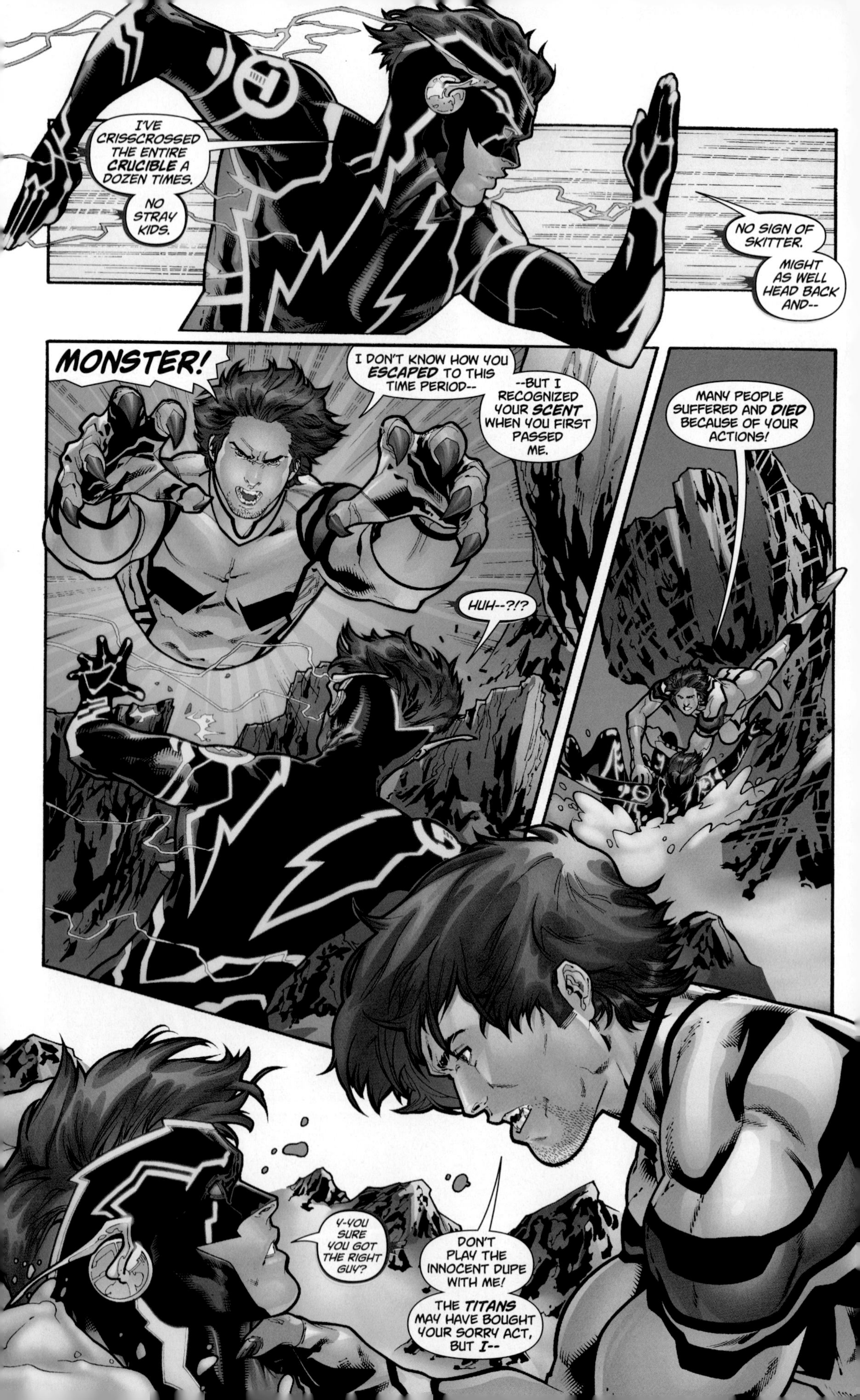
I'VE CRISSCROSSED THE ENTIRE CRUCIBLE A DOZEN TIMES.
NO STRAY KIDS.
NO SIGN OF SKITTER.
MIGHT AS WELL HEAD BACK AND--
MONSTER!
I DON'T KNOW HOW YOU ESCAPED TO THIS TIME PERIOD--
--BUT I RECOGNIZED YOUR SCENT WHEN YOU FIRST PASSED ME.
HUH--?!?
MANY PEOPLE SUFFERED AND DIED BECAUSE OF YOUR ACTIONS!
Y-YOU SURE YOU GOT THE RIGHT GUY?
DON'T PLAY THE INNOCENT DUPE WITH ME!
THE TITANS MAY HAVE BOUGHT YOUR SORRY ACT, BUT I--

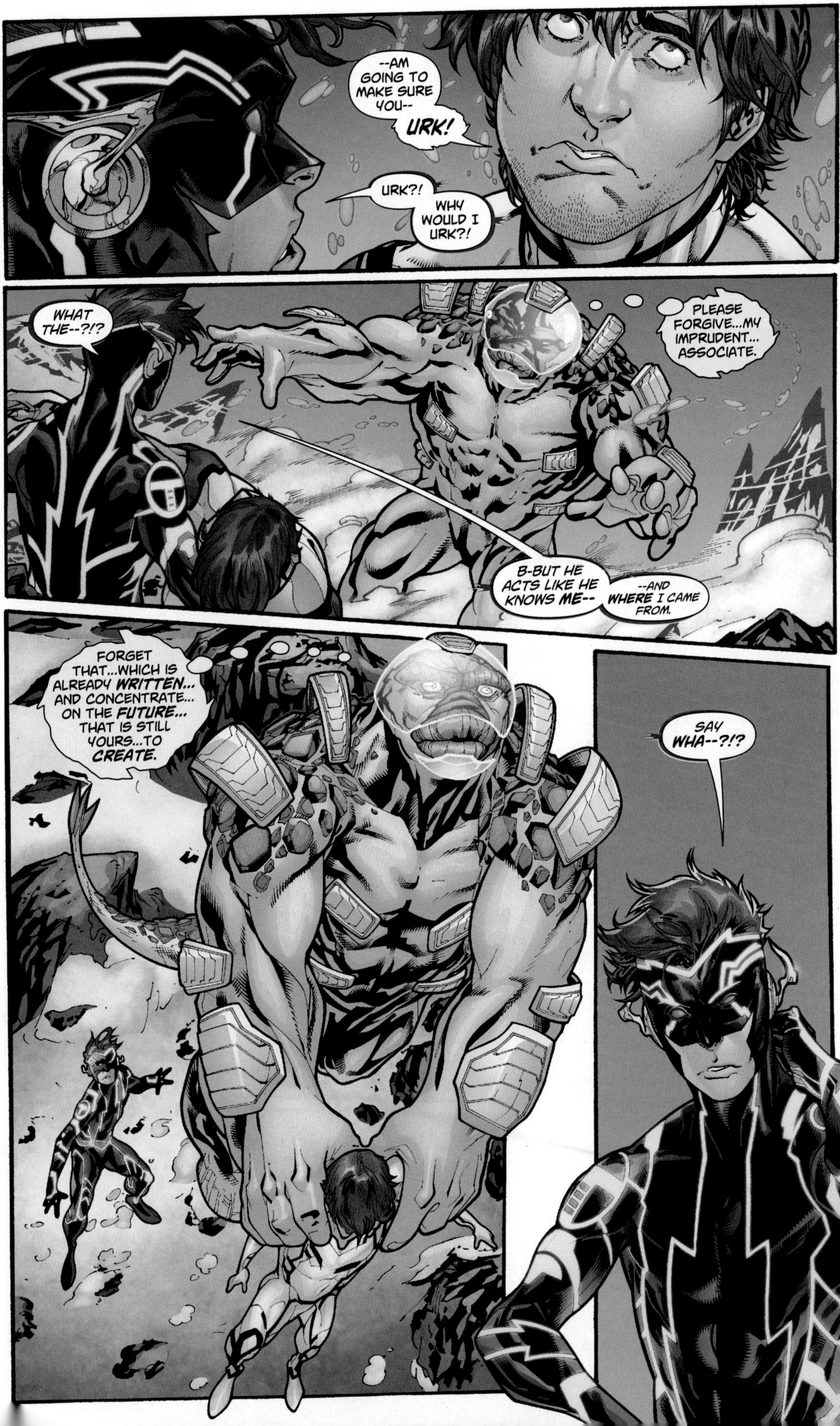
--AM GOING TO MAKE SURE YOU--
URK!
URK?!
WHY WOULD I URK?!
WHAT THE--?!?
PLEASE FORGIVE...MY IMPRUDENT... ASSOCIATE.
B-BUT HE ACTS LIKE HE KNOWS ME--
--AND WHERE I CAME FROM.
FORGET THAT...WHICH IS ALREADY WRITTEN... AND CONCENTRATE... ON THE FUTURE... THAT IS STILL YOURS...TO CREATE.
SAY WHA--?!?

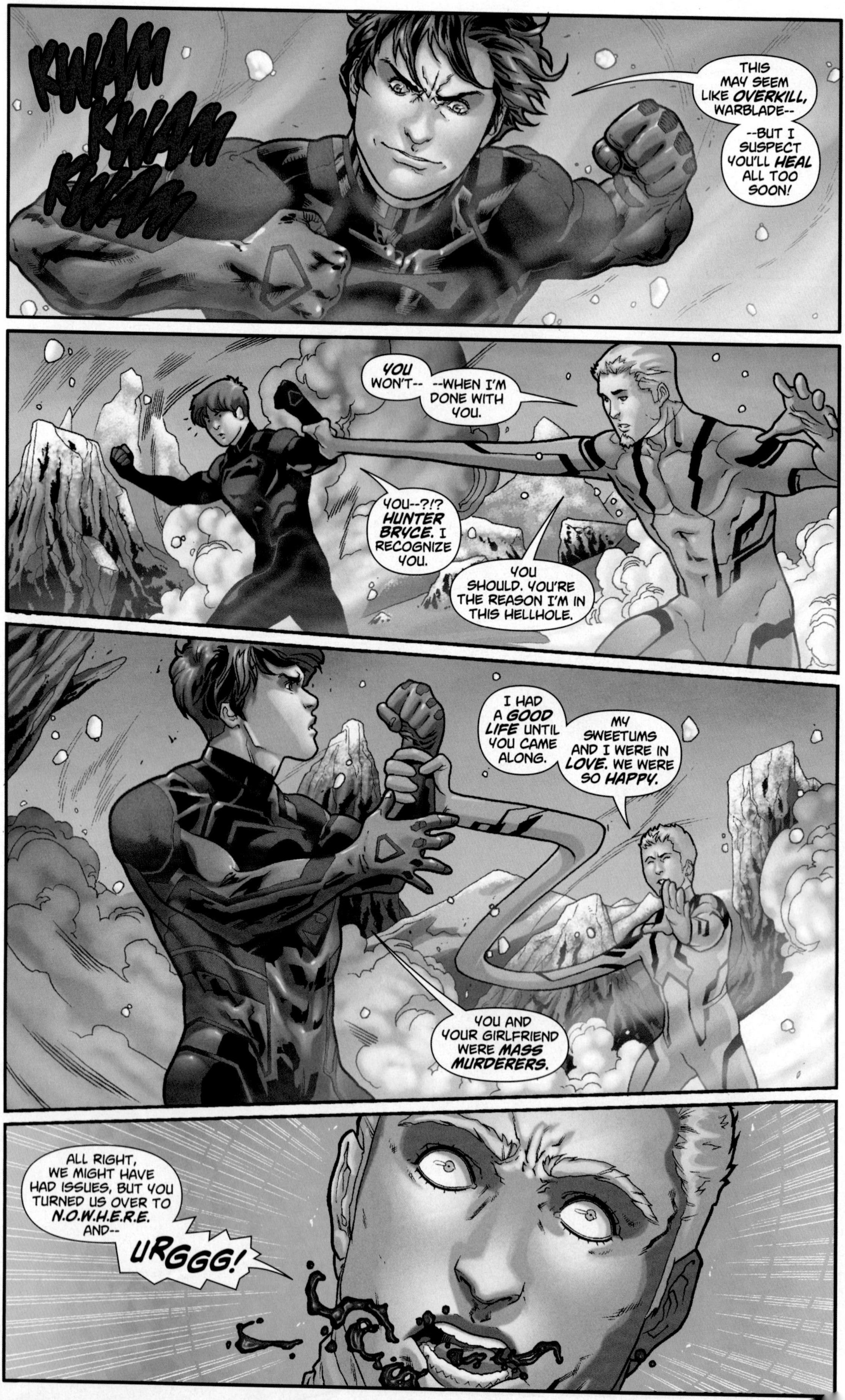
KWAM KWAM KWAM
THIS MAY SEEM LIKE OVERKILL, WARBLADE--
--BUT I SUSPECT YOU'LL HEAL ALL TOO SOON!
YOU WON'T--
--WHEN I'M DONE WITH YOU.
YOU--?!? HUNTER BRYCE. I RECOGNIZE YOU.
YOU SHOULD. YOU'RE THE REASON I'M IN THIS HELLHOLE.
I HAD A GOOD LIFE UNTIL YOU CAME ALONG.
MY SWEETUMS AND I WERE IN LOVE. WE WERE SO HAPPY.
YOU AND YOUR GIRLFRIEND WERE MASS MURDERERS.
ALL RIGHT, WE MIGHT HAVE HAD ISSUES, BUT YOU TURNED US OVER TO N.O.W.H.E.R.E. AND--
URGGG!

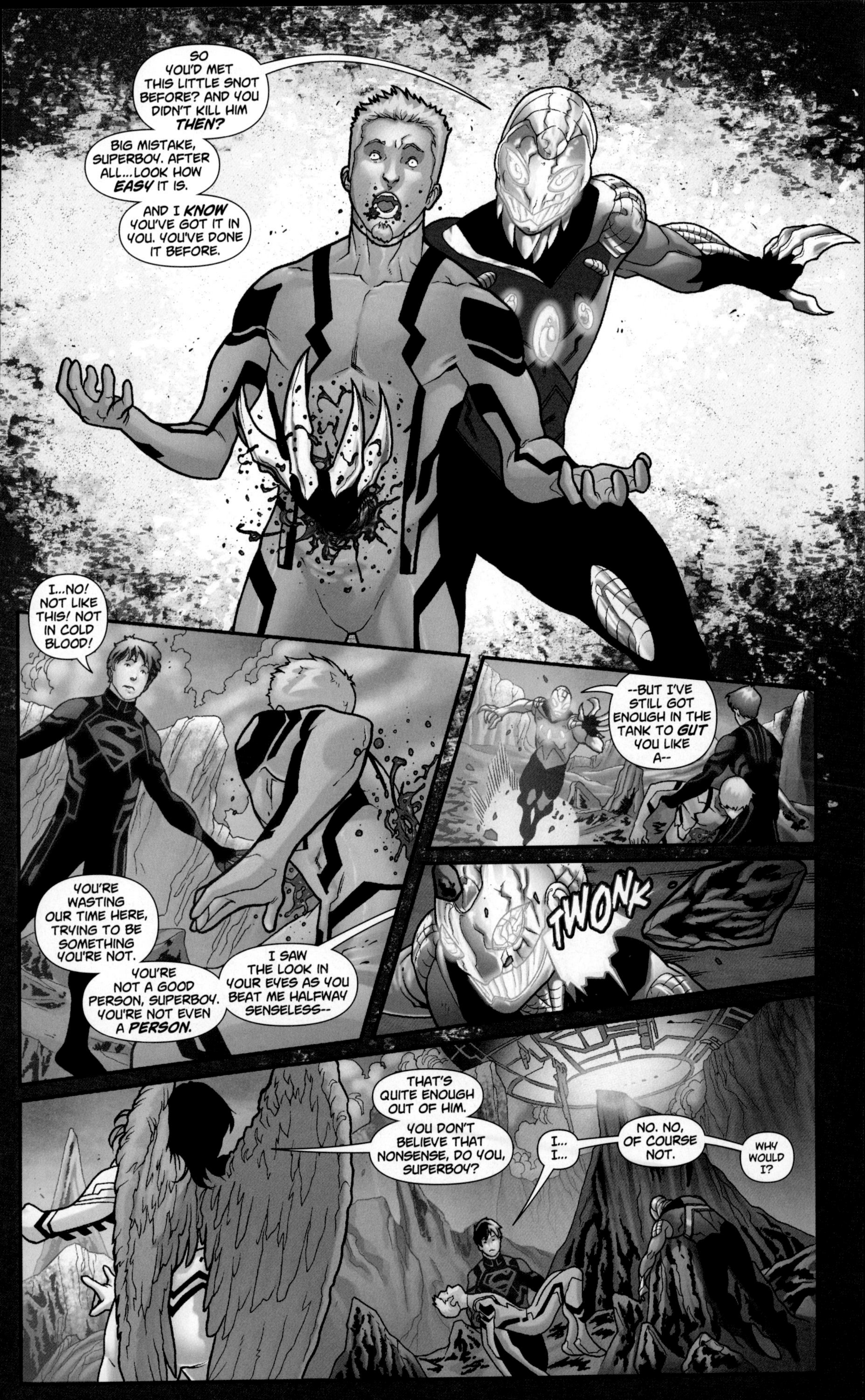

SO YOU'D MET THIS LITTLE SNOT BEFORE? AND YOU DIDN'T KILL HIM *THEN?*
BIG MISTAKE, SUPERBOY. AFTER ALL...LOOK HOW *EASY* IT IS.
AND I *KNOW* YOU'VE GOT IT IN YOU. YOU'VE DONE IT BEFORE.
I...NO! NOT LIKE THIS! NOT IN COLD BLOOD!
YOU'RE WASTING OUR TIME HERE, TRYING TO BE SOMETHING YOU'RE NOT.
YOU'RE NOT A GOOD PERSON, SUPERBOY. YOU'RE NOT EVEN A *PERSON.*
I SAW THE LOOK IN YOUR EYES AS YOU BEAT ME HALFWAY SENSELESS--
--BUT I'VE STILL GOT ENOUGH IN THE TANK TO *GUT* YOU LIKE A--
TWONK
THAT'S QUITE ENOUGH OUT OF HIM.
YOU DON'T BELIEVE THAT NONSENSE, DO YOU, SUPERBOY?
I... I...
NO. NO, OF COURSE NOT.
WHY WOULD I?

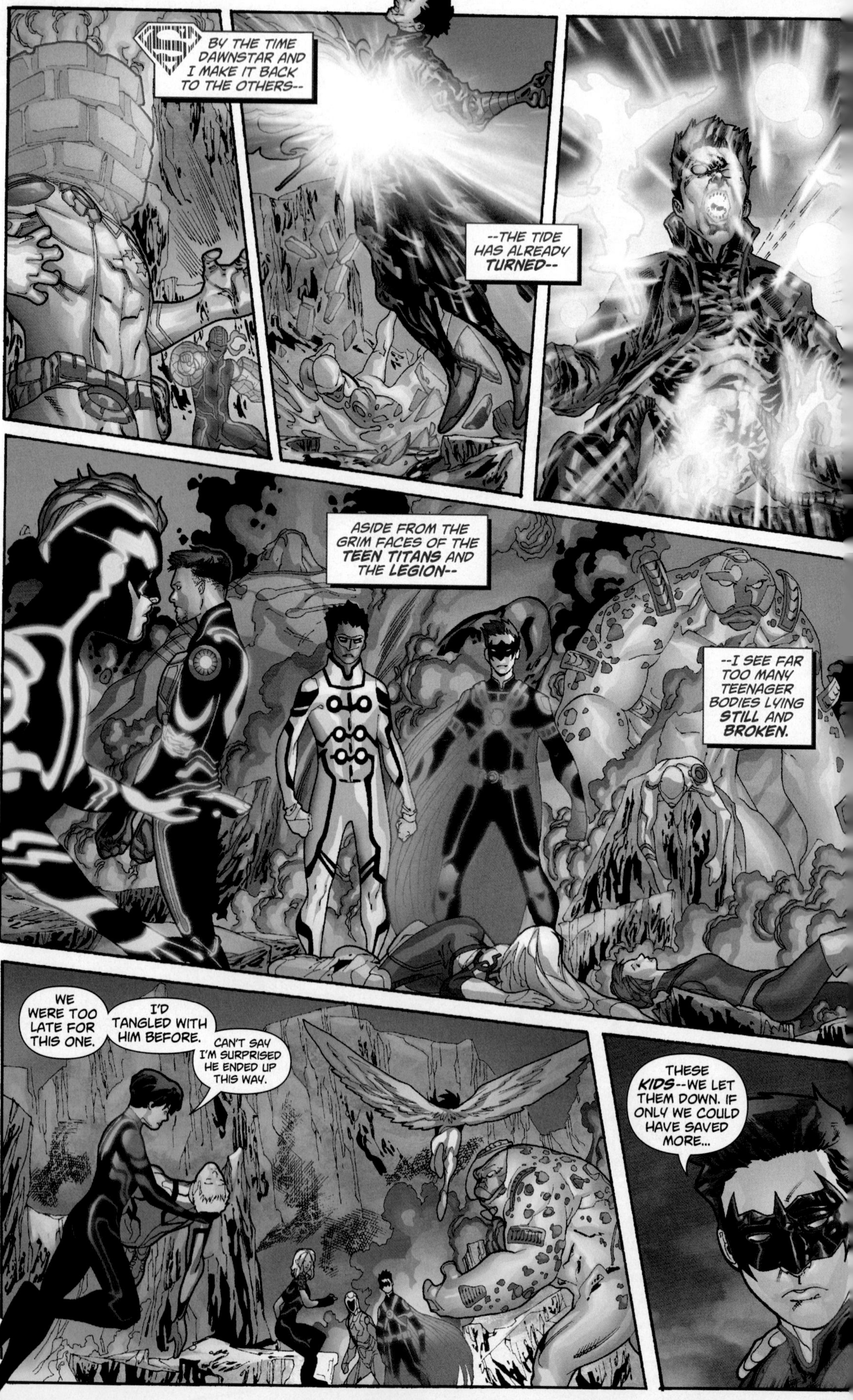
BY THE TIME DAWNSTAR AND I MAKE IT BACK TO THE OTHERS--
--THE TIDE HAS ALREADY TURNED--
ASIDE FROM THE GRIM FACES OF THE TEEN TITANS AND THE LEGION--
--I SEE FAR TOO MANY TEENAGER BODIES LYING STILL AND BROKEN.
WE WERE TOO LATE FOR THIS ONE.
I'D TANGLED WITH HIM BEFORE.
CAN'T SAY I'M SURPRISED HE ENDED UP THIS WAY.
THESE KIDS--WE LET THEM DOWN. IF ONLY WE COULD HAVE SAVED MORE...

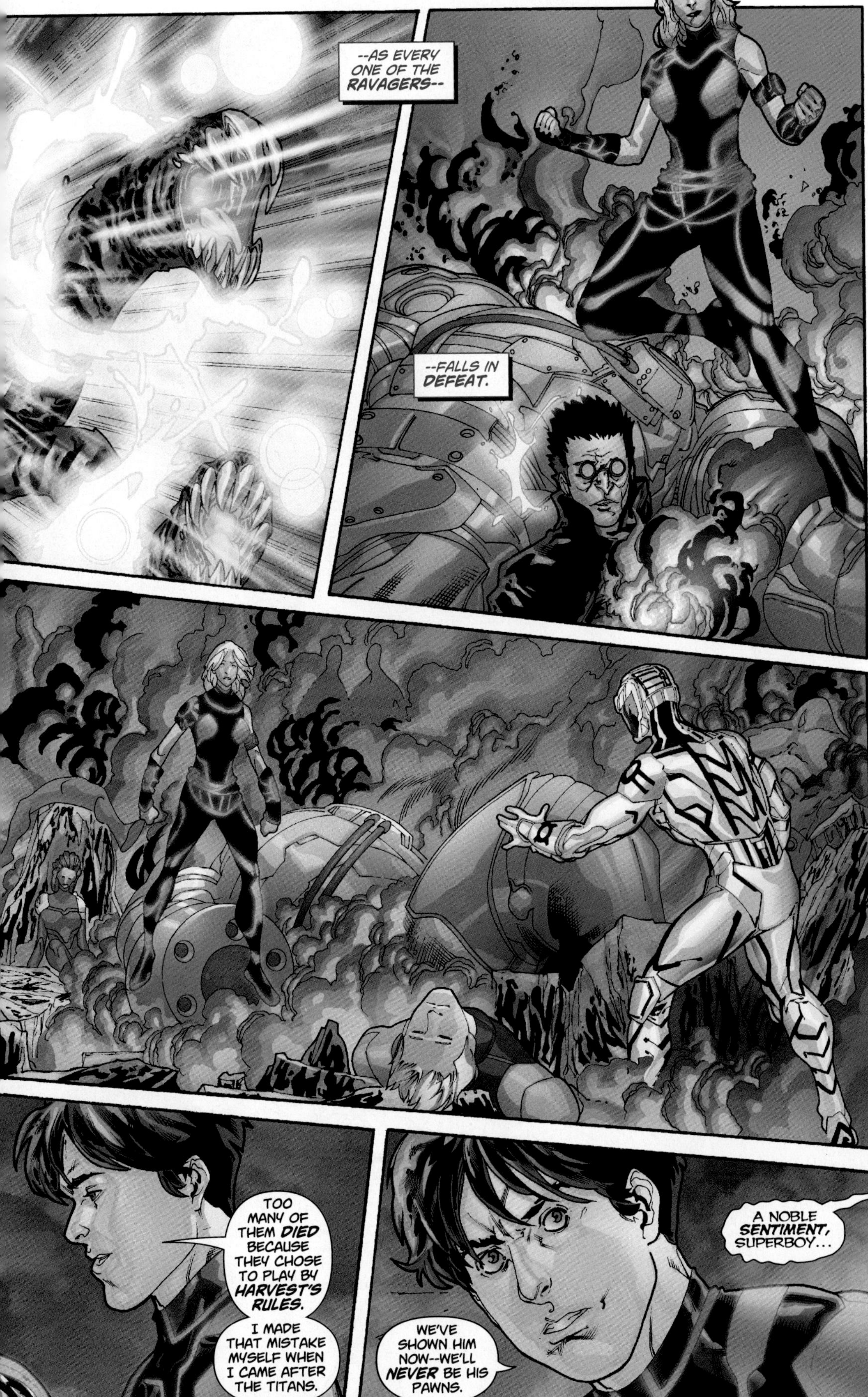
--AS EVERY ONE OF THE RAVAGERS--
--FALLS IN DEFEAT.
TOO MANY OF THEM DIED BECAUSE THEY CHOSE TO PLAY BY HARVEST'S RULES.
I MADE THAT MISTAKE MYSELF WHEN I CAME AFTER THE TITANS.
WE'VE SHOWN HIM NOW--WE'LL NEVER BE HIS PAWNS.
A NOBLE SENTIMENT, SUPERBOY...

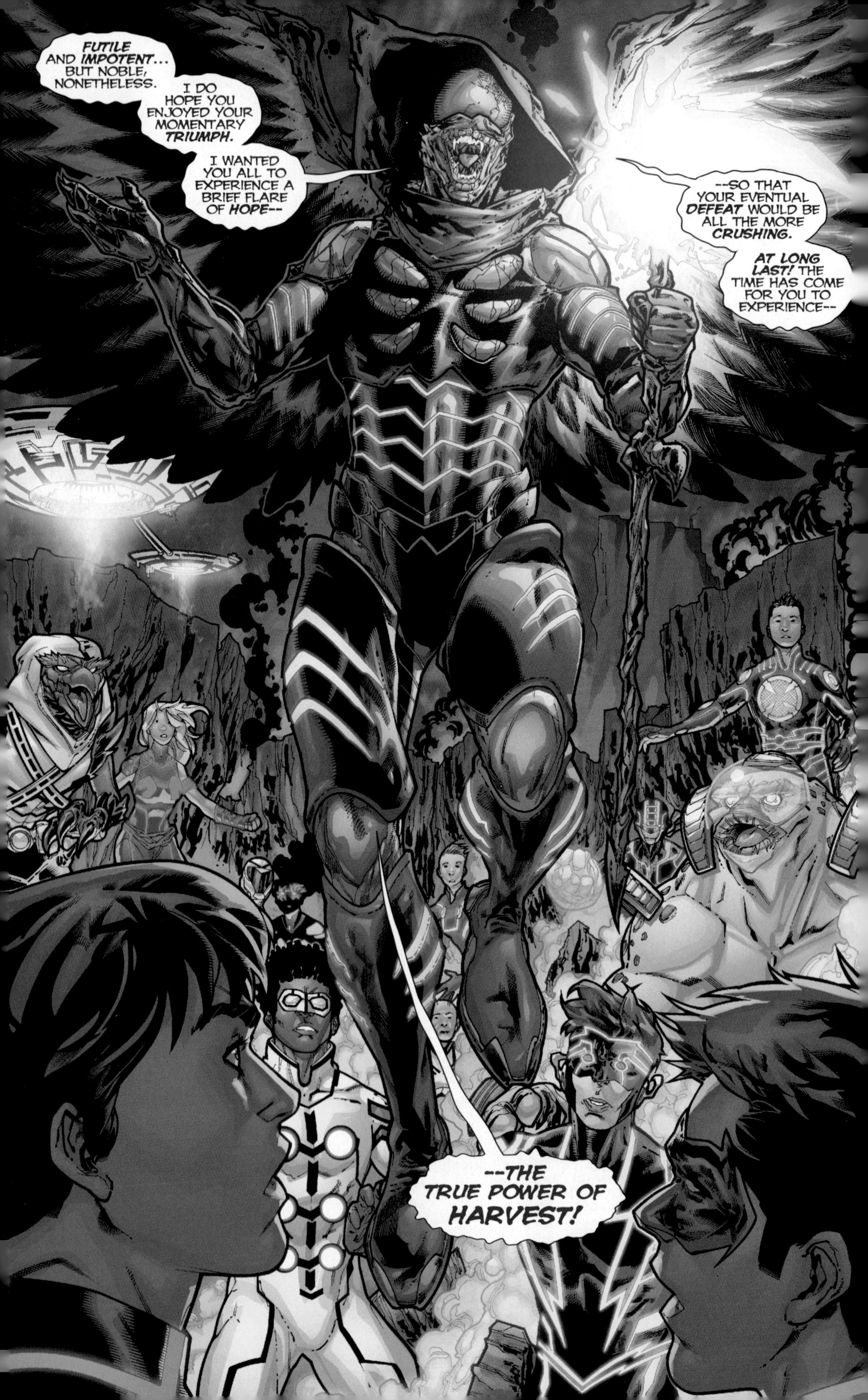
FUTILE AND IMPOTENT... BUT NOBLE, NONETHELESS.
I DO HOPE YOU ENJOYED YOUR MOMENTARY TRIUMPH.
I WANTED YOU ALL TO EXPERIENCE A BRIEF FLARE OF HOPE--
--SO THAT YOUR EVENTUAL DEFEAT WOULD BE ALL THE MORE CRUSHING.
AT LONG LAST! THE TIME HAS COME FOR YOU TO EXPERIENCE--
--THE TRUE POWER OF HARVEST!

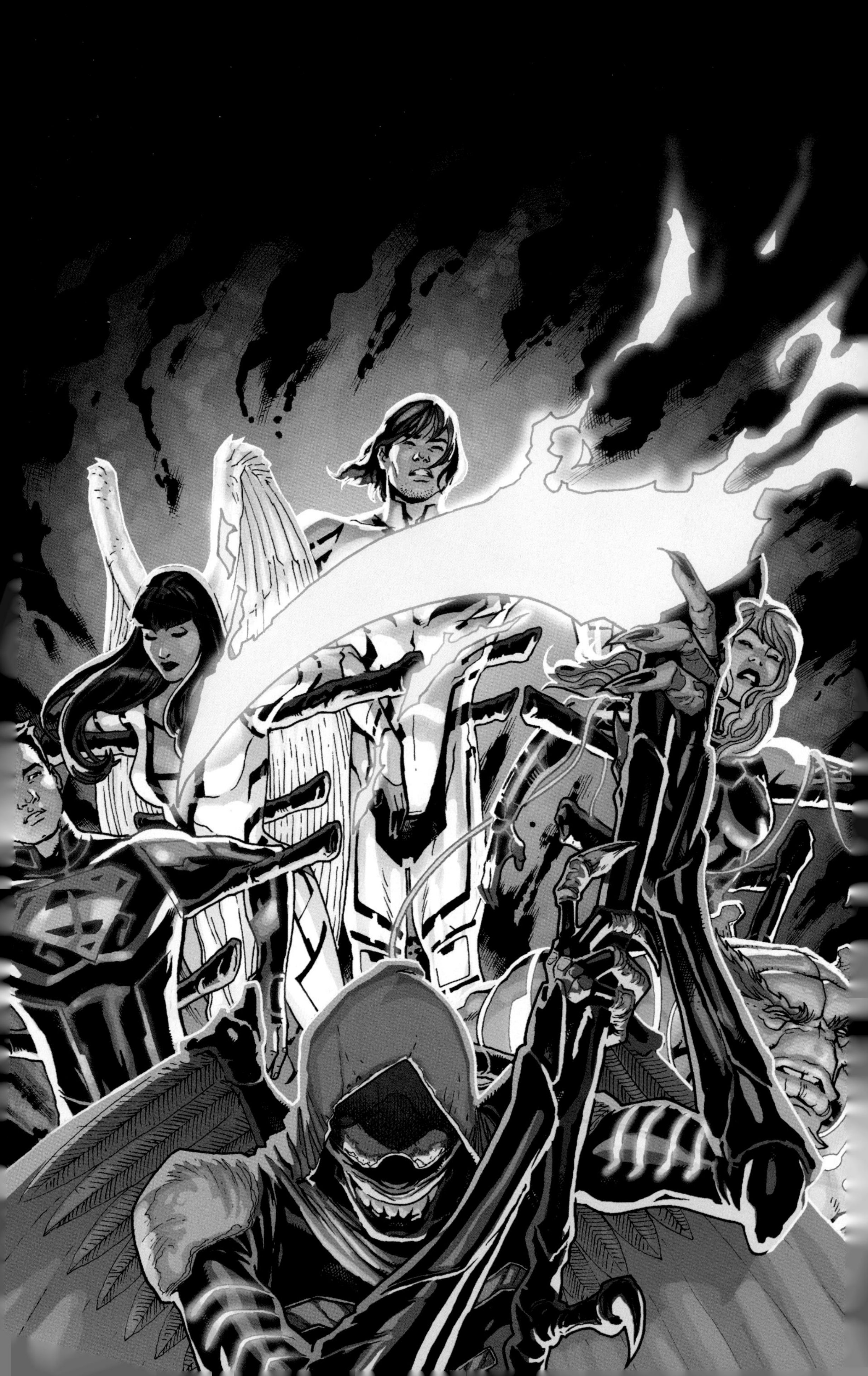

THE CULLING PART THREE: UNBEATABLE
TOM DEFALCO writer   PETE WOODS artist
cover art by PETE WOODS & BRAD ANDERSON

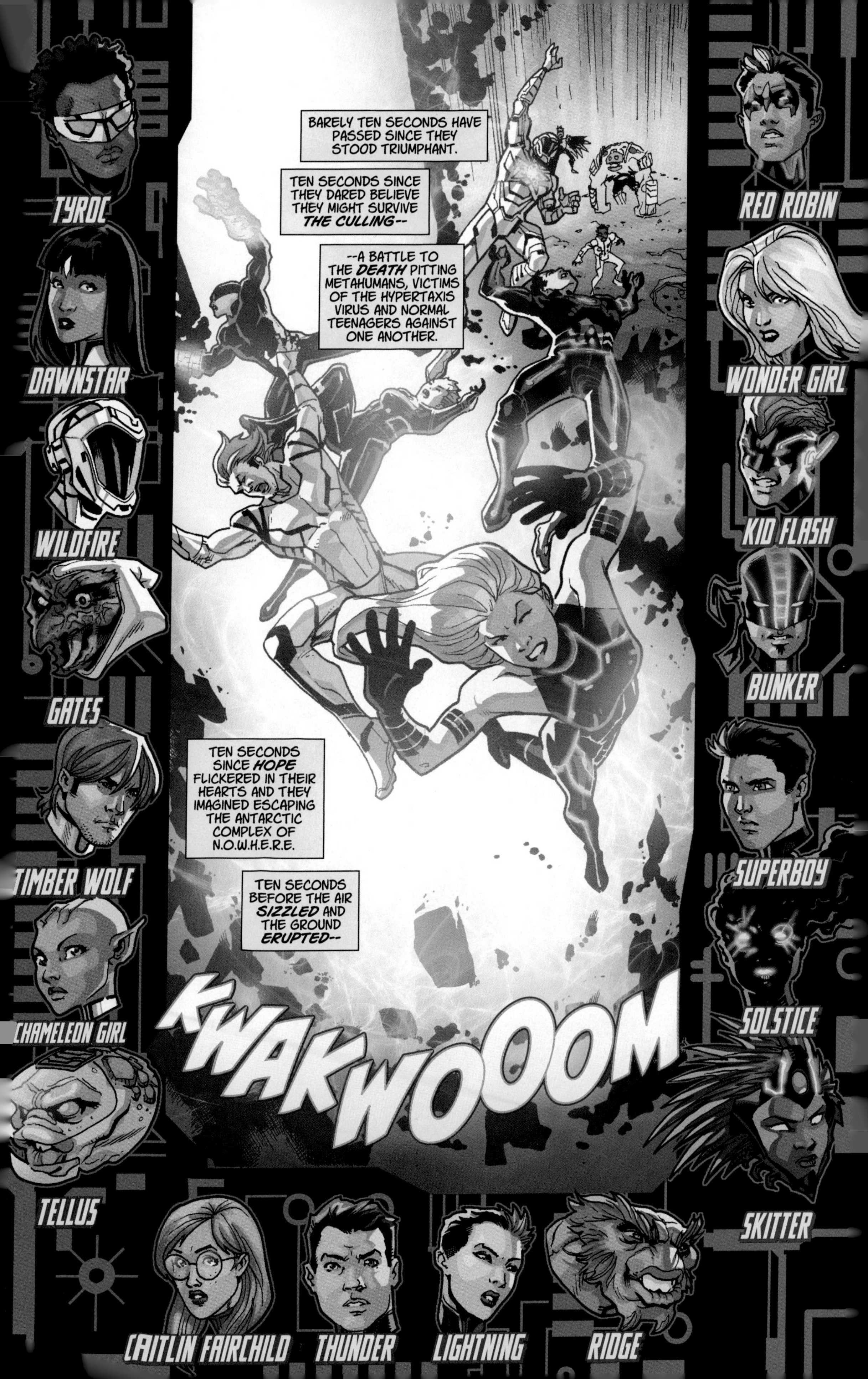
TYROC
DAWNSTAR
WILDFIRE
GATES
TIMBER WOLF
CHAMELEON GIRL
TELLUS
BARELY TEN SECONDS HAVE PASSED SINCE THEY STOOD TRIUMPHANT.
TEN SECONDS SINCE THEY DARED BELIEVE THEY MIGHT SURVIVE THE CULLING--
--A BATTLE TO THE DEATH PITTING METAHUMANS, VICTIMS OF THE HYPERTAXIS VIRUS AND NORMAL TEENAGERS AGAINST ONE ANOTHER.
TEN SECONDS SINCE HOPE FLICKERED IN THEIR HEARTS AND THEY IMAGINED ESCAPING THE ANTARCTIC COMPLEX OF N.O.W.H.E.R.E.
TEN SECONDS BEFORE THE AIR SIZZLED AND THE GROUND ERUPTED--
KWAKWOOOOM
RED ROBIN
WONDER GIRL
KID FLASH
BUNKER
SUPERBOY
SOLSTICE
SKITTER
CAITLIN FAIRCHILD
THUNDER
LIGHTNING
RIDGE

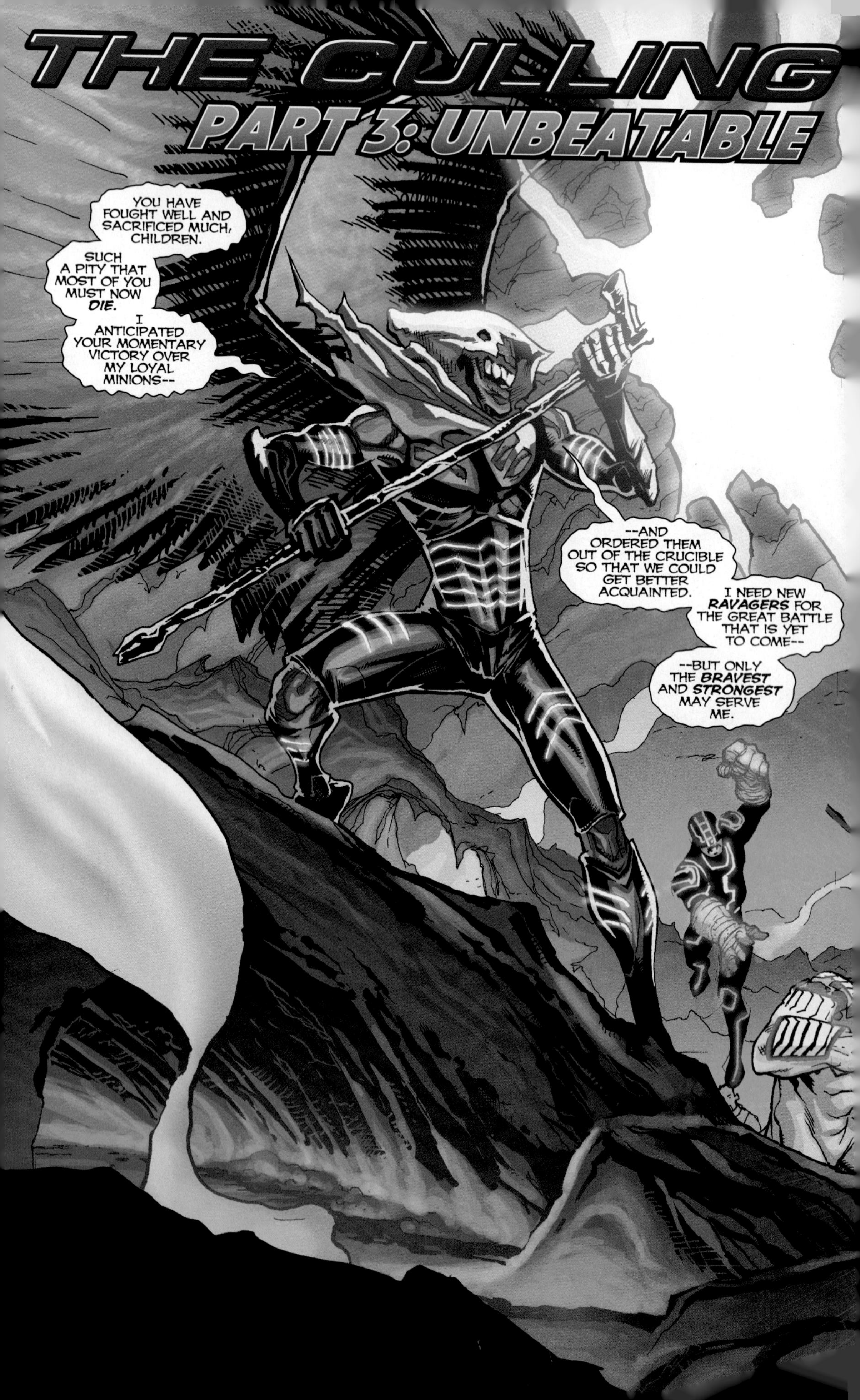
THE CULLING
PART 3: UNBEATABLE
YOU HAVE FOUGHT WELL AND SACRIFICED MUCH, CHILDREN.
SUCH A PITY THAT MOST OF YOU MUST NOW DIE.
I ANTICIPATED YOUR MOMENTARY VICTORY OVER MY LOYAL MINIONS--
--AND ORDERED THEM OUT OF THE CRUCIBLE SO THAT WE COULD GET BETTER ACQUAINTED.
I NEED NEW RAVAGERS FOR THE GREAT BATTLE THAT IS YET TO COME--
--BUT ONLY THE BRAVEST AND STRONGEST MAY SERVE ME.

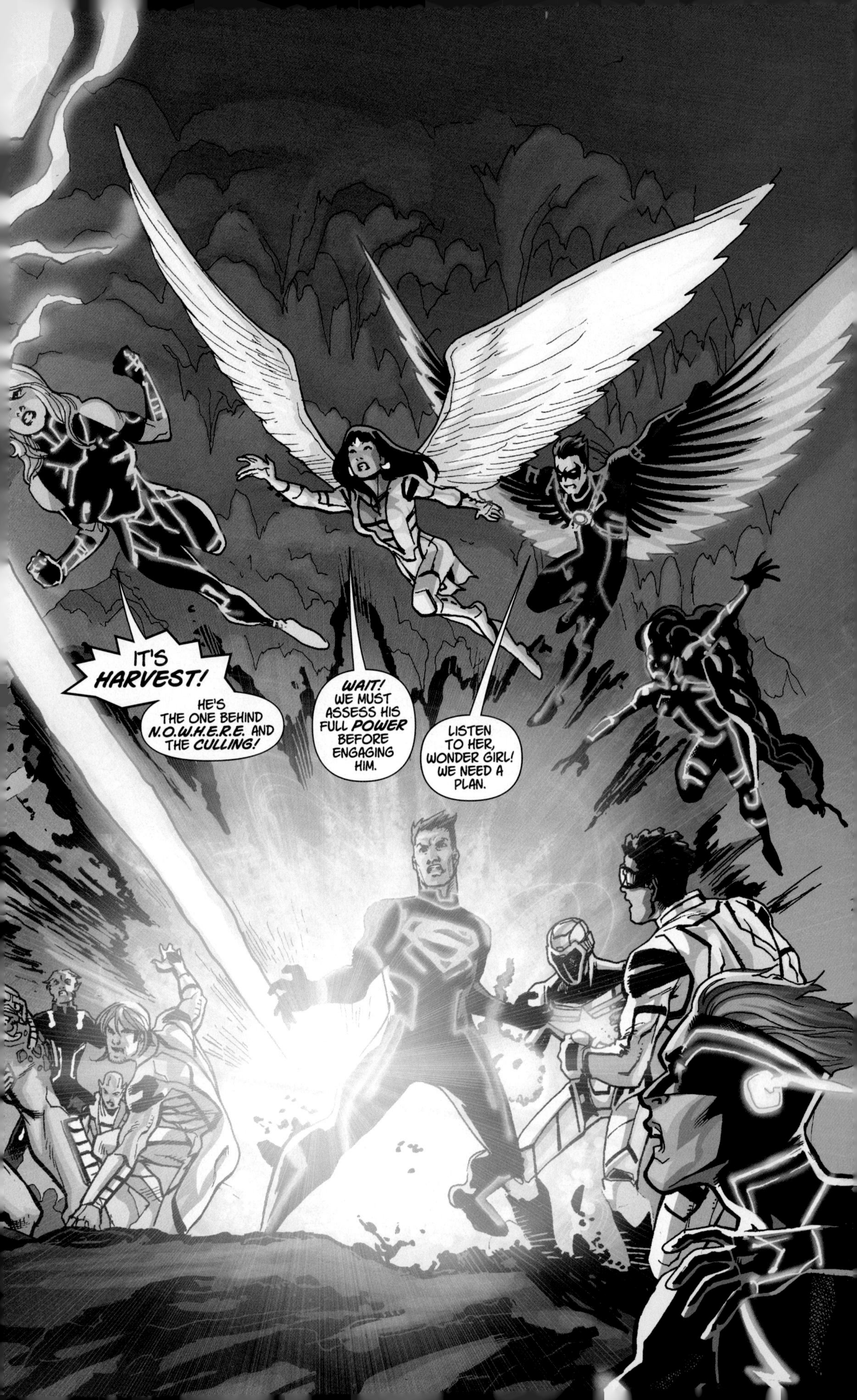
IT'S HARVEST!
HE'S THE ONE BEHIND N.O.W.H.E.R.E. AND THE CULLING!
WAIT! WE MUST ASSESS HIS FULL POWER BEFORE ENGAGING HIM.
LISTEN TO HER, WONDER GIRL! WE NEED A PLAN.

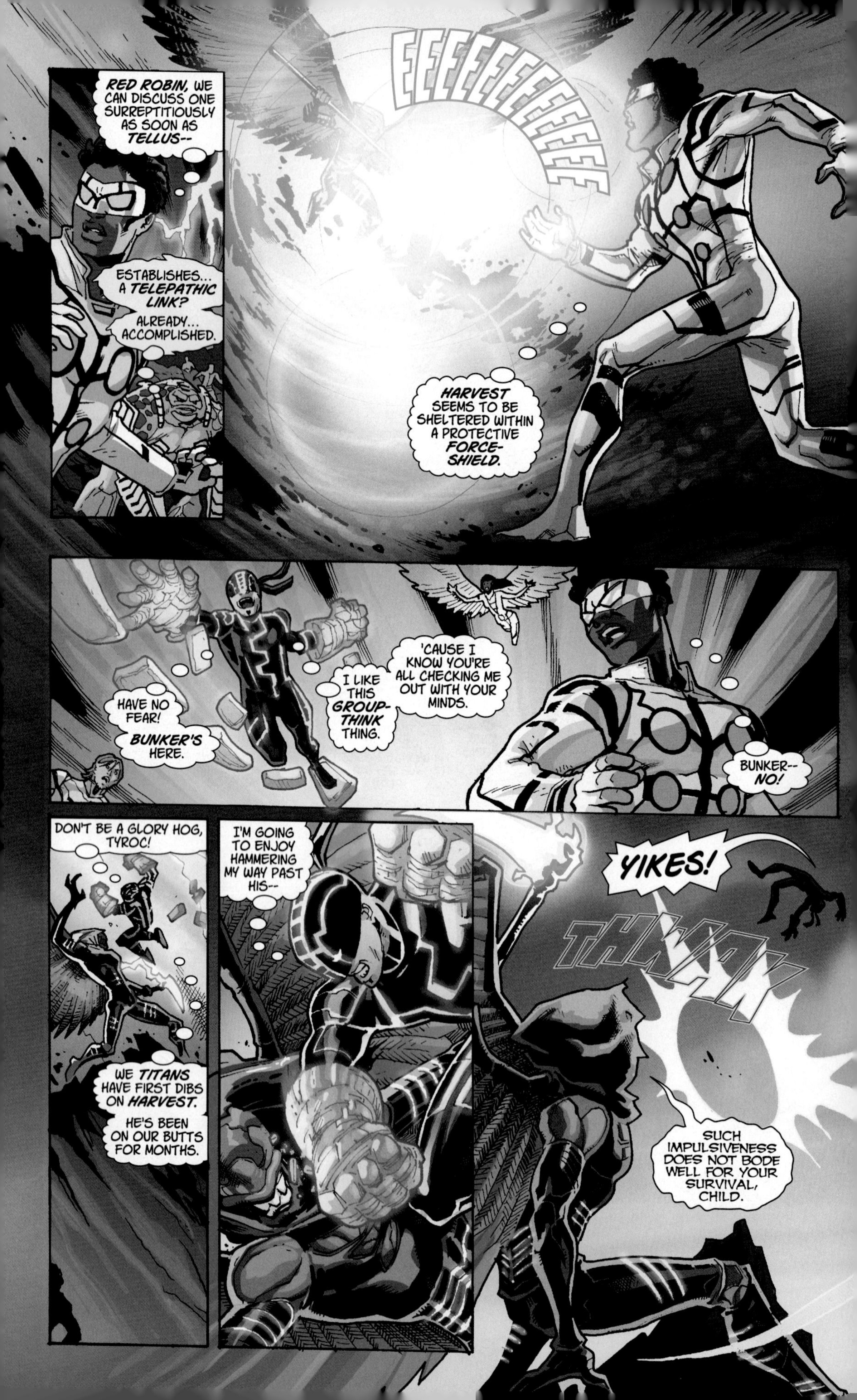

EEEEEEEEEEEE
RED ROBIN, WE CAN DISCUSS ONE SURREPTITIOUSLY AS SOON AS TELLUS--
ESTABLISHES... A TELEPATHIC LINK?
ALREADY... ACCOMPLISHED.
HARVEST SEEMS TO BE SHELTERED WITHIN A PROTECTIVE FORCE-SHIELD.
HAVE NO FEAR!
BUNKER'S HERE.
I LIKE THIS GROUP-THINK THING.
'CAUSE I KNOW YOU'RE ALL CHECKING ME OUT WITH YOUR MINDS.
BUNKER-- NO!
DON'T BE A GLORY HOG, TYROC!
WE TITANS HAVE FIRST DIBS ON HARVEST.
HE'S BEEN ON OUR BUTTS FOR MONTHS.
I'M GOING TO ENJOY HAMMERING MY WAY PAST HIS--
YIKES!
THWAK
SUCH IMPULSIVENESS DOES NOT BODE WELL FOR YOUR SURVIVAL, CHILD.

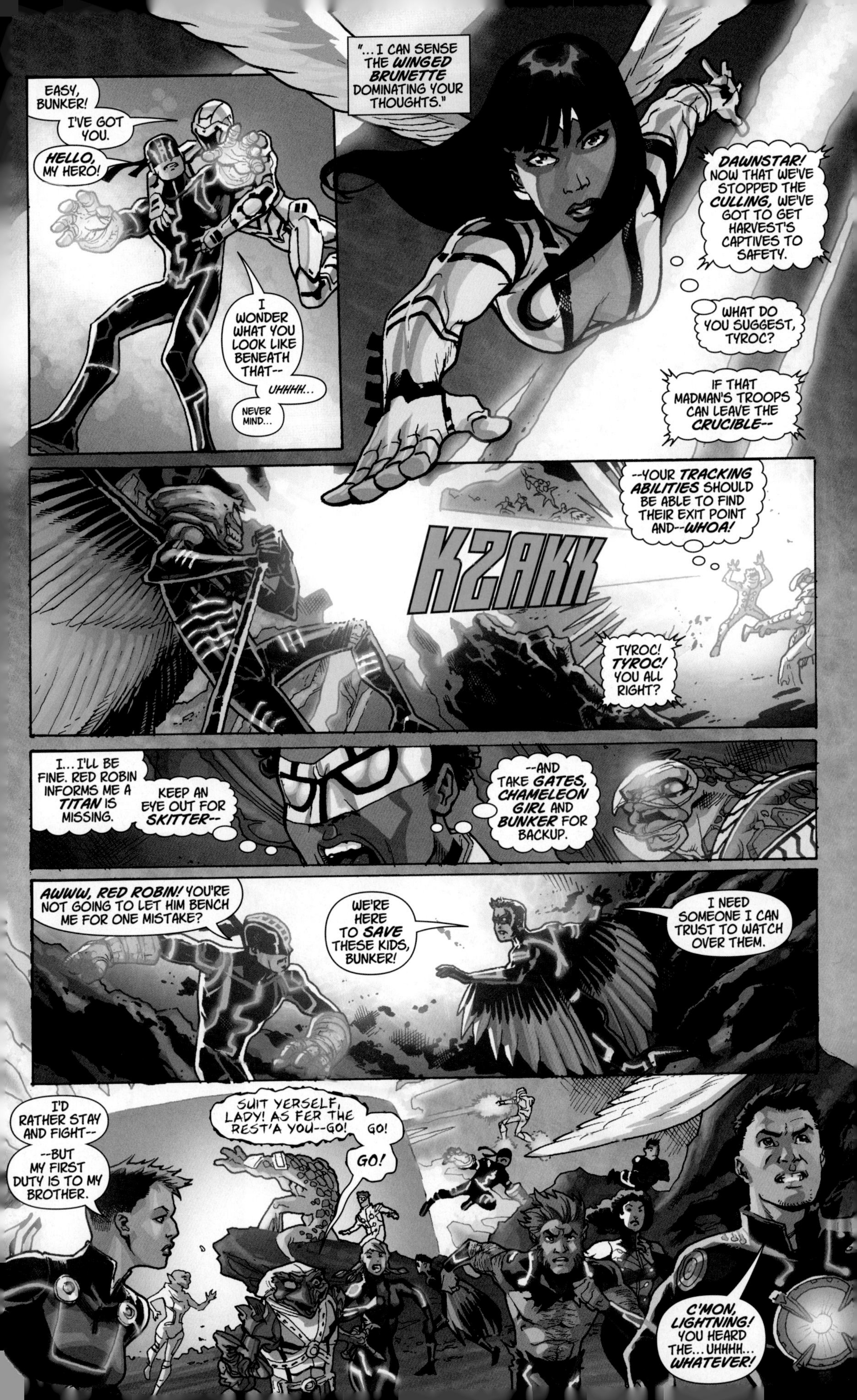
EASY, BUNKER! I'VE GOT YOU.
HELLO, MY HERO!
I WONDER WHAT YOU LOOK LIKE BENEATH THAT--
UHHHH...
NEVER MIND...
"...I CAN SENSE THE WINGED BRUNETTE DOMINATING YOUR THOUGHTS."
DAWNSTAR! NOW THAT WE'VE STOPPED THE CULLING, WE'VE GOT TO GET HARVEST'S CAPTIVES TO SAFETY.
WHAT DO YOU SUGGEST, TYROC?
IF THAT MADMAN'S TROOPS CAN LEAVE THE CRUCIBLE--
--YOUR TRACKING ABILITIES SHOULD BE ABLE TO FIND THEIR EXIT POINT AND--WHOA!
KZAKK
TYROC! TYROC! YOU ALL RIGHT?
I...I'LL BE FINE. RED ROBIN INFORMS ME A TITAN IS MISSING.
KEEP AN EYE OUT FOR SKITTER--
--AND TAKE GATES, CHAMELEON GIRL AND BUNKER FOR BACKUP.
AWWW, RED ROBIN! YOU'RE NOT GOING TO LET HIM BENCH ME FOR ONE MISTAKE?
WE'RE HERE TO SAVE THESE KIDS, BUNKER!
I NEED SOMEONE I CAN TRUST TO WATCH OVER THEM.
I'D RATHER STAY AND FIGHT--
--BUT MY FIRST DUTY IS TO MY BROTHER.
SUIT YERSELF, LADY! AS FER THE REST'A YOU--GO!
GO!
GO!
C'MON, LIGHTNING! YOU HEARD THE...UHHHH... WHATEVER!

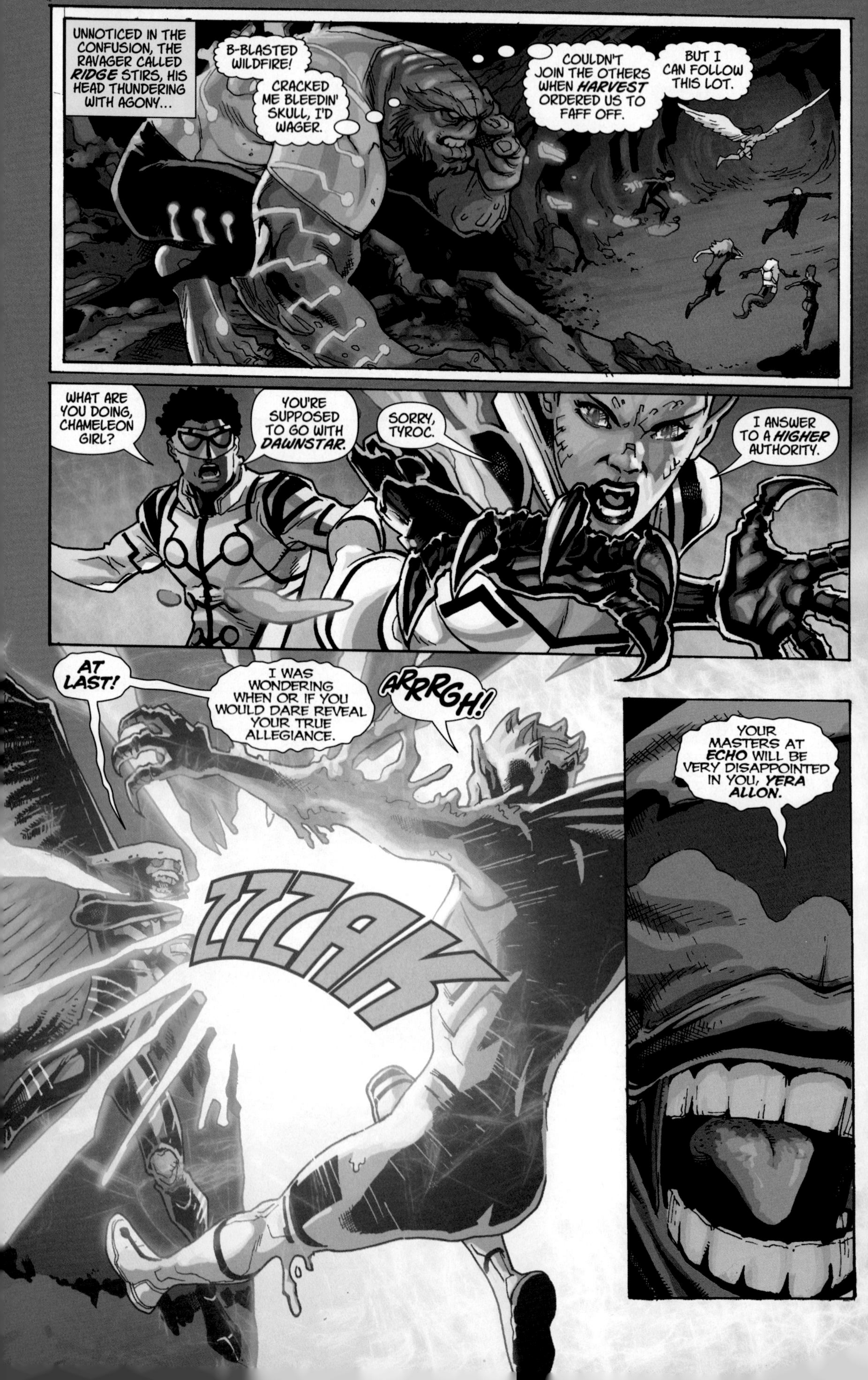
UNNOTICED IN THE CONFUSION, THE RAVAGER CALLED RIDGE STIRS, HIS HEAD THUNDERING WITH AGONY...
B-BLASTED WILDFIRE!
CRACKED ME BLEEDIN' SKULL, I'D WAGER.
COULDN'T JOIN THE OTHERS WHEN HARVEST ORDERED US TO FAFF OFF.
BUT I CAN FOLLOW THIS LOT.
WHAT ARE YOU DOING, CHAMELEON GIRL?
YOU'RE SUPPOSED TO GO WITH DAWNSTAR.
SORRY, TYROC.
I ANSWER TO A HIGHER AUTHORITY.
AT LAST!
I WAS WONDERING WHEN OR IF YOU WOULD DARE REVEAL YOUR TRUE ALLEGIANCE.
ARRRGH!
ZZZAK
YOUR MASTERS AT ECHO WILL BE VERY DISAPPOINTED IN YOU, YERA ALLON.

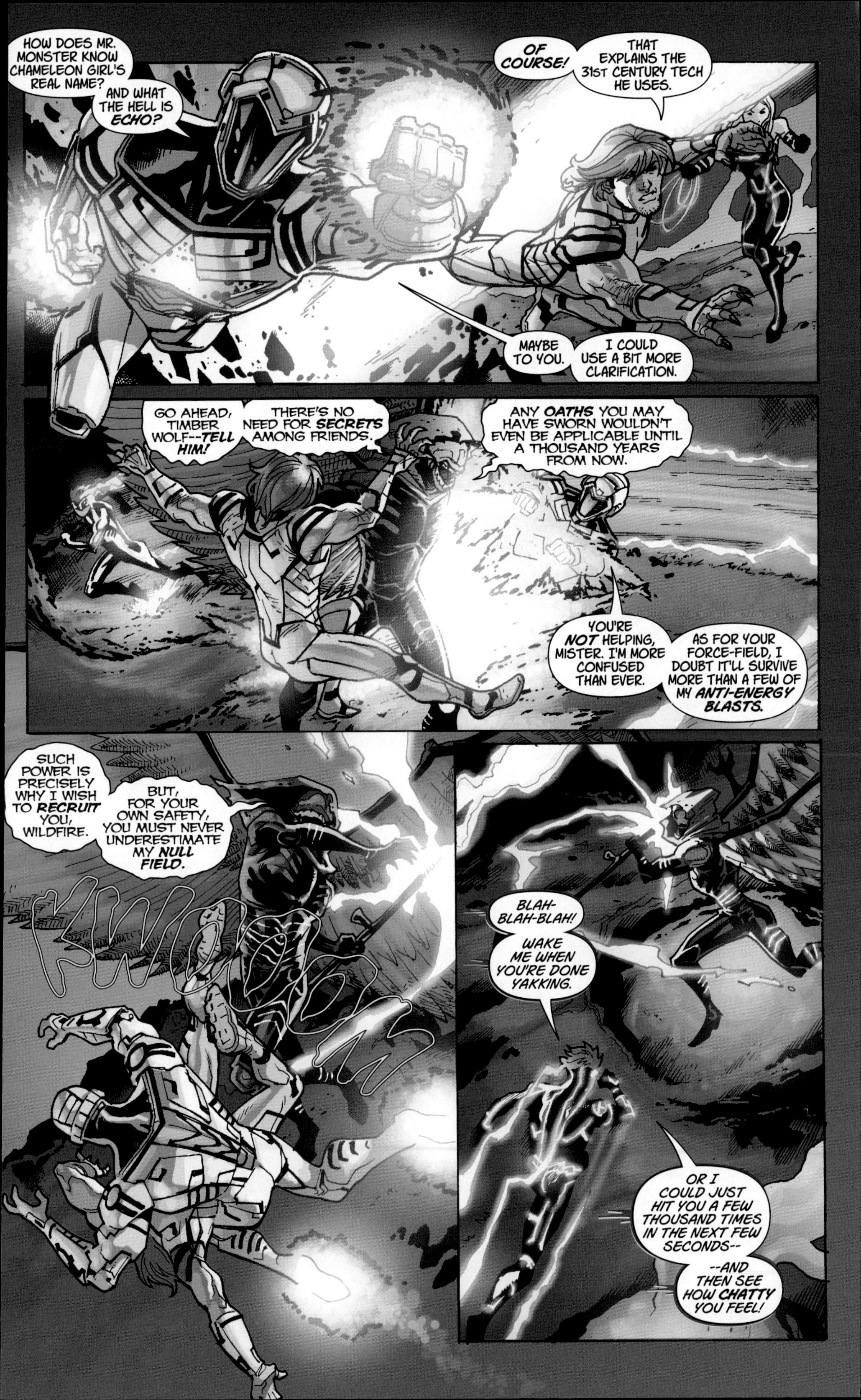
HOW DOES MR. MONSTER KNOW CHAMELEON GIRL'S REAL NAME?
AND WHAT THE HELL IS ECHO?
OF COURSE!
THAT EXPLAINS THE 31ST CENTURY TECH HE USES.
MAYBE TO YOU.
I COULD USE A BIT MORE CLARIFICATION.
GO AHEAD, TIMBER WOLF--TELL HIM!
THERE'S NO NEED FOR SECRETS AMONG FRIENDS.
ANY OATHS YOU MAY HAVE SWORN WOULDN'T EVEN BE APPLICABLE UNTIL A THOUSAND YEARS FROM NOW.
YOU'RE NOT HELPING, MISTER. I'M MORE CONFUSED THAN EVER.
AS FOR YOUR FORCE-FIELD, I DOUBT IT'LL SURVIVE MORE THAN A FEW OF MY ANTI-ENERGY BLASTS.
SUCH POWER IS PRECISELY WHY I WISH TO RECRUIT YOU, WILDFIRE.
BUT, FOR YOUR OWN SAFETY, YOU MUST NEVER UNDERESTIMATE MY NULL FIELD.
KWOOOOM
BLAH-BLAH-BLAH!
WAKE ME WHEN YOU'RE DONE YAKKING.
OR I COULD JUST HIT YOU A FEW THOUSAND TIMES IN THE NEXT FEW SECONDS--
--AND THEN SEE HOW CHATTY YOU FEEL!

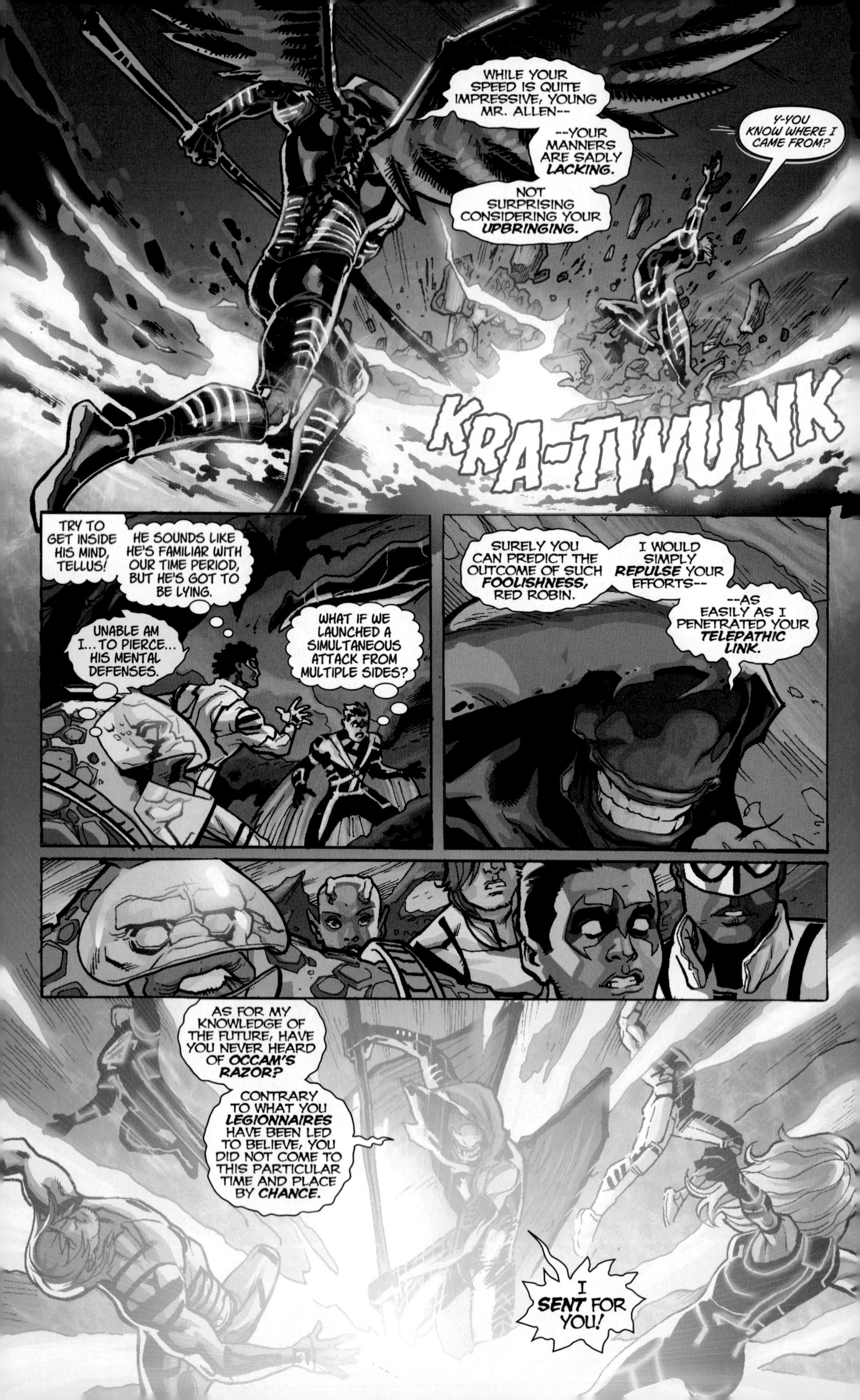
WHILE YOUR SPEED IS QUITE IMPRESSIVE, YOUNG MR. ALLEN--
--YOUR MANNERS ARE SADLY LACKING.
NOT SURPRISING CONSIDERING YOUR UPBRINGING.
Y-YOU KNOW WHERE I CAME FROM?
KRA-TWUNK
TRY TO GET INSIDE HIS MIND, TELLUS!
HE SOUNDS LIKE HE'S FAMILIAR WITH OUR TIME PERIOD, BUT HE'S GOT TO BE LYING.
UNABLE AM I... TO PIERCE... HIS MENTAL DEFENSES.
WHAT IF WE LAUNCHED A SIMULTANEOUS ATTACK FROM MULTIPLE SIDES?
SURELY YOU CAN PREDICT THE OUTCOME OF SUCH FOOLISHNESS, RED ROBIN.
I WOULD SIMPLY REPULSE YOUR EFFORTS--
--AS EASILY AS I PENETRATED YOUR TELEPATHIC LINK.
AS FOR MY KNOWLEDGE OF THE FUTURE, HAVE YOU NEVER HEARD OF OCCAM'S RAZOR?
CONTRARY TO WHAT YOU LEGIONNAIRES HAVE BEEN LED TO BELIEVE, YOU DID NOT COME TO THIS PARTICULAR TIME AND PLACE BY CHANCE.
I SENT FOR YOU!

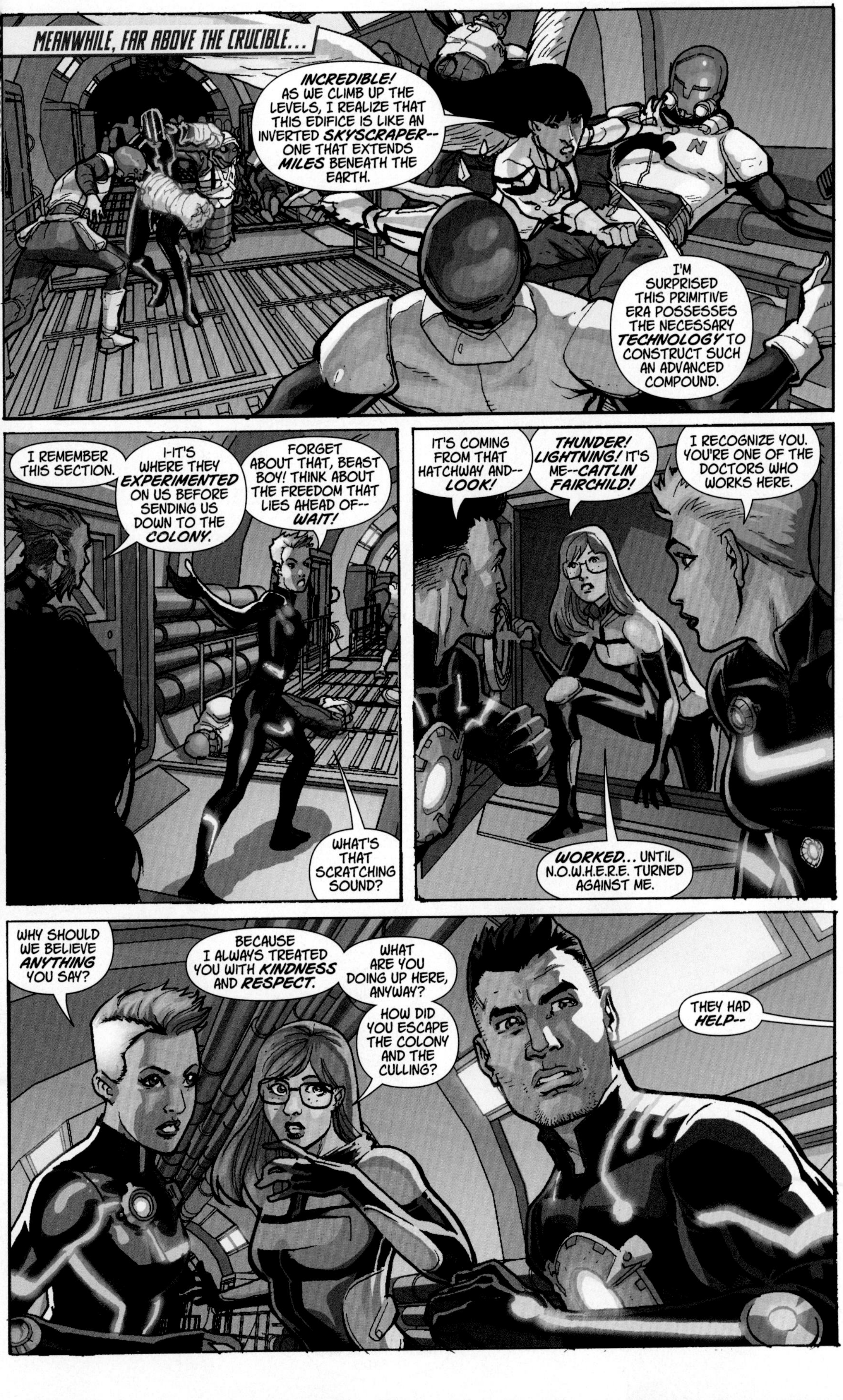
MEANWHILE, FAR ABOVE THE CRUCIBLE...
INCREDIBLE! AS WE CLIMB UP THE LEVELS, I REALIZE THAT THIS EDIFICE IS LIKE AN INVERTED SKYSCRAPER-- ONE THAT EXTENDS MILES BENEATH THE EARTH.
I'M SURPRISED THIS PRIMITIVE ERA POSSESSES THE NECESSARY TECHNOLOGY TO CONSTRUCT SUCH AN ADVANCED COMPOUND.
I REMEMBER THIS SECTION.
I-IT'S WHERE THEY EXPERIMENTED ON US BEFORE SENDING US DOWN TO THE COLONY.
FORGET ABOUT THAT, BEAST BOY! THINK ABOUT THE FREEDOM THAT LIES AHEAD OF-- WAIT!
WHAT'S THAT SCRATCHING SOUND?
IT'S COMING FROM THAT HATCHWAY AND-- LOOK!
THUNDER! LIGHTNING! IT'S ME--CAITLIN FAIRCHILD!
I RECOGNIZE YOU. YOU'RE ONE OF THE DOCTORS WHO WORKS HERE.
WORKED... UNTIL N.O.W.H.E.R.E. TURNED AGAINST ME.
WHY SHOULD WE BELIEVE ANYTHING YOU SAY?
BECAUSE I ALWAYS TREATED YOU WITH KINDNESS AND RESPECT.
WHAT ARE YOU DOING UP HERE, ANYWAY?
HOW DID YOU ESCAPE THE COLONY AND THE CULLING?
THEY HAD HELP--

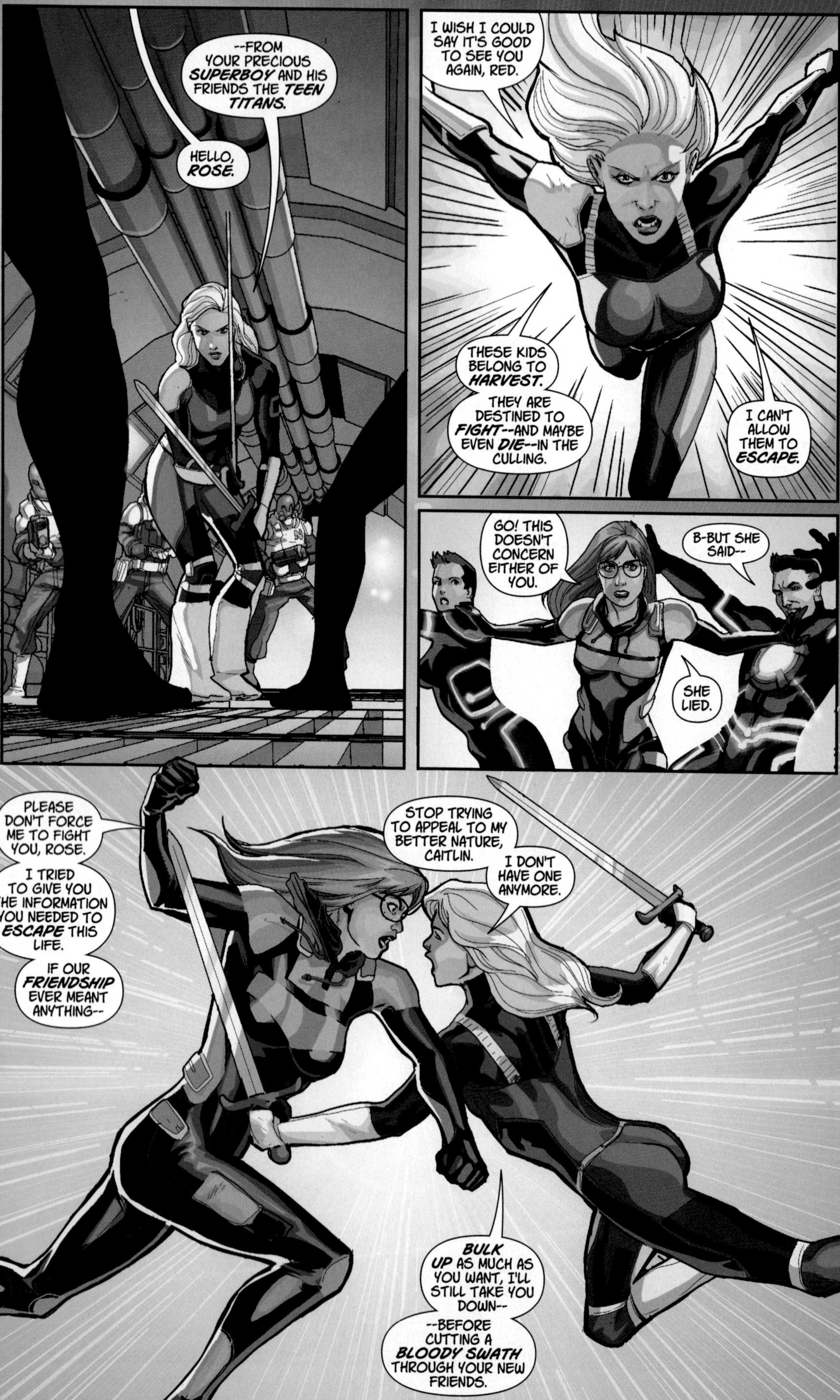
--FROM YOUR PRECIOUS SUPERBOY AND HIS FRIENDS THE TEEN TITANS.
HELLO, ROSE.
I WISH I COULD SAY IT'S GOOD TO SEE YOU AGAIN, RED.
THESE KIDS BELONG TO HARVEST.
THEY ARE DESTINED TO FIGHT--AND MAYBE EVEN DIE--IN THE CULLING.
I CAN'T ALLOW THEM TO ESCAPE.
GO! THIS DOESN'T CONCERN EITHER OF YOU.
B-BUT SHE SAID--
SHE LIED.
PLEASE DON'T FORCE ME TO FIGHT YOU, ROSE.
I TRIED TO GIVE YOU THE INFORMATION YOU NEEDED TO ESCAPE THIS LIFE.
IF OUR FRIENDSHIP EVER MEANT ANYTHING--
STOP TRYING TO APPEAL TO MY BETTER NATURE, CAITLIN.
I DON'T HAVE ONE ANYMORE.
BULK UP AS MUCH AS YOU WANT, I'LL STILL TAKE YOU DOWN--
--BEFORE CUTTING A BLOODY SWATH THROUGH YOUR NEW FRIENDS.

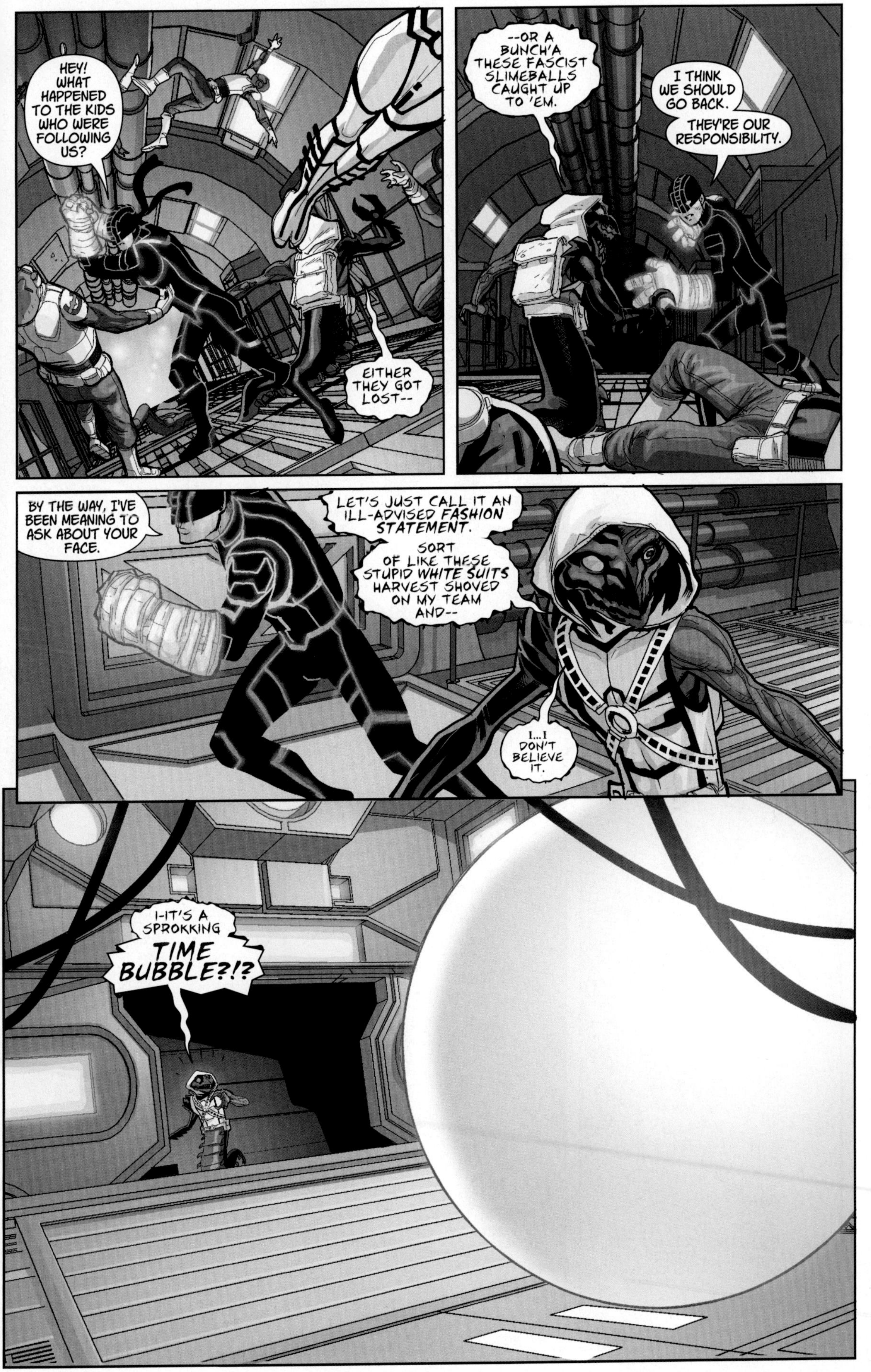
HEY! WHAT HAPPENED TO THE KIDS WHO WERE FOLLOWING US?
EITHER THEY GOT LOST--
--OR A BUNCH'A THESE FASCIST SLIMEBALLS CAUGHT UP TO 'EM.
I THINK WE SHOULD GO BACK.
THEY'RE OUR RESPONSIBILITY.
BY THE WAY, I'VE BEEN MEANING TO ASK ABOUT YOUR FACE.
LET'S JUST CALL IT AN ILL-ADVISED FASHION STATEMENT.
SORT OF LIKE THESE STUPID WHITE SUITS HARVEST SHOVED ON MY TEAM AND--
I...I DON'T BELIEVE IT.
I-IT'S A SPROKKING
TIME BUBBLE?!?

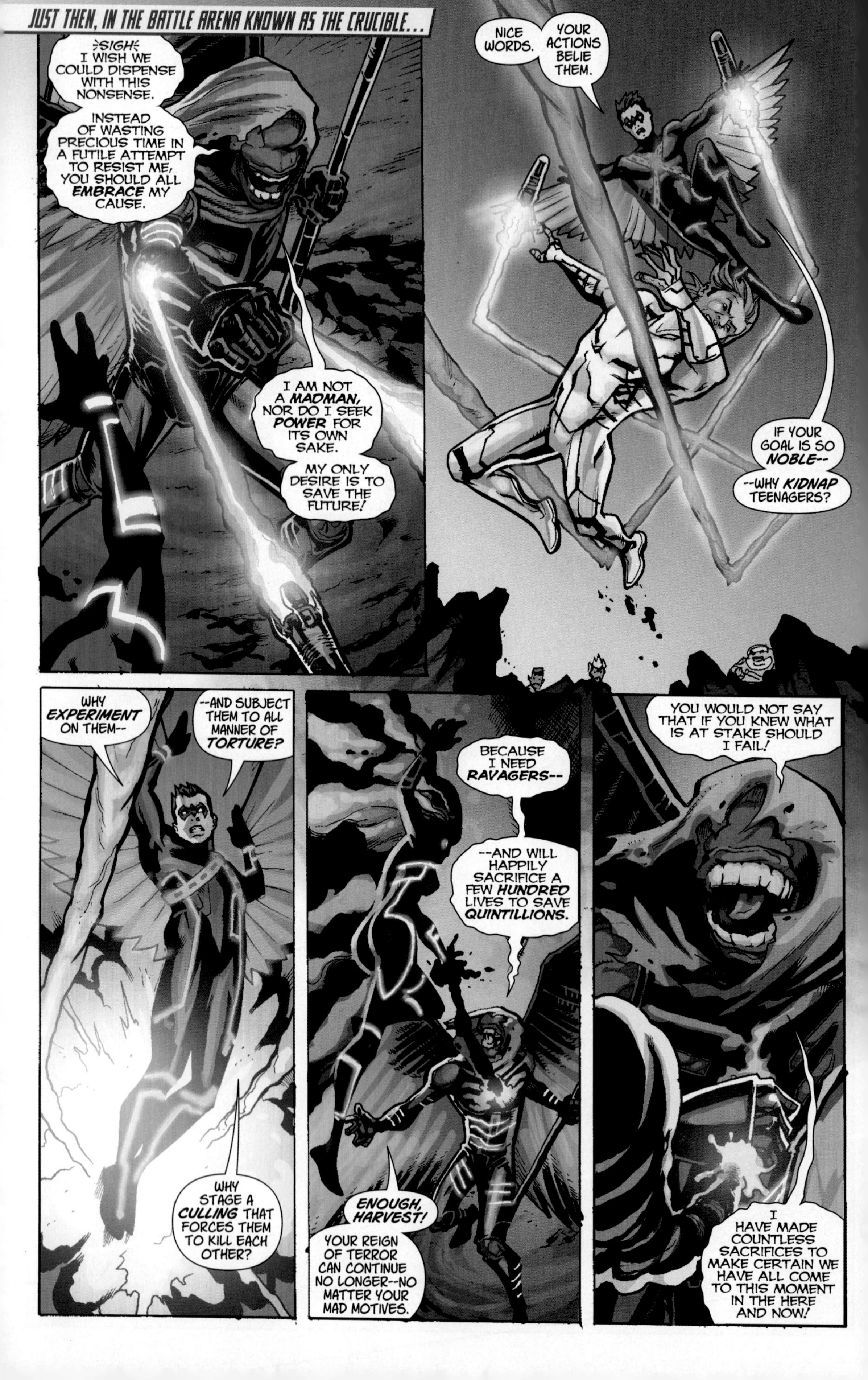
JUST THEN, IN THE BATTLE ARENA KNOWN AS THE CRUCIBLE...
SIGH I WISH WE COULD DISPENSE WITH THIS NONSENSE.
INSTEAD OF WASTING PRECIOUS TIME IN A FUTILE ATTEMPT TO RESIST ME, YOU SHOULD ALL EMBRACE MY CAUSE.
I AM NOT A MADMAN, NOR DO I SEEK POWER FOR ITS OWN SAKE.
MY ONLY DESIRE IS TO SAVE THE FUTURE!
NICE WORDS.
YOUR ACTIONS BELIE THEM.
IF YOUR GOAL IS SO NOBLE--
--WHY KIDNAP TEENAGERS?
WHY EXPERIMENT ON THEM--
--AND SUBJECT THEM TO ALL MANNER OF TORTURE?
WHY STAGE A CULLING THAT FORCES THEM TO KILL EACH OTHER?
BECAUSE I NEED RAVAGERS--
--AND WILL HAPPILY SACRIFICE A FEW HUNDRED LIVES TO SAVE QUINTILLIONS.
ENOUGH, HARVEST!
YOUR REIGN OF TERROR CAN CONTINUE NO LONGER--NO MATTER YOUR MAD MOTIVES.
YOU WOULD NOT SAY THAT IF YOU KNEW WHAT IS AT STAKE SHOULD I FAIL!
I HAVE MADE COUNTLESS SACRIFICES TO MAKE CERTAIN WE HAVE ALL COME TO THIS MOMENT IN THE HERE AND NOW!

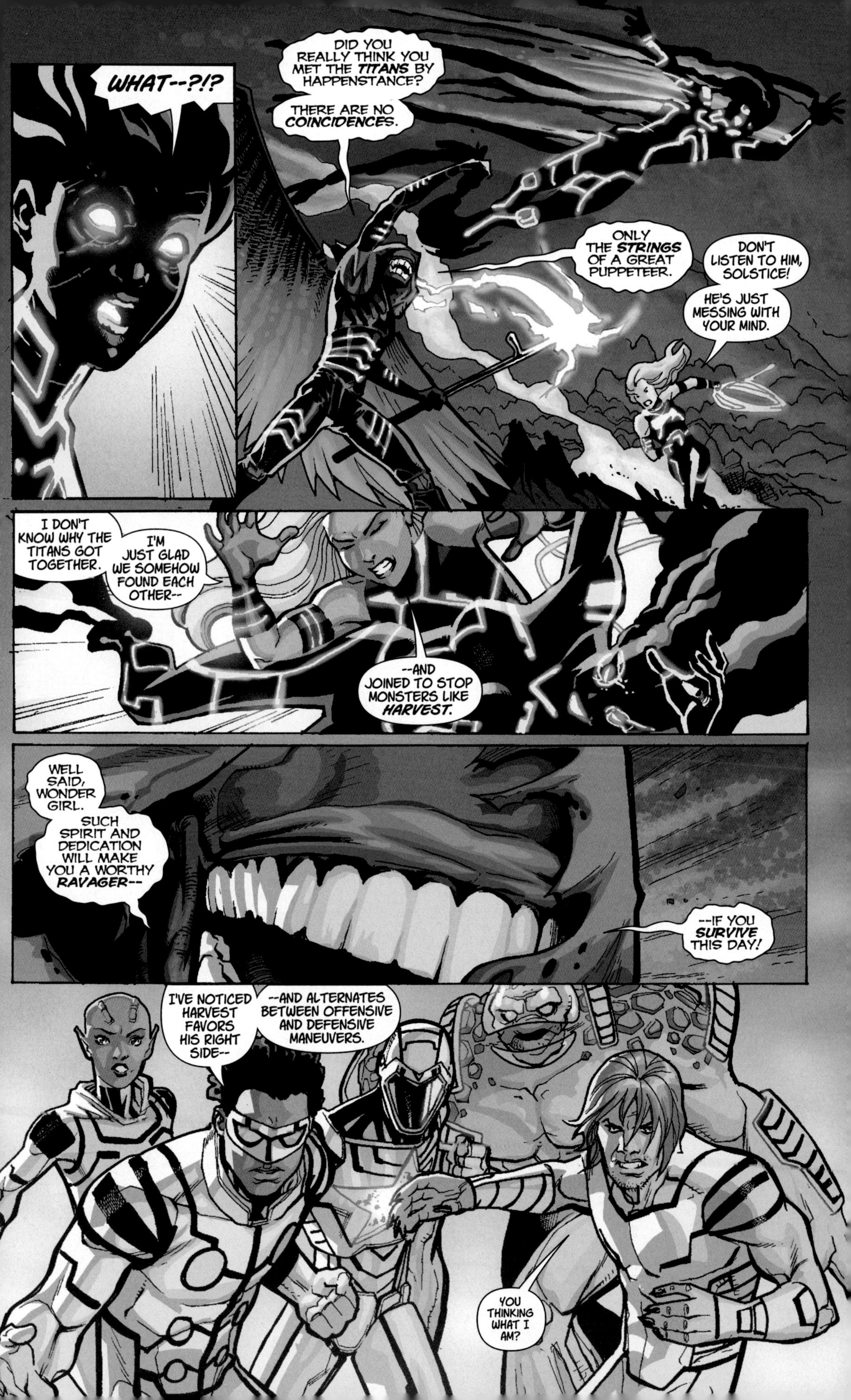
WHAT--?!?
DID YOU REALLY THINK YOU MET THE TITANS BY HAPPENSTANCE?
THERE ARE NO COINCIDENCES.
ONLY THE STRINGS OF A GREAT PUPPETEER.
DON'T LISTEN TO HIM, SOLSTICE!
HE'S JUST MESSING WITH YOUR MIND.
I DON'T KNOW WHY THE TITANS GOT TOGETHER.
I'M JUST GLAD WE SOMEHOW FOUND EACH OTHER--
--AND JOINED TO STOP MONSTERS LIKE HARVEST.
WELL SAID, WONDER GIRL.
SUCH SPIRIT AND DEDICATION WILL MAKE YOU A WORTHY RAVAGER--
--IF YOU SURVIVE THIS DAY!
I'VE NOTICED HARVEST FAVORS HIS RIGHT SIDE--
--AND ALTERNATES BETWEEN OFFENSIVE AND DEFENSIVE MANEUVERS.
YOU THINKING WHAT I AM?

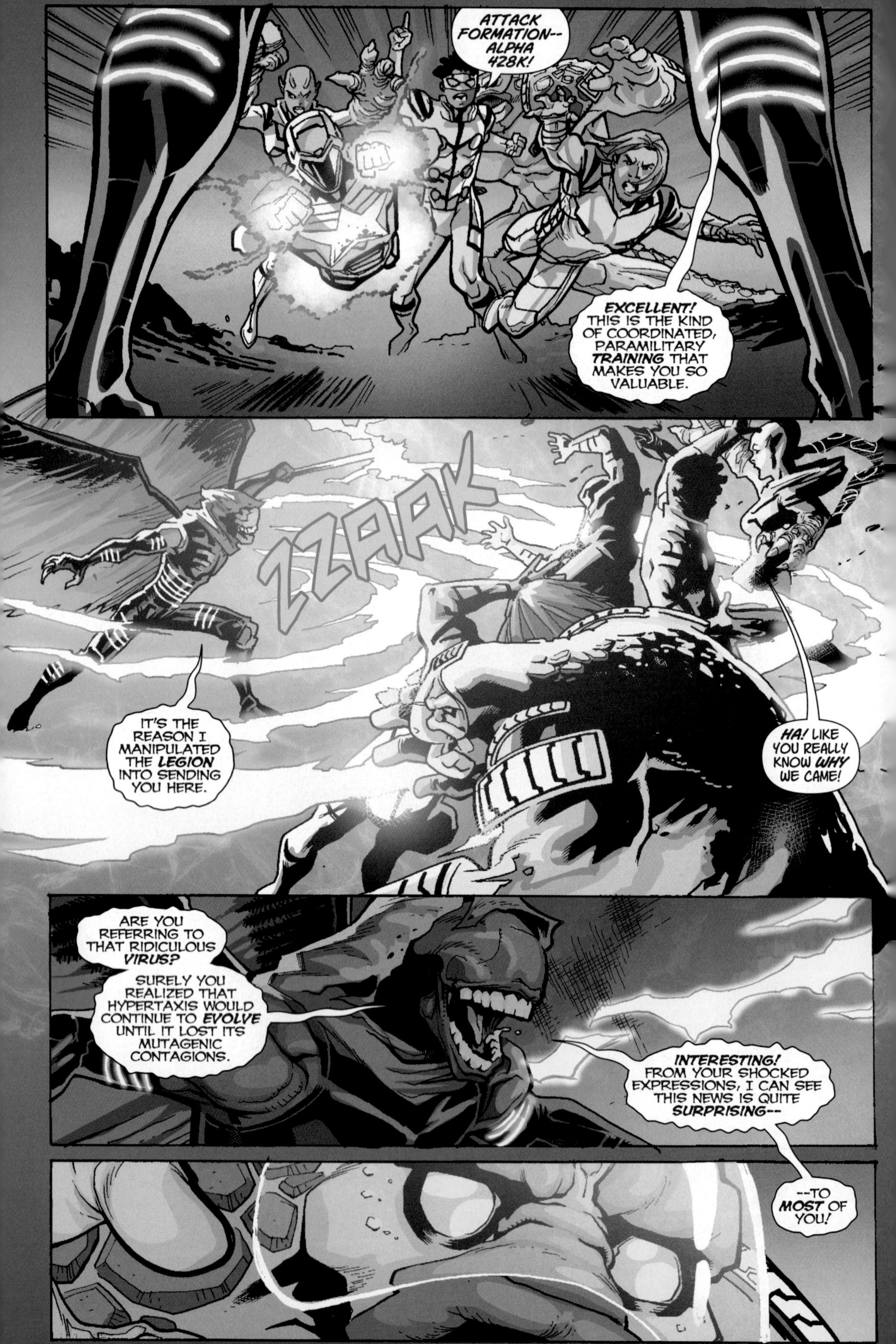
ATTACK FORMATION-- ALPHA 428K!
EXCELLENT! THIS IS THE KIND OF COORDINATED, PARAMILITARY TRAINING THAT MAKES YOU SO VALUABLE.
ZZAAK
IT'S THE REASON I MANIPULATED THE LEGION INTO SENDING YOU HERE.
HA! LIKE YOU REALLY KNOW WHY WE CAME!
ARE YOU REFERRING TO THAT RIDICULOUS VIRUS?
SURELY YOU REALIZED THAT HYPERTAXIS WOULD CONTINUE TO EVOLVE UNTIL IT LOST ITS MUTAGENIC CONTAGIONS.
INTERESTING! FROM YOUR SHOCKED EXPRESSIONS, I CAN SEE THIS NEWS IS QUITE SURPRISING--
--TO MOST OF YOU!

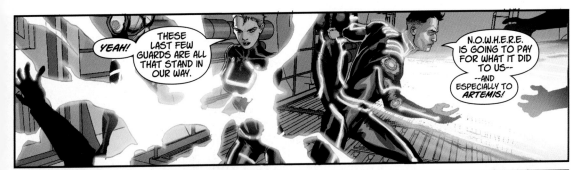

YEAH! THESE LAST FEW GUARDS ARE ALL THAT STAND IN OUR WAY.

N.O.W.H.E.R.E. IS GOING TO PAY FOR WHAT IT DID TO US-- --AND ESPECIALLY TO *ARTEMIS!*

COME ALONG, KIDDIES! YOU CAN PLAN ALL THE *VENGEANCE* YOU WANT--

--AFTER YOU'VE ESCAPED THIS *MADHOUSE!*

YOU *BETRAYED* ME, RED!

YOU *LIED* FROM THE BEGINNING.

IF YOU MEAN ABOUT N.O.W.H.E.R.E.-- IT'S *TRUE!* I HEARD ABOUT THEIR PLAN TO *CAPTURE, CORRUPT* OR *KILL* YOUNG METAHUMANS--

--AND VOWED TO *STOP* THEM!

IF YOU'RE TALKING ABOUT *US,* ROSE--

SHUT UP!

I DON'T *CARE* ANYMORE.

I ONCE SAID THAT IT WOULD BE *BAD BUSINESS* TO KILL YOU FOR *FREE.*

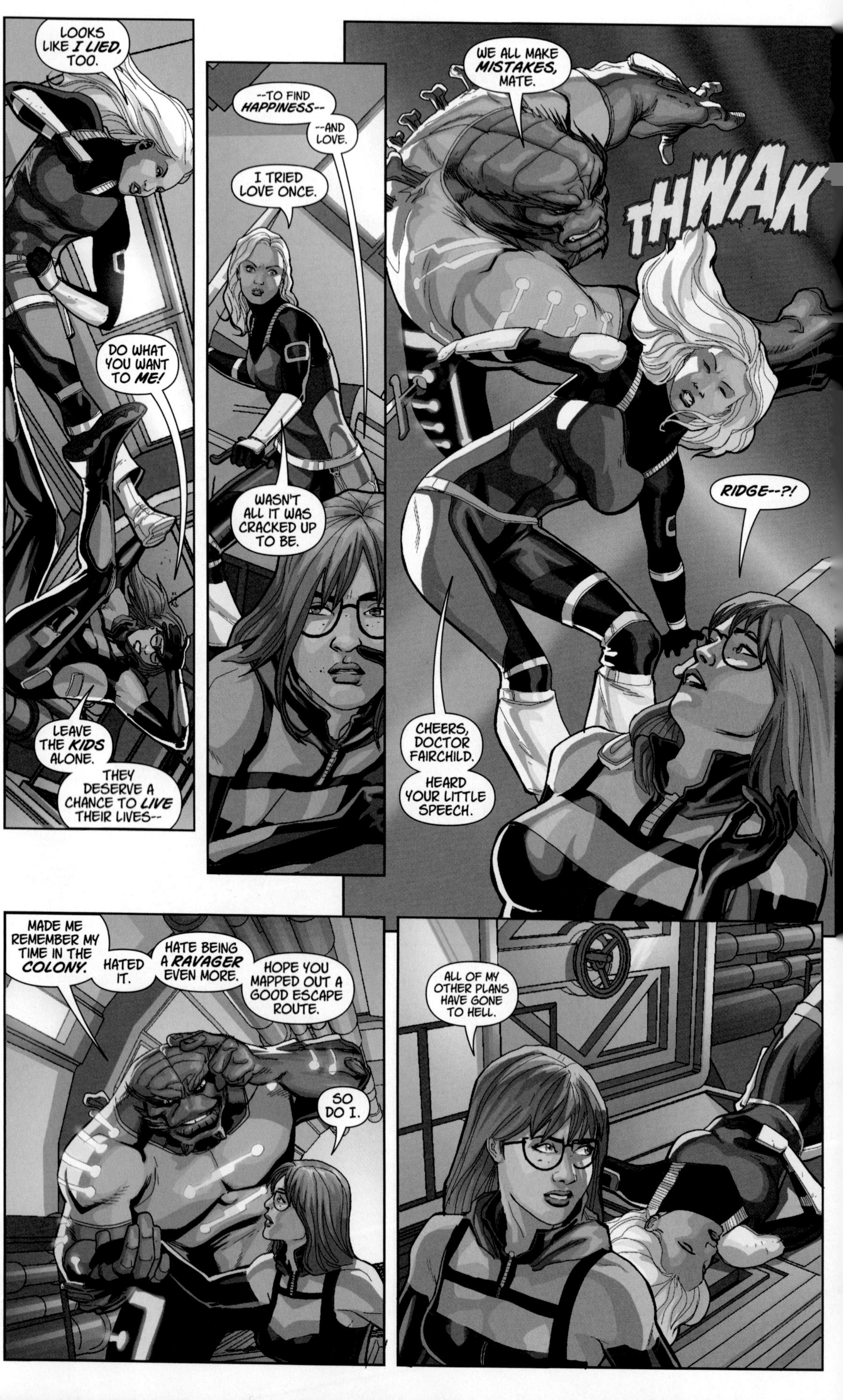
LOOKS LIKE I LIED, TOO.
DO WHAT YOU WANT TO ME!
LEAVE THE KIDS ALONE.
THEY DESERVE A CHANCE TO LIVE THEIR LIVES--
--TO FIND HAPPINESS--
--AND LOVE.
I TRIED LOVE ONCE.
WASN'T ALL IT WAS CRACKED UP TO BE.
WE ALL MAKE MISTAKES, MATE.
THWAK
RIDGE--?!
CHEERS, DOCTOR FAIRCHILD.
HEARD YOUR LITTLE SPEECH.
MADE ME REMEMBER MY TIME IN THE COLONY.
HATED IT.
HATE BEING A RAVAGER EVEN MORE.
HOPE YOU MAPPED OUT A GOOD ESCAPE ROUTE.
SO DO I.
ALL OF MY OTHER PLANS HAVE GONE TO HELL.

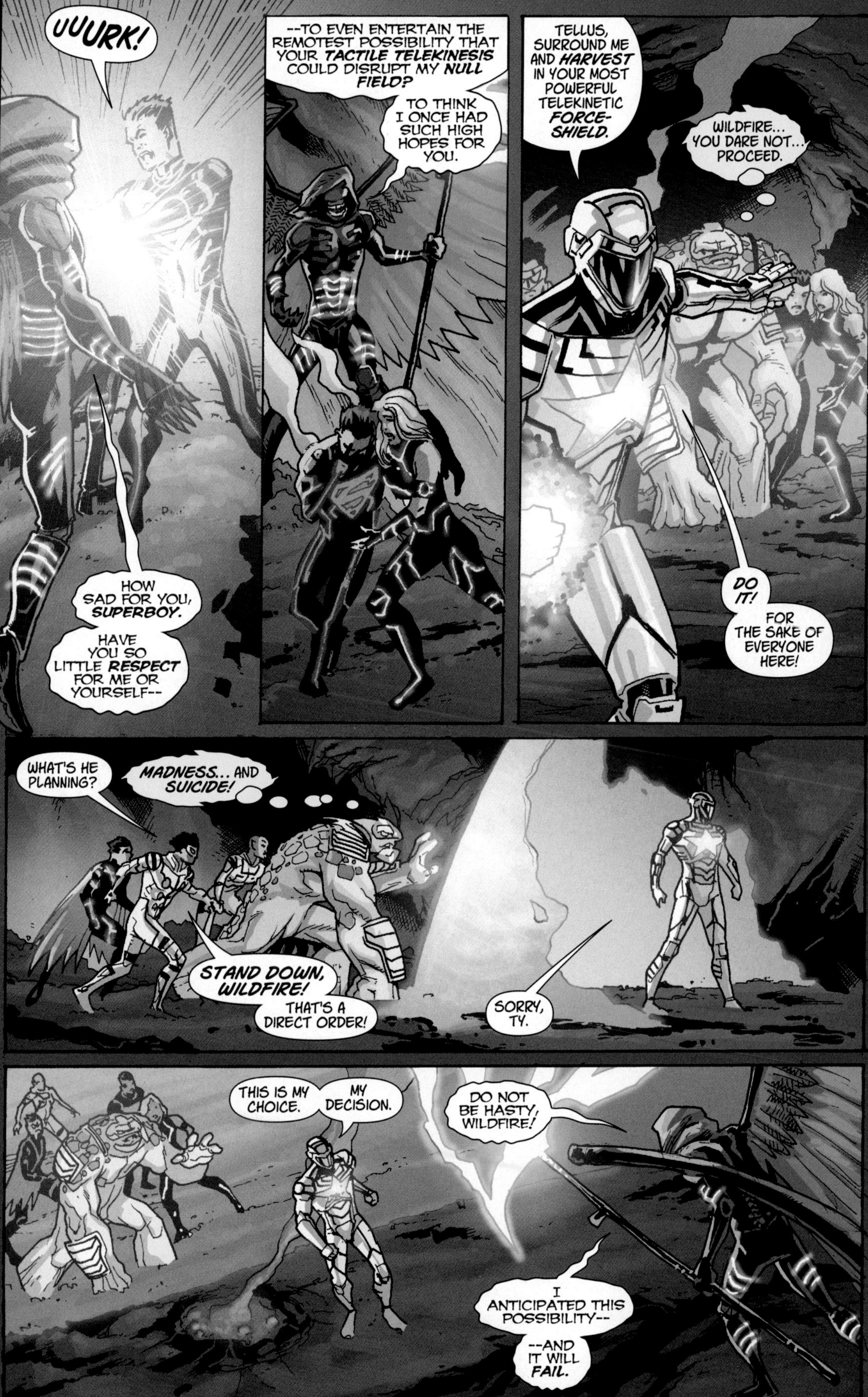
UUURK!
HOW SAD FOR YOU, SUPERBOY.
HAVE YOU SO LITTLE RESPECT FOR ME OR YOURSELF--
--TO EVEN ENTERTAIN THE REMOTEST POSSIBILITY THAT YOUR TACTILE TELEKINESIS COULD DISRUPT MY NULL FIELD?
TO THINK I ONCE HAD SUCH HIGH HOPES FOR YOU.
TELLUS, SURROUND ME AND HARVEST IN YOUR MOST POWERFUL TELEKINETIC FORCE-SHIELD.
WILDFIRE... YOU DARE NOT... PROCEED.
DO IT!
FOR THE SAKE OF EVERYONE HERE!
WHAT'S HE PLANNING?
MADNESS... AND SUICIDE!
STAND DOWN, WILDFIRE!
THAT'S A DIRECT ORDER!
SORRY, TY.
THIS IS MY CHOICE.
MY DECISION.
DO NOT BE HASTY, WILDFIRE!
I ANTICIPATED THIS POSSIBILITY--
--AND IT WILL FAIL.

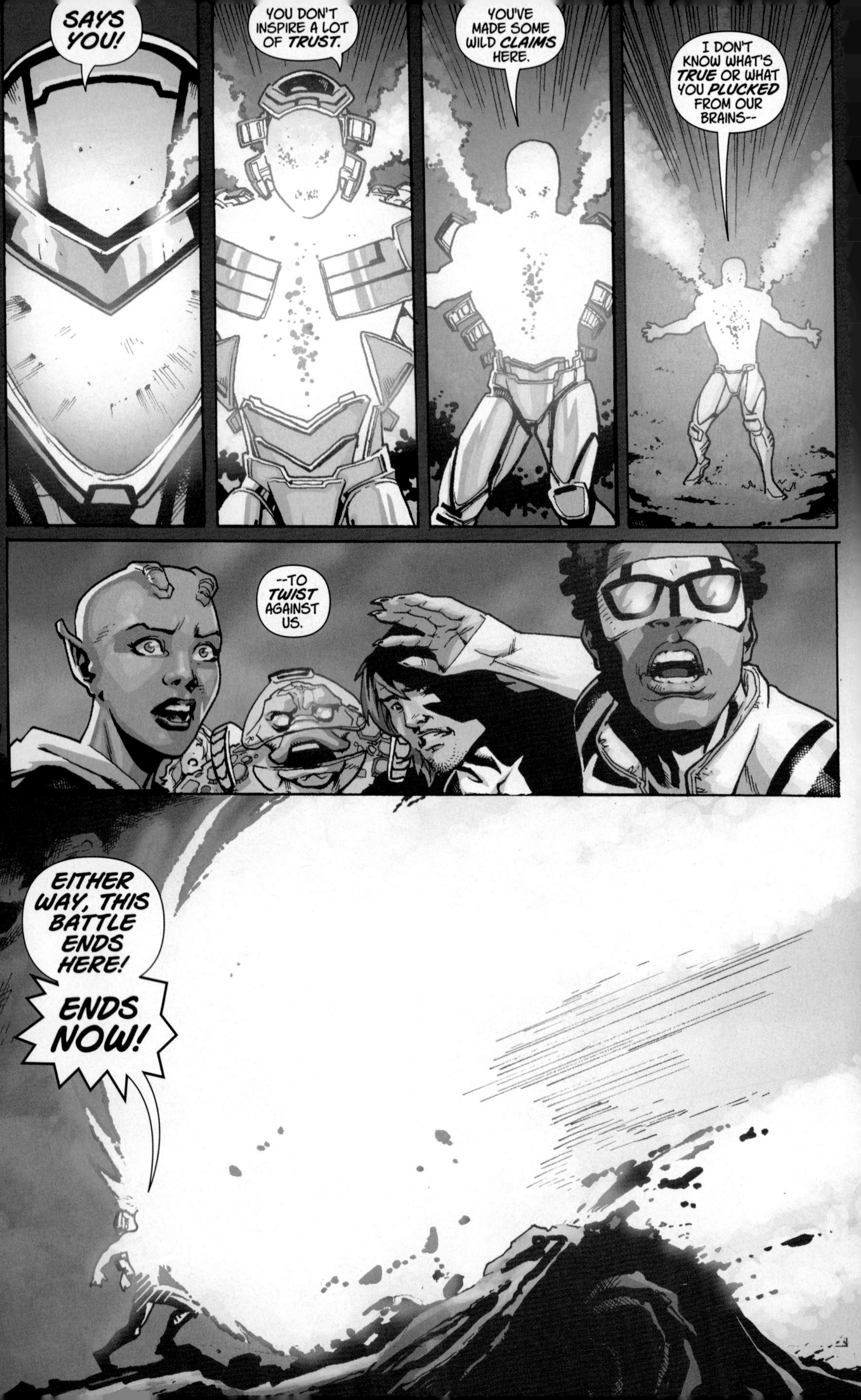
SAYS YOU!
YOU DON'T INSPIRE A LOT OF TRUST.
YOU'VE MADE SOME WILD CLAIMS HERE.
I DON'T KNOW WHAT'S TRUE OR WHAT YOU PLUCKED FROM OUR BRAINS--
--TO TWIST AGAINST US.
EITHER WAY, THIS BATTLE ENDS HERE!
ENDS NOW!

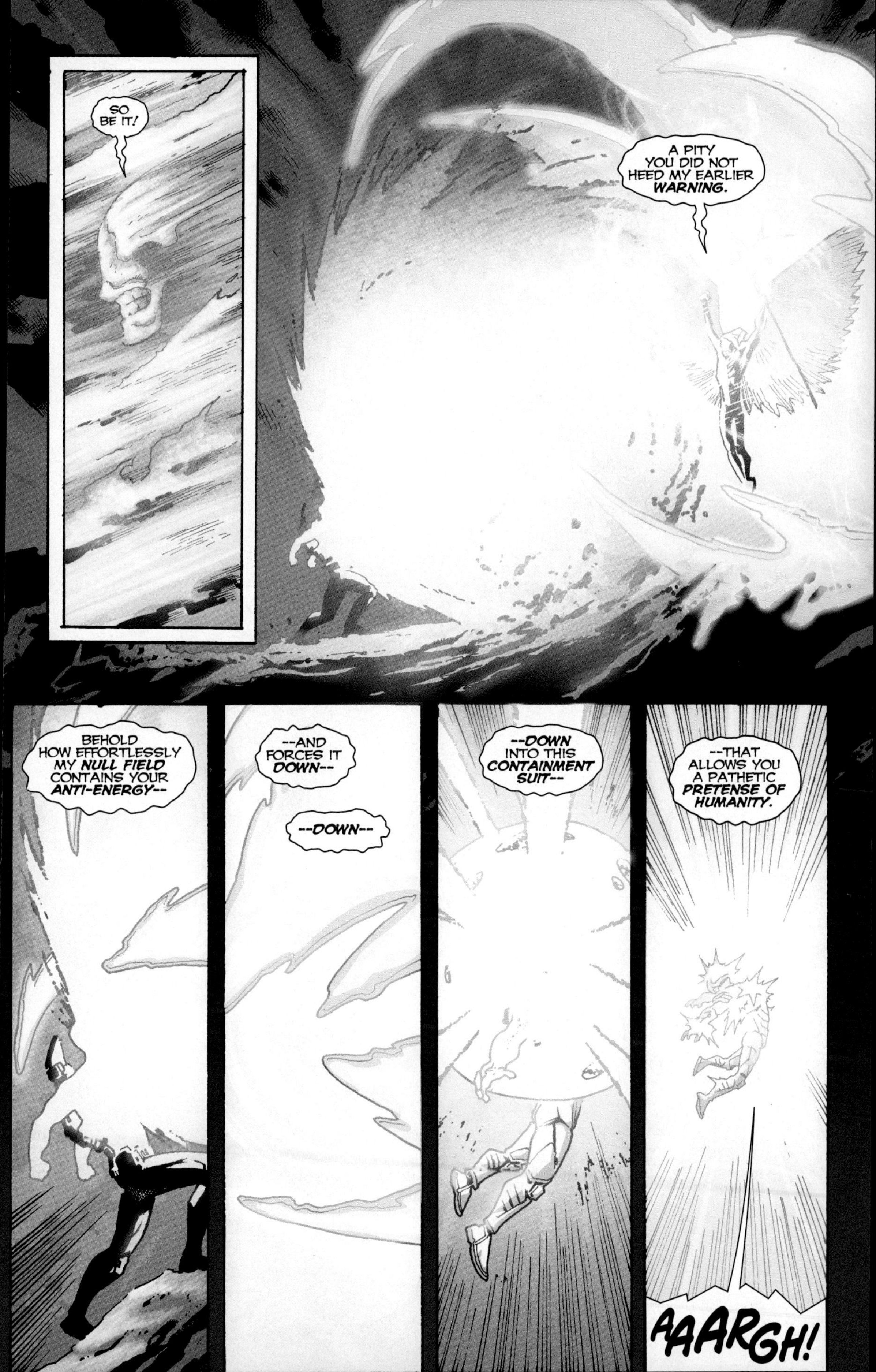
SO BE IT!
A PITY YOU DID NOT HEED MY EARLIER WARNING.
BEHOLD HOW EFFORTLESSLY MY NULL FIELD CONTAINS YOUR ANTI-ENERGY--
--AND FORCES IT DOWN--
--DOWN--
--DOWN INTO THIS CONTAINMENT SUIT--
--THAT ALLOWS YOU A PATHETIC PRETENSE OF HUMANITY.
AAARGH!

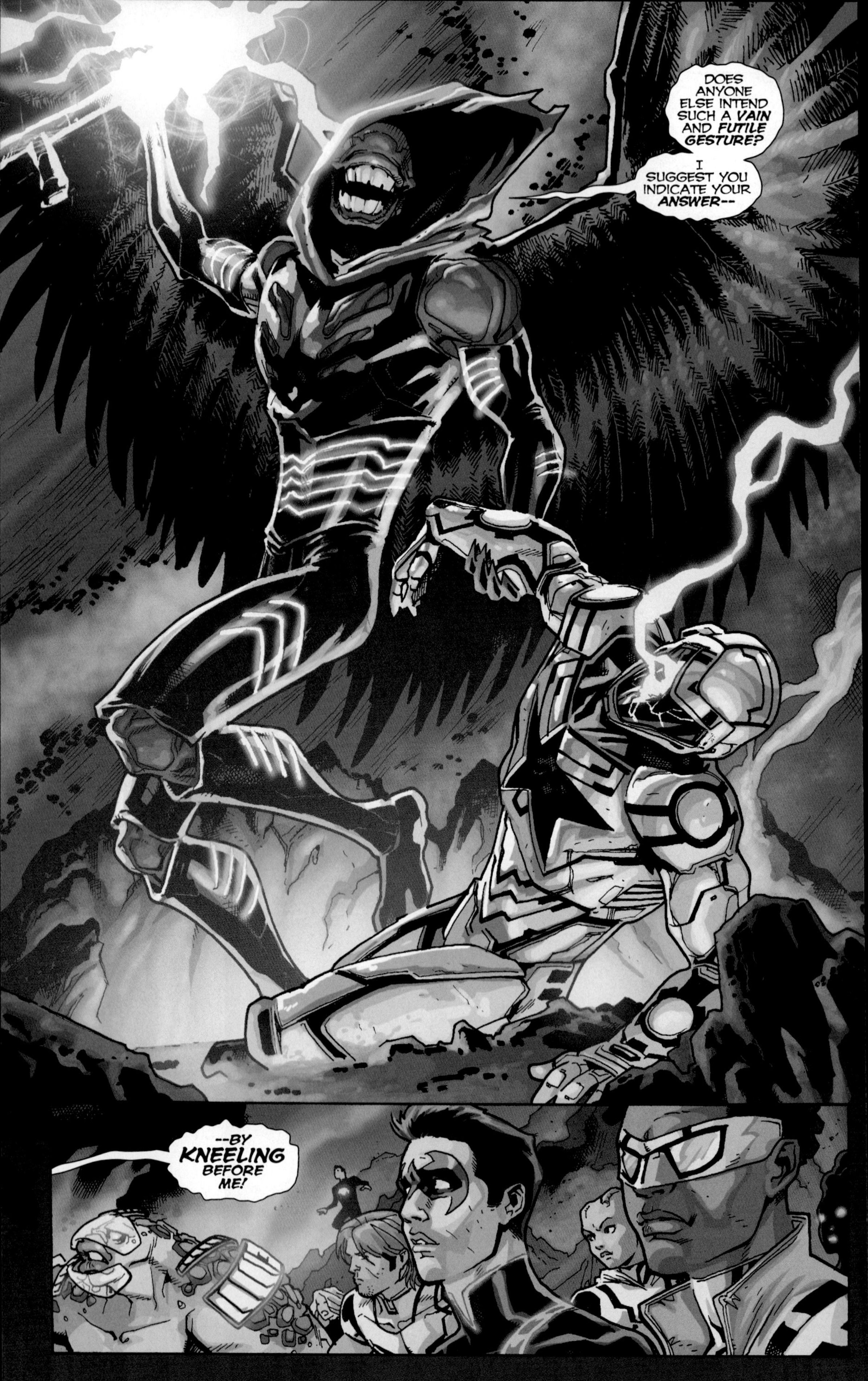
DOES ANYONE ELSE INTEND SUCH A VAIN AND FUTILE GESTURE?
I SUGGEST YOU INDICATE YOUR ANSWER--
--BY KNEELING BEFORE ME!

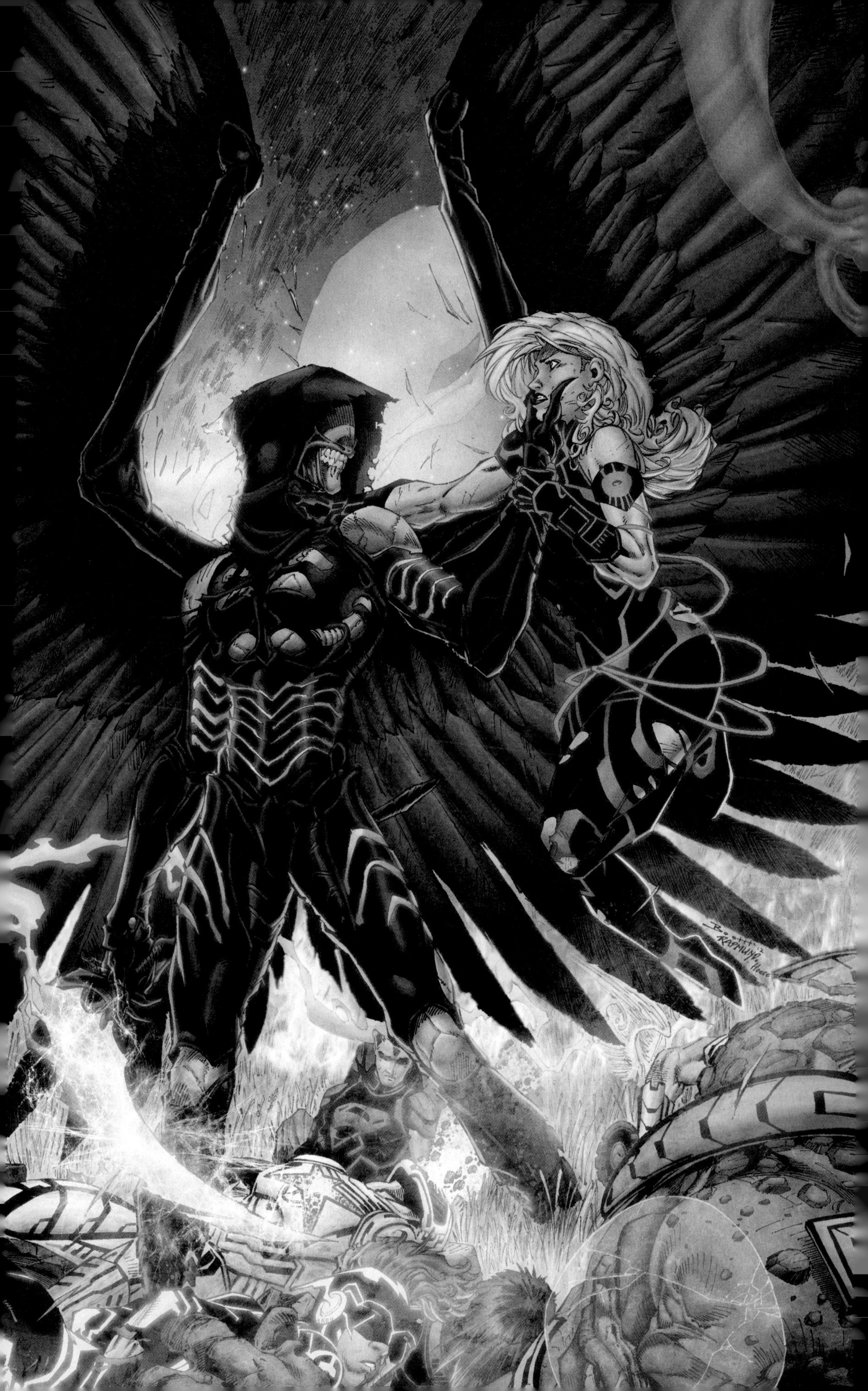

THE CULLING PART FOUR: IF THIS BE VICTORY – !

SCOTT LOBDELL & TOM DEFALCO writers IG GUARA penciller JP MAYER inker
cover art by BRETT BOOTH, NORM RAPMUND & ANDREW DALHOUSE

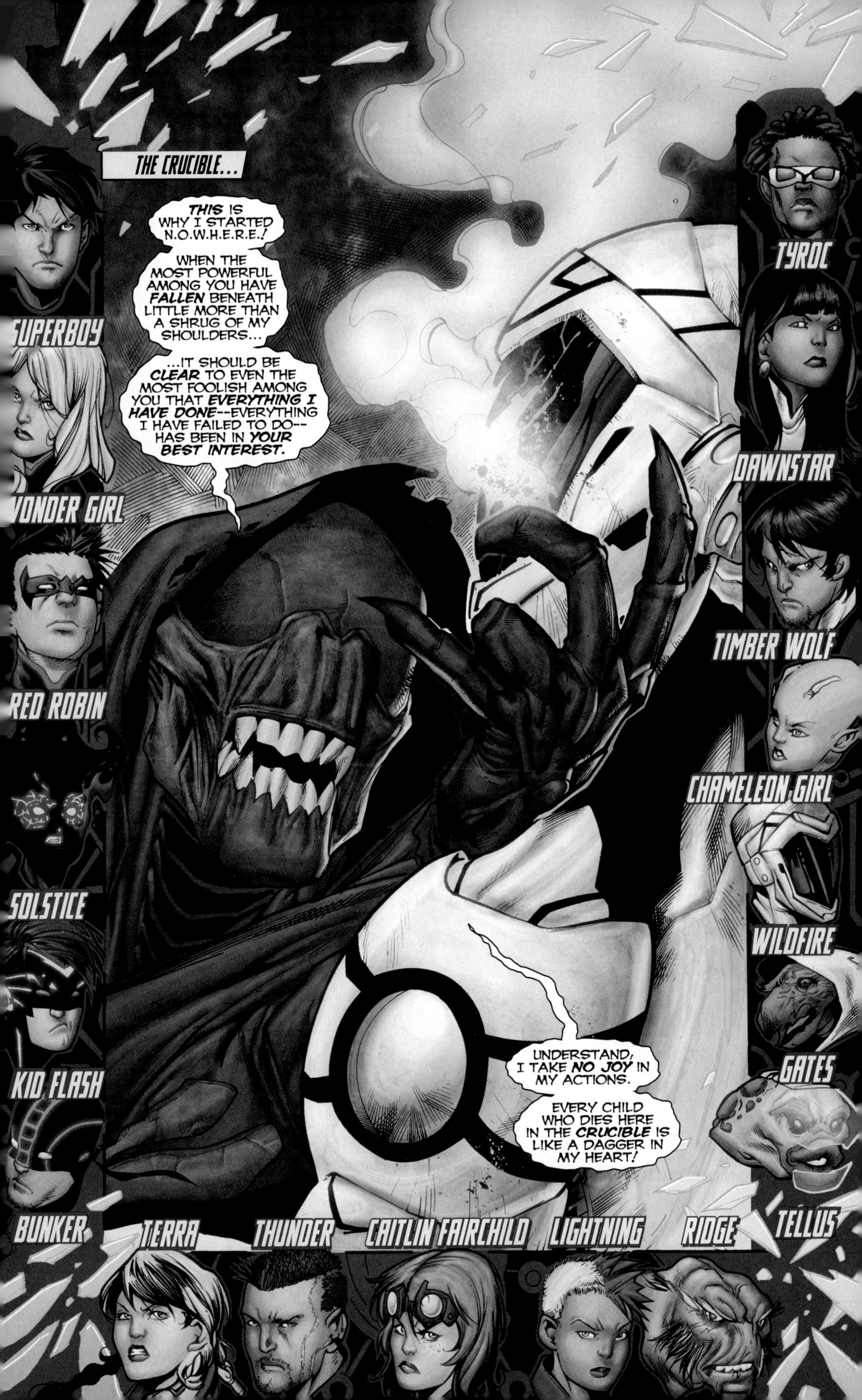
THE CRUCIBLE...
THIS IS WHY I STARTED N.O.W.H.E.R.E.! WHEN THE MOST POWERFUL AMONG YOU HAVE FALLEN BENEATH LITTLE MORE THAN A SHRUG OF MY SHOULDERS...
...IT SHOULD BE CLEAR TO EVEN THE MOST FOOLISH AMONG YOU THAT EVERYTHING I HAVE DONE--EVERYTHING I HAVE FAILED TO DO--HAS BEEN IN YOUR BEST INTEREST.
UNDERSTAND, I TAKE NO JOY IN MY ACTIONS.
EVERY CHILD WHO DIES HERE IN THE CRUCIBLE IS LIKE A DAGGER IN MY HEART!
SUPERBOY
WONDER GIRL
RED ROBIN
SOLSTICE
KID FLASH
BUNKER
TYROC
DAWNSTAR
TIMBER WOLF
CHAMELEON GIRL
WILDFIRE
GATES
TELLUS
TERRA
THUNDER
CAITLIN FAIRCHILD
LIGHTNING
RIDGE

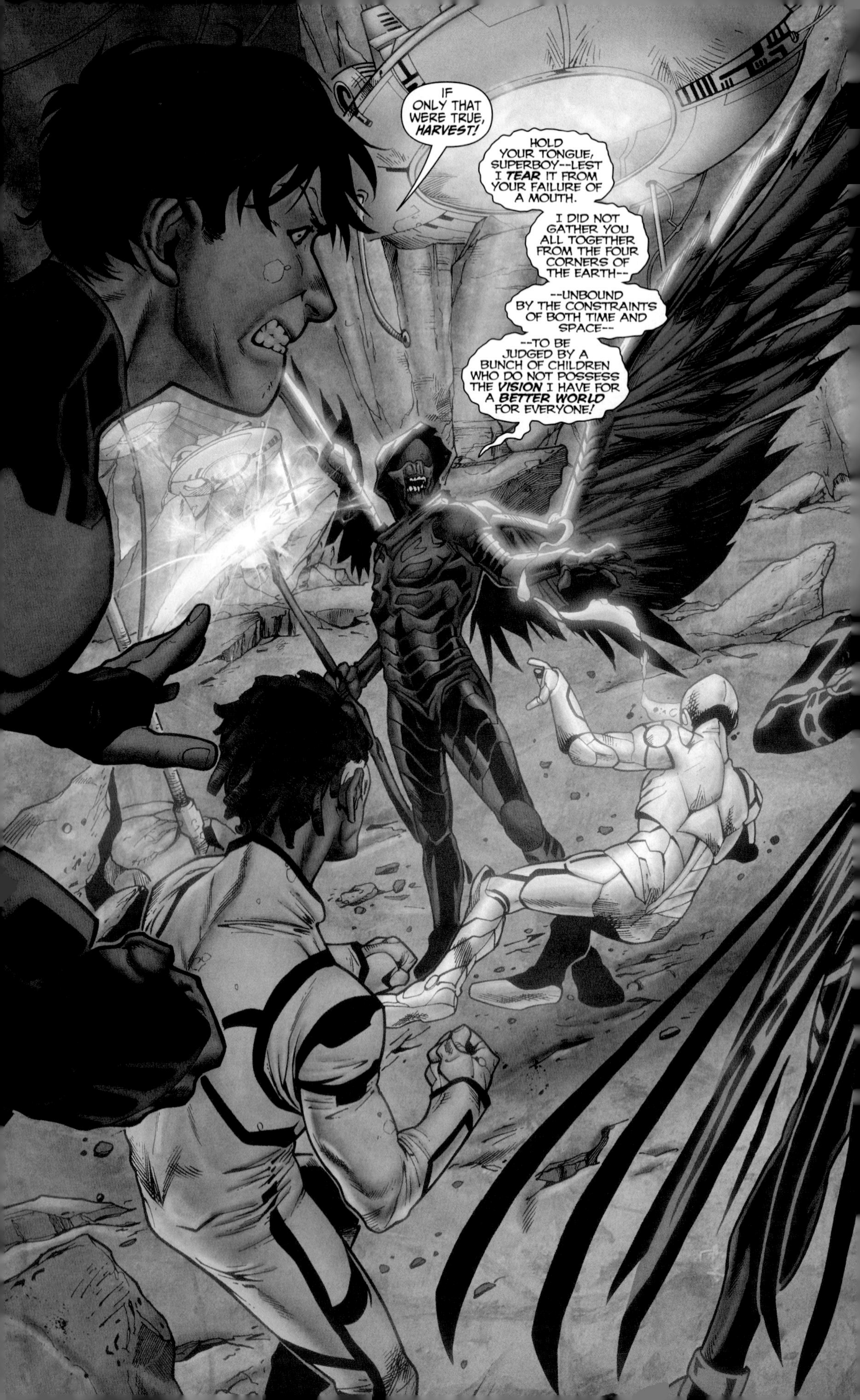

IF ONLY THAT WERE TRUE, HARVEST!
HOLD YOUR TONGUE, SUPERBOY--LEST I TEAR IT FROM YOUR FAILURE OF A MOUTH.
I DID NOT GATHER YOU ALL TOGETHER FROM THE FOUR CORNERS OF THE EARTH--
--UNBOUND BY THE CONSTRAINTS OF BOTH TIME AND SPACE--
--TO BE JUDGED BY A BUNCH OF CHILDREN WHO DO NOT POSSESS THE VISION I HAVE FOR A BETTER WORLD FOR EVERYONE!

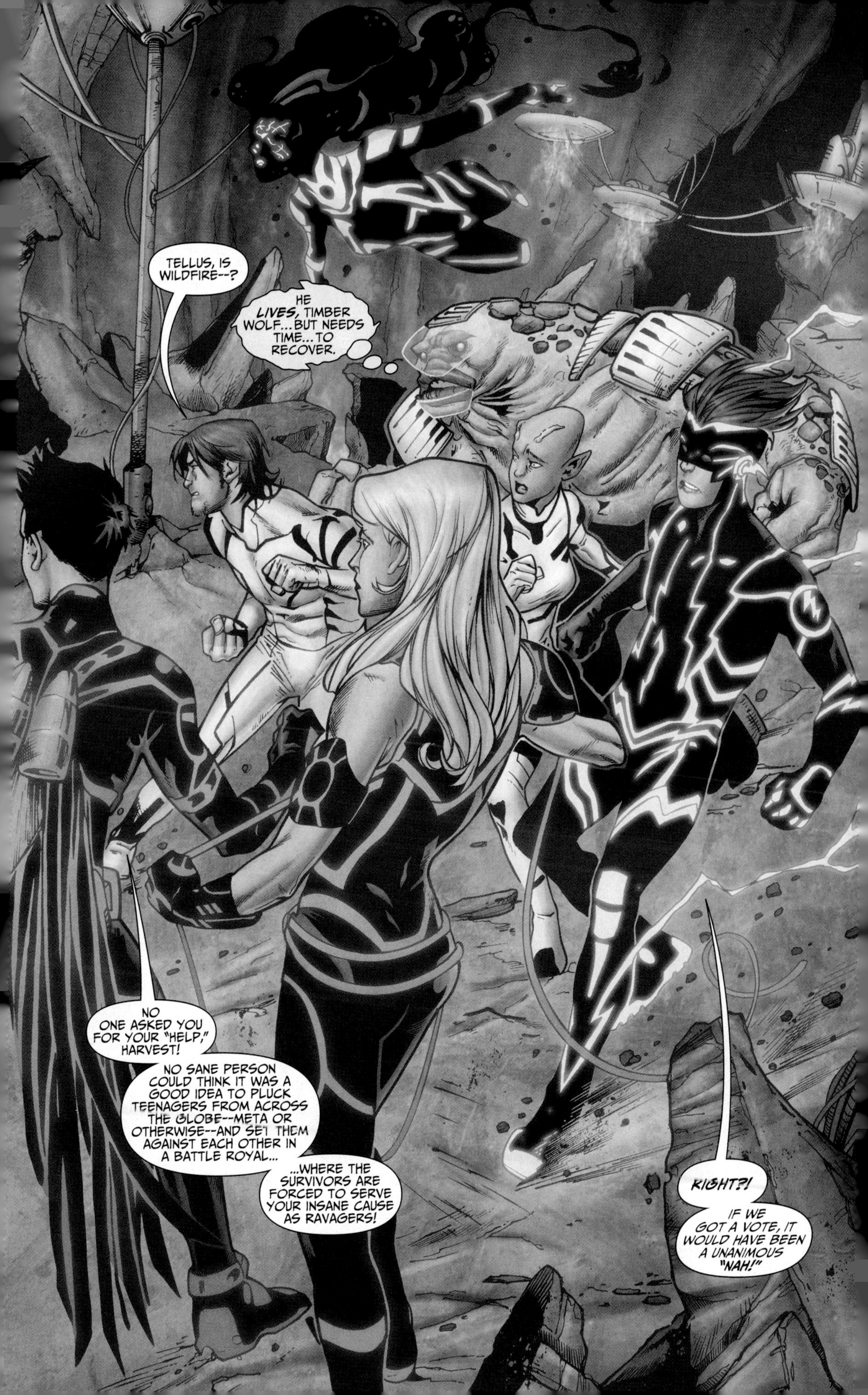
TELLUS, IS WILDFIRE--?
HE LIVES, TIMBER WOLF...BUT NEEDS TIME...TO RECOVER.
NO ONE ASKED YOU FOR YOUR "HELP," HARVEST!
NO SANE PERSON COULD THINK IT WAS A GOOD IDEA TO PLUCK TEENAGERS FROM ACROSS THE GLOBE--META OR OTHERWISE--AND SET THEM AGAINST EACH OTHER IN A BATTLE ROYAL...
...WHERE THE SURVIVORS ARE FORCED TO SERVE YOUR INSANE CAUSE AS RAVAGERS!
RIGHT?!
IF WE GOT A VOTE, IT WOULD HAVE BEEN A UNANIMOUS "NAH!"

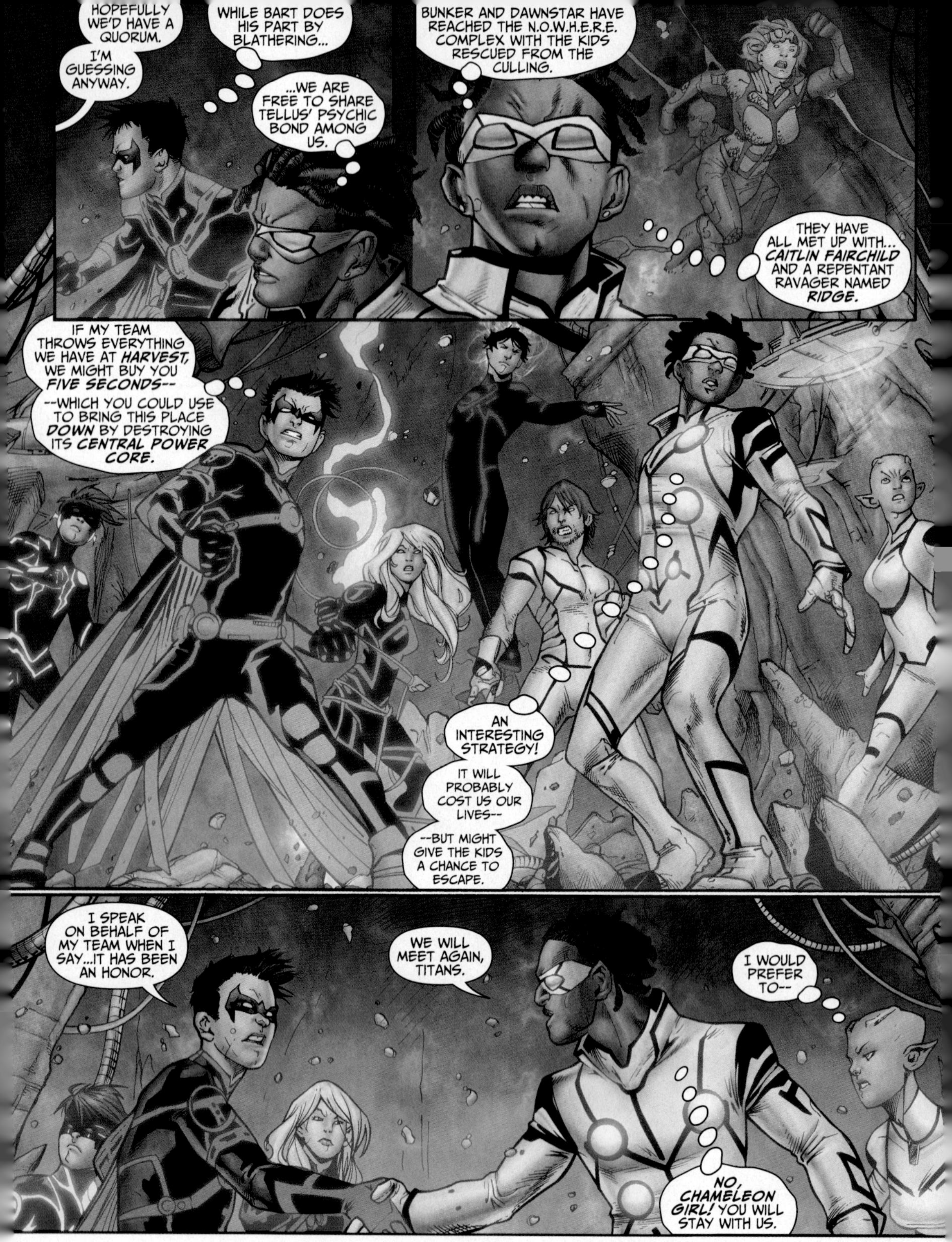
HOPEFULLY WE'D HAVE A QUORUM.
I'M GUESSING ANYWAY.
WHILE BART DOES HIS PART BY BLATHERING...
...WE ARE FREE TO SHARE TELLUS' PSYCHIC BOND AMONG US.
BUNKER AND DAWNSTAR HAVE REACHED THE N.O.W.H.E.R.E. COMPLEX WITH THE KIDS RESCUED FROM THE CULLING.
THEY HAVE ALL MET UP WITH... CAITLIN FAIRCHILD AND A REPENTANT RAVAGER NAMED RIDGE.
IF MY TEAM THROWS EVERYTHING WE HAVE AT HARVEST, WE MIGHT BUY YOU FIVE SECONDS--
--WHICH YOU COULD USE TO BRING THIS PLACE DOWN BY DESTROYING ITS CENTRAL POWER CORE.
AN INTERESTING STRATEGY!
IT WILL PROBABLY COST US OUR LIVES--
--BUT MIGHT GIVE THE KIDS A CHANCE TO ESCAPE.
I SPEAK ON BEHALF OF MY TEAM WHEN I SAY...IT HAS BEEN AN HONOR.
WE WILL MEET AGAIN, TITANS.
I WOULD PREFER TO--
NO, CHAMELEON GIRL! YOU WILL STAY WITH US.

THE CULLING

PART 4: IF THIS BE VICTORY--!

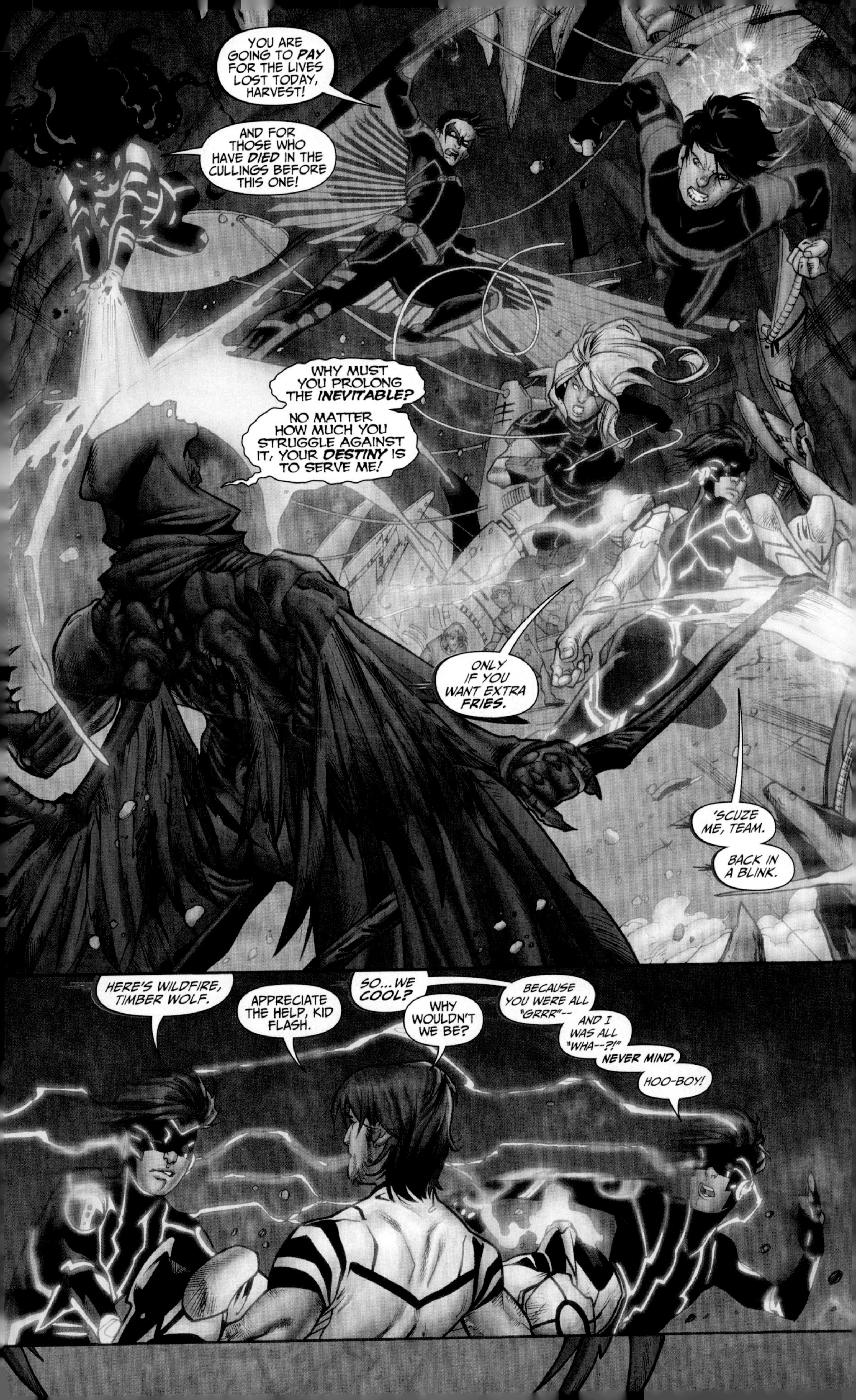
YOU ARE GOING TO PAY FOR THE LIVES LOST TODAY, HARVEST!
AND FOR THOSE WHO HAVE DIED IN THE CULLINGS BEFORE THIS ONE!
WHY MUST YOU PROLONG THE INEVITABLE?
NO MATTER HOW MUCH YOU STRUGGLE AGAINST IT, YOUR DESTINY IS TO SERVE ME!
ONLY IF YOU WANT EXTRA FRIES.
'SCUZE ME, TEAM.
BACK IN A BLINK.
HERE'S WILDFIRE, TIMBER WOLF.
APPRECIATE THE HELP, KID FLASH.
SO...WE COOL?
WHY WOULDN'T WE BE?
BECAUSE YOU WERE ALL "GRRR"--
AND I WAS ALL "WHA--?!"
NEVER MIND.
HOO-BOY!

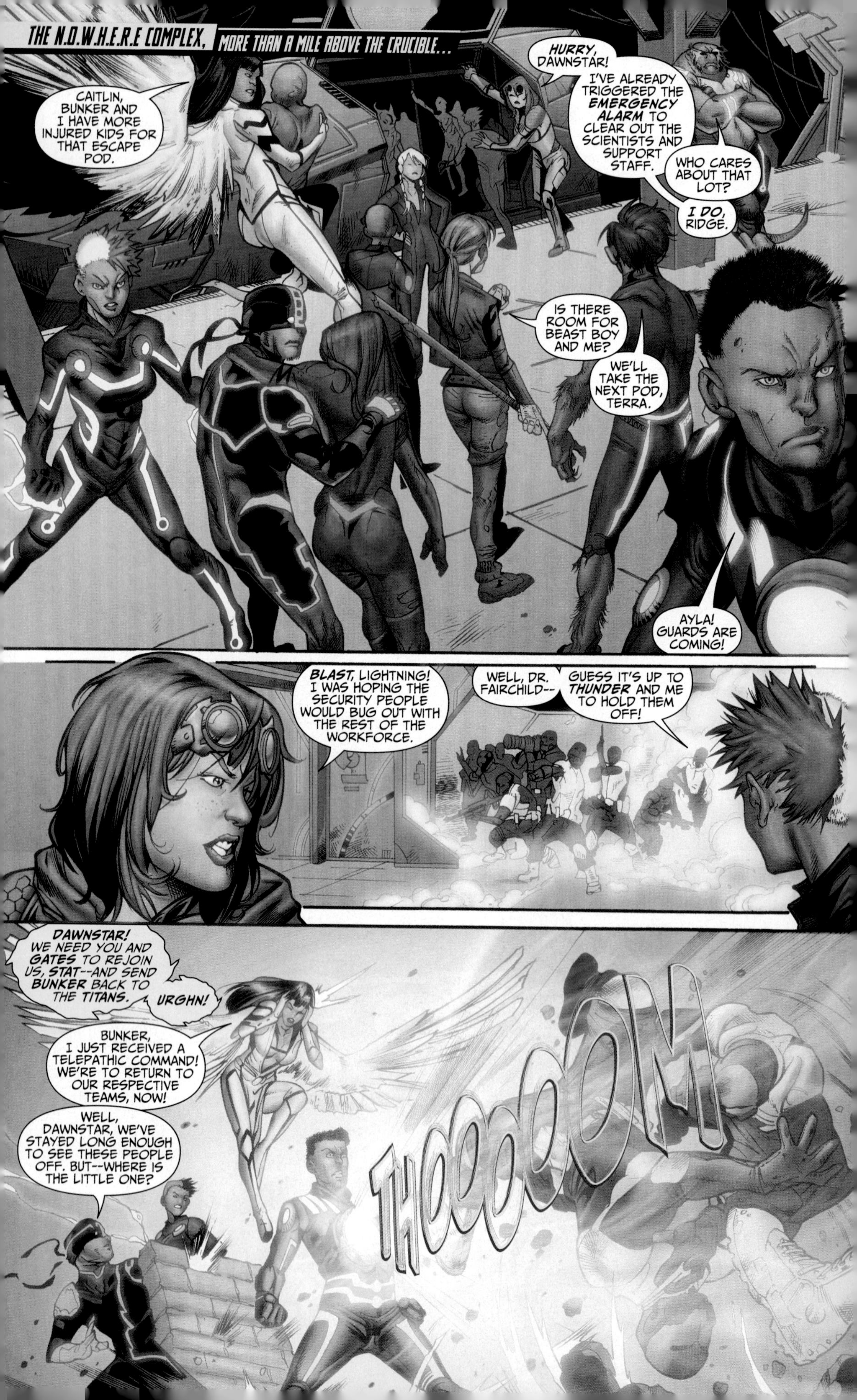
THE N.O.W.H.E.R.E COMPLEX, MORE THAN A MILE ABOVE THE CRUCIBLE...
CAITLIN, BUNKER AND I HAVE MORE INJURED KIDS FOR THAT ESCAPE POD.
HURRY, DAWNSTAR!
I'VE ALREADY TRIGGERED THE EMERGENCY ALARM TO CLEAR OUT THE SCIENTISTS AND SUPPORT STAFF.
WHO CARES ABOUT THAT LOT?
I DO, RIDGE.
IS THERE ROOM FOR BEAST BOY AND ME?
WE'LL TAKE THE NEXT POD, TERRA.
AYLA! GUARDS ARE COMING!
BLAST, LIGHTNING! I WAS HOPING THE SECURITY PEOPLE WOULD BUG OUT WITH THE REST OF THE WORKFORCE.
WELL, DR. FAIRCHILD--
GUESS IT'S UP TO THUNDER AND ME TO HOLD THEM OFF!
DAWNSTAR! WE NEED YOU AND GATES TO REJOIN US, STAT--AND SEND BUNKER BACK TO THE TITANS.
URGHN!
BUNKER, I JUST RECEIVED A TELEPATHIC COMMAND! WE'RE TO RETURN TO OUR RESPECTIVE TEAMS, NOW!
WELL, DAWNSTAR, WE'VE STAYED LONG ENOUGH TO SEE THESE PEOPLE OFF. BUT--WHERE IS THE LITTLE ONE?
THOOOOOM

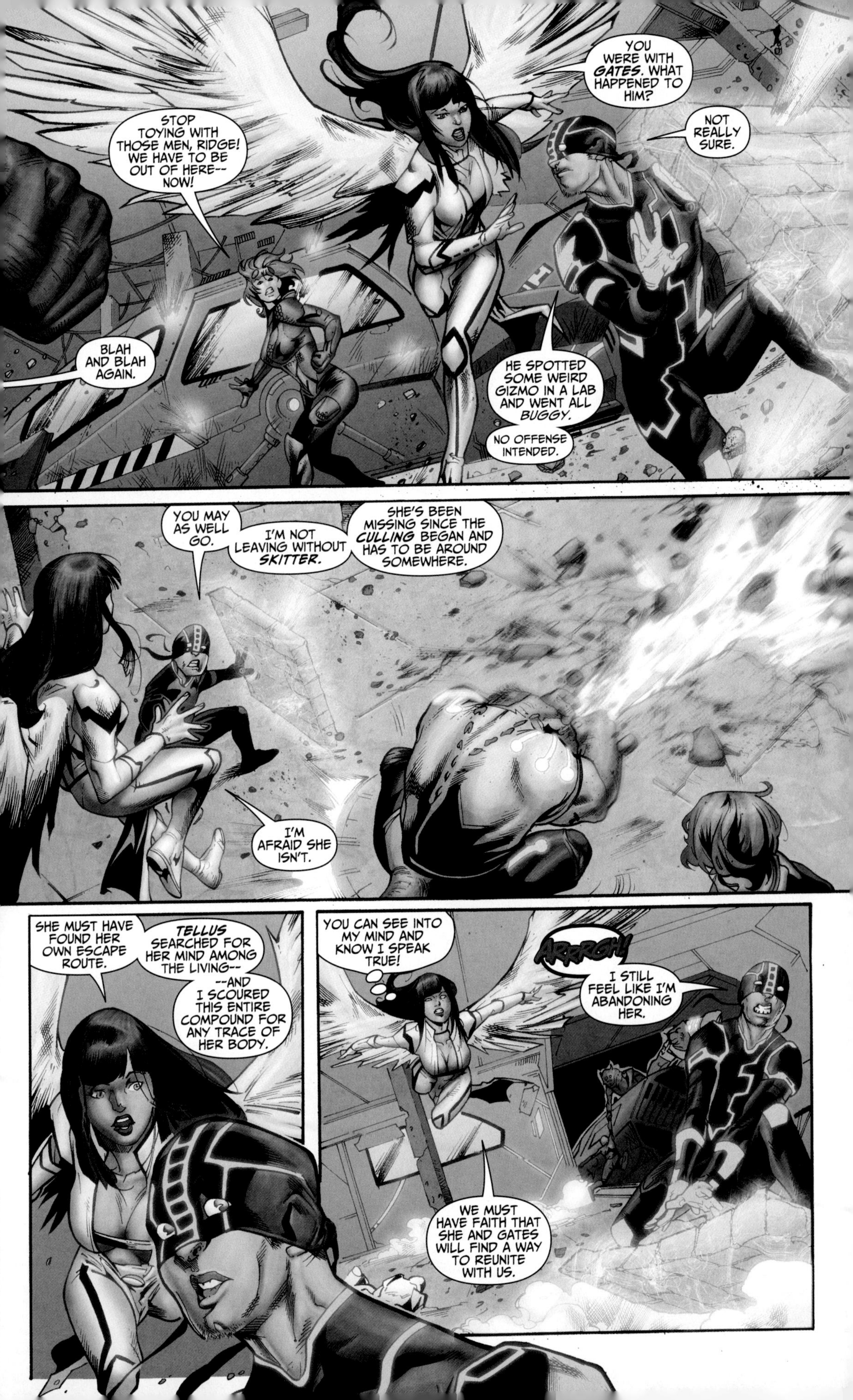
STOP TOYING WITH THOSE MEN, RIDGE! WE HAVE TO BE OUT OF HERE-- NOW!
YOU WERE WITH GATES. WHAT HAPPENED TO HIM?
NOT REALLY SURE.
BLAH AND BLAH AGAIN.
HE SPOTTED SOME WEIRD GIZMO IN A LAB AND WENT ALL BUGGY.
NO OFFENSE INTENDED.
YOU MAY AS WELL GO.
I'M NOT LEAVING WITHOUT SKITTER.
SHE'S BEEN MISSING SINCE THE CULLING BEGAN AND HAS TO BE AROUND SOMEWHERE.
I'M AFRAID SHE ISN'T.
SHE MUST HAVE FOUND HER OWN ESCAPE ROUTE.
TELLUS SEARCHED FOR HER MIND AMONG THE LIVING--
--AND I SCOURED THIS ENTIRE COMPOUND FOR ANY TRACE OF HER BODY.
YOU CAN SEE INTO MY MIND AND KNOW I SPEAK TRUE!
ARRRGH!
I STILL FEEL LIKE I'M ABANDONING HER.
WE MUST HAVE FAITH THAT SHE AND GATES WILL FIND A WAY TO REUNITE WITH US.

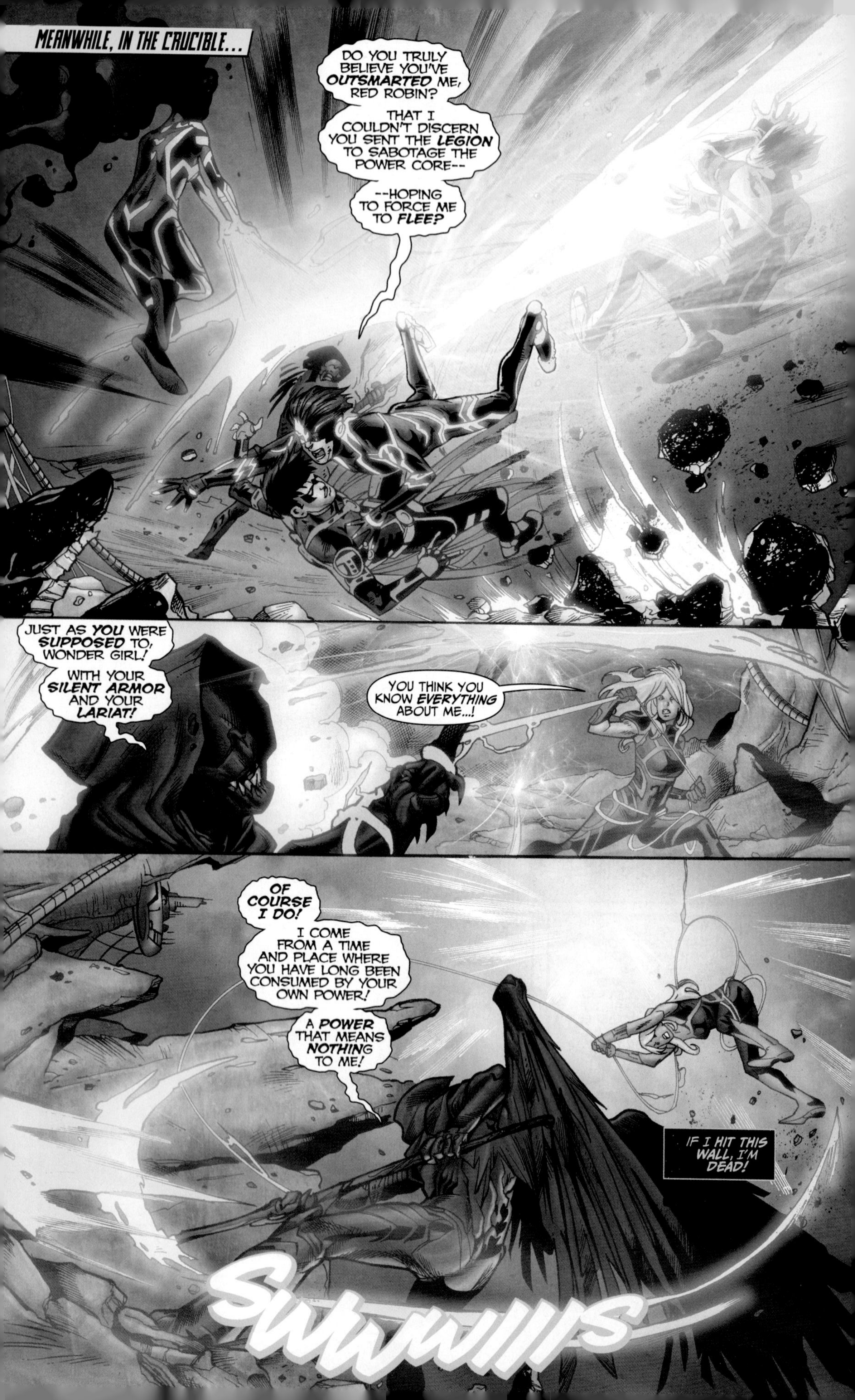
MEANWHILE, IN THE CRUCIBLE...
DO YOU TRULY BELIEVE YOU'VE OUTSMARTED ME, RED ROBIN?
THAT I COULDN'T DISCERN YOU SENT THE LEGION TO SABOTAGE THE POWER CORE--
--HOPING TO FORCE ME TO FLEE?
JUST AS YOU WERE SUPPOSED TO, WONDER GIRL!
WITH YOUR SILENT ARMOR AND YOUR LARIAT!
YOU THINK YOU KNOW EVERYTHING ABOUT ME...!
OF COURSE I DO!
I COME FROM A TIME AND PLACE WHERE YOU HAVE LONG BEEN CONSUMED BY YOUR OWN POWER!
A POWER THAT MEANS NOTHING TO ME!
IF I HIT THIS WALL, I'M DEAD!
SWWIIIS

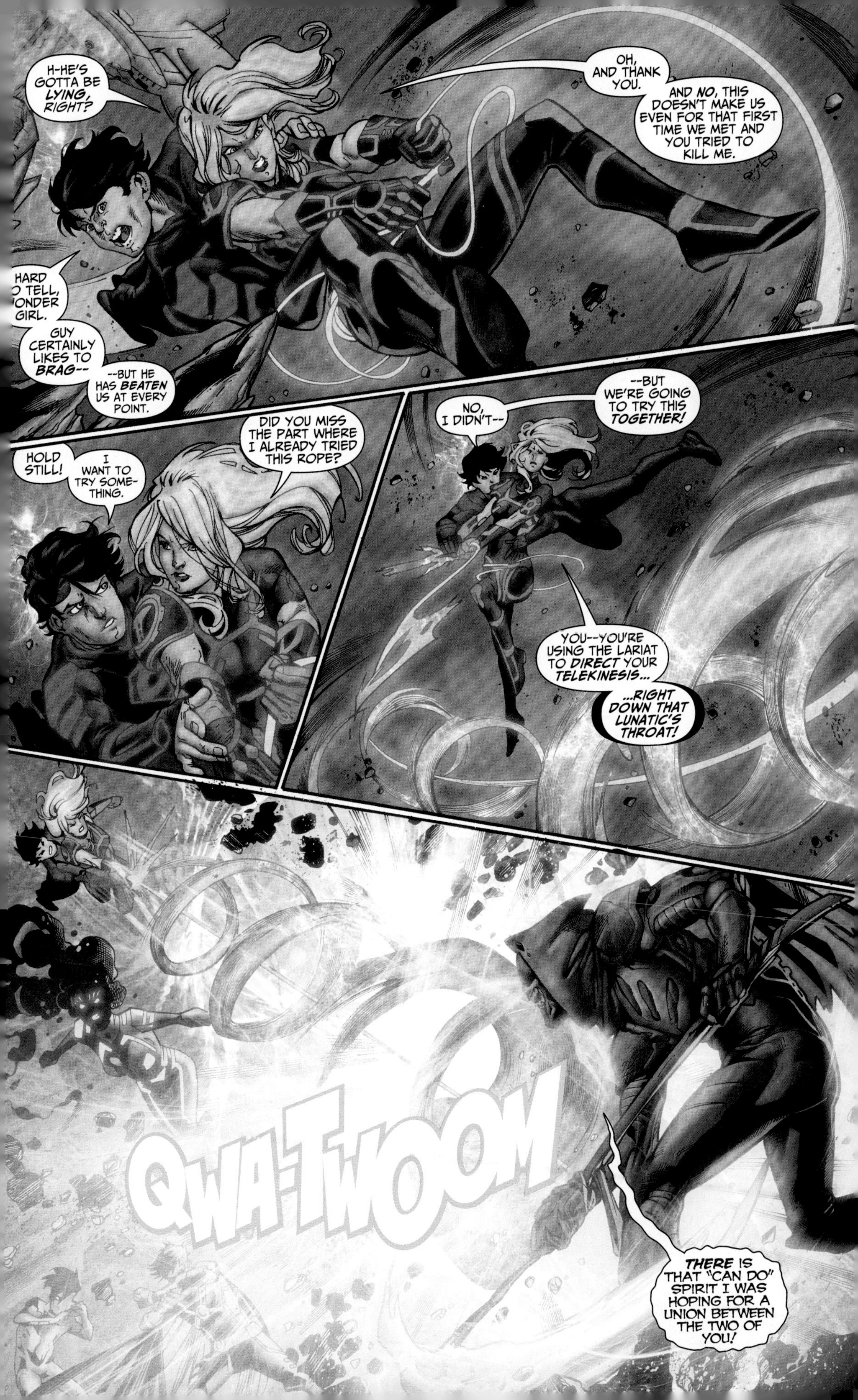
H-HE'S GOTTA BE LYING, RIGHT?
OH, AND THANK YOU.
AND NO, THIS DOESN'T MAKE US EVEN FOR THAT FIRST TIME WE MET AND YOU TRIED TO KILL ME.
HARD TO TELL, WONDER GIRL.
GUY CERTAINLY LIKES TO BRAG--
--BUT HE HAS BEATEN US AT EVERY POINT.
HOLD STILL!
I WANT TO TRY SOME-THING.
DID YOU MISS THE PART WHERE I ALREADY TRIED THIS ROPE?
NO, I DIDN'T--
--BUT WE'RE GOING TO TRY THIS TOGETHER!
YOU--YOU'RE USING THE LARIAT TO DIRECT YOUR TELEKINESIS...
...RIGHT DOWN THAT LUNATIC'S THROAT!
QWA-TWOOM
THERE IS THAT "CAN DO" SPIRIT I WAS HOPING FOR A UNION BETWEEN THE TWO OF YOU!

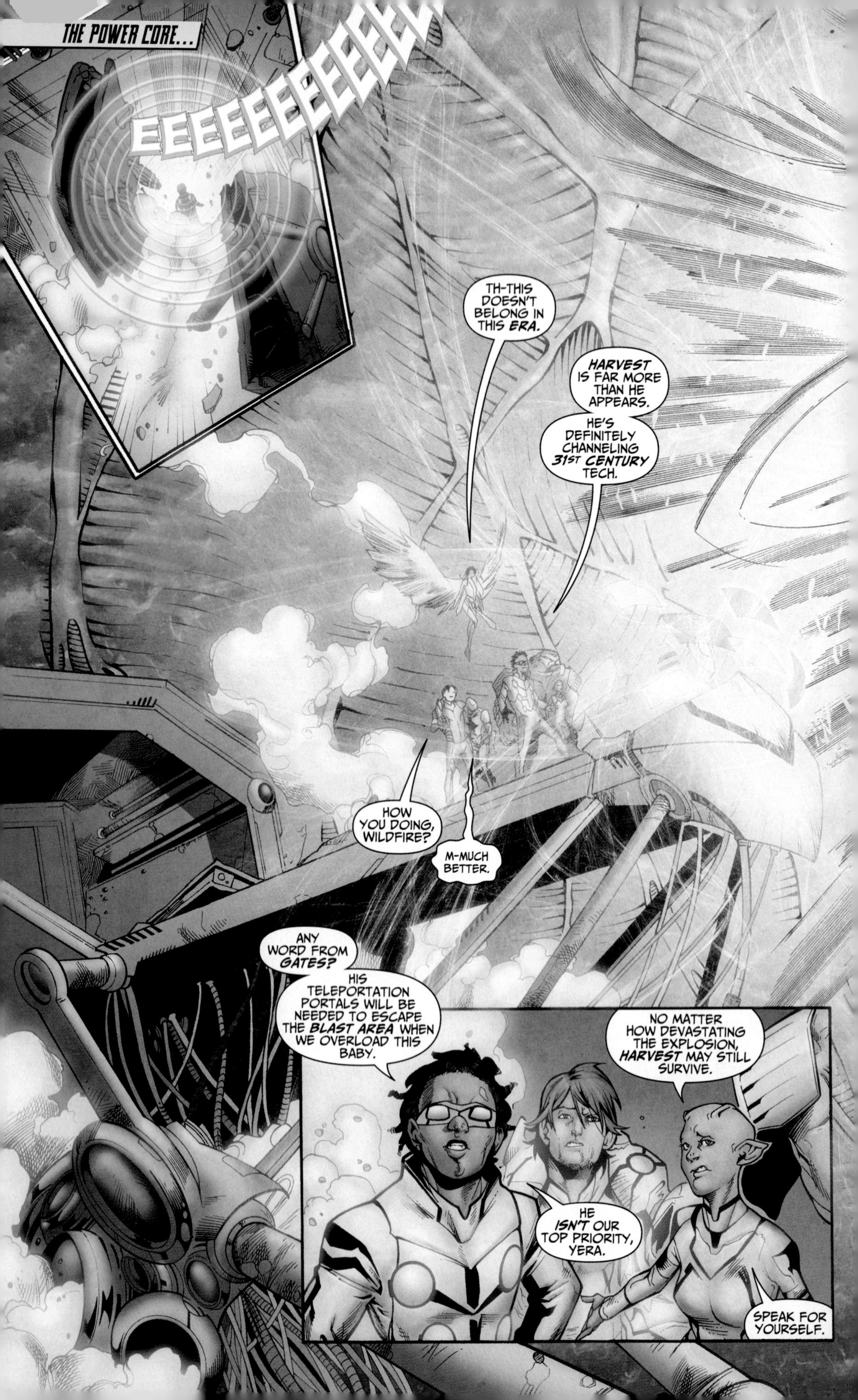
THE POWER CORE...
EEEEEEEEEEEEEEL
TH-THIS DOESN'T BELONG IN THIS *ERA.*
HARVEST IS FAR MORE THAN HE APPEARS.
HE'S DEFINITELY CHANNELING *31ST CENTURY* TECH.
HOW YOU DOING, WILDFIRE?
M-MUCH BETTER.
ANY WORD FROM *GATES?*
HIS TELEPORTATION PORTALS WILL BE NEEDED TO ESCAPE THE *BLAST AREA* WHEN WE OVERLOAD THIS BABY.
NO MATTER HOW DEVASTATING THE EXPLOSION, *HARVEST* MAY STILL SURVIVE.
HE *ISN'T* OUR TOP PRIORITY, YERA.
SPEAK FOR YOURSELF.

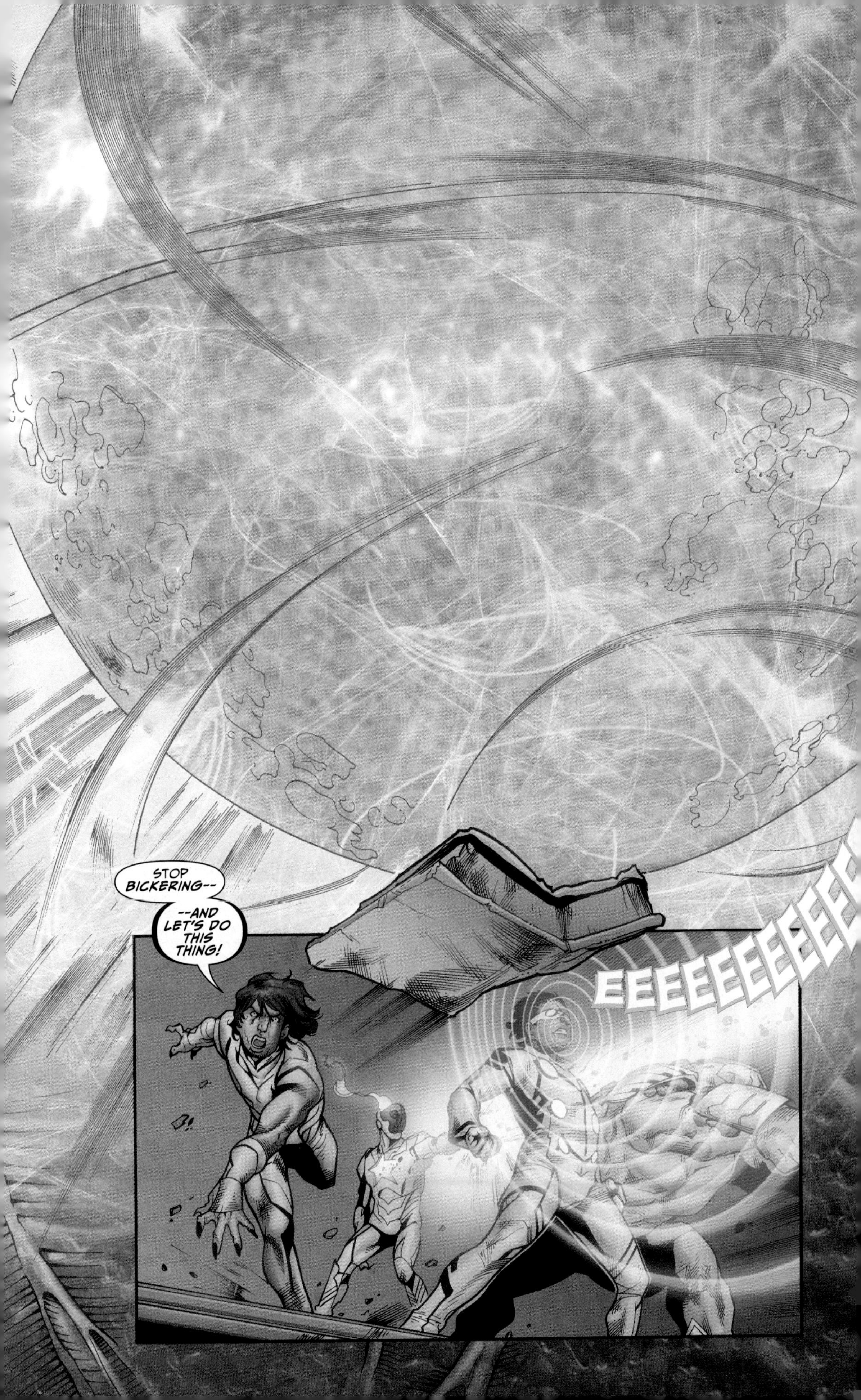
STOP BICKERING--
--AND LET'S DO THIS THING!
EEEEEEEEEEEEEEEEEE

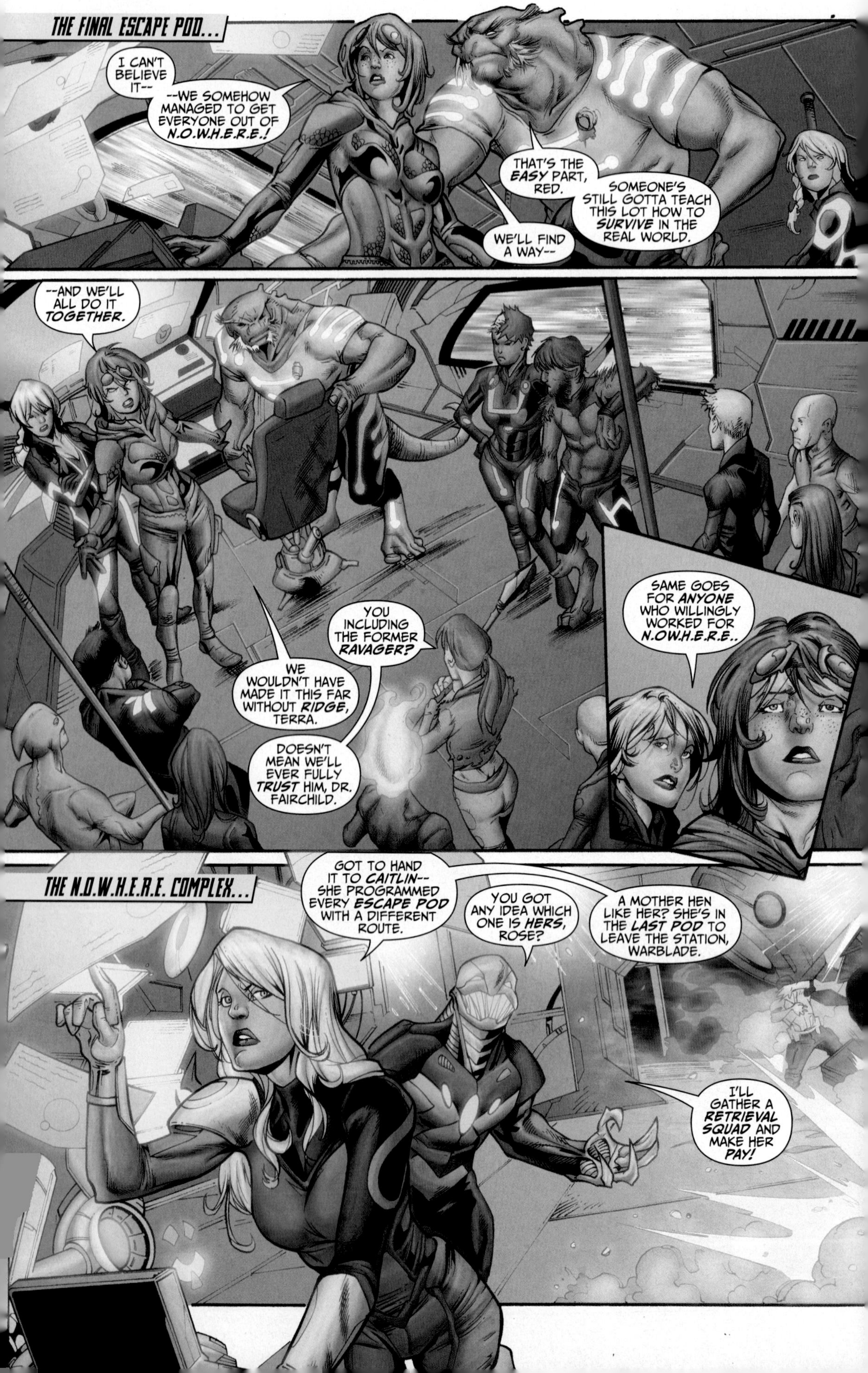
THE FINAL ESCAPE POD...
I CAN'T BELIEVE IT--
--WE SOMEHOW MANAGED TO GET EVERYONE OUT OF N.O.W.H.E.R.E.!
THAT'S THE EASY PART, RED.
SOMEONE'S STILL GOTTA TEACH THIS LOT HOW TO SURVIVE IN THE REAL WORLD.
WE'LL FIND A WAY--
--AND WE'LL ALL DO IT TOGETHER.
YOU INCLUDING THE FORMER RAVAGER?
WE WOULDN'T HAVE MADE IT THIS FAR WITHOUT RIDGE, TERRA.
DOESN'T MEAN WE'LL EVER FULLY TRUST HIM, DR. FAIRCHILD.
SAME GOES FOR ANYONE WHO WILLINGLY WORKED FOR N.O.W.H.E.R.E..
THE N.O.W.H.E.R.E. COMPLEX...
GOT TO HAND IT TO CAITLIN-- SHE PROGRAMMED EVERY ESCAPE POD WITH A DIFFERENT ROUTE.
YOU GOT ANY IDEA WHICH ONE IS HERS, ROSE?
A MOTHER HEN LIKE HER? SHE'S IN THE LAST POD TO LEAVE THE STATION, WARBLADE.
I'LL GATHER A RETRIEVAL SQUAD AND MAKE HER PAY!

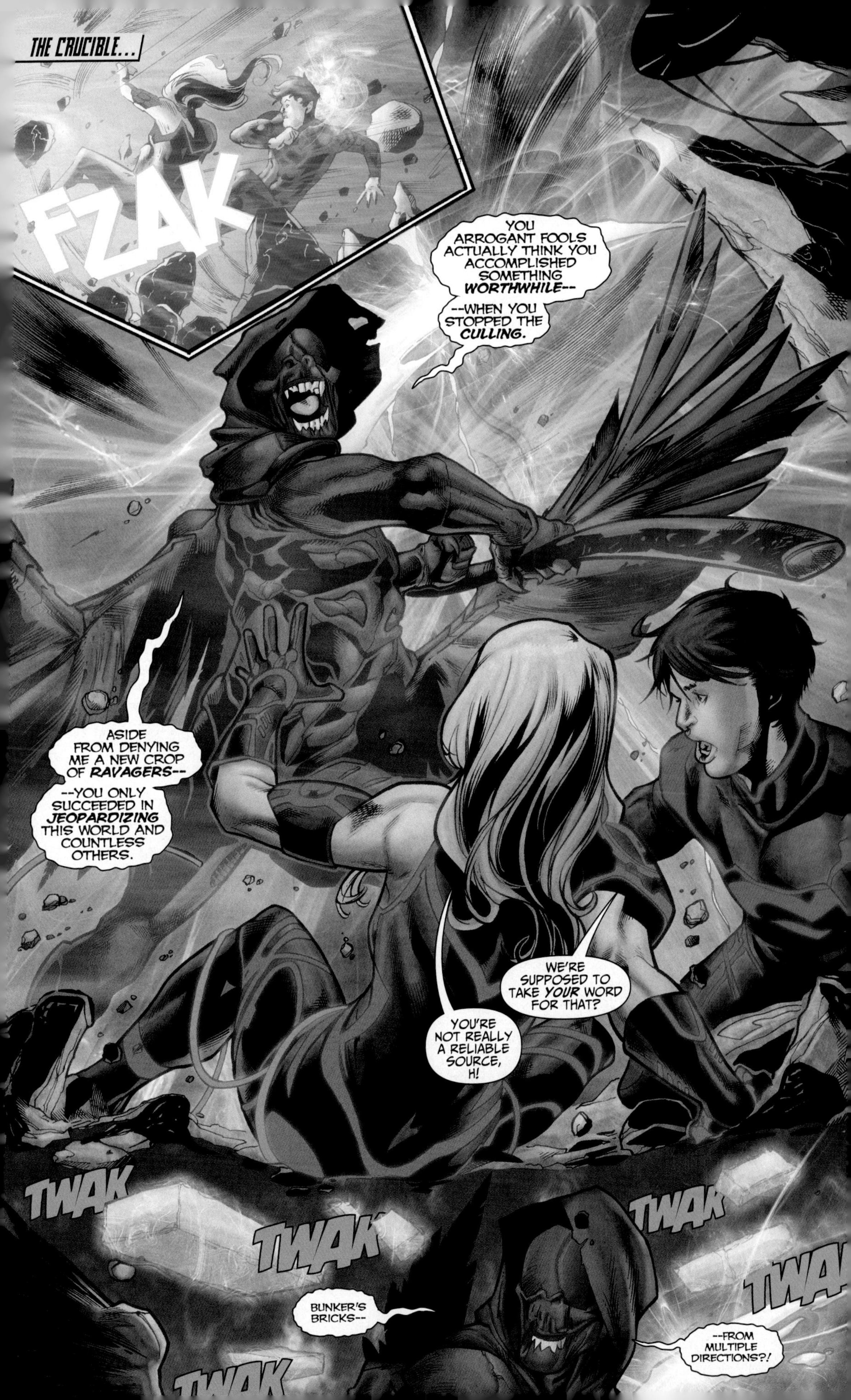
THE CRUCIBLE...
FZAK
YOU ARROGANT FOOLS ACTUALLY THINK YOU ACCOMPLISHED SOMETHING WORTHWHILE--
--WHEN YOU STOPPED THE CULLING.
ASIDE FROM DENYING ME A NEW CROP OF RAVAGERS--
--YOU ONLY SUCCEEDED IN JEOPARDIZING THIS WORLD AND COUNTLESS OTHERS.
WE'RE SUPPOSED TO TAKE YOUR WORD FOR THAT?
YOU'RE NOT REALLY A RELIABLE SOURCE, H!
TWAK
TWAK
TWAK
TWAK
BUNKER'S BRICKS--
--FROM MULTIPLE DIRECTIONS?!
TWAK

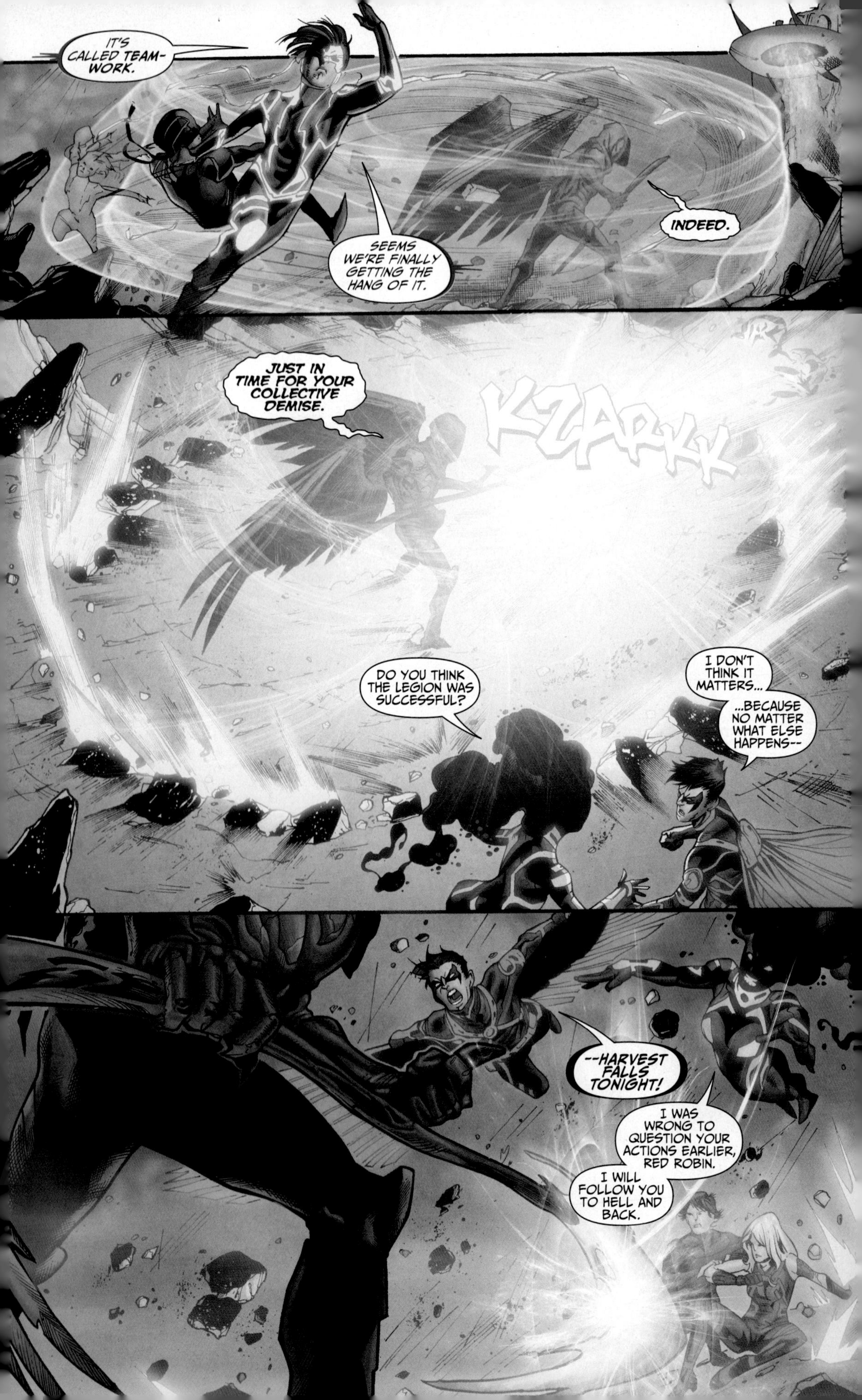
IT'S CALLED TEAM-WORK.
SEEMS WE'RE FINALLY GETTING THE HANG OF IT.
INDEED.
JUST IN TIME FOR YOUR COLLECTIVE DEMISE.
KZARKK
DO YOU THINK THE LEGION WAS SUCCESSFUL?
I DON'T THINK IT MATTERS...
...BECAUSE NO MATTER WHAT ELSE HAPPENS--
--HARVEST FALLS TONIGHT!
I WAS WRONG TO QUESTION YOUR ACTIONS EARLIER, RED ROBIN.
I WILL FOLLOW YOU TO HELL AND BACK.

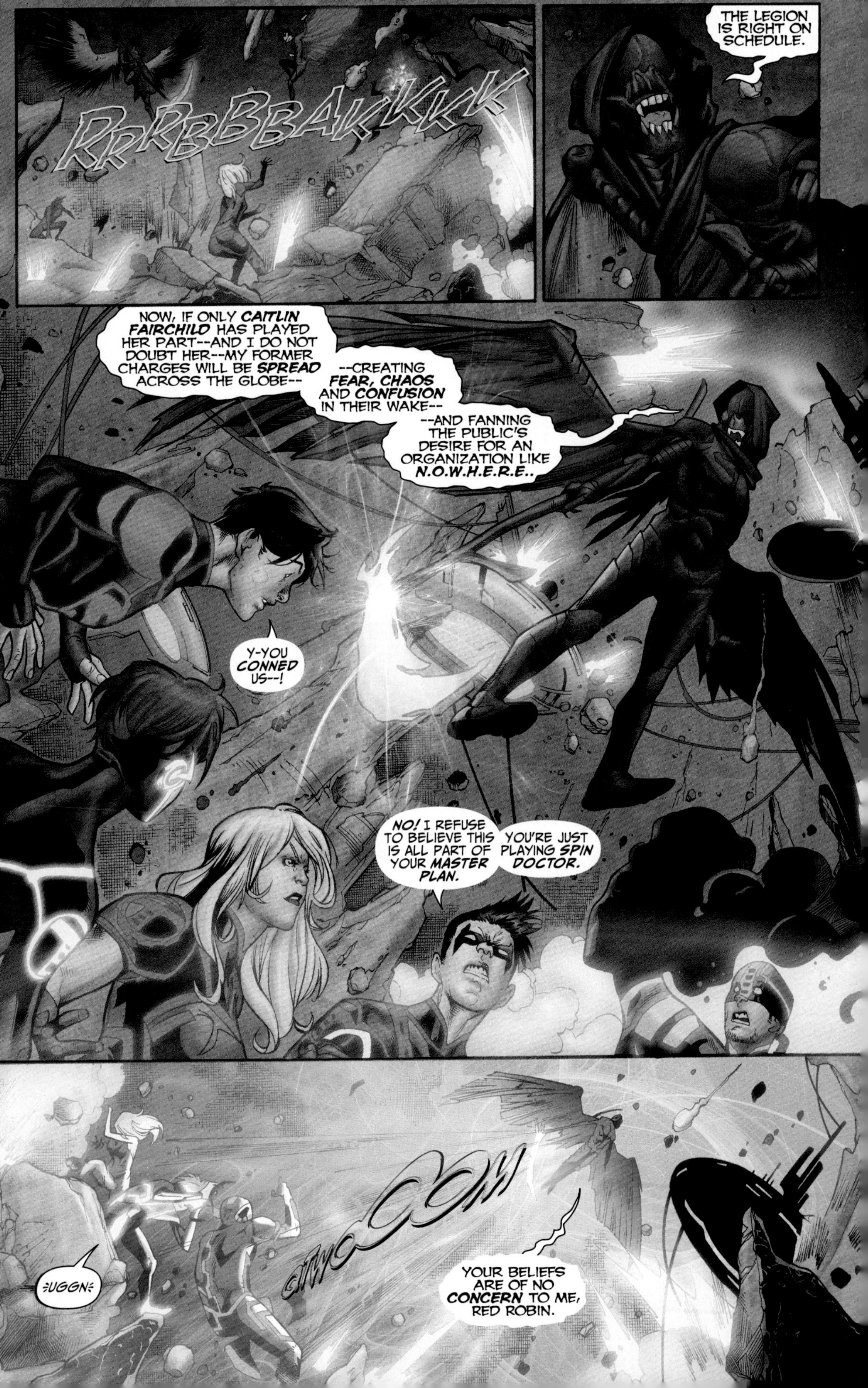
THE LEGION IS RIGHT ON SCHEDULE.
NOW, IF ONLY CAITLIN FAIRCHILD HAS PLAYED HER PART--AND I DO NOT DOUBT HER--MY FORMER CHARGES WILL BE SPREAD ACROSS THE GLOBE--
--CREATING FEAR, CHAOS AND CONFUSION IN THEIR WAKE--
--AND FANNING THE PUBLIC'S DESIRE FOR AN ORGANIZATION LIKE N.O.W.H.E.R.E..
Y-YOU CONNED US--!
NO! I REFUSE TO BELIEVE THIS IS ALL PART OF YOUR MASTER PLAN.
YOU'RE JUST PLAYING SPIN DOCTOR.
UGGN
YOUR BELIEFS ARE OF NO CONCERN TO ME, RED ROBIN.

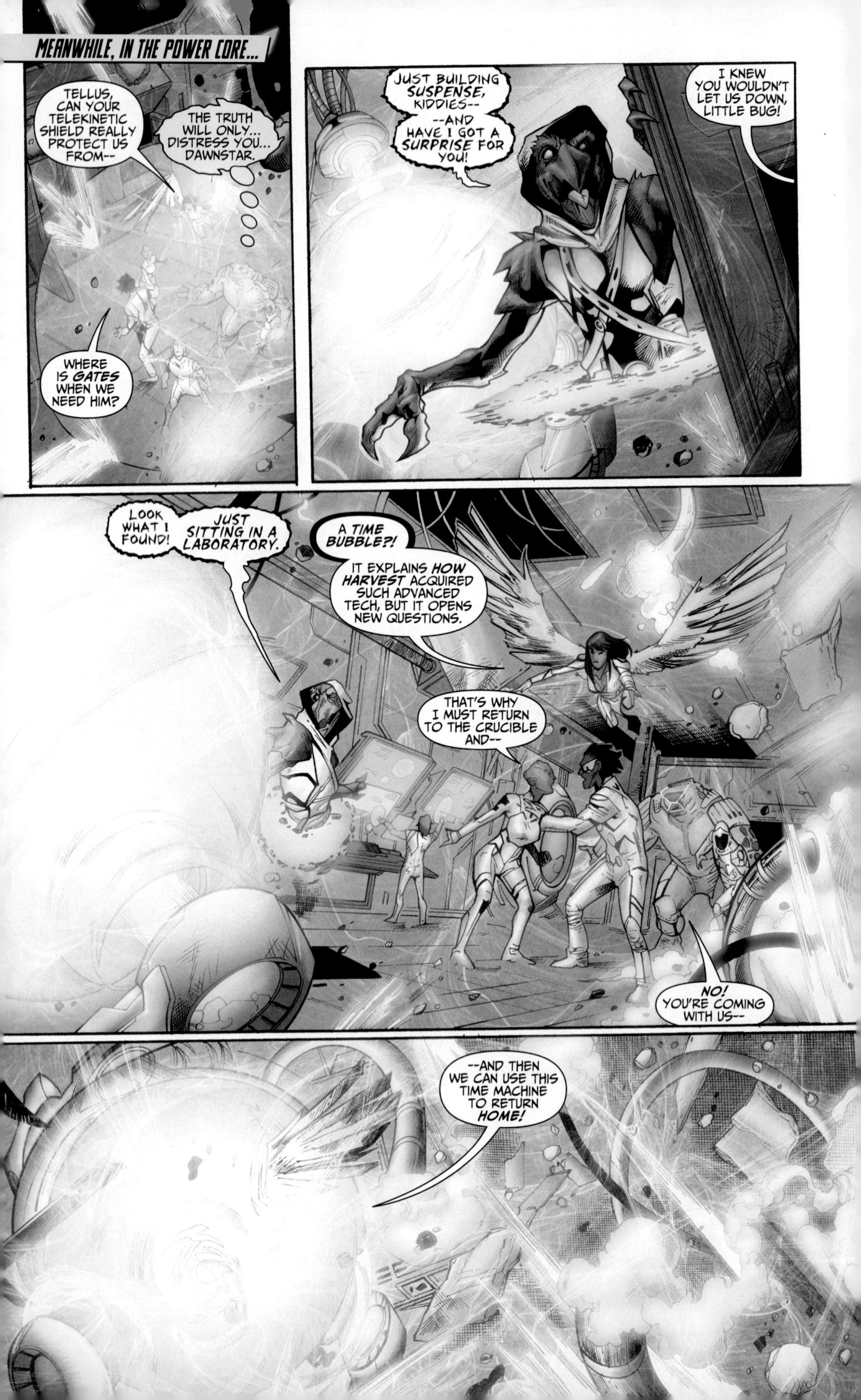
MEANWHILE, IN THE POWER CORE...
TELLUS, CAN YOUR TELEKINETIC SHIELD REALLY PROTECT US FROM--
THE TRUTH WILL ONLY... DISTRESS YOU... DAWNSTAR.
WHERE IS GATES WHEN WE NEED HIM?
JUST BUILDING SUSPENSE, KIDDIES--
--AND HAVE I GOT A SURPRISE FOR YOU!
I KNEW YOU WOULDN'T LET US DOWN, LITTLE BUG!
LOOK WHAT I FOUND!
JUST SITTING IN A LABORATORY.
A TIME BUBBLE?!
IT EXPLAINS HOW HARVEST ACQUIRED SUCH ADVANCED TECH, BUT IT OPENS NEW QUESTIONS.
THAT'S WHY I MUST RETURN TO THE CRUCIBLE AND--
NO! YOU'RE COMING WITH US--
--AND THEN WE CAN USE THIS TIME MACHINE TO RETURN HOME!

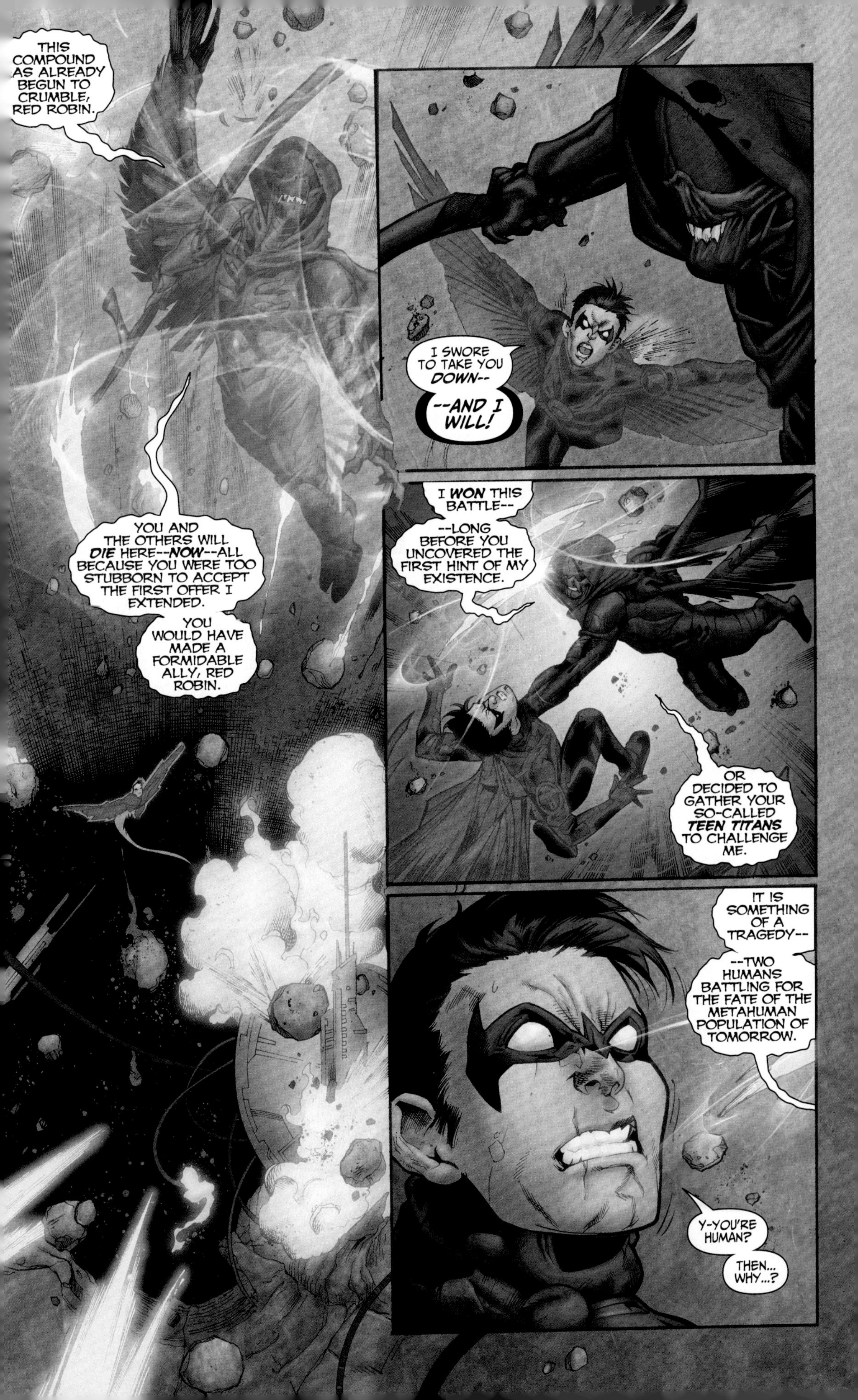
THIS COMPOUND HAS ALREADY BEGUN TO CRUMBLE, RED ROBIN.
I SWORE TO TAKE YOU DOWN--
--AND I WILL!
YOU AND THE OTHERS WILL DIE HERE--NOW--ALL BECAUSE YOU WERE TOO STUBBORN TO ACCEPT THE FIRST OFFER I EXTENDED.
YOU WOULD HAVE MADE A FORMIDABLE ALLY, RED ROBIN.
I WON THIS BATTLE--
--LONG BEFORE YOU UNCOVERED THE FIRST HINT OF MY EXISTENCE.
OR DECIDED TO GATHER YOUR SO-CALLED TEEN TITANS TO CHALLENGE ME.
IT IS SOMETHING OF A TRAGEDY--
--TWO HUMANS BATTLING FOR THE FATE OF THE METAHUMAN POPULATION OF TOMORROW.
Y-YOU'RE HUMAN?
THEN... WHY...?

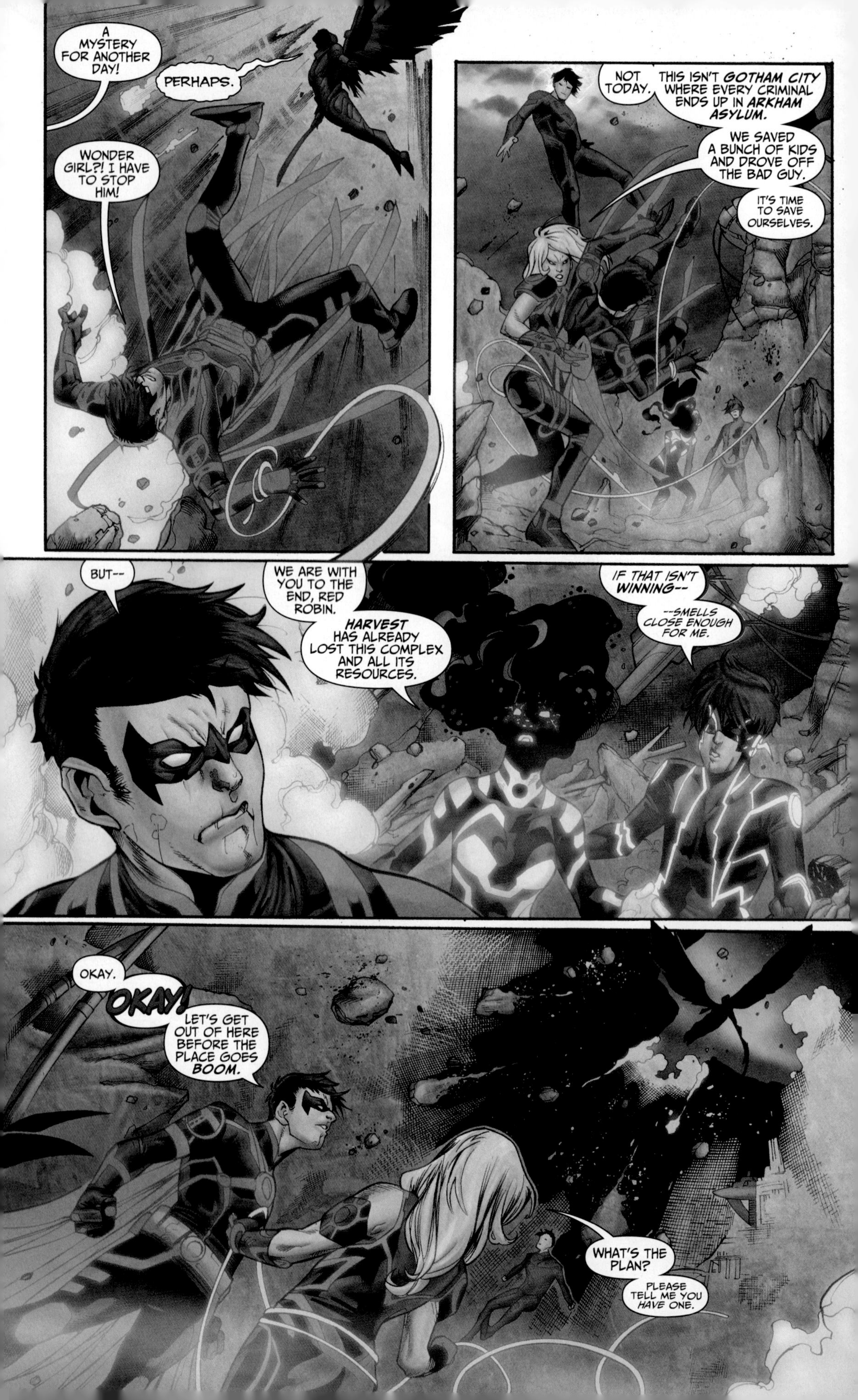
A MYSTERY FOR ANOTHER DAY!
PERHAPS.
WONDER GIRL?! I HAVE TO STOP HIM!
NOT TODAY.
THIS ISN'T GOTHAM CITY WHERE EVERY CRIMINAL ENDS UP IN ARKHAM ASYLUM.
WE SAVED A BUNCH OF KIDS AND DROVE OFF THE BAD GUY.
IT'S TIME TO SAVE OURSELVES.
BUT--
WE ARE WITH YOU TO THE END, RED ROBIN.
HARVEST HAS ALREADY LOST THIS COMPLEX AND ALL ITS RESOURCES.
IF THAT ISN'T WINNING--
--SMELLS CLOSE ENOUGH FOR ME.
OKAY.
OKAY!
LET'S GET OUT OF HERE BEFORE THE PLACE GOES BOOM.
WHAT'S THE PLAN?
PLEASE TELL ME YOU HAVE ONE.

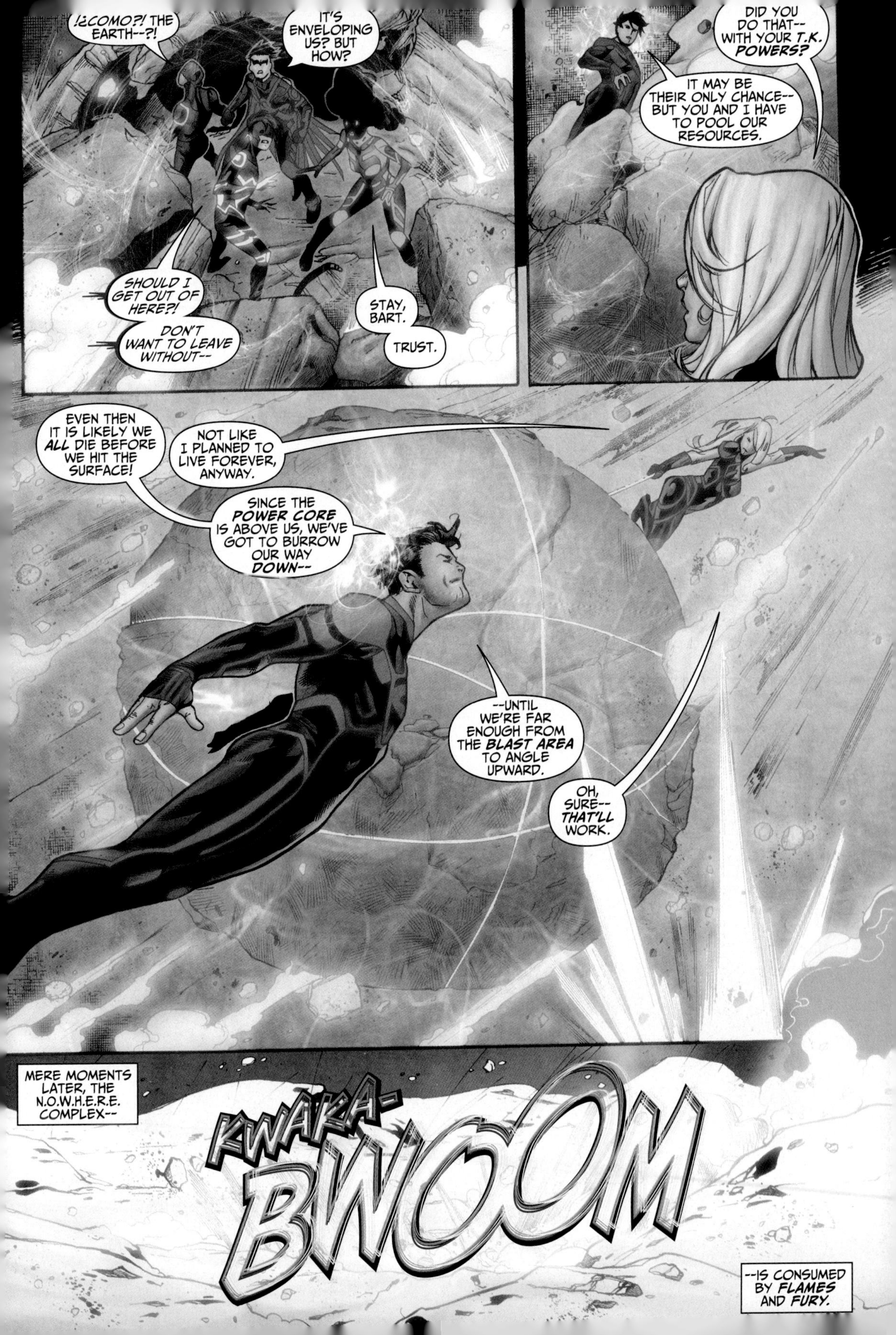
¡¿COMO?! THE EARTH--?!
IT'S ENVELOPING US? BUT HOW?
SHOULD I GET OUT OF HERE?!
DON'T WANT TO LEAVE WITHOUT--
STAY, BART.
TRUST.
DID YOU DO THAT--WITH YOUR T.K. POWERS?
IT MAY BE THEIR ONLY CHANCE--BUT YOU AND I HAVE TO POOL OUR RESOURCES.
NOT LIKE I PLANNED TO LIVE FOREVER, ANYWAY.
EVEN THEN IT IS LIKELY WE ALL DIE BEFORE WE HIT THE SURFACE!
SINCE THE POWER CORE IS ABOVE US, WE'VE GOT TO BURROW OUR WAY DOWN--
--UNTIL WE'RE FAR ENOUGH FROM THE BLAST AREA TO ANGLE UPWARD.
OH, SURE--THAT'LL WORK.
MERE MOMENTS LATER, THE N.O.W.H.E.R.E. COMPLEX--
KWAKA-BWOOM
--IS CONSUMED BY FLAMES AND FURY.

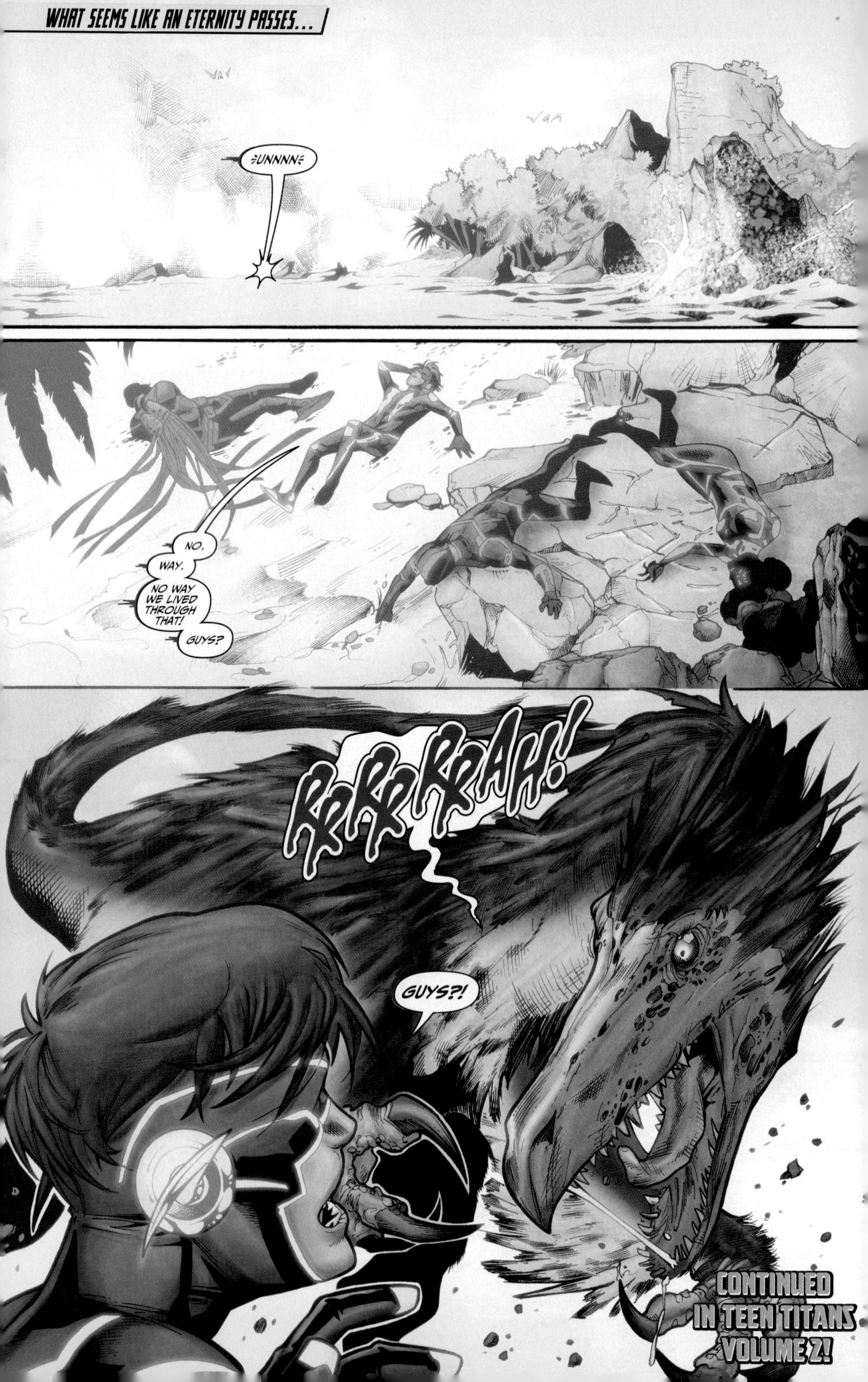
WHAT SEEMS LIKE AN ETERNITY PASSES...
UNNNN
NO.
WAY.
NO WAY WE LIVED THROUGH THAT!
GUYS?
RRRRRRAH!
GUYS?!
CONTINUED IN TEEN TITANS VOLUME 2!

THE COLONY

Design by Brett Booth

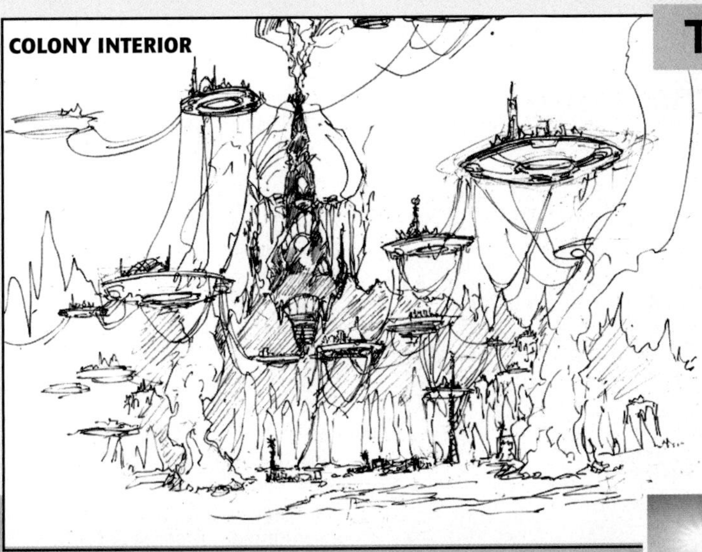
COLONY INTERIOR

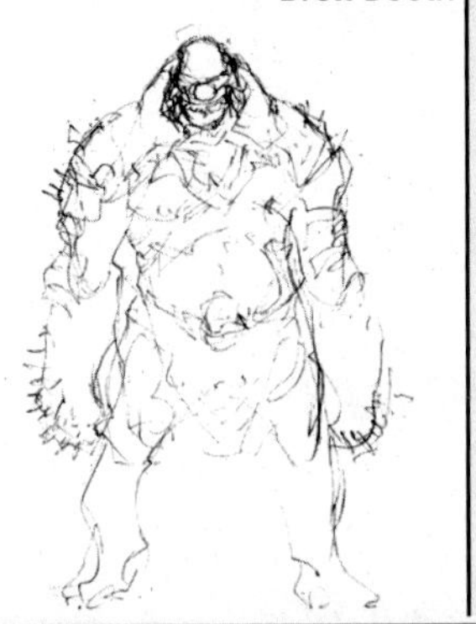

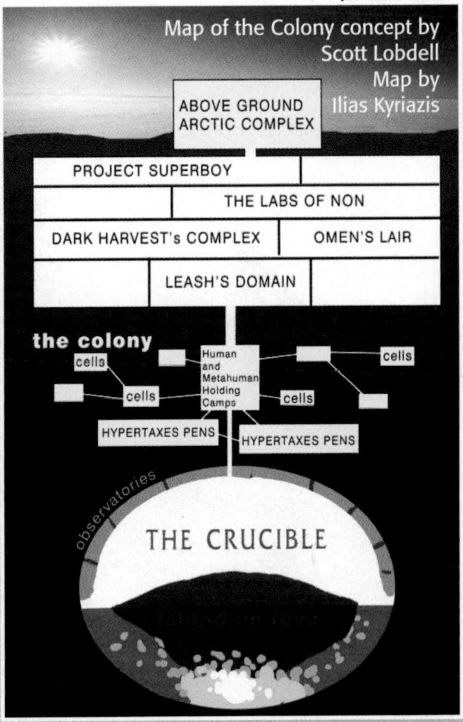
ABOVE GROUND ARCTIC COMPLEX
PROJECT SUPERBOY
THE LABS OF NON
DARK HARVEST's COMPLEX
OMEN'S LAIR
LEASH'S DOMAIN
the colony
cells
cells
Human and Metahuman Holding Camps
cells
cells
HYPERTAXES PENS
HYPERTAXES PENS
observatories
THE CRUCIBLE

Map of the Colony concept by Scott Lobdell
Map by Ilias Kyriazis

N.O.W.H.E.R.E., an international organization with a nefarious interest in young metahumans, has created **The Colony** – a huge complex built deep underground. Miles wide and miles high – in it, young metahumans are left alone to survive. Some live, some die. It is survival of the fittest. They fight for food, and they fight for water. They fight – because that is what N.O.W.H.E.R.E. wants. They will be hardened, they will be toughened – or they will be dead.

The Colony (HARVEST's UNDERGROUND EMPIRE) is based on terraforming technology and goes on for miles underground. There are platforms built high up into the walls and tendrils, used as ladders, that reach to the ground. The trick is to avoid the towers of volcanic glass, walls of volcanic rock, the mysterious vents, and the lava, falling everywhere. The Colony is like a ghetto of horror and despair, as dozens of teenagers go about their daily business here in "hell."

Most of the kids here are hungry and dirty and dressed in N.O.W.H.E.R.E.-provided clothing. No one is over nineteen years old. Some are metahuman, some are human, some have cybernetic implants and some are alien/human combinations as the result of being infected with the Hypertaxis virus.

Even the metahuman teenagers have restraining devices meant to dampen their powers inside the Colony.

It is clear that everyone here views each other with suspicion. Sure, there might be alliances established in the Colony, but they are all very tenuous marriages of convenience…untrustworthy alliances.

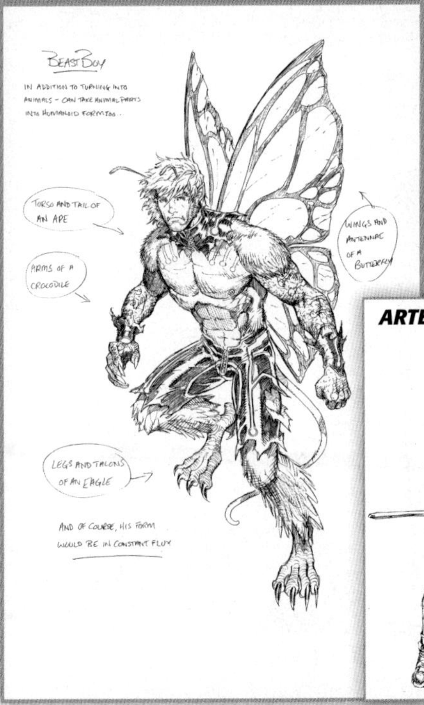
BEAST BOY
IN ADDITION TO TURNING INTO ANIMALS - CAN TAKE ANIMAL PARTS INTO HUMANOID FORM TOO.
TORSO AND TAIL OF AN APE
WINGS AND ANTENNAE OF A BUTTERFLY
ARMS OF A CROCODILE
LEGS AND TALONS OF AN EAGLE
AND OF COURSE, HIS FORM WOULD BE IN CONSTANT FLUX

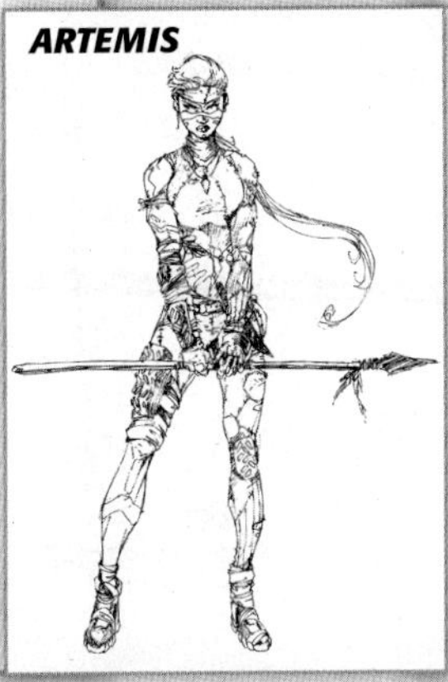
ARTEMIS

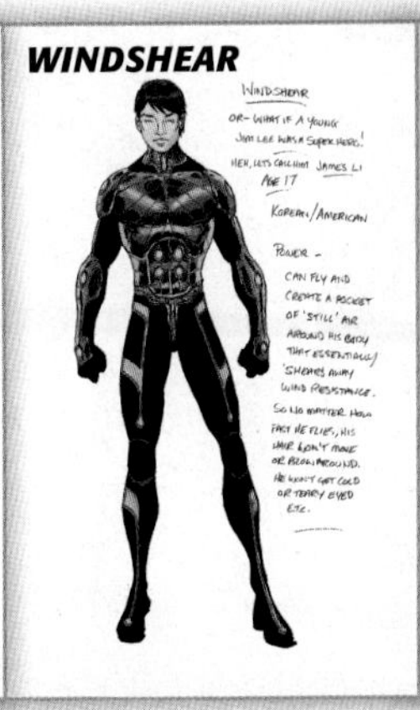
WINDSHEAR

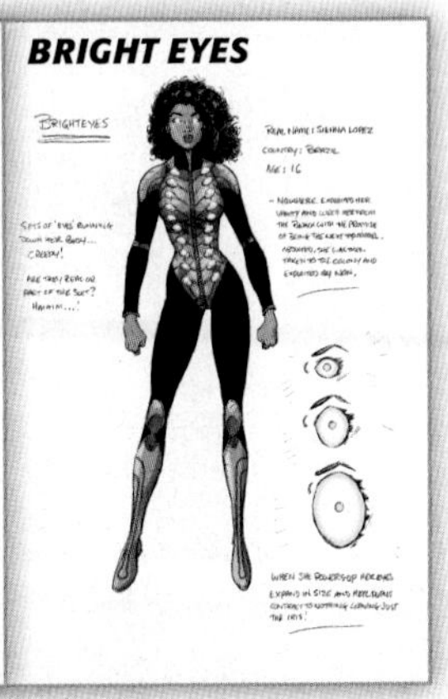
BRIGHT EYES

Initial character sketches by Brett Booth (Artemis) and Ian Churchill (all others)

THE CRUCIBLE

Periodically, there is a ***Culling*** – a process of thinning the herd. All food, water and any other basic necessities of life are withdrawn. Select inhabitants of the Colony are sent into **The Crucible**, a high-tech arena, and told they must fight to survive.

The Crucible...the Culling fields. Surrounded by a river of lava, it is an island filled with nooks and crannies, stalagmites and stalactites – anything that would help serve as a battleground filled with rough terrain. It is the environment of those who will "kill or be killed."

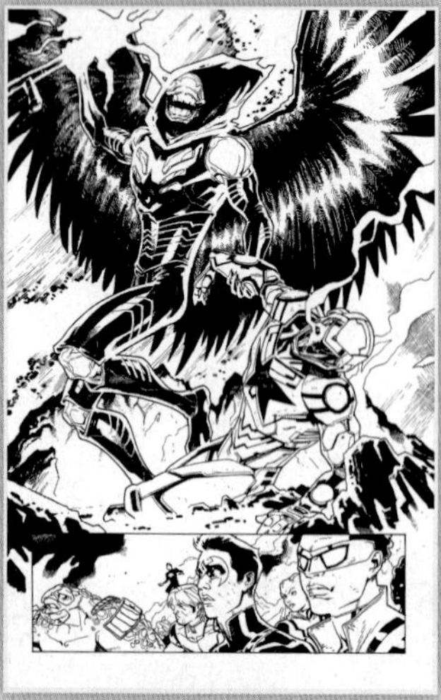

Harvest battles Wildfire in Legion Lost #9

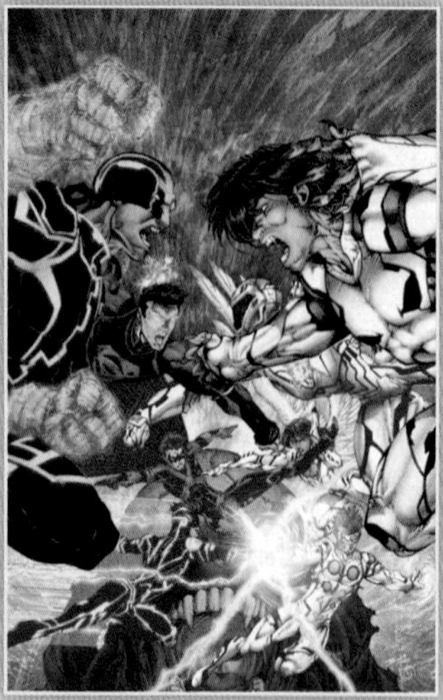

Teen Titans vs. Legion Lost in The Crucible

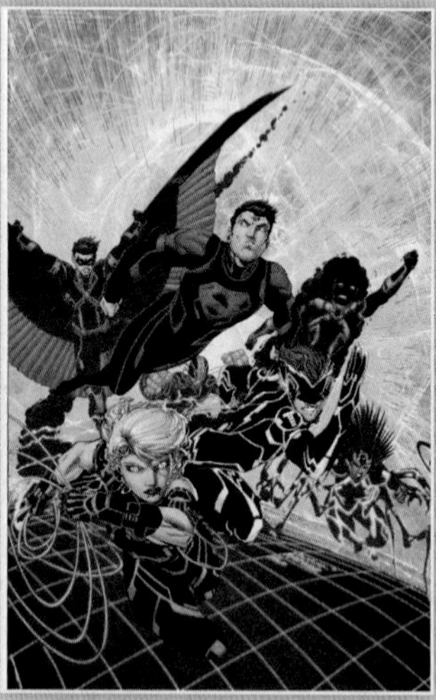

The Teen Titans donning the colors of Harvest

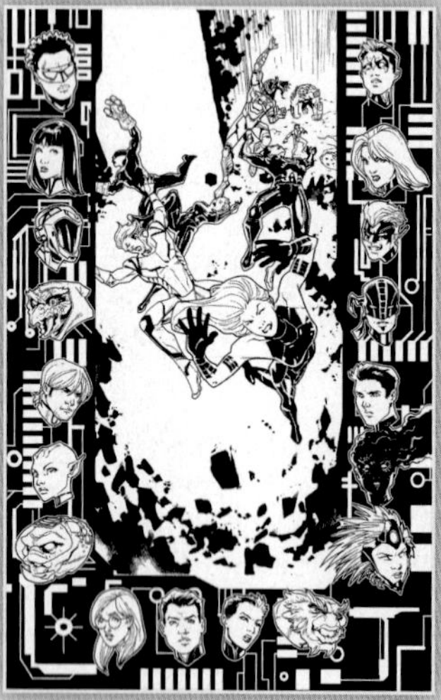

Legion Lost falling into The Crucible in Legion Lost #9

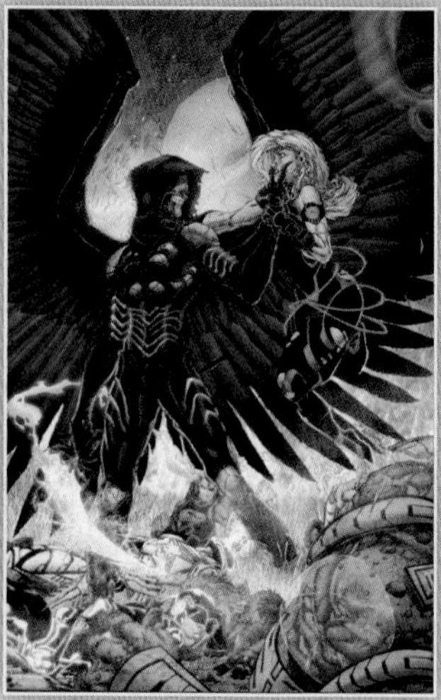

Wonder Girl vs. Harvest!

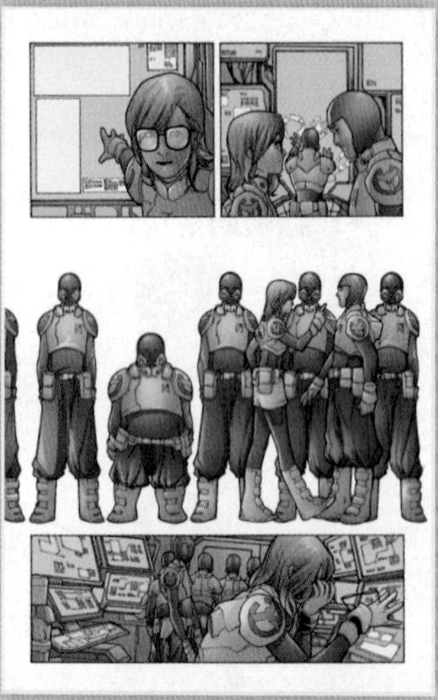

Caitlin Fairchild behind the scenes of N.O.W.H.E.R.E. in Superboy #1

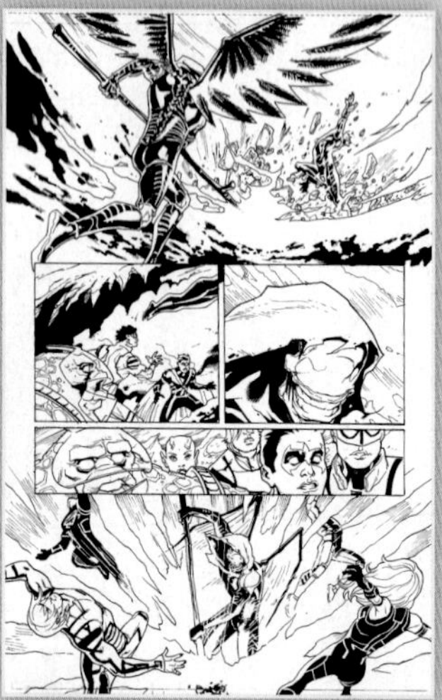

The Legion and The Teen Titans fight for freedom in Legion Lost #9

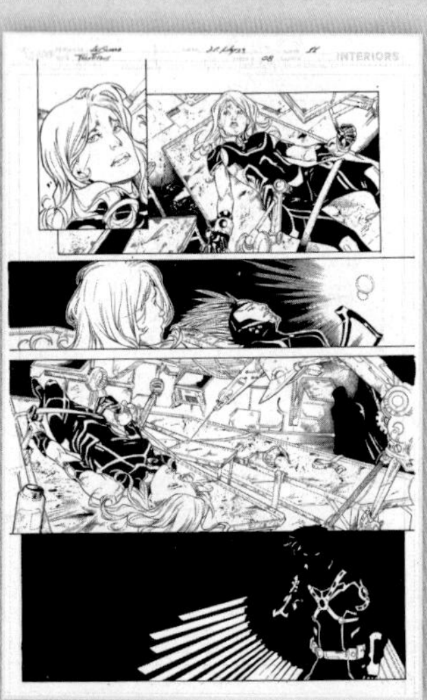

Teen Titans being prepared for The Culling in Teen Titans #8

N.O.W.H.E.R.E.'s leader is a cold, calculating and ruthless man out of time. His ultimate goal is humanitarian, at least in his own mind – to reshape the future through sheer force of will. He plans to control the next generation of metahumans…even if it means killing off the current one. His army is made up of past and present Ravagers, the winners of The Culling.

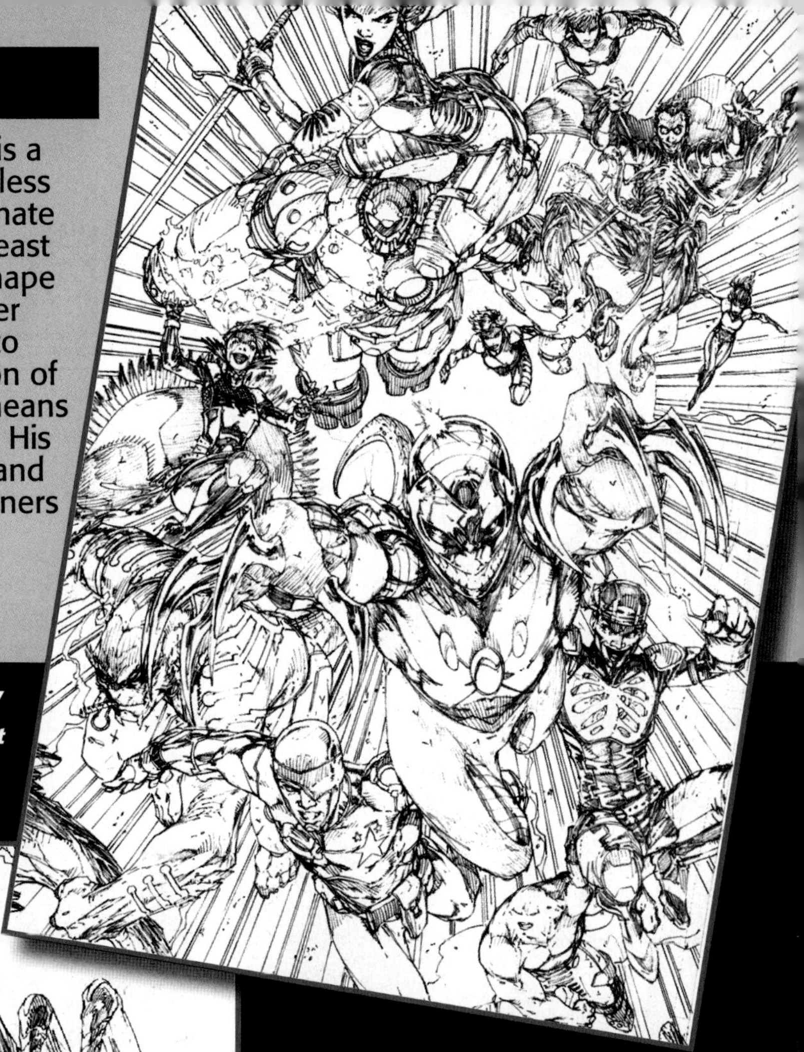

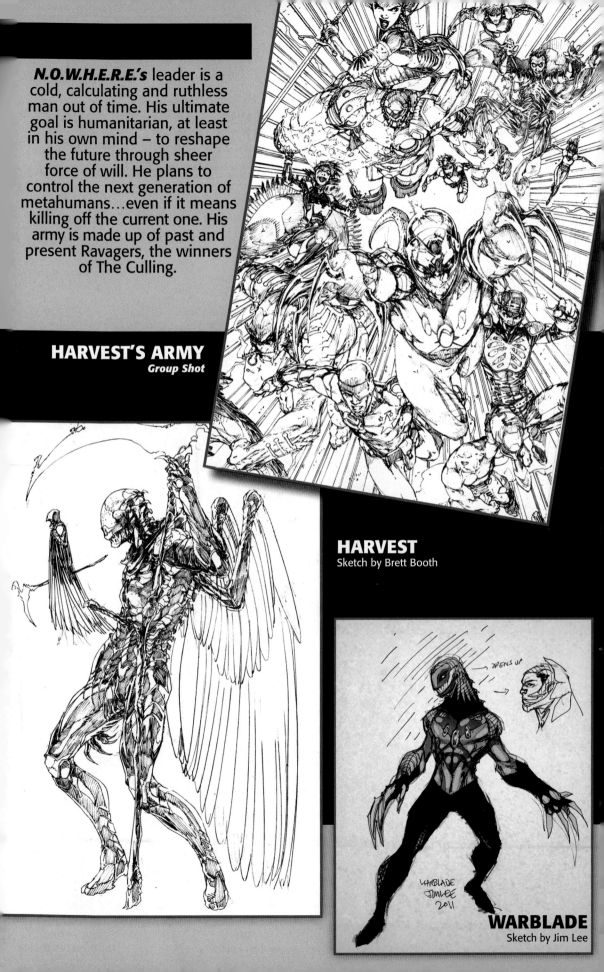

HARVEST'S ARMY
Group Shot

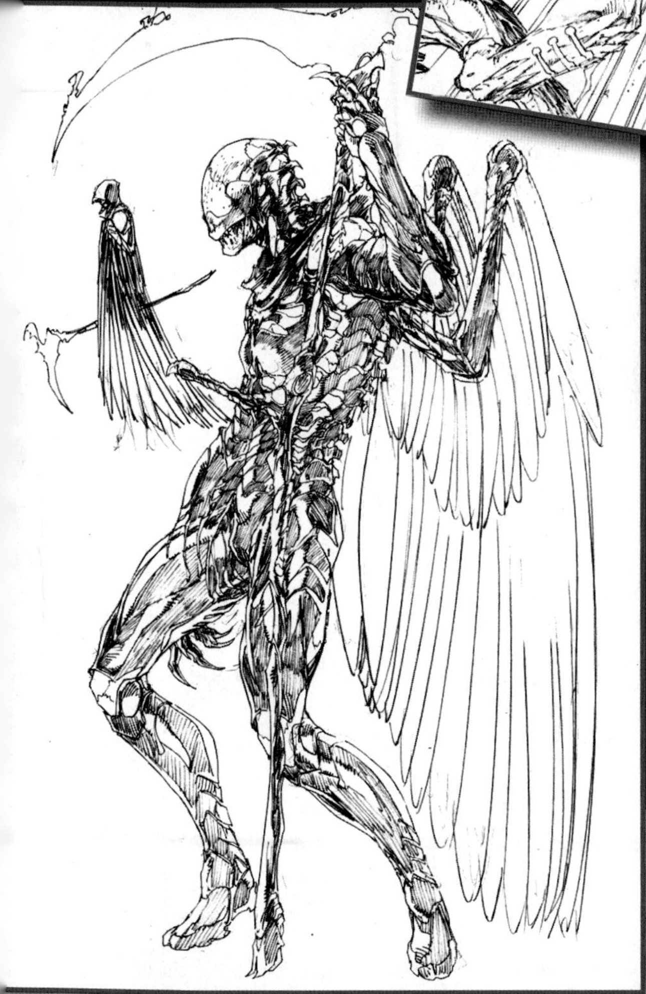

HARVEST
Sketch by Brett Booth

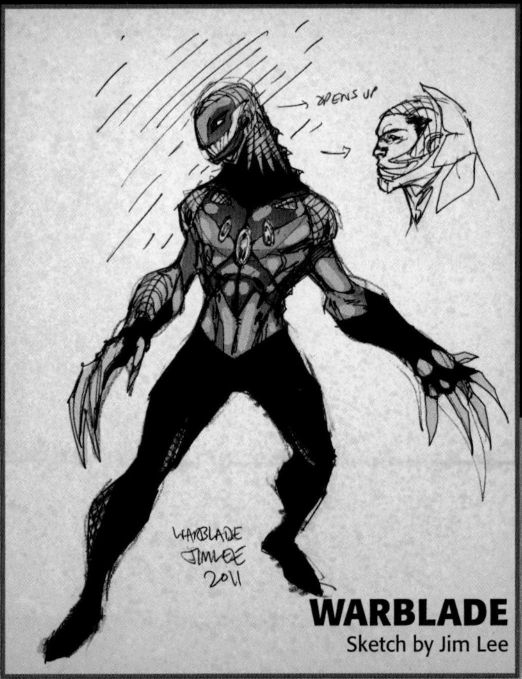
OPENS UP
WARBLADE
JIM LEE
2011

WARBLADE
Sketch by Jim Lee

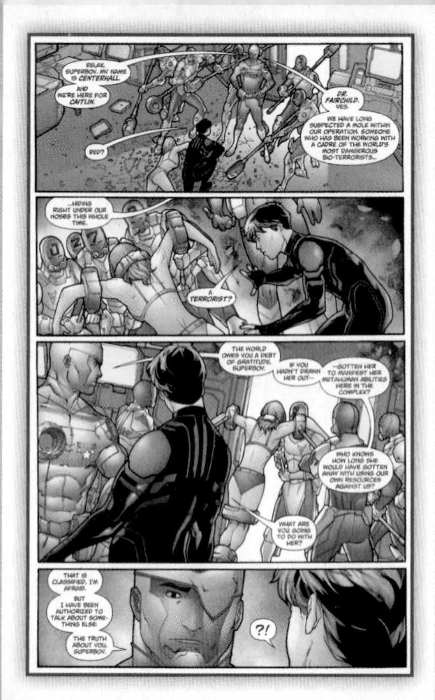
RELAX, SUPERBOY. MY NAME IS CENTERHALL.
AND WE'RE HERE FOR CAITLIN.
RED?
DR. FAIRCHILD, YES.
WE HAVE LONG SUSPECTED A MOLE WITHIN OUR OPERATION. SOMEONE WHO HAS BEEN WORKING WITH A CADRE OF THE WORLD'S MOST DANGEROUS BIO-TERRORISTS...
...HIDING RIGHT UNDER OUR NOSES THIS WHOLE TIME.
A TERRORIST?
THE WORLD OWES YOU A DEBT OF GRATITUDE, SUPERBOY.
IF YOU HADN'T DRAWN HER OUT--
--GOTTEN HER TO MANIFEST HER METAHUMAN ABILITIES HERE IN THE COMPLEX?
WHO KNOWS HOW LONG SHE WOULD HAVE GOTTEN AWAY WITH USING OUR OWN RESOURCES AGAINST US?
WHAT ARE YOU GOING TO DO WITH HER?
THAT IS CLASSIFIED, I'M AFRAID.
BUT I HAVE BEEN AUTHORIZED TO TALK ABOUT SOME-THING ELSE:
THE TRUTH ABOUT YOU, SUPERBOY.
?!

SUPERBOY WITH CENTERHALL
FROM
SUPERBOY #4 & 5
by RB Silva

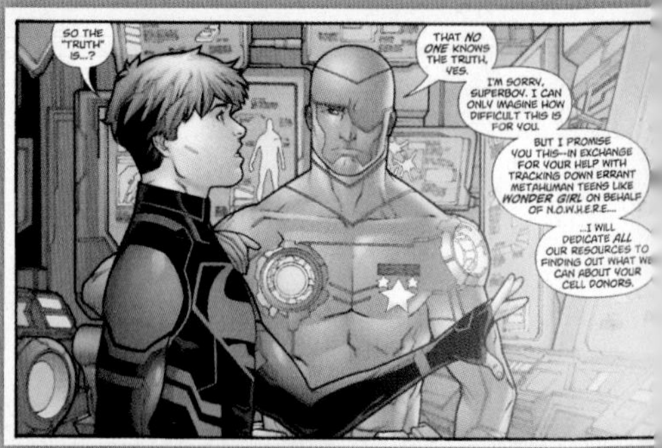
SO THE "TRUTH" IS...?
THAT NO ONE KNOWS THE TRUTH, YES.
I'M SORRY, SUPERBOY. I CAN ONLY IMAGINE HOW DIFFICULT THIS IS FOR YOU.
BUT I PROMISE YOU THIS--IN EXCHANGE FOR YOUR HELP WITH TRACKING DOWN ERRANT METAHUMAN TEENS LIKE WONDER GIRL ON BEHALF OF N.O.W.H.E.R.E...
...I WILL DEDICATE ALL OUR RESOURCES TO FINDING OUT WHAT W CAN ABOUT YOUR CELL DONORS.

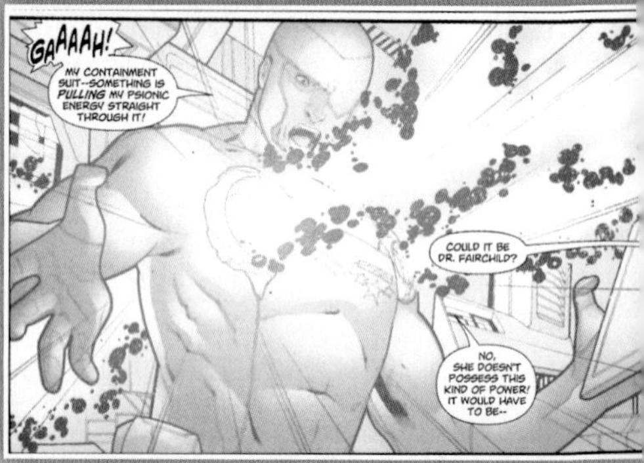
GAAAAH!
MY CONTAINMENT SUIT--SOMETHING IS PULLING MY PSIONIC ENERGY STRAIGHT THROUGH IT!
COULD IT BE DR. FAIRCHILD?
NO, SHE DOESN'T POSSESS THIS KIND OF POWER! IT WOULD HAVE TO BE--

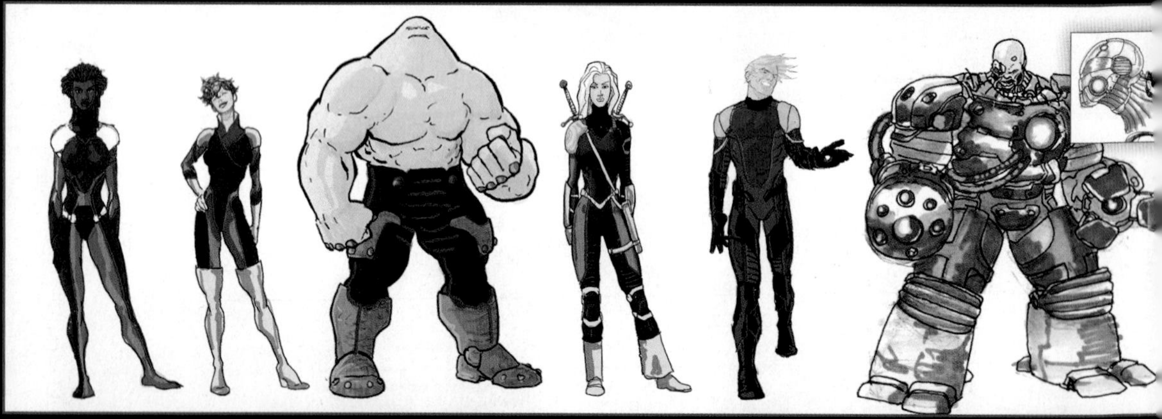

1. CRUSH
2. MISBELIEF
3. HAMMERSMITH
4. ROSE WILSON
5. WINDSTROM
6. PSYKILL

Designs by
Aaron Kuder

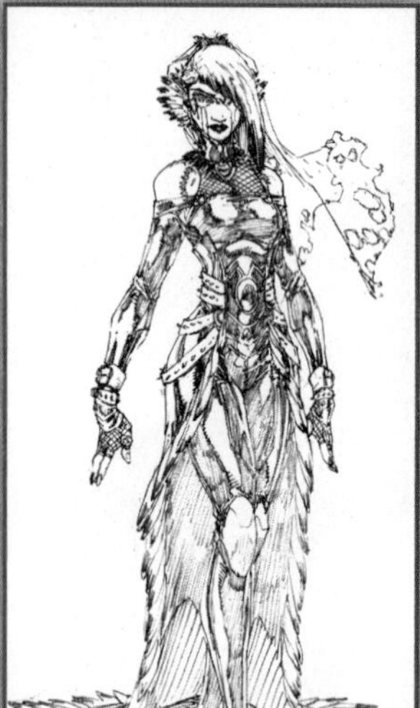

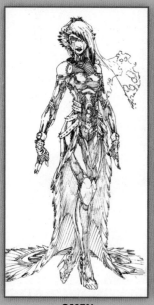

OMEN
by Brett Booth

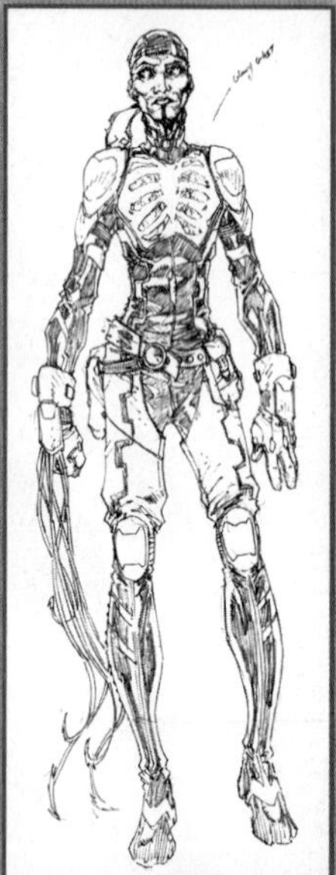

LEASH
by Brett Booth

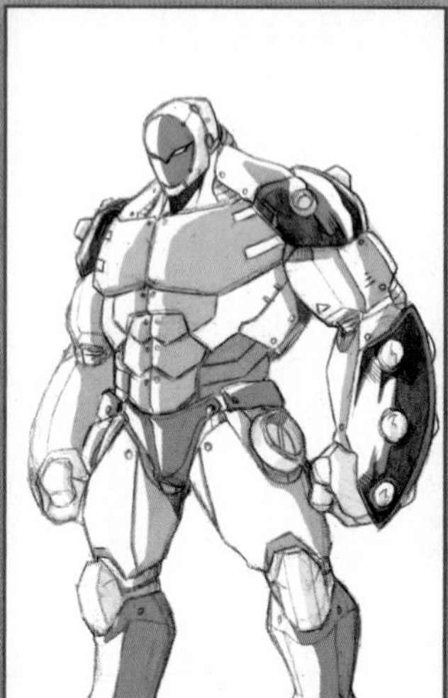

FUJI
by Iban Coello

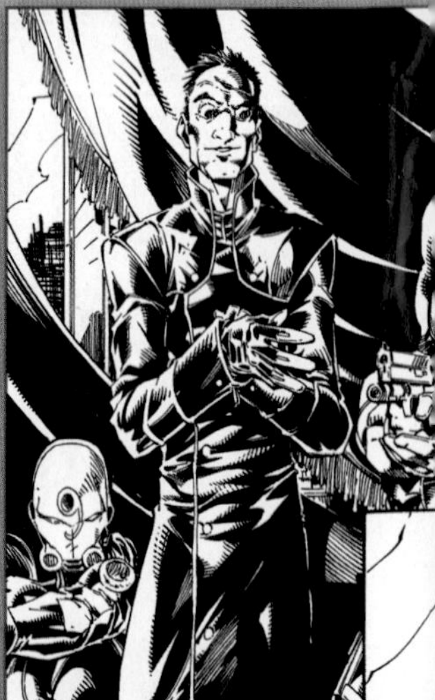

TEMPLAR
by Brett Booth